An Introduction to the Counseling Profession

An Introduction to the Counseling Profession

DUANE BROWN
University of North Carolina at Chapel Hill

DAVID J. SREBALUS
West Virginia University

PRENTICE HALL, ENGLEWOOD CLIFFS, NEW JERSEY 07632

LIBRARY OF CONGRESS
Library of Congress Cataloging-in-Publication Data

Brown, Duane.
   An introduction to the counseling profession / Duane Brown, David
J. Srebalus.
      p.   cm.
   ISBN 0-13-481540-8
   1. Counseling. 2. Counseling--Practice.   I. Srebalus, David J.
II. Title.
BF637.C6B745 1988
   158'.3--dc19   87-29145
                                                     CIP

Cover design: 20/20 Services, Inc.
Manufacturing buyer: Margaret Rizzi

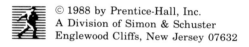 © 1988 by Prentice-Hall, Inc.
A Division of Simon & Schuster
Englewood Cliffs, New Jersey 07632

Printed in the United States of America
10 9 8 7 6 5 4 3 2 1

ISBN 0-13-481540-8

Prentice-Hall International (UK) Limited, *London*
Prentice-Hall of Australia Pty. Limited, *Sydney*
Prentice-Hall Canada Inc., *Toronto*
Prentice-Hall Hispanoamericana, S.A., *Mexico*
Prentice-Hall of India Private Limited, *New Delhi*
Prentice-Hall of Japan, Inc., *Tokyo*
Simon & Schuster Asia Pte. Ltd., *Singapore*
Editora Prentice-Hall do Brasil, Ltda., *Rio de Janeiro*

To Cassandra, Kindra, Jeffrey, and Tamara Brown
John and Cathy Srebalus

Contents

Preface

Counseling is a fledgling profession that is growing rapidly in size and in recognition, but it is not without its problems. To provide students entering the field with a sense of the profession they are choosing—both its promise and its problems—this book discusses the historical roots, the current status, and the future of the counseling profession.

The book also has a secondary purpose: to provide students with an overview of the varied theories, techniques, and procedures used by counselors as they strive to help those they serve. The richness and diversity of these approaches illustrate that counselors have the means to make a positive difference in the lives of individuals and in society as a whole.

Along with the diversity of the techniques employed, this volume illustrates the diversity of the profession itself. There is no single prototypical counselor; there are probably dozens of them. There are school counselors, mental health counselors, employment counselors, career counselors, rehabilitation counselors, and many others, each title reflecting a setting in which counselors work and, to some degree, clients that they serve.

Counselors, the techniques they employ, and the settings in which they work are important but would not, in and of themselves, justify calling counseling a profession. Ethical principles, legal guidelines, credentialing, and training standards are the fabric of which a profession is woven. This book discusses these issues and others in depth since they are, in many ways, the most important topics neophyte counselors can consider on their journey to becoming professionals.

The Plan of the Book

The book is divided into five parts. Part One, in addition to providing an overview, describes the foundations upon which the counseling profession is built.

Part Two develops an understanding of how counselors serve clients in the counseling and consultation processes. A major agenda of this part is to develop the reader's awareness of, and appreciation for, the special needs of cross-cultural clients, women, handicapped people, and other client groups. The position of this book, and of the counseling profession in general, is that understanding the uniqueness of clients is a prerequisite to successful practice.

Part Three contains three chapters, one dealing with the ethical underpinnings of the counseling profession, one with legal concerns, and one with the credentialing of counselors. The chapter dealing with ethics outlines ethical principles, whereas the chapter on legal concerns identifies the major legal issues facing counselors. The latter chapter also suggests ways to avoid legal entanglements. The credentialing chapter is more factual, providing some definitions of and guidelines for the credentialing process.

The work settings of the counselor are considered in Part Four. While the position of this book is that counselors need a general set of skills and knowledge bases, it would be naive to assert that there is no need for specialization or that the setting in which the counselor functions does not influence the manner in which his or her skills are implemented. Thus, Part Four contains three chapters on the work setting, including one chapter each on counselors in educational settings, mental health agencies, and business and industry.

Part Five deals with the issues currently confronting the counseling profession. One chapter discusses research and evaluation, and another covers career issues for counselors. Chapter 17, the book's final chapter, deals with unresolved issues and offers recommendations for the continued development of the profession.

For the curious, this book will provide information. For the interested, it should provide a reference point for assessing one's own potential as a counselor. For the dedicated, it will provide a springboard for continued professional growth and development.

No book can be produced without assistance from many individuals. Lyda Beemer and Jane Trexler deciphered and typed the manuscript developed by the senior author and deserve much credit for his work. Much credit also goes to several graduate students, particularly Alan Cunningham, who did leg work, proofed the manuscript, and provided initial response to the material in this volume.

D.B.
D.J.S.

1

Counseling and Counselors: An Overview

GOALS OF THE CHAPTER

The primary goal of this chapter is to present a historical as well as a current view of how the counseling profession strives to serve society. A secondary goal of the chapter is to prognosticate about the future of the profession.

CHAPTER PREVIEW

1. The history of the counseling profession will be presented.
2. The mental health needs of our society will be discussed.
3. Counselors' roles in meeting current mental health problems will be identified.
4. An assessment of the current status of the profession will be made.

INTRODUCTION

This book is about the counseling profession. The discussions herein will range broadly, focusing variously upon the history, future, strengths, limitations, theories, and techniques of the profession. For the most part, the theories and techniques are shared with other professions, namely psychology and social work. To some degree, counseling is historically linked to psychology as well.

In this first chapter the history of the profession will be outlined. This will be followed by a discussion of the mental health needs of our society and how counselors are particularly well positioned to address many of these needs. Finally, the current status of the counseling profession will be addressed, with attention given to both its strengths and its limitations.

HISTORY OF THE COUNSELING PROFESSION

Pre–20th Century

Because of the diversity within the counseling profession, it is impossible to identify definitely a historical point at which the profession began. Some (e.g., Gibson & Mitchell, 1986) attempt to link the work of Plato and Aristotle to the origins of the profession because of their early insights regarding the functioning of the individual. Belkin (1975) also has placed the origins of the profession in this period, drawing specifically from the work of Plato. It is unquestionably the case that Plato, Aristotle, and a number of other early Western philosophers addressed the matter of how individuals learn and develop and, in some instances, attempted to generalize their thinking to practical processes such as teaching and counseling. Their philosophy can still be found in the fabric of the profession.

While the roots of counseling can be tenuously tied to philosophers in early Greece, a more definite historical linkage can be made to Europe and the middle ages. Zytowski (1972) identified a number of books devoted to specific occupations aimed at helping people make career choices. The earliest of these seems to have been *The Mirror of Men's Lives,* authored by a bishop of the Roman Catholic Church, Rodrigo Sanches, which describes occupations within the church and crafts careers in 15th-century Europe. This book, according to Zytowski, appeared in illustrated form in 1472 and had German, French, and Spanish editions over its 125-year life span. During the decades that followed, a number of other books were published that were the forerunners of much of today's thinking. Included among these are Juan Huartis' *The Examination of Men's Wits* (1575), which expounded upon Plato's beliefs that people differ in their abilities; and Powell's *Tom of All Trades* (1631) and *Pathway to Preferment* (1631), which are analogous to current books that detail occupational information. Ten such books were published during the 1700s, including an anonymously authored work called *A General Description of All Trades* (1747). Zytowski (1972) reports that this trend of publishing books regarding careers accelerated in the 19th century, when at least 65 were published. A number of these volumes were published in America.

The early American guides to occupations, including *A Treatise of the Vocations* by William Perkins (1603), and *The Parents and Guardians Direc-*

tory and the *Youth's Guide in the Choice of a Profession or Trade* by Joseph Collyer (1761), emphasize the work ethic and the importance of moral training. Also, in keeping with the Puritan emphasis of the time, the uniqueness of the individual was emphasized in these early works (Picchioni & Bonk, 1983). Picchioni and Bonk trace how this emphasis upon the individual plus the Puritan belief in self-discipline through work and education combined with laissez-faire economics (individual enterprise) to form a philosophy of individualism—a philosophy that still pervades the counseling profession.

The 19th century was particularly influential in historical development of the profession, partly because of the growing emphasis upon career guidance. But there were forces outside the field that were later to have great impact. Wilhelm Wundt established the first psychological laboratory in Germany in 1879. In 1883 G. Stanley Hall started the first psychology laboratory devoted to the study of children. These two laboratories would provide the impetus for scientific psychology in the United States. Also, in 1890 a little-known physician, Sigmund Freud, began the treatment of mental patients with an unknown technique, psychoanalysis, which along with Pavlovian psychology in Russia and Gestalt psychology in Germany would provide the impetus for many current theories of human behavior.

The pre–Civil War period in America was characterized by rapid industrial expansion in the North and a flourishing agriculturally based economy in the South. The Civil War accelerated the industrial movement, specialization in the work force, and awareness of the need for vocational education and guidance (Picchioni & Bonk, 1983). In 1881 Salmon Richards published what may have been the first true call for counselors. In his book *Vocophy,* he called for vocophers to be located in every town who could provide vocational assistance to those in need. Brewer (1942) stopped short of giving credit to Richards for founding the vocational guidance movement. However, Picchioni and Bonk recognize him as the first individual to call for a counseling profession.

The Early 20th Century

Not surprisingly, given the rapid industrialization at the turn of the century, programs aimed at providing career guidance were springing to life, primarily in public school settings. Brewer (1942) reports that the first vocational guidance program began in Cogswell High School, San Francisco, in 1888. This program included vocational exploration through work samples, counseling for vocational choice, vocational training, and job placement. In 1897 Jessie B. Davis began a program of moral and vocational guidance in Detroit, where he served as 11th-grade counselor until 1907, when he became principal of Grand Rapids High School. Davis (1904) was later to publish a book detailing his approaches, *Vocational and Moral Guidance*. Eli Weaver in New York and Anna Reed in Seattle also established school-based guidance programs in the early 1900s.

Two things should be clear at this point. There was no single starting point for the counseling profession, and a number of individuals made contributions to its inception. In spite of this, one man, Frank Parsons, is generally identified as the founder of the guidance movement in the United States (Aubrey, 1977; Brewer, 1942; Picchioni & Bonk, 1983; Whitely, 1984). In order to understand why, the man and his contributions must be fully explored.

Parsons was born in Mount Holly, New Jersey, in 1854. Early on, he demonstrated high academic ability and entered Cornell at age 15, graduating three years later with a degree in civil engineering. During the subsequent years he served as a railroad engineer, common laborer, high school teacher, lawyer, and politician. However, his most salient characteristic lay not in the traits associated with any of these jobs, but in his penchant for social reform. He rejected Social Darwinism, the belief that social evolution was based upon the survival of the fittest, and developed his own philosophy of Mutualism (Miller, 1961; Picchioni & Bonk, 1983)., Mutualism held that the common good of society was based to a large extent upon cooperative efforts to ensure benefits for all. Parsons advocated urban renewal projects, educational reform, women's suffrage, uniform divorce laws, and a host of other social changes.

In 1905 Parsons was asked to establish what became known as the Breadwinner's College in the famous Civic Service House in Boston. The Civic Service House had been created in 1901 as a continuing education center for immigrant and native youth. Parsons' Breadwinner's Institute, as it was renamed, thrived, and in 1907 he asked Mrs. Quincy Adams Shaw, benefactor of the Civic Service House, to underwrite what was to become the Vocational Bureau of Boston in 1908. Parsons died a few months later. Soon after his death, his book *Choosing a Vocation* (Parsons, 1909) was published. In this volume he set forth a tripartite model of career counseling: (1) self-analysis, (2) analysis of occupations, and (3) choosing a career using true reasoning.

In 1905 Alfred Binet and Theodore Simon, working with the Paris schools, published the first standardized intelligence tests, which were to provide the impetus for the testing movement. A scientific basis for self-analysis, unavailable to Parsons, was beginning to evolve. During World War I and into the 1920s, the production of tests to measure human traits would reach a peak unparalleled since. The Great Depression would result in the publication of the forerunners of the *Occupational Outlook Handbook* and, in 1939, the *Dictionary of Occupational Titles*. These provided a device by which counselors could help students conduct an analysis of occupations.

Parsons' work and that of the other pioneers spawned numerous guidance programs throughout America. Much of this early effort was directed at improving vocational guidance. In 1910 the First National Conference on Vocational Guidance was convened in Boston. Three years later the National Vocational Guidance Association was formed as the first professional organization for counselors. In 1915 it published the first journal, the *Vocational Guidance Bulletin*, which was the forerunner of today's *Career Development Quarterly*.

In another movement that focused to some degree on vocationally related services, the National Civilian Rehabilitation Conference was formed in 1924. The purpose of this organization, now titled the National Rehabilitation Association, was to enhance services to the handicapped through counseling, vocational assessment, and placement.

Early developments in the counseling profession were not restricted to schools or community agencies, nor were they limited to vocational concerns. Student personnel programs variously emphasizing guidance, counseling, and discipline were being formed across the United States. Generally, these programs were headed by deans, a title later widely copied by high schools. Northwestern University was the first to establish an extensive student personnel program, while Teachers College at Columbia University pioneered the training of student personnel workers (Picchioni & Bonk, 1983).

It is probably clear that much of the activity detailed to this point focused on guidance programs and services rather than other forms of counseling. To be sure, counseling as an activity was being talked and written about, particularly by E. G. Williamson (1939) in *How to Counsel Students* and others at the University of Minnesota. In a parallel movement, Freud and neo-Freudians were having a tremendous impact upon psychiatry and the fledgling psychology profession. However, counselors were largely unaffected by this influence.

From Guidance to Counseling: The 1940s, 1950s, and 1960s

In 1942 Carl Rogers published *Counseling and Psychotherapy*. This was followed nearly a decade later by *Client-Centered Therapy* (Rogers, 1951) and 19 years later by *On Becoming a Person* (Rogers, 1961). While it is difficult to pinpoint any single turning point in the development of any profession, Carl Rogers and his publications probably contributed more than any other phenomenon to the transition of the counseling profession from a focus on group-delivered guidance services, such as classroom units on choosing a career, to a group that provided counseling services (Aubrey, 1977; Bradley, 1978; Picchioni & Bonk, 1983). His emphasis upon Humanism and his nondirective approach to counseling captured the imagination of counselors because of its positive nature and its departure from the medical model that characterized people with problems as medically ill. Counseling, not testing or guidance, became the central thrust of a young profession (Aubrey, 1977).

The fifties and sixties were characterized by many significant developments. In 1949 Eli Ginzburg was the first to present a theory why people choose occupations over the life span (Ginzburg, 1984), a theory he published in 1951 (Ginzberg, Ginsburg, Axelrod, and Herma, 1951). In 1953 Super published what was to become, and remains, one of the dominant career development theories. It was, and is, the major competitor to the trait-and-factor theory initiated by Parsons and popularized by E. G. Williamson and others.

But theorizing did not dominate the growth of the profession in the forties, fifties, and sixties. The development of professional structures did. In 1951, after nearly 20 years of collaborative efforts, the National Vocational Guidance Association and the American College Personnel Association voted to merge under an umbrella organization, the American Personnel and Guidance Association (APGA). A third organization, the National Association of Deans of Women, long a collaborator, declined to join. At the first meeting of the APGA in Los Angeles in 1952, two additional associations had become chartered members: National Association of Guidance Supervisors and Trainers, and Student Personnel Association for Teacher Education. Robert Shaffer became the first president of the association and Donald Super its first president-elect.

Following the formation of APGA, the growth of a fledgling profession took a predictable path. Scholarly journals were added (e.g., *The Personnel and Guidance Journal,* 1958), standards for counselor preparation were promulgated (1958), a proposed code of ethics was published in *The Personnel and Guidance Journal* in 1959, and the profession began to support legislation that corresponded to its goals (Picchioni & Bonk, 1983).

Just as Carl Rogers' publications propelled the counseling profession toward counseling, the launching of a Russian satellite in 1957 and the nation's response in the form of the National Defense Education Act (NDEA) in 1958 provided a springboard for the rapid development of the profession. Title V-A of NDEA provided monies to support school counseling programs and V-B established funds to support the training of counselors. The result was a rapid expansion of secondary school counseling programs and a parallel increase in both the number and size of training programs.

In 1964 the limited focus of NDEA was expanded to include elementary schools, junior colleges, and technical schools. The major impact of this amendment was to legitimize elementary school counseling and, as Faust (1968) noted, provide a major impetus for this movement.

A period that had been initiated by the development of the theories of Rogers and Super was to be characterized by the presentation of a variety of theories that would underpin the work of many counselors. Rational-Emotive Therapy was developed by Albert Ellis (1978) during the 1950s, as was Reality Therapy (Glasser & Zunin, 1978). Behavioral counseling also surfaced during this period, introduced first by Wolpe (Chambliss & Goldstein, 1979), but probably brought most forcefully to the attention of counselors by John D. Krumboltz (1966) in works such as *Revolution in Counseling.* A professional group dedicated in the practice of counseling had a whole new set of theoretical constructs to consider.

Career choice and career development also received much attention from theorists in the fifties and sixties: Anne Roe published the first comprehensive view of the career choice and development process in 1956; John Holland presented his theory of occupational choice in 1959, and Tiedemann and O'Hara put forth their framework for career decision making in 1963. These theories, along with Super's framework, would dominate the field into the 1980s (Brown & Brooks, 1984).

The Professionalization Era

The roots of the profession can be traced to 1913 and beyond. However, during the last 20 years, those roots have borne fruit. In 1978 APGA established an independent training program accreditation body, now known as the *Council for the Accreditation of Counseling and Related Educational Programs* (CACREP). While efforts to establish standards for training counselors had been underway for more than 30 years, much of that time under the leadership of Robert Stripling, this was a public affirmation of the importance of preparation standards. APGA also provided vigorous leadership in the area of individual credentialing and established a Licensure Commission chaired by Thomas Sweeney in 1974. In 1976 Virginia became the first state to pass a licensure law for professional counselors, a move followed by 17 other states in the next 12 years. Currently, almost all states have active legislative programs aimed at securing licensing for counselors.

Credentialing of another sort also reflects the rapid professionalization of the early 1980s. The American Mental Health Counselors Association, the American Rehabilitation Counselors Association, and the National Vocational Guidance Association (now National Career Development Association) embarked upon programs to certify counselors in the counseling specialties they represented. The American Association for Counseling and Development also established the National Board for Certified Counselors as a certifying agency for all counselors. The basic purpose of all of the councils and commissions established by these organizations is to recognize counselors who have met certain criteria, including certain training requirements (e.g., supervised practicums in the area of specialty), and who possess a knowledge base as reflected by sucessfully passing an examination. A second purpose of certification is to encourage maintenance of skills and knowledge by requiring continuing education for maintenance of the certification.

Finally, during the 1980s a number of associations, including the parent organization, the American Personnel and Guidance Association, changed their names, partly because some of the names no longer adequately reflected the purposes of the organizations, and partly to reflect the organizations' emphasis on counseling. APGA became the American Association for Counseling and Development (AACD), the Association for Non-White Concerns became the Association for Multicultural Counseling and Development (AMCD), the National Vocational Guidance Association became the National Career Development Association, and the Association for Measurement and Evaluation in Guidance became the Association for Measurement and Evaluation in Counseling and Development.

THE NEED FOR COUNSELING SERVICES

A decade ago it was conventional wisdom that one in ten persons in the general population was in need of mental health services at any given time. Currently that estimate has been revised to one in five. Of these approximately 45 million people who are in need of services, no more than 2.5 million can be classified as chronically mentally ill (Bates, 1985). The remainder, some over 40 million people, have problems ranging from a temporary need for support to one that requires long-term psychotherapy. This section will be devoted to identifying the scope of the mental health problem confronting our society, and to a brief discussion of the need for development and preventive services. This discussion will be followed by one that illustrates how members of the counseling profession are positioned to deal with these problems.

At the outset, it may be useful to note that the mental health problems in our society are not restricted to a single age group. Children, adolescents, adults, and the elderly all have problems that vary in type to a considerable degree. To illustrate this point, let us consider some of the recent factual reports that have surfaced for these groups.

Children

The major problems confronting children in our society can be directly related to poverty and instability in the family. The Children's Defense Fund (1985) reports that black children in particular are victims of these forces, and the results are alarming: Black children are twice as likely as white children to die before age one, three times as likely as their white counterparts to live in poverty, only one-quarter as likely to live with either parent, five times more likely to be on welfare, and 12 times as likely to live with an unmarried parent. Hispanic children are also likely to find themselves living in poverty: More than 70% live in this condition (Children's Defense Fund, 1985).

Divorce has also had a dramatic impact on children. In 1983 *alone*, 1,091,000 children under age 18 saw their parents' marriages dissolve. This, coupled with the fact that there are 19.5 million working mothers in our society (Bureau of Labor Statistics, 1986), has led to a situation where as many as 7 million children may go unsupervised during a portion of each year (Children's Defense Fund, 1984). The result is that the social support network for children has evaporated in many instances and, predictably, mental health problems have skyrocketed.

Physical, sexual, and psychological abuse of children has also received increasing attention with nearly a million cases being reported each year (Bureau of the Census, 1985). The result is that all states have enacted legislation that requires that abuse be reported by individuals who care for children, including physicians, teachers, and counselors. The gradual lessening of taboos regarding the discussion of incest has also contributed to the identification and reporting of sexual abuse.

Without question, child abuse is related to a number of other problems. For example, 36% of 10–18-year-old runaways reported that they had either been sexually or physically abused (National Network of Runaway and Youth Services, 1985). Abuse, along with poverty and other family problems, also contributes to other mental health problems manifested by children and to problems that surface later in life, including suicide and depression.

Adolescents

The mental health needs of adolescents are among those most often studied, perhaps because they can easily be surveyed through the public schools. The result is that there is a vast amount of data suggesting that adolescents have a variety of serious mental health concerns. For example, a study conducted by the University of Michigan Institute for Social Research (Johnston, 1985) indicated the drug abuse was once again on the upswing among young people after half a decade of decline. Alcohol abuse continued to lead the list of abused substances, with 37% of the responding students reporting an occasion of heavy drinking—defined as consuming five or more drinks in a row—during the two weeks prior to the study. Five percent of the respondents in the study reported daily use of alcohol.

The University of Michigan study reported a continued decline in the use of such illegal substances as amphetamines, methaqualine, and LSD. However, this was offset to some degree by an upswing in the use of cocaine: 17% of the respondents reported that they had tried cocaine. A total of 61% of those surveyed reported experimenting with an illegal drug at some time, of which 40% indicated that it was a substance other than marijuana.

Sargent (1984) reports that substance abuse, along with medical and psychological illnesses and family problems, distinguished an increasing number of adolescents who attempt and succeed at suicide. The suicide rate among white adolescent males in 1978 was 138 per million, white adolescent females 34 per million, black adolescent males 75 per million, and black adolescent females 16 per million (Lipsitz, 1985). There is every reason to believe that these numbers are increasing rapidly, although the increase may be accounted for by more accurate reporting procedures (Sargent, 1984). One of the troublesome events that characterizes suicide patterns in the '80s is what appears to be waves of imitational suicide; that is, a high incidence of suicide after a highly publicized suicide in a given community.

Just as it is difficult to get an accurate estimate of the number of adolescents involved in either successful or unsuccessful suicide attempts, accurate figures regarding mental health problems of adolescents are difficult to obtain. However, Lipsitz (1985) reports after a survey of the literature in this area that about one-fifth of the individuals treated for depression are under age

18, and that approximately 15–16% of adolescents need some form of mental health services, although many are not receiving the assistance they need.

Teen-age pregnancy cannot be interpreted as a mental health problem, although it is an area where adolescents need assistance. In an editorial appearing in the *American Journal of Public Health* (1985), it was reported that the statistics in this area have remained relatively stable. There are approximately 5 million sexually active adolescents in this country. The result is 1.15 million pregnancies annually, of which approximately 460,000 are terminated by abortion and 153,000 by miscarriage. Of the 537,000 births that occur among adolescents, 268,000 are to unmarried mothers. The National Center for Educational Statistics (NCES, 1983) reports that 23% of the women who left school prior to graduation did so because they were pregnant. The media have often dramatized this problem as children having children. The results of teenage pregnancy can indeed be dramatic: Adolescent mothers attempt suicide seven times as often as their peers, 72% of all teen marriages end in divorce, and over 70% of teen mothers will be on welfare for one to five years (The Crier, 1985).

Pregnant girls are not the only ones to leave school prematurely, although, as noted above, they represent a substantial portion of the nearly 25% who fail to complete high school. Among certain groups (e.g., Hispanics in large cities and Native Americans), the drop-out rate may range from 50% to 85% (NCES, 1983). Reasons given for leaving school prematurely vary widely, including financial needs (had to support family), expulsion, poor academic performance, low motivation, inability to get along with other students or teachers, and so forth (NCES, 1983). The consequences are much more predictable: lower chances of gaining and keeping jobs and lowered lifetime earnings. The result is that 51% of the males and 55% of the females who dropped out reported that leaving school was not a good idea (NCES, 1983). The unemployment rate among adolescents is generally two to three times that of their adult counterparts, although it is likely to be twice that for black 16–19 year olds.

Unemployment, drug abuse, and other problems already mentioned are related to the adolescent crime rate and the number of runaways. Adolescents commit 20% of all crimes reported (Youth Policy, 1984), and 1.5 million 10–18-year-olds run away each year (National Network of Runaway Youth Services, 1985). These facts, in turn, can be tied to many of the problems facing our society generally, such as poverty and discrimination, and to the problems of the parents of adolescents, which will be discussed in the next section.

Adults

As we have seen in the two preceding sessions, the problems of children and adolescents are, to a large degree, tied to adults. While it would be impossible to pinpoint a predominant causal force, divorce would have to be one of the leaders. Divorce rates declined slightly during the 1982 to 1984 period, but went up again in 1985, with an estimated 1,186,000 couples dissolving their marriages during this period. This was an increase of 2% according to the National Center for Health Statistics over the 1984 period (NCHS, 1985a, b). As reported earlier, more than a million children are involved in these marital dissolutions each year (NCHS, 1983). The mental health consequences of divorce upon adults can be severe. Depression and suicide attempts are often the most dramatic result. Even those adults who manage to escape psychologically debilitating symptoms are often beset by stress resulting from role changes, such as entering or re-entering the job market, becoming a single parent, and/or re-entering the "dating scene."

Alcoholism and drug abuse are widespread maladies among adults, although their exact dimensions are not fully known. One estimate is that 10% of all employees in this country are impaired by psychological or substance abuse problems (Turkington, 1985), costing businesses untold millions of dollars in profits. Substance abuse is also a prime contributor to marital breakup, child and spouse abuse, and a variety of health problems.

The unemployment rate during the 1980s has ranged from approximately 7% to 10% of the working force. In real terms, this means that probably 7 to 10 million people are out of work at any given time. Some of these job losses are the result of seasonal fluctuations (e.g., farm workers), economic downturns, and occupational structural changes (e.g., manufacturing to information processing). Those changes that occur precipitously and have the potential for being long-term in nature produce the greatest stress and hence are more likely to have a deleterious effect on the mental health of the individuals concerned. It is not uncommon to see depression, substance abuse, and child and spouse abuse rise soon after job loss, although some workers seem to rebound psychologically quite quickly (Herr & Cramer, 1984).

Dealing with families and work are two of the major problems confronting adults, and it appears that nearly 10 million individuals could benefit from assistance in these areas alone. Other aspects of adulthood that may be related to mental health concerns are accepting one's mortality, adjusting to declining physical prowess, health problems, particularly those that are life threatening, and loss of parents. These stressors can and do precipitate a variety of difficulties, including anxiety, depression, and psychosomatic illnesses (e.g., lower back pain).

There is also an increasing possibility that adults (and others as well) will become, directly or indirectly, the victims of a violent crime. Criminals have long been the focus of rehabilitation counseling efforts. However, it is only recently that attention has been given to the victims of crime. In 1983 nearly 79,000 cases of rape, more than 639,000 cases of aggravated assault, 3 million burglaries, and just about 20,000 murders were reported. Herrington (1985) concluded that 6,000,000 people were the victims of violent crimes in 1984. An American Psychological Association task force (Siegel, 1985) on the victims of

Table 1.1 A Schematic of Concerns for the Generations

Area of concern	Age group/generation				
	Child/adolesc. 1–19	Young adult 20–35	Mid-life 36–54	Young/old 55–74	Old/old 75–100
Education	XXXXXXXXXXXX				
Identity	XXXXXXXXX				
Intimacy	XXXXXXX				
Marriage		XXXXXXXXXXXXXXXXXXXXXXXXXXX			
Parenthood	XXXXXXXXXXXXXXXXXXXXXXXXXXXXXXXXXXXXXXXXXXXXXXXX				
Generativity		XXXXXXXXXXXXXXXXXXXXXX			
Mid-life crisis		XXXXXXXXXXXXX			
Financial stress		XXXXXXXXXXX		XXXXXXXXXXXXXXX	
Filial crisis			XXXXXXXXXXXXXXXXXXXXXXXX		
Grandparenthood			XXXXXXXXXXXXXXXXXXXXXXXXXX		
Retirement				XXXXXXXXXXXXXXXX	
Life review	XX	XX	XX	XX	XX XX
Widow(er)hood			X X X X X X X	XXXXXXXXXX	
Institutionalization					XXXXXXXXXXXXX

Note. From "Common Crises in the Family Life of Older Workers" (p. 36) by I. C. Siegler and L. A. Hyer. In *A Family Approach to Health Care of the Elderly* (p. 33–50) by D. Blazen and I. C. Siegler, eds., 1984, Reading MA: Addison-Wesley. Reprinted by permission.

crime concluded that many of these individuals suffer post-traumatic stress disorders, ranging from short- to long-term in duration, characterized variously by fear of vulnerability, the perception of being deviant, and/or a sense of inequity.

The Elderly

In 1900 only 4% of the population in the United States was over age 65. The latest report places this percentage at 12.5, and it is increasing (U.S. Committee on Aging, 1985–86). This same report notes that the fastest-growing age group is the over-85 group. These figures dramatize not only what has been termed the graying of America, but the increasing longevity of older people. By 2050 one-third of our population will be over 55 and one-fifth over 65 (U.S. Committee on Aging, 1985–86). With these figures comes the sobering reality that counselors and other mental health professionals must prepare to assist the elderly to cope with mental health concerns.

In the previous section it was observed that many Americans will need assistance because they will be victims of violent crimes. The elderly are disproportionately represented in this group since they are viewed as vulnerable by many criminals. However, retirement, marital relationships, widow(er)hood, grandparenting, institutionalization, and coming to grips with one's mortality represent the major developmental crises of the elderly. Siegler and Hyer (1984) have summarized not only the common crises affecting older persons, but those impairing other age groups as well. Their conclusions are presented in Table 1.1.

Of the common crises listed in Table 1.1, two or three deserve special attention because of the sheer number of individuals involved. Coping with retirement is certainly one of the leading concerns. Currently, men spend nearly 14 years in retirement, and women, because of their longer life expectancy, spend more than 20 years.

The retirement period is characterized by greatly reduced incomes. Families headed by persons over age 65 have average incomes less than two-thirds of the average for families headed by persons between 25 and 64. There is also evidence that minorities and white women who are older fare considerably less well than older white males with regard to income (U.S. Committee on Aging, 1985–86). The financial situations of most groups of older persons is greatly exacerbated by the need for increasing expenditures for health care.

Adjusting to chronic health problems such as arthritis, hypertension, hearing loss, heart conditions, orthopedic impairment, sinusitis, and visual impairment are also major concerns of the elderly. Heart disease, cancer, and stroke, which are the leading causes of death among the elderly, often result in serious adjustment problems for the patients and their families.

Older people appear to have fewer mental problems than other age groups. However, cognitive impairment was a problem for about 14% of the elderly. Although National Institute of Mental Health studies found that persons 65 years of age and older had the lowest incidence of eight common disorders, suicides among the group were the highest for any age group, varying from 19 per 100,000 for 65–74-year-olds to about 15 per 100,000 for persons 85 and older (U.S. Committee on Aging, 1985–86).

In addition to the so-called common crises and to the other problems discussed above, the elderly also experience many of the problems of the other age groups, including physical, psychological, and sexual abuse (Fisher, 1985), alcohol and substance abuse, and psychosomatic complaints.

COUNSELORS AND MENTAL HEALTH PROBLEMS

The result of the historically unprecedented demand for mental health services has been a veritable explosion in the numbers of mental health practitioners, including psychologists, psychiatrists, psychiatric nurses, social workers, and counselors. The latter group, counselors, are in a very real sense newcomers, although, as we saw, the roots of the counseling profession go back at least three-quarters of a century. As newcomers, counselors have assumed fewer of the trappings of an established profession, such as extended training programs, certification boards, and aggressive enforcement of ethical codes, although these are rapidly being put into place. However, no group is better situated to address the mental health problems confronting members of our society.

Any of the aforementioned groups may take at least three approaches to dealing with mental health problems. One of these, the *developmental–primary prevention approach,* focuses upon programs and techniques that will keep mental health problems from arising. Drug education programs are an example of this approach to mental health problems. *Secondary prevention approaches* attempt to control mental health problems that have already surfaced, such as keeping mild substance abuse from becoming chronic. In the *tertiary approach,* mental health practitioners work to prevent serious mental health problems from becoming chronic or life threatening. Counselors primarily work with primary and secondary mental health prevention programs and techniques.

There are approximately 125,000 to 150,000 counselors in the United States, of whom about 55,000 belong to the American Association for Counseling and Development (AACD, 1985–86). Of these, large numbers are situated in public schools, colleges and universities, churches, rehabilitation agencies, employment offices, and mental health agencies. Additionally, a growing number of counselors offer counseling services as a part of business and industry, and as practitioners in consulting firms.

The number of counselors and the far-ranging nature of their placement are impressive in terms of their potential to meet the growing mental health problems. The general orientation of counselors to health and wellness, as opposed to psychopathology and mental illness, also enables counselors to deal with the burgeoning mental health concerns of our society. Some counselors are prepared to design and implement educational programs aimed at preventing mental health problems, to deal with short-term developmental crises such as divorce or death of a loved one, and to assist people to cope with developmental difficulties. These counselors may work in such areas as interpersonal relationships, career choice and development issues, time and stress management, developing decision-making skills, making education decisions, coping with authority figures, anger management, achievement motivation, adjusting to or coping with disabilities, and so on. Others are prepared to deliver long-term psychotherapy to those more seriously impaired. Among mental health practitioners, only counselors and counseling psychologists share this orientation, although there is some movement by other groups in this direction.

Not only does the orientation of counselors make them ideally suited to meet the mental health needs of our society, their placement in public agencies provides them with an opportunity to provide the needed services as well.

CURRENT STATUS OF THE PROFESSION

As can be discerned from the foregoing sections, the counseling profession has made giant strides toward assuming the trappings of a profession and is well positioned to assume a major role in the delivery of mental health services. Training standards are in place, a code of ethics has been adopted, certification programs have been established for a number of counseling specialties, and, in a number of states, legislatures have legally recognized counselors by passing licensure laws that regulate the use of the title *counselor* in the private sector. Another form of recognition has been accorded counselors in some states, such as Alabama and Florida, in the form of third-party payments by insurance companies for the provision of mental health services. School counseling has also been increasingly recognized as central to the process of schooling.

However, there are still issues to be addressed. The training standards for counselors are not uniform and are still somewhat lower than those for social workers, among whom the two-year Masters in Social Work (MSW) is the accepted norm (although some social workers practice with a bachelor's degree). For psychologists, of course, the doctoral degree is expected in most states. The Association for Mental Health Counselors is now pressing for a training standard that would be equivalent to the MSW and the two-year training program required for entering school psychology, in terms of both coursework and clinical experience. Little consideration is being given to the doctorate as a training standard for counselors, although many institutions offer the degree.

Because the counseling profession has not adopted the doctorate as a training standard, interest in the training programs at this level has waned at many institutions. As a result, many major counselor preparation institutions have converted their counselor education doctorates to counseling psychology training programs. One result of this has been to exacerbate the job hunting problem for individuals with a doctorate in counseling, since most of these institutions now require degrees in counseling psychology for employment. A second result is that individuals from major research institutions do not participate to the same degree in the affairs of the counseling profession, and thus a source of leadership has been lost. Finally, the move from counselor education to counseling psychology has in some instances focused research efforts on issues more related to psychology than to counseling, with the result that the empirical bases for certain aspects of the counseling profession have not grown as one would expect. To be sure, much of the research relating to counseling psychology pertains to counselors because of their common interests and focus.

Recognition of the counseling profession by governmental groups such as CHAMPUS (U.S. Office of Civilian Health and Medical Programs of the Uniformed Services) and by insurance companies has been slow in coming, but progress had been steady. Harold (1985) reports that some, but not all, counselors in Massachusetts, Montana, Colorado, Alabama, Virginia, and Florida received third-party payments. However, in some instances, counselors have to be supervised by psychiatrists or psychologists in order to be eligible for payment. One counselor (Covin, undated) has even developed a guide for collecting third-party payments from insurance carriers. States such as Florida, where freedom-of-choice legislation requires insurance companies to recognize counselors along with psychiatrists and psychologists, appear to be the most successful in this domain.

The enforcement of ethical behavior is one of the true hallmarks of a professional group. Until recently the Ethics Committee of AACD has been relatively inactive and many state branches of AACD do not have active ethics committees. While a number of states are moving ahead aggressively to remedy this situation, the degree of enforcement of ethical behavior remains a problem.

A companion problem to enforcing ethical behavior is legislative recognition of privileged communication between counselors and clients, which protects counselors from disclosing information gained in counseling. Subsectors of all licensing and certification laws deal with this problem and grant counselors immunity from disclosure. In other instances counselors have lobbied for, and been granted, privileged communication by legislatures independent of licensing laws. The fact remains that in some states, the counselors have not been accorded privileged communication. This is particularly problematic for counselors working in the public sector in institutions such as schools or rehabilitation agencies.

Finally, counselors have, at times, either not been included in the state mental health system, or found themselves supervised by psychologists or psychiatrists. To be sure, in some states, counselors are accorded the same status as other mental health professionals, but this is not always the case. These problems and the others mentioned are being aggressively addressed by the profession and will be resolved. Just how this is being done will be covered in later chapters.

SUMMARY

At the outset of the chapter, a brief history of the counseling profession was presented. An important part of the heritage of the profession is its ties to career choice-making, a part that still remains as a central focus of the profession. However, more recently, the profession has increased its focus on dealing with the myriad of personal problems confronting our society. Counselors, because of their placement and training, are well suited to deal with both sets of problems.

The current status of the profession was also addressed, and will continue to be addressed throughout the book. As was obvious, the counseling profession is in a state of dynamic growth and development at this time.

REVIEW QUESTIONS

1. Identify the key developmental periods in the development of the counseling profession. What did each contribute to the current status of the profession?
2. Given the vast number of problems confronting our society, can we justify a mental health strategy that concentrates on remediation? Provide a rationale for your answer.
3. Discuss the pros and cons of adopting a master's-level training standard for the counseling profession.

4. What does the counseling profession have to offer to our society that other mental health professions such as social work and psychology do not?

5. Write a prescription for the future development of the counseling profession.

REFERENCES

American Association for Counseling and Development. (1985–86). *AACD today.* Washington, DC: American Association for Counseling and Development.

American Journal of Public Health. (1984). Editorial, *75,* p. 1.

Aubrey, R. F. (1977). Historical developments of guidance and counseling and implications for the future. *Personnel and Guidance Journal, 55*(6), 288–295.

Bates, J. (1985). Families could aid mentally ill. *APA Monitor, 16*(7), 14.

Beers, C. (1908). *A mind that found itself.* New York: Longmans, Green, & Co.

Belkin, G. S. (1975). *Practical counseling in the schools.* Dubuque, IA: W. C. Brown Publishers.

Bradley, M. K. (1978). Counseling past and present: Is there a future? *Personnel and Guidance Journal, 57*(1), 42–45.

Brewer, J. M. (1942). *History of vocational guidance: Origins of early developments.* New York: Harper and Brothers.

Brown, D., & Brooks, L. (Eds.). (1984). *Career choice and development.* San Francisco: Jossey-Bass.

Bureau of the Census (1985). *Statistical abstracts of the United States 1985.* Washington, DC: Bureau of the Census.

Bureau of Labor Statistics (1986). *Facts on U.S. working women* (fact sheet #86–2). Washington, DC: U.S. Department of Labor.

Chambliss, D. L., & Goldstein, A. J. (1979). Behavioral psychotherapy. In R. J. Corsini (Ed.), *Current psychotherapies* (pp. 230–272). Itasca, IL: F. E. Peacock.

Children's Defense Fund (1984). News release. Washington, DC: Children's Defense Fund.

Children's Defense Fund (1985). News release cited in *Washington Post,* Tuesday, June 4, 1985.

Covin, T. M. (undated). *How to collect third-party payments: The professional counselor's guide to third-party reimbursement.* Ozark, AL: Center for Counseling and Human Development, Inc.

Crier, The (1985). Research on teenage pregnancy. Charlotte, NC: The Junior League.

Davis, J. B. (1904). *Moral and vocational development.* Boston: Ginn and Company.

Ellis, A. (1978). Rational-emotive therapy. In R. J. Corsini (Ed.), *Current psychotherapies* (pp. 185–229). Itasca, IL: F. E. Peacock.

Faust, V. (1968). *History of elementary school counseling.* Boston: Houghton Mifflin.

Fisher, K. (1985). Experts probe who, what, whys of elderly abuse. *APA Monitor, 16*(12), 24–26.

Gibson, R. L., & Mitchell, M. H. (1986). *Introduction to guidance.* New York: Macmillan.

Ginzberg, E. (1984). Career development. In D. Brown & L. Brooks (Eds.), *Career choice and development* (pp. 169–191). San Francisco: Jossey-Bass.

Ginzberg, E. Ginsburg, S. W., Axelrad, S., & Herma, J. (1951). *Occupational choice: An approach to a general theory.* New York: Columbia University Press.

Glaser, W., & Funin, L. M. (1978). Reality therapy. In R. J. Corsini (Ed.), *Current psychotherapies* (pp. 302–339). Itasca, IL: F. E. Peacock.

Harold, M. (1985). AMHCA updates third-party payment situation. *Guidepost, 28*(9), 1–6.

Herr, E. L., & Cramer, S. H. (1984). *Career guidance and counseling through the life span: Systematic approaches* (2nd ed.). Boston: Little, Brown & Co.

Herrington, L. H. (1985). Victims of crime: Their plight, our response. *American Psychologist, 40*(1), 99–103.

Johnston, L. D. (1985). News release. Ann Arbor, MI: News and Information Services, The University of Michigan Institute for Social Research.

Krumboltz, J. D. (Ed.). (1966). *Revolution in counseling.* Boston: Houghton Mifflin.

Lipsitz, J. (1985). A statistical portrait of American adolescents. *Common Focus, 6*(1), 1–5.

Miller, C. H. (1961). *Foundations of guidance.* New York: Harper & Row.

National Network of Runaway Youth Services (1985). News release. Washington, DC: National Network of Runaway Youth Services.

NCES (1983). *High school and beyond.* Washington, DC: National Center for Educational Statistics.

NCHS (1985a). Births, marriages, divorces, and deaths for September 1985. *NCHS Monthly Vital Statistics Report, 34*(9), 1–3.

NCHS (1985b). Advance report of final divorce statistics, 1983. *NCHS Monthly Vital Statistics Report, 34*(8) (Supplement), 1–13.

Parsons, F. (1909). *Choosing a vocation.* Boston: Houghton Mifflin.

Picchioni, A. P., & Bonk, E. C. (1983). *A comprehensive history of guidance in the United States.* Austin, TX: Texas Personnel and Guidance Association.

Rogers, C. R. (1942). *Counseling and psychotherapy.* Boston: Houghton Mifflin.

Rogers, C. R. (1951). *Client-centered therapy.* Boston: Houghton Mifflin.

Rogers, C. R. (1961). *On becoming a person.* Boston: Houghton Mifflin.

Sargent, M. (1984). Adolescent suicide: Studies reported. *APA MHA News, 10*(7), 8.

Siegel, M. (1985). Executive summary: Final report of the APA task force on victims of crime and violence. *American Psychologist, 40*(1), 107–112.

Siegler, I. C., & Hyer, L. A. (1984). Common crises in the family life of older workers. In D. Blazen & I. C. Siegler (Eds.), *A family approach to health care of the elderly* (pp. 33–50). Reading, MA: Addison-Wesley.

Super, D. E. (1953). A theory of vocational development. *American Psychologist, 8*(2), 185–190.

Turkington, C. (1985). EAPS: Healthier employees, lower cost spur growth of programs. *APA Monitor, 16*(8), 22–23.

U.S. Committee on Aging (1985–86). *Aging America: Trends and projections.* Washington, DC: U.S. Senate Special Committee on Aging.

Whitely, J. M. (1984). Counseling psychology: A historical perspective. *The Counseling Psychologist, 12*(1), 7–95.

Williamson, E. G. (1939). *How to counsel students.* New York: McGraw-Hill.

Zytowski, D. G. (1972). Four hundred years before Parsons. *Personnel and Guidance Journal, 50*(6), 443–450.

2

Normal Development
and Adjustment

GOAL OF THE CHAPTER

The aim of this chapter is to provide an overview of social and emotional development, factors that must be considered when one is planning counseling interventions.

CHAPTER PREVIEW

1. Development and adjustment will be defined.
2. Historic influences in the counseling profession that have promoted a developmental perspective toward clients will be presented.
3. Developmental theories that have influenced the counseling profession will be discussed.
4. A composite picture of developmental issues effecting clients will be drawn.

INTRODUCTION

Understanding human development and using it as a basis for helping clients is a major emphasis in counseling. At one time developmental change was a concept most often applied to the young; it is now used to understand persons of all ages. Its prominence in current thinking has altered views about delivery of human services. This chapter will provide an overview of the use of developmental theory in the counseling profession. Important developmental concepts and theories will be abstracted, and a sketch of developmental issues at each important period in a person's life will be presented. This treatment will become a basis for many of the ideas developed in later chapters.

DEFINING DEVELOPMENT

Development can be defined simply as change over time. Observation of a person's behavior from birth to death would reveal numerous behavior changes. Lefrancois (1984) notes that development involves growth, maturation, and learning, with each term having its own meaning. Growth refers to physical changes; mautration, to changes relatively independent of the environment; learning, to lasting changes attributable not to maturation but to experiences in the environment. Development is the composite outcome in terms of adaptability for the person; it represents not short-term learning but gradual adaptation over many years. Thus, adults have a better chance for survival than infants simply because they are better developed. In light of this, the counseling profession promotes human development as a way of helping clients adapt.

DEFINING ADJUSTMENT

The terms adjustment and adaptation are frequently used interchangeably. We stated above that adaptation is the outcome of the process of development. Adaptation is linked to human survival and the capabilities required to achieve it. At its most basic level, adjustment is a requisite for survival.

We expect more from adjusted persons than simple survival. Adjustment consists of coming to terms with the important features in human life. Certainly this includes reconciling oneself to those forces in nature that humans cannot control. It also includes coming to terms with other human beings, becoming able to coexist with them in relative harmony. In addition to involving an adaptation to physical and social environments, adjustment also entails evolving a relationship with self.

Coming to terms with oneself is a rich adjustment arena. This process consists of the meeting of needs that ascend into a hierarchy from survival to self-actualization (Maslow, 1954). Adjustment to self becomes a journey inward, with intense attention being given to the development and management of goals, values, and fundamental identity. At first reading this may sound confusing, since adjusting to self may sound as if a person is made of two different entities. Friedman (1976) calls it "aiming at the self"; each person must carefully attend to the establishment of a relationship with the unattended parts of personal experience. If one does not do this, unattended personal needs and unexamined wishes become troublesome or conflictual, limiting the actualization of potential.

Adjustment can become even more complex. Some developmentalists (e.g., Stensrud & Stensrud, 1984) contend that this adjustment process eventually must even go beyond self. Advocates of a holistic perspective have labeled some issues "transpersonal," which means going beyond a personal identity to one that unites self with larger realities. Transpersonal issues are relationship issues between people and the universe. Included are the recognition, acceptance, and realization of such states as illumination, mystical union, transcendence, and cosmic unity (Clark, 1977). There is for many (but not for all) a deeply spiritual side of adjustment.

PROMOTING DEVELOPMENT THROUGH COUNSELING AND CONSULTATION

The counseling profession has a rich tradition with regard to promoting development. This had been particularly true in school counseling. Reference to developmental issues appears very early in the history of counseling and guidance (Little & Chapman, 1955). Mathewson (1962) was a pioneer in attempting to articulate the role of the school counselor. He drew a continuum, with the practice of intense psychotherapy at one end and the practice of casework at the other; between these extremes he placed school counseling and guidance. Counselors were seen as utilizing to a degree the intense, personal relationship found in psychotherapy while also intervening broadly in the client's social environment. Thus, the early view of a counselor's role was somewhere between psychotherapist and case-oriented social worker.

Later Peters (1966) and Dinkmeyer (1966) elaborated on this view. They emphasized counselor effort at team-building, that is, working with other professional service-providers such as teachers, school administrators, and other social service professionals to promote the acquisition of adaptive behavior on the part of young clients. Fundamental to this position was the realization that many individuals and forces contribute to adjustment. At first the articulation of developmental counseling was general in nature. As increased effort was made to provide counseling and consultation services to elementary school–age children, the need for more precise developmental theories and concepts became evident (Dinkmeyer, 1966; Dinkmeyer & Caldwell, 1970).

Counselors over the last decade and a half took this beginning, did their homework in developmental psychology, and evolved what now is an elaborate developmental framework. Reliance on developmental concepts in counseling now goes far beyond school counseling and efforts with children to include work with clients of all ages. The chapter will survey the salient developmental concepts currently practiced in the counseling profession.

Key Concept: "The Developmental Mainstream."   To understand counselor involvement in promoting development is to understand the power and extent of developmental forces in combination with one another. To appreciate this one must have a belief in the general positive value of combined life experience. If one agrees that most people end up as decent, competent human beings if given access to "normal" life experience, then one can appreciate the value of planned developmental experience.

In other words, the developmental mainstream can be visualized as a sequence of varied experiences that promote positive growth, maturation, and learning. As long as individuals remain within this mainstream of experience, they will turn out all right. Of course, mainstream development does not preclude encounters with pain, challenge, unhappiness, and stress, but as this process runs its course, people will be better able to cope and find meaning. However, if people fall or are pushed out of this flow of normal development, they will miss opportunities, possibly to the point that they become handicapped in meeting the stresses of everyday life. From this can be seen the close connection between development and adjustment.

This view does not suggest that the mainstream of development cannot be enriched; each generation may, in fact, do this. Indeed recent generations, by virtue of their assault on prejudice, have widened the mainstream, enabling more individuals to benefit from it. Certainly the more that is understood about the process of mainstream development, the more it can be improved.

Global developmental forces have also produced some wreckage; persons have been damaged by the developmental mainstream. For example, adolescents commonly experience considerable peer pressure to experiment with alcohol and drugs. Sexual contact is accepted as a means for gaining social status. The importance of peer acceptance often propels youngsters into such areas long before they are developmentally ready for them. But, because contemporary counseling recognizes the value of the developmental mainstream for the most part, promoting human potential by keeping people healthy is an effort that is given greater emphasis than healing those who are sick and injured.

Both the healthy and the injured are the concern of counselors, who try to maintain health by keeping people within the mainstream while they strive to enhance it. Counselors work with the injured with the constant objective of reinstating them into the mainstream so that they may benefit from it. Counselors look first at developmental strengths and accomplishments, followed by an assessment of lost opportunities. Then is it possible to appraise deficiencies by viewing them as developmental omissions or delays.

This emphasis on normal development is extremely important in understanding counseling as a profession. A major achievement on the part of counselors has been the sensible recognition of who should get the credit for what happens to people. Both healing and keeping people healthy result from cooperative, combined efforts on the part of many.

STUDENT LEARNING EXERCISE

Read the following descriptions of incidents and indicate whether what the counselor is doing utilizes positive developmental forces. Circle Y for yes or N for no.

1. A school counselor pressures a mental health center to have its therapists see student clients at school so the children will not miss classes while being transported to the mental health center.   Y   N

2. A counselor in a group home for adolescents encourages residents to join other intramural teams instead of forming their own.   Y   N

3. A family counselor refuses to mediate a dispute between a teenager and her parents.   Y   N

IMPORTANT DEVELOPMENTAL CONCEPTS AND THEORIES

In addition to the concept of the developmental mainstream, it is important for counselors to understand the components of that mainstream. Hence a brief primer on prominent developmental concepts and theories will be attempted.

Some developmental theories attempt to explain human change over time by dividing all or part of the lifespan into steps or stages through which people evolve; the stages usually are connected to chronological age. Other theories describe the kinds of changes that occur in persons as they develop. According to such theories developmental stages begin and end when some significant change takes place; chronological age may or may not predict the change. This chapter will refer to some of the developmental theories as *stage-progression theories* and others as *stage-hierarchy theories*. These labels are used because they are descriptive of the essential nature of the theories classified.

The first group of theories in effect divides all or part of the lifespan into stages that signal different challenges, which ideally prompt new and different strategies in coping. No one stage is "better" than another; stages are simply different; they are more relevant to one age group than another. For example, adolescence can be viewed as a different developmental stage from childhood, but not necessarily a better one. Stage-hierarchy theories attempt to describe qualitative changes that occur in some dimension of human functioning. Later stages are clearly viewed as more advanced, "superior" levels of human existence.

The qualitative changes in human performance described by these theories are generally based on the notion that some structural development has occurred "inside" the individual. The person has a new implement or structure to use in dealing with the world. Such structures are not directly observable; their presence is based on the observation of response changes. For example, up to a certain age a child thinks a ribbon of clay becomes smaller when it is rolled into a tight ball. When a specific structure is formed in the intellect (called the Principle of the Conservation of Matter—by Piaget), a further developed child will recognize that both the ribbon of clay and the ball of clay contain the same amount of clay.

Moral development provides another example. Altruism, a selfless form of love, is not part of a person in the early stages of moral development. Rather, self-oriented pleasure-seeking is more representative of people at these stages (Kohlberg, 1969). Thus, self-sacrifice for the welfare of another would be unimaginable as a worthwhile and meaningful activity. This is so because the structure containing the idea of altruism has yet to be developed.

Stage-hierarchy theories provide use with an architectural view of self-development, whether the theory applies to cognition, the making of moral decisions, or ego development. Study of these theories can enhance one's ability to conceptualize how adaptive resources build in an individual. Such theories are mostly descriptive; that is, they describe different levels of development without saying much about what it is that influences the advance to the next developmental level.

Both progression and the hierarchy theories, popular among counselors, are epigenetic in nature, which means that the theories see earlier stages of development as the basis for later stages (Lidz, 1976). Development in later stages utilizes as a foundation that which was achieved in previous stages. In stage-progression theories, if an individual does not achieve at least baseline objectives in an earlier stage, the person will have a poor basis for gaining the full benefit of developmental experiences at later stages. This deficit will be carried through the entire balance of that person's developmental history. However, the individual will progress on to later developmental stages. At a later stage the person with earlier developmental problems will not meet the challenges of that period as well as others who did not suffer the earlier difficulty. For example, identity formation is the key issue in adolescence, according to Erikson (1968). In early adulthood the principal developmental objective is the formation of intimate relationships. If identity formation does not progress well for the adolescent, adult intimacy is also in jeopardy, since it is best built upon a stable self-image.

In stage-hierarchy theories, if a person gets "hung up" or stopped at a particular developmental stage, there can occur no further development in the particular area of functioning the theory is describing. If the issue is moral development, for example, a person may reach a certain stage of moral decision-making and not advance to higher levels (Kohlberg, 1969). Individuals of the same chronological age will respond differently to the same moral dilemmas depending on the different stages of moral development each has attained.

The counseling profession has drawn upon many of the developmental approaches that fit into this category. The most popular is Erik Erikson's eight ages of man (1963). More recently adult development has been the dominant focus of attention in the literature. Counselors have enriched their therapeutic practice by incorporating key concepts concerning adult life changes. In the counseling literature, Daniel Levinson and his colleagues (Levinson, Darrow, Klein, Levinson, & McKee, 1978) are the most frequently quoted contributors to understanding adult development. Gail Sheehy's best-selling *Passages* (1974) was based on Levinson's principal concepts.

Erik Erikson's Developmental Theory

Erik Erikson is a fascinating author. Among his many works are his general theory of development (1963), numerous comments on social issues (e.g., nuclear war, racial tensions, changing sex roles, etc), and several biographies of great men. One of these biographies, *Gandhi's Truth* (1969), won a Pulitzer Prize.

Erikson's theory of development is considered to be neo-Freudian; it is an expansion on Freud's psychosexual stages. Erikson looks at both psychological and social development over the lifespan, mapping development by means of eight psychosocial stages (see Table 2.1). Each stage is differentiated from the other by means of the separate issues or "crises" a person must face at a particular stage. For example, in Stage 2 a child struggles for increased independence and resistance to control by parents, yet maintains a lingering awareness of vulnerablility and the need for protection. A clash of wills, symbolized by toilet training, represents this particular stage.

In coping with the crises at each stage of development, according to Erikson, people risk both positive and negative outcomes, such as autonomy versus shame and guilt. Obviously, favorable development strives for more of the positive; at least it is hoped that positive outcomes will predominate over negative ones. Since Erikson's theory is epigenetic in nature, each stage builds on earlier ones, mandating stage-related successes as the foundation for later development.

Social involvement is integral to Erikson's theory. As a person matures, social contact expands. During the first three stages parents and the family are central; broader involvements follow. The peer group is central to Stage 5. Partners and lasting friendships follow in Stage 6. Finally, in Stage 8 union with the brotherhood of mankind becomes the ultimate social issue.

Throughout Erikson's theory, but especially during adolescence, identity formation is a chief point of emphasis. People at all ages are asking themselves who they are. Just as synthesis is considered one of the highest mental functions, a synthesized view of self (identity) is a life-long goal. At adolescence the struggle for identity reaches a crisis (Erikson, 1968). This is not surprising in light of the fact that adolescents have just developed a new body with new urges. New pressures develop, especially around education and career. Erikson (1968) notes that adolescents will experiment with many iden-

Table 2.1 Worksheet Summarizing the Eight Stages of Development

Stage	A Psychosocial crises	B Radius of significant relations	C Related elements of social order	D Psychosocial modalities	E Psychosexual stages
1	Trust versus mistrust	Maternal person	Cosmic order	To get To give in return	Oral-respiratory, sensory-kinesthetic (incorporative modes)
2	Autonomy versus shame, doubt	Parental persons	"Law and order"	To hold (on) To let (go)	Anal-urethral, muscular (retentive-eliminative)
3	Initiative versus guilt	Basic family	Ideal prototypes	To make (= going after) To "make like" (= playing)	Infantile-genital, locomotor (intrusive, inclusive)
4	Industry versus inferiority	"Neighborhood," school	Technological elements	To make things (= completing) To make things together	"Latency"
5	Identity and repudiation versus identity diffusion	Peer groups and out-groups; models of leadership	Ideological perspectives	To be oneself (or not to be) To share being oneself	Puberty
6	Intimacy and solidarity versus isolation	Partners in friendship, sex, competition, cooperation	Patterns of cooperation and competition	To lose and find oneself in another	Genitality
7	Generativity versus self-absorption	Divided labor and shared household	Currents of education and tradition	To make be To take care of	
8	Integrity versus despair	"Mankind" "My kind"	Wisdom	To be, through having been To face not being	

tities through participation in different peer groups, clubs, and political movements. Affluent youth may find they have too many choices; disadvantaged youth may succumb to the negative identity repeatedly pressed upon them.

Levinson's Theory of Adult Development

Levinson's theory originated in his early study of men's lives (1977, 1978), with an emphasis on mid-life, the years between 40 and 45. His theory has been extended to women (1987) and represents a pioneering attempt to chart changes adults experience.

Besides developing a theory that at present describes nine developmental periods in adulthood, Levinson introduces a series of global concepts to capture the chain of events in people's lives. One such concept is *life course*. Levinson (1986) believes that life needs to be studied as it unfolds over the years in order to account for stability and change, continuity and discontinuity, orderly progression as well as stasis and chaotic fluctuation. In studying life course, one must look at life in all its complexity at a given time to include all its components and their evolution. Beyond life course is *life cycle*, which is divided into various segments or seasons, just as the year is divided into seasons. *Eras* are broad segments of the life cycle; preadulthood, early adulthood, middle adulthood, and late adulthood are the eras of Levinson's theory.

Within each era there are stable periods and periods of flux or change. The work done on what Levinson calls the *life structure* determines stability or flux. As people go through life they work on forming an underlying pattern or design that is called the life structure. Relationships are the primary determiner of a person's life structure at any given time. The relationships can be with people, self, groups, institutions, culture, or a particular object or place. Most important are relationships with marriage and family and with occupation.

At different times a person will follow a given life structure for 5 to 7 years, but will eventually recognize that the life structure is not satisfying all needs. Momentum will build to question that life structure, to evaluate it with the intent to change or rebuild it in some way. As this happens the person begins another 5-to-7–year period of transition between one structure and another. Half of a person's life is spent in transition (Levinson, 1986). A particularly negative and intense transition is called a crisis.

Like many other developmental theories, Levinson's assigns special tasks to be worked on at different periods (see Figure 2.1). The developmental tasks are like questions asked of everyone. Answers to the questions can vary infinitely. How a given person answers these questions relates to the work done on forming a life structure. Overall, if one looks at the life course as an order shaped by eras and by periods of life structure development, the underlying order to human life becomes apparent. Stage-progression theories make sense out of experiences that as single events lose meaning.

Kohlberg's Theory of Moral Development

As portrayed in Table 2.2, Lawrence Kohlberg (1969) offers a useful stage-hierarchy theory of moral development. In it he proposes the progressive acquisition of three levels of moral judgment. The earliest level is based on reward and punishment, followed by a conventional morality based on rules, and finally a stage of relativistic values based on universal principles. Within the levels

Figure 2.1 Developmental Periods in the Eras of Early and Middle Adulthood. *Note.* From "Developmental Periods in the Eras of Early and Middle Adulthood from a Conception of Adult Development," by Daniel J. Levinson, 1986, *American Psychologist*, 41(1), p. 3. An earlier version appeared in Daniel J. Levinson with C. N. Darrow, E. B. Klein, M. H. Levinson, and B. McKee, *The Seasons of a Man's Life,* Copyright © 1978 by Alfred A. Knopf, Inc. Reprinted by permission.

Table 2.2 Kohlberg's Stages of Moral Development

Level	Stage	Description of stage
Preconventional	Punishment/obedience	Decisions based on physical consequences
	Instrumental hedonism	Seek pleasure and avoid pain
Conventional	Good-boy, nice-girl	Seek approval of others
	Law and order	Uncritical following of authority
Autonomous	Social contract	Obey contract arrived at democratically, will of the people
	Individual conscience	Ethics self-chosen based on universal principles

are stages of moral development that further define how individuals make moral decisions. Since clients often seek counselors when an important decision must be made, Kohlberg's theory can help in understanding the decision-making process and some of its outcomes.

Like many theories, Kohlberg's sequence of development has not always been verified by research findings (Holstein, 1976). Of considerable interest in such stage-hierarchy theories is the description of the process by which one can achieve the highest level. For Kohlberg this is altruism. This is especially relevant to counselors, who have devoted themselves to caring for others.

Loevinger's Theory of Ego Development

Jane Loevinger (1976) has attempted an integrative theory of ego development in which moral judgment, character formation, socialization, and intellectual development are treated. As represented in Table 2.3, the student of human development, through Loevinger, can examine and integrate concepts from Erikson, Piaget, and Kohlberg, and others.

STUDENT LEARNING EXERCISE
Read the following statements and indicate whether the counselor's action is consistent with the developmental theories just reviewed. Circle Y for yes or N for no.

1. A high school counselor spends considerable time training students to be peer counselors.   Y   N
2. A mental health counselor believes that depression is more likely at certain ages than at others because of predictable life changes.   Y   N
3. A child counselor rarely works with the parents of his child clients.   Y   N

Table 2.3 Some Milestones of Ego Development

Stage	Impulse control, character development	Interpersonal style	Conscious preoccupations	Cognitive style
Presocial		Autistic		
Symbiotic		Symbiotic	Self versus nonself	
Impulsive	Impulsive, fear of retaliation	Receiving, dependent, exploitative	Bodily feelings, especially sexual and aggressive	Stereotyping, conceptual confusion
Self-protective	Fear of being caught, externalizing blame, opportunistic	Wary, manipulative, exploitative	Self-protection, trouble, wishes, things, advantage, control	
Conformist	Conformity to external rules, shame, guilt for breaking rules	Belonging, superficial niceness	Appearance, social acceptability, banal feelings, behavior	Conceptual simplicity, stereotypes, cliches
Conscientious-conformist	Differentiation of norms, goals	Aware of self in relation to group, helping	Adjustment, problems, reasons, opportunities (vague)	Multiplicity

Stage	Impulse Control, Character Development	Interpersonal Style	Conscious Preoccupations	Cognitive Style
Conscientious	Selfevaluated standards, self-criticism, guilt for consequences, long-term goals and ideals	Intensive, responsible, mutual, concern for communication	Differentiated feelings, motives for behavior, self-respect, achievements, traits, expression	Conceptual complexity, idea of patterning
Individualistic	Add: Respect for individuality	Add: Dependence as an emotional problem	Add: Development, social problems, differentiation of inner life from outer	Add: Distinction of process and outcome
Autonomous	Add: Coping with conflicting inner needs, toleration	Add: Respect for autonomy, interdependence	Add: Vividly conveyed feelings, integration of physiological and psychological, psychological causation of behavior, role conception, self-fulfillment, self in social context	Increased conceptual complexity, complex patterns, toleration for ambiguity, broad scope, objectivity
Integrated	Add: Reconciling inner conflicts, renunciation of unattainable	Add: Cherishing of individuality	Add: Identity	

Note: "Add" means in addition to the description applying to the previous level. From *Ego Development: Conceptions and Theories* (pp. 24–25) by J. Loevinger, 1976, San Francisco: Jossey-Bass. Reprinted by permission.

MERGING THEORIES OF DEVELOPMENT

The composite picture of human growth and development resulting from theory-building and related research helps the counselor to monitor the progress and problems of clients. This section provides a synopsis of selected but important challenges facing clients at different periods in their lifespan, hopefully introducing ideas that help with decisions regarding what a counselor can do to wisely assist clients. The discussion treats three broad life periods: childhood, adolescence, and adulthood. Social and emotional development are emphasized.

Developmental Issues During Childhood

Much of the developmental literature associated with early childhood emphasizes the importance of the parenting received by the infant and toddler. If the persons caring for the child are comfortable with their role and nurturing to the child, it is likely that the child's future relationships will be positive. In these early relationships the basis for bonding with others is established. Attachment and loss are relationship issues of enormous magnitude in human life; they appear repeatedly regardless of the age of a client. Early separations from the primary-care adult can have a major impact on the long-term emotional health of a person (Bowlby, 1969).

While some parent-child relationship factors may be subtle with regard to their long-range impact, issues of abuse and neglect are not. Each year thousands of children in the United States are sufficiently abused that intervention from social agencies is required. Regrettably the most seriously injured are usually the very young. Counselors who work exclusively with adults will likely deal with clients who portray in later years the crippling effects of early abuse (Leehan & Wilson, 1985). Another paramount issue in rearing children is their socialization in the family. This includes the important topic of discipline. Ideally parents help a child learn respect for the rights of others and how to conform to arrangements that lead to harmonious social relationships while concurrently maintaining and enhancing personal autonomy.

An important landmark in development is the first time a youngster says "no" (Spitz, 1957); this event marks the development of one of those internal structures by which it can be ascertained that the child has differentiated self from important others. From that point on there exists the potential for a conflict of will. Effective parenting does not defeat the child's effort to exercise the will and at the same time provides experience in the beneficial nature of cooperative relationships. A breakdown in the resolution of this important developmental issue can lead to the extremes of either an overly compliant individual or one obsessed with power and control. Later, as such a child enters school, repercussions from this unresolved developmental struggle can result in problems of both discipline and achievement (Dreikurs, Grunwald, & Pepper, 1982).

Schooling constitutes much of the developmental mainstream in middle childhood. During these years peer relationships and personal achievement replace dependence on caretakers as central challenges. Sullivan (1953) associates childhood friendships with meaningful and lasting relationships in adulthood. For this reason the ability to assess peer acceptance and rejection (utilize such techniques as sociometry) is an important competency for both teachers and counselors. Through relationships with peers youngsters manufacture much of their self-esteem. In turn self-esteem constitutes much of the raw energy used to fuel academic achievement.

The ease or difficulty that a child has in meeting academic requirements warrants careful attention. Although there are some negative consequences associated with giftedness (e.g., feeling different), the repeated experience of failure in the classroom eventually wears down adaptive resources. Contemporary counselors, with the help of other professionals, can more fully understand such difficulties. Minimal brain dysfunction and specific learning disabilities, important contributors to school failure, have been better understood in recent years. However, these and other factors that contribute to developmental delays are not easily diagnosed. Estimates are that 2–4% of U.S. students have identifiable learning disabilities (Johnson & Morasky, 1980). Learning disabled individuals are of normal intelligence but have difficulty in one or more subject areas. Some learning disabled individuals can be identified through visual, motor, or speech/hearing problems; others are less obvious, appearing restless or inattentive.

From this brief overview of childhood development several critical features stand out as worthy of monitoring by the counselor. These include parental nurturing and discipline, a child's over-compliance or oppositional behavior, emotional energy and self-esteem, peer relations/social withdrawal, and school failure or uneven achievement. Important but not discussed in this abbreviated summary are both language and physical development.

Developmental Issues During Adolescence

Physical development and its primary psychological counterpart, body image, achieve major significance in adolescence. Since pubescence marks the beginning of this period, sexual self-image is an essential part of the teenager's effort to form an acceptable identity. Adolescents are extremely self-conscious about their bodies and their behavior. Elkind (1980) describes this self-consciousness as a feeling of being perpetually "on stage"; adolescents unconsciously sense that everyone is watching them, waiting for them to make a mistake so they can be ridiculed.

Coleman (1981) lists the following as important issues that arise in counseling adolescent males: changing relationships, masturbation, premarital sex, unwanted pregnancy of a sexual partner, venereal disease, and drug problems. Sexual preference and considerable uneasiness regarding homosexuality combine with initial attempts at personal intimacy to dominate the teenager's view of sexuality.

Adolescence is certainly one of the most intense periods of social development. Dunphy (1963) describes the evolution of adolescent social relationships. This process begins with isolated same-sex groups, the higher status members of which begin to form heterosexual cliques. The formation of heterosexual cliques spreads to others with considerable interaction among the various cliques, leading to what is often referred to as "the crowd." However, in late adolescence "the crowd" begins to disintegrate into a loose network of couples. Of major concern developmentally are those individuals who do not achieve membership in heterosexual groups; they remain on the periphery of the adolescent social world.

Late adolescence is the most common time for an individual to come to grips with questions of sexual preference. A consistent pattern of "childhood gender nonconformity" (Bell, Weinberg, & Hammersmith, 1981) and an increasing awareness of feeling "different" begin to engender very difficult questions. Most people who eventually develop a homosexual identity begin dating as heterosexuals (Bell & Weinburg, 1978), but they experience closeness with members of the opposite sex as lacking in physical attraction. Concurrently they begin to experience undeniable awareness of their strong sexual attraction toward members of the same sex. During late adolescence or early 20s most begin to acknowledge, often with difficulty, and eventually come to accept their homosexuality. With this acceptance begins an evolution toward a workable lifestyle.

Adolescents are frequently accused of being moody. They do frequently become depressed, and in fact suicide has been found to be the leading cause of adolescent death (Klagsbrun, 1976).

A major factor that contributes to the unevenness of mood and behavior among adolescents is the still-developing sense of identity (Erikson, 1968). As the self-image becomes more secure, behavior becomes more stable. Unfortunately self-concept development is the basis for career decision-making (Super, 1957), and often teenagers are pushed to make extremely important initial career decisions while their self-concepts are still somewhat unstable. This sometimes forces impulsive choices, ones much less appropriate than choices made later when a better developed self-image acts as a guide. Planning for the future is a paramount concern at this time of life, and it generates within the young person considerable anxiety.

Going to college or becoming employed has great symbolic meaning in connection with the adolescent's struggle to separate from parents. Counselors know full well how common tensions are among teenagers and their parents. In fact authority figures in general often do not interpret the rebelliousness of youth as an effort on their part to gain a sense of control over the various roles they must play.

Developmental Issues During Adulthood

Levinson and his associates (1978) identify the real beginning of adulthood as that day in a person's life when he leaves his parents' home realizing that it will never again be his home. Adult development differs from that of childhood and adolescence in that it is less closely linked with chronological age. It begins with the challenges of economic independence and intimate relationships.

In contrast to earlier generations, where heterosexual marriage and children were seemingly the only acceptable courses, contemporary adulthood has many more lifestyle options. Remaining single, choosing a homosexual lifestyle, and living with another person of the opposite sex without getting married have become more acceptable than they were earlier. Regardless of chosen lifestyle, the questions facing adults remain the same; people simply execute a greater variety of answers. Will I marry? Will I have children? Will I attempt to use my employment as a major source of gratification? These and others are common questions for the adult.

Early Adulthood.   If leaving home, both physically and psychologically, marks the beginning of adulthood, the developmental challenge is to reach out to others without the security of knowing that they are part of one's family. Most views of adult development portray the 20s as a time to further complete a sense of personal identity by making commitments to relationships, a career, and possibly a community. Making such choices provides a concrete representation of who we are trying to become. In addition to including spouses/living partners and young children, early adulthood involves other important relationships. One such relationship can be with a mentor. This individual, according to Levinson and associates (1978), is a person one-half a generation older who promotes especially one's career development through sponsorship and teaching of the subtle, success-related maneuvers. Relationships with mentors, while beneficial, require additional energy, which further complicates this life period.

The difficulty of combining the themes just mentioned with learning to manage finances and household, and possibly beginning a family, taxes the adaptive resources of the person. Early adulthood ends with a period of transition from the late 20s to the mid-30s during which relationships and values are reappraised. Pressure intensifies to make significant career gains during just the period when one's challenge at home may be to adjust to growing children. It is a time to reevaluate a marriage that is likely different from how it began. For the unmarried who would like to be married it is a time to reconcile with a single lifestyle. As adults, men and women face the same questions, though some differences do occur. In particular, it may be that women face especially important career questions a little later than men because of an earlier absorption with marriage and children (Fitzgerald & Crites, 1980).

Middle Adulthood.   The last half of the 30s can be a fulfilling period marked with career success and improved psychological autonomy. This only precedes the much-publicized "midlife crisis" or transition. At approximately age 40 people go through a stage that is second only to adolescence for being explosive and unstable. Neugarten (1976) provides the key indicator of midlife: Prior to it people thank of how old they are; after it they think of how many years they have left.

Midlife is a time for intense reevaluation. It is a time when many compare achievements to goals, with the former never quite matching the latter. It is common for an individual to experience at this time what in retrospect will be viewed as the peak of his or their career; most people also become very aware of the magnitude of what they have sacrificed for their career achievements. The questions often faced during this period are fundamental to the search for meaning. What makes it all the more difficult for many people are the challenges to deal also with teenage children, the recognition of clear signs of personal aging, and possibly the need to care for aged parents.

This self-examination, while at times painful, has the value of enabling individuals to balance out their personalities, fulfill neglected needs, and possibly repair damaged relationships with important others. As in earlier transitional periods it helps launch the person into a new level of maturity. A significant outcome of this growth often is more genuine and complete self-acceptance.

Such a transition in life is described by many as a mellowing of the individual. If successful in dealing with the changes of adulthood to this point, an individual can broaden her or his involvements and become less driven by a handful of life goals. Certainly health problems can become more significant, and financial pressures continue even for the middle-class with the need to finance college for children.

The themes developed following the midlife evaluation continue as middle adulthood enters its last phase. At this point such issues as preparing for retirement or adjusting to the loss of a mate become more important.

Late Adulthood.   Some caution needs be mentioned regarding generalizations that can be made about persons in their 60s and beyond. A major investigation conducted by the Social Security Administration (Irelan, Motley, Schwab, Sherman, & Murray, 1976) presents evidence that suggests major differences among groups of retirees at six-year intervals. This suggests a new generation of retirees at approximately each half decade. As the proportion of our population becomes older, better educated, better prepared for the last era of life, we are strongly encouraged to reevaluate and revise our theories of old age (Sarason, Sarason, & Cowden, 1975). In summary, the verdict about what it means to be elderly in the last decade or two of the 20th century is as yet not available.

COUNSELING APPLICATIONS

From the study of human growth and development can be drawn some specific principles to guide counselor practice. First, it is evident that clients at different developmental levels possess differing capacities to cognitively process events, to accomplish moral reasoning, and to make decisions. Both Elkind (1980) from a Piagetian position and Swensen (1980) from a Loevinger-based ego development point of view argue for the selection of counseling strategy with developmental level as a major criterion. For example, Swensen suggests that certain clients might benefit more from a behavioral approach than from one of the "actualizing" therapies because these clients remain at a developmental stage in which their behavior is influenced by external consequences and they are not yet at a level at which an evolving autonomy can be fostered so as to strengthen their ability to transcend such external controls.

Counselors would be wise to integrate into their practice another of Swensen's (1980) recommendations: to be cognizant of the fact that within each counseling dyad the ego development of the counselor may need to be more advanced than that of the client in order for the latter to benefit optimally from the relationship. The self-development of the counselor may determine the ceiling for client self-development as a result of that treatment, provided Swensen is correct. If the profession is to treat all persons, including well-functioning individuals in search of additional personal growth, the above implies two powerful mandates: (1) careful selection of candidates for the profession and (2) the continued self-development of counselors and other helpers.

The developmental literature uses the concept of readiness to describe optimal periods during which it is possible for an individual to make a significant advance in development. To prompt the development of a particular capability prior to that time, though not impossible, requires more effort than it is ultimately worth. Any gain achieved, beyond what another individual at the same developmental level could accomplish without special effort, would be lost at a later date. Hopefully the recognition of this phenomenon encourages among members of the counseling profession a deep respect for "nature" and the order that has evolved over time.

Probably the most impelling impression a counselor would experience upon reviewing normal developmental histories is of the intensity of the struggle that is inherent in growing up. It is no simple task to take advantage of all the opportunities for becoming more mature. Many developmentalists describe the process involved in progressive and positive development as the "stretching" of a person. If a challenge lies too far beyond the capability of an individual, it provides an opportunity for failure, discouragement, and defeat. If a challenge is too easy, it does not help the individual build further upon his or her repertoire of adaptive capabilities. Ideally, from a developmental point of view, a life challenge should be just a little beyond what is comfortable for a person to attain (McCoy, Ryan, & Lichtenberg, 1978). The individual must "reach" or "stretch" in order to succeed in the effort. This optimal distance promotes progressive, positive development by providing the incentive for enlarging one's repertoire of adaptive responses.

Beginning counselors have difficulty achieving this ideal balance; they vacillate between being overly protective and overly confrontive. At times they encourage their clients to escape from some of the pain necessary to overcome important problems and conflicts. In other situations beginning counselors get impatient and tend to hurry a client through the careful deliberation of changes at a transitional stage in life. With experience comes a greater capacity to set reasonable expectations during the intital phase of work with a client, and also the self-confidence and security to adjust or change treatment plans in accord with what will promote client growth.

Finally, one might reflect again on the fact that an understanding of normal development certifies the frequent anxieties and uncertainties people experience as they live out the human experience. As Moreland (1979) points out, confusion, feeling out-of-control, and being depressed are common to individuals going through predictable life transitions. Yet such feelings are often diagnosed by counselors as clear indicators of psychopathology. Familiarity with normal development assists the counselor in both avoiding the misdiagnosis of problems and in timing appropriate treatments. A thorough understanding of human development is certainly one of the most important factors in the knowledge foundation of a competent counselor.

SUMMARY

This chapter reviewed the respect for and the utilization of normal developmental forces in the work of counselors. Maturation was described as a life-long process that helps build adaptive skills in people. In part the building process results from being forced to meet predictable challenges at regular intervals in life. Counselors attempt to understand these challenges to help their clients increase the benefit achieved from these experiences. In this way natural forces instead of aritificial ones are used to enhance the development of clients.

REVIEW QUESTIONS

1. Compare the period in the history of the counseling profession when developmental concepts began to influence practice with other historic influences of the same period (see Chapter 1).
2. List developmental theories other than the ones treated in this chapter that also can be classified as "stage-progression" or "stage-hierarchy."
3. List the key concepts in this chapter. Look up those concepts in the index at the back of the text to note other places where they are discussed.
4. List the issues one can expect to meet when counseling adolescent clients.

5. What is the explanation for the developmental changes adults experience?
6. What are some developmental explanations for anxiety?
7. What sexual issues are likely to arise during different developmental periods?
8. How do interpersonal relationships change as one matures? What relationships are likely to cause problems for clients at different life stages?

REFERENCES

Bell, A. P., Weinberg, M. S. (1978). *Homosexualities: A study of diversity among men and women.* New York: Simon and Schuster.

Bell, A. P., Weinberg, M. S., & Hammersmith, S. K. (1981). *Sexual preference: Its development in men and women.* Bloomington, IN: Indiana University Press.

Bowlby, J. (1969). *Attachment and loss* (Vol. I). New York: Basic Books.

Clark, F. V. (1977). Transpersonal perspectives in psychotherapy. *Journal of Humanistic Psychology. 17*(1), 69–81.

Coleman, E. (1981). Counseling adolescent males. *Personnel and Guidance Journal, 60*(4), 215–218.

Dinkmeyer, D. (1966). Developmental counseling in the elementary school. *Personnel and Guidance Journal, 45*(3), 262–266.

Dinkmeyer, D., & Caldwell, E. (1970). *Developmental counseling and guidance: A comprehensive school approach.* New York: McGraw-Hill.

Dreikurs, R., Grunwald, B. R., & Pepper, F. C. (1982). *Maintaining sanity in the classroom: Illustrated teaching techniques* (2nd. ed). New York: Harper and Row.

Dunphy, D. C. (1963). The social structure of urban adolescent peer groups. *Sociometry, 26*(3), 230–246.

Elkind, D. (1980). Child development and counseling. *Personnel and Guidance Journal, 58*(5), 353–357.

Erikson, E. H. (1963). *Childhood and society* (2nd. ed.). New York: W. W. Norton.

Erikson, E. H. (1968). *Identity: Youth in crisis.* New York: W. W. Norton.

Erikson, E. H. (1980). *Identity and the life cycle.* New York: W. W. Norton.

Fitzgerald, L. F., & Crites, J. O. (1980). Toward a career psychology of women: What do we know? What do we need to know? *Journal of Counseling Psychology, 27*(1), 44–62.

Freidman, M. (1976). Aiming at the self: The paradox of encounter and the human potential movement. *Journal of Humanistic Psychology, 16*(1), 5–34.

Gould, R. L. (1978). *Transformations: Growth and change in adult life.* New York: Simon and Schuster.

Havighurst, R. J. (1972). *Developmental tasks and education* (3rd. ed.). New York: David McKay.

Holstein, C. B. (1976). Irreversible stepwise sequence in the development of moral judgment: A longitudinal study of males and females. *Child Development, 47*(1), 51–61.

Irelan, L. M., Motley, D. K., Schwab, K., Sherman, S. R., & Murray, J. (1976). *Almost 65: Baseline data from the retirement history study.* Washington, DC: U.S. Government Printing Office.

Johnson, W. W., & Morasky, R. L. (1980). *Learning disabilities* (2nd. ed.). Boston: Allyn and Bacon.

Klagsbrun, F. (1976). *Youth and suicide.* Boston: Houghton Mifflin.

Kohlberg, L. (1969). Stage and sequence: The cognitive developmental approach to socialization. In D. A. Goslin (Ed.), *Handbook of socialization theory and research.* Chicago: Rand McNally.

Leehan, J., & Wilson, L. P. (1985). *Grown-up abused children.* Springfield, IL: Charles C Thomas Publisher.

Lefrancois, G. R. (1984). *The lifespan.* Belmont, CA: Wadsworth Publishing Company.

Levinson, D. J. (1977). The mid-life transition. *Psychiatry, 40*(1), 99–112.

Levinson, D. J. (1986). A conception of adult development. *American Psychologist, 41* (1), 3–13.

Levinson, D. J. (1987). *The seasons of a woman's life.* New York: Knopf.

Levinson, D. J., Darrow, C. N., Klein, E. B., Levinson, M. H., & McKee, B. (1978). *The seasons of a man's life.* New York: Ballantine Books.

Lidz, T. (1976). *The person: His and her development throughout the life cycle* (Revised edition). New York: Basic Books.

Little, W., & Chapman, A. L. (1955). *Developmental guidance in the secondary school.* New York: McGraw-Hill.

Loevinger, J. (1976). *Ego development.* San Francisco: Jossey-Bass.

McCoy, V. R., Ryan, C., & Lichtenberg, J. W. (1978). *The adult life cycle: Training manual and reader.* Lawrence, KS: Adult Life Resource Center.

Maslow, A. H. (1954). *Motivation and personality.* New York: Harper & Row.

Mathewson, R. H. (1962). *Guidance policy and practice.* New York: Harper & Row.

Moreland, J. R. (1979). Some implications of life-span development for counseling psychology. *Personnel and Guidance Journal, 57,* 299–304.

Neugarten, B. L. (1976). The psychology of aging: An overview. *Master lectures on developmental psychology.* Washington, DC: American Psychological Association.

Peters, H. J. (1966). Developmental counseling. *Clearing House, 41,* 111–117.

Sarason, D. B., Sarason, E. K., & Cowden, P. (1975). Aging and the nature of work. *American Psychologist, 30*(5), 584–592.

Sheehy, G. (1974). *Passages: Predictable crises of adult life.* New York: E. P. Dutton and Company.

Spitz, R. A. (1957). *No and yes.* New York: International Universities Press.

Stensrud, R., & Stensrud, K. (1984). Holistic health through holistic counseling: Toward a unified theory. *The Personnel and Guidance Journal, 62*(7), 421–424.

Sullivan, H. S. (1953). *The interpersonal theory of psychiatry.* New York: W. W. Norton.

Super, D. E. (1957). *The psychology of careers.* New York: Harper and Row.

Swensen, C. H. (1980). Ego development and a general model for counseling and psychotherapy. *Personnel and Guidance Journal, 58,* 382–388.

3

Counseling: Theory
and Practice

GOAL OF THE CHAPTER

The purpose of this chapter is to survey popular counseling theories and how they are developed and used.

CHAPTER PREVIEW

1. The historic development of the practice of counseling as distinct from psychotherapy will be explored.
2. An overview of the characteristics and components of counseling theories will be presented.
3. Major counseling approaches will be summarized.

INTRODUCTION

This is the first of two chapters designed to acquaint readers with the theory and practice of counseling. Counseling will be defined. The similarities and differences between counseling and psychotherapy will be reviewed, with emphasis on the search for effective, short-term therapies. Following a brief historical review, short-term treatment will be explored. Ways of classifying counseling approaches will be discussed; components of theoretical systems in counseling will be examined. Several popular approaches to counseling will be outlined. In Chapter 4 the discussion begun here will be completed with a discussion of some general aspects of the counseling process.

HELPING PEOPLE CHANGE

Helping people change has always been a concern of advancing cultures. For centuries Western Civilization has sanctioned some of its members as helpers for others in this change process. For a little less than a century one general way to help has been through talk, persuasion, and caring. Individuals trained to do this well have been called either counselors or psychotherapists. Both work in similar ways; they are trained healers who help suffering people primarily though words, acts, and rituals (Frank, 1973). While differences between these two disciplines exist (to be discussed later), the need to help people change is a common reason for the existence of each.

Most texts identify Freud and psychoanalysis as the beginning of modern psychotherapy. In its classical form, psychoanalysis was an expensive, long-term treatment. In addition, it was not useful in treating all clients.

Clients seek assistance for a number of reasons. First, some people are in need of remedial help. They not only lack means to adapt to life challenges, but also have other characteristics or behaviors that are troublesome and best abandoned. Other individuals, by societal standards are considered functional, maybe even successful. However, they desire to live more fully, to actualize themselves, to grow. The changes they seek are additive to what they already are capable of doing. They do not seek remediation.

A second distinction, related to those in need of remedial help, separates those unable to function independently in society from others who can get through difficult life challenges, but suffer emotional pain. The former, if left alone, could be dangerous to themselves or others; the latter would not. For the latter group a third distinction emerges. Some of them struggle because of acute circumstances; others have lasting characteristics that make their emotional pain cyclical or chronic.

Classical psychoanalysis did not treat all these different kinds of clients; it was intended to serve the functionally capable but emotionally troubled. Left untreated via psychotherapy were the severely mentally ill, the client seeking growth, and the people in crisis. While psychiatry made advances in treating the more severe conditions, an alliance of many helping professions worked on finding more brief treatments for less disabled clientele.

The impetus for brief treatments (less than one year) gained strength during the last four to five decades. Through the work of Carl Rogers (1942, 1951) therapists learned how to establish effective working relationships with clients in a short time. The behavior therapies, developed during the last three decades, helped to streamline treatment by encouraging work toward more modest objectives, instead of the more global personality changes posed by early therapies. Many of the cognitive therapies, also developed in the last three decades, quickened the pace of treatment through emphasis on more direct confrontation of problems. These and many other innovations streamlined the talking therapies.

Counseling versus Psychotherapy

Many different therapy approaches have developed during the last 30 years. Nisenholz (1983) lists more than 100 different approaches. No doubt the variety of clients seeking help has influenced the proliferation of approaches. To date no one has taken all these therapies and divided them between counseling and psychotherapy. Belkin (1984), as have others, concludes that many similarities and differences exist between counseling and psychotherapy. They both rely on verbal interaction within a trusting interpersonal relationship to help clients understand problems, plan, and enact changes. However, the setting in which the treatment occurs and the severity of client problems in part distinguish the two treatments. Counseling signifies a more brief treatment for less severely disturbed clients who seek assistance in educational and community settings. Psychotherapy usually signifies a more long-term treatment for more chronic and severe problems conducted in a medical setting. A number of professions such as psychiatry, clinical psychology, and social work label their treatment psychotherapy.

However, it is not uncommon, for example, for someone to work for several years at a school and to be thought of as doing counseling. This same person may become employed at a residential treatment setting for youth of the same age as those in educational setting. But since the clients at the residential center are considered more disturbed than those at the school, the counselor now becomes viewed as a therapist who performs psychotherapy. The same person may do many of the same things in trying to help. Some things will change. If nothing else, the latter treatment probably will be of longer duration. Because the client may be more troubled, more at risk, other help-givers may be involved with the client (e.g., a consulting psychiatrist). In this setting psychotherapy may be the traditional label for interactions between client and therapist that in another setting would be called counseling.

The counseling profession shows a preference for brief therapies with particular application to a broad spectrum of clients. Counselors are not deterred from using an approach to helping if it is called psychotherapy as long as it has that broad application and is more or less a short-term treatment. In line with Wolberg's (1980) view of short-term therapy, counselors often select treatment strategies with the following in mind:

1. Those strategies that fit in a time period not to exceed one year.
2. Strategies that assume the client to be an active and willing participant in treatment. While clients may be resistant at times, such

resistances can be treated directly and resolved. The client will be able to form a relationship with the counselor.

3. Strategies that emphasize client strengths and allow for the minimization of deficits. The focus is on learning new ways to solve problems along with how this learning generalizes to other situations.

4. Strategies that assume clients will be able to endure periods in treatment when their anxiety will be raised as a result of the direct confrontation of problems.

5. Strategies that apply to outpatient treatment, that is, with clients who "walk in" for weekly treatment and can cope with life stresses between sessions.

6. Strategies that can be learned within the framework of a master's degree program. While these strategies are further developed over a lifetime of actual practice, the recent master's counseling graduate can be certified as competent to practice those strategies.

In general, it is very difficult (probably impossible) to distinguish between counseling and short-term psychotherapy, especially if both offer a supportive relationship and are educational in nature. In mental health settings in which a client in crisis may require medication (antidepressants or tranquilizers), the accompanying talk therapy very often is labeled counseling even though the client would be considered at much greater risk without the medication. At least over a brief period the condition of the client is serious. Thus, the more versus less severely troubled client often does not distinguish counseling from psychotherapy.

There are some advantages to using the label counseling. This label has less stigma attached to it and is more palatable to more people. Also, less liability is incurred as a counselor than as a psychotherapist. Some may prefer the label of counseling over the more generic label therapy, since the latter is understood as a treatment for some disorder. As mentioned earlier, counselors have the opportunity to treat nondisordered clients, those already functioning well but in search of further growth. Counseling is useful in more efficiently coping with predictable life changes and challenges. Thus, counseling deserves its own title, one that historically has come to represent a broad set of short-term strategies aimed at helping a wide variety of people.

STUDENT LEARNING EXERCISE

Read the statements below and indicate whether they represent the nature of counseling or not. Circle T for true and F for false.

1. Counseling and other forms of short-term therapy were developed to serve clients not served by the early forms of psychotherapy.   T   F

2. Seeking greater self-actualization is a valid reason for a client to pursue counseling.   T   F

3. The differences between counseling and psychotherapy are clear and straightforward.   T   F

CHARACTERISTICS OF COUNSELING APPROACHES

Counseling theories are specialized theories of behavior change. Most of them emerge from broader views of human behavior. Theorizing about human behavior could begin with very broad philosophical concepts regarding being and how one comes to know about that which exists. This is a branch of philosophy called metaphysics. Usually it is more practical to see theories of counseling as emerging from theories of personality. These theories speculate on how humans adjust or adapt to the many challenges of life. Special attention is paid to those characteristics allowing humans to survive and possibly evolve the species to an even higher form.

A subset of personality theory is the study of psychopathology (problem behavior), that is, a description and explanation of what happens when individuals are not able to cope well with life's challenges. Also part of the study of personality is speculation on how human behavior changes. When such principles of behavior change are applied to a situation in which one person tries to influence another primarily through verbal communication, a theory of counseling or psychotherapy emerges. Thus, many major theories of personality have spawned theories of counseling.

Theories of counseling or psychotherapy can begin as more or less pure speculation. They are nothing more than ideas or concepts linked together to form hypotheses. Several hypotheses linked together form the theory. A few counseling theories are well structured into hypotheses called postulates, theorems, and corollaries—much like the euclidean geometry studied in high school. Other theories are rambling narratives about a theorist's experiences as a therapist. When one reads most of the original sources written on a particular counseling theory, it is like sitting down with an experienced practitioner to "talk" counseling. Most theory books have sections in which concepts are defined and discussed. These references frequently make the ideas live through case illustrations and examples. Thus, reading counseling theory is exposure to real life; the emphasis is on helping people solve problems in living.

It is important to recognize that a theory is first and foremost a set of ideas used as a convenience in explaining what happens when the counselor and client work together. An idea is an abstraction that only exists in the mind. They are not able to exist by themselves, i.e., outside of human minds. In many instances one idea can explain reality (possibly several different realities) just as well as another idea. Pure speculation eventually is shown to be useful or not useful through the experience of those who use the ideas. Since two different ideas can be equally useful in explaining the same aspect of our experience, it is difficult to determine one set of ideas as being better than another set.

For some sets of ideas (theories), there is more experience or evidence verifying (or proving) the ideas to be useful. A theory is proved by gathering evidence in favor of the explanations provided. Different disciplines and schools of thought within a discipline argue about what constitutes valid evidence in support of theories. For example, in counseling some practitioners will accept as evidence only tightly controlled empirical research. Others argue that the "court" hearing a case for a counseling approach should admit more evidence than empirical data. For example, subjective experience of participants that is carefully analyzed and recorded may be just as valid evidence as simulations (analogues) of counseling, empirically studied in the human relations laboratory. The most productive method for advancing the practice of counseling is to develop counseling theories as a consequence of the research and experience of its practitioners. Admitting evidence too restrictively or too liberally can negatively affect this development. In the former, knowledge is lost through narrow bias; in the latter, knowledge is buried in nonsense.

Generally, theories tend to mature over time. In the beginning a theoretical approach may be identified with one person as its founder but later becomes associated with many different persons as the approach expands and is verified. However, as time passes some approaches seem to lose popularity, even though they are still useful. Transactional Analysis is an example of this process. People in the field seem to tire of the concepts, replacing it with a more recent or more novel approach.

The better counseling/psychotherapy theories tend to have application for a wider variety of clientele. They are parsimonious; they neither over or under explain the issues. Their explanations are believable.

Making a believable explanation is not easy. A theorist will begin to explain something new by relying on familiar ideas. The theorist then draws an analogy from the old to the new. For example, scientists had the idea of the solar system before a scheme existed for the atom. They used the solar system as a conceptual model for the structure of the atom.

Theorists use metaphors; that is, they denote one idea by relating it to another. For example, someone familiar with auto mechanics might explain counseling as "like [analogous to] overhauling an internal combustion engine." We would learn about counseling through the engine overhaul metaphor. Theories can be judged according to the quality of the metaphors used. One metaphor can "grab" us, while another stimulates little involvement.

The point should be made again that counseling theories are meant to be convenient ways of explaining what goes on when one counsels. It is better to say that a theoretical approach is useful rather than that it is *the* truth. There are many truths when it comes to finding ways to explain how counseling works, just as there are many stories or parables that can portray a belief.

effective: minimal age, client motivation as a result of emotional pain, absence of thought disorders (psychosis), and so forth.

Counselor Characteristics.   A very important part of any counseling theory is the description of the attitudes and behavior of the counselor. Mention may be made of the training required.

Relationship Between Counselor and Client.   Historically, the relationship between the counselor and the client in counseling and psychotherapy has been viewed as one of the most important elements in achieving favorable outcome. However, differences in the type of relationship developed produce sharp distinctions among different approaches.

Diagnosis of Client Problems.   The type and importance of diagnosis is another differentiating factor among approaches, with significant implications regarding necessary training for the counselor. Diagnosis is usually tied to the theory's view of problem behavior (psychopathology) and how it is manifested by the client.

Counseling Goals.   Treatment objectives can be divided into terminal and process goals. The former refer to final outcomes upon completion of the process; the latter are accomplishments arrived at during the process of treatment. Goals are usually connected to the diagnosis of client difficulties; often they are the antitheses of the problems. Some counseling approaches utilize broad goals applicable to every client; others are more specific, with particular goals applied to individual clients depending on their circumstances and needs.

Techniques.   Techniques are the methods used by the counselor to explore, define, and attain treatment objectives. They include ways of saying things, special procedures enacted during an interview, and tactics used by both counselor and client between (outside of) interviews.

The Process.   A well-developed counseling theory will describe shifts and changes that occur during the treatment. From early in the process, to the middle, and finally to the end, the movement to be observed may be noted, possibly through the identification of stages in the process. The theory may note that a certain condition must precede another. Critical periods may be noted, such as times when attrition is most probable or when setbacks usually occur.

How to Evaluate Outcome.   A counseling theory should identify the type of evidence it views as valid in determining progress or the lack of it. Criteria should be offered to assist the counselor in determining when the process can be terminated, when outcomes have been achieved.

STUDENT LEARNING EXERCISE

Read the following statements and indicate whether they reflect an appropriate use of counseling theory or not. Circle T for true and F for false.

1. A counselor has used a particular theory with satisfactory results with one client population, but in working with another, finds that the theory does not explain how clients respond to stress in a session. The counselor decides the theory is wrong.   T   F

2. In assessing the value of a particular counseling theory, different people may draw different conclusions because they use different evidence to test the usefulness of the theory.   T   F

3. The many different counseling theories can be classified according to how feelings, thoughts, and observable behavior are emphasized.   T   F

MAJOR COUNSELING APPROACHES

Client-Centered Therapy

If one recognizes that prior to Carl Rogers very little was written regarding how one actually does counseling and psychotherapy, the importance of his contributions become even more significant. Some of his earliest writings (Rogers, 1942) demonstrate his keen interest in the actual practice of counseling and psychotherapy.

The central emphasis in Client-centered therapy is the relationship between counselor and client. The primary goal of treatment, to free the actualizing tendency of the client, is best achieved by creating an interpersonal environment full of warmth and understanding and free of constraint. This is achieved by having the counselor offer the conditions of empathy, unconditional positive regard, and congruence. If the client is able to perceive these conditions, in part by being physically present to the counselor, and is motivated to change because the difficulties make the client feel anxious or vulnerable, Rogers (1957) argued that positive personality change would result. This constitutes the essence of Rogers' theory; nothing else is needed.

The goal of counseling, to make the client more fully functioning, is represented during the process of therapy by increasing levels of self-acceptance. As counseling continues, the client's actual self-image becomes more congruent with his or her ideal self-image. When a counselor enters the subjective world of a client, understanding it and communicating that understanding (empathy) to the client, the counselor lowers the client's defenses to more honestly evaluate experiences.

Feeling safe in the relationship as a result of the warmth and caring (unconditional positive regard) of the therapist, the client reflects this greater openness in deeper levels of self-disclosure. As the counselor remains genuine (congruent), showing no pretense or phoniness, the client also becomes congruent; his self-concept begins to coincide more with the ideal he has for himself.

During his long career Rogers applied his approach to many different types of individuals, to groups, and to married and other committed couples. In addition, his ideas have been applied to educational, interracial, and international problems. More recently Rogers (1977) suggested that his approach be called the *person-centered approach,* since its emphasis ultimately is to return power and control to the individual.

Client-centered therapy has stood the test of time; its ability to achieve its stated treatment goals has been documented repeatedly. Its position on the necessity of offering the conditions described earlier has been accepted by the majority of professional help-givers. As will be described in Chapter 8, training procedures have been carefully refined to teach counselors-in-training how to communicate empathy, positive regard, and congruence. Few helping professionals will be unaffected in their career by the teachings of Carl Rogers. He died in 1987 of heart disease.

Adlerian Counseling

Adlerian or individual psychology has come to practitioners in this country primarily from the work of Rudolf Driekurs (1953), a follower and careful interpreter of Alfred Adler's ideas. Ansbacher and Ansbacher (1956) have been responsible for collecting the writings of Adler, while Don Dinkmeyer and co-workers (Dinkmeyer, Pew, & Dinkmeyer, 1979) have applied Adlerian psychology to elementary school counseling. Adlerian concepts have been directed extensively toward parenting and child-rearing (Driekurs & Soltz, 1964).

Adlerian counseling seeks to correct mistakes in perception and logic that people make in their effort to fit into social relationships and to overcome feelings of inferiority. According to this view, people are born with feelings of inferiority. Certainly the need to rely on caretakers so long reinforces those feelings in the young child.

As a result of conclusions drawn about early experiences in the extended family, clients adopt "mistaken goals." Rather than pursuing social interest, they strive for attention, power, revenge, or the showing of inadequacy. Depending on the mistaken goal, the client will formulate other supportive misconceptions. The complex of this faulty logic leads to a particular lifestyle or way of acting consistent with the logic.

The counselor attempts to develop a positive relationship with the client in order to discover the mistaken goals of faulty logic. In other words, if the counselor can find out what the client is up to (goals), all the rest of his or her behavior will be understandable. Once discovered, the logic is interpreted to the client. Dreams and early recollections reveal the logic clearly. Recollections are vivid memories of very early experiences retained out of the millions of brief life episodes. They are remembered because they support (defend) the faulty (private) logic of the client. To simplify the use of dreams, early recollections, and beliefs regarding the client's role in the family (family constellation), the Adlerians have developed a structured way to inventory them, called a lifestyle questionnaire (Mosak, 1972). Once discovered and interpreted, the client's faulty logic is repeatedly confronted and challenged in an effort to demonstrate its flaws. Persuasion and paradoxical intention (wish for unwanted consequences) are also used. In addition, Adlerian counselors encourage clients to try behaviors between sessions that they would ordinarily not use because of their faulty beliefs. Such practice, followed by favorable consequences, may help clients change their minds about themselves and what they might be able to achieve.

The Adlerian approach, while not well researched, utilizes common techniques (e.g., interpretation) favored by many other approaches. In this respect it is a "mainstream" form of intervention.

Reality Therapy

William Glasser, the founder of reality therapy, is one of many contemporary therapists who have tried to demystify the process of helping. Glasser has had a particular interest in developing a common sense approach that can be used by parents, teachers, and all kinds of professional help-givers besides those with extensive training and experience.

Reality therapy is a very optimistic, highly involved way of helping people confront the problems of modern society. To achieve, and in particular to learn to accept oneself, individuals must develop a success identity (Glasser & Zunin, 1979). While being loved and accepted by others helps develop a success identity, those without it can only develop one through actions that lead to accomplishments. Such accomplishments then lead to self-acceptance.

According to Glasser and Zunin (1979), people who are unhappy, who get into trouble, and who develop many different emotional problems are persons with a failure identity. This identity leads to loneliness, poor contact with reality, and the giving up of responsibility. Responsibility is a key word in reality therapy (Glasser, 1965); by it Glasser means learning how to fulfill one's own needs so that the needs of others are not violated.

During the process of helping change a client's failure identity and subsequent irresponsible behavior, acting or doing is emphasized. Glasser believes it is easier to change behavior than to change feelings and cognitions (Glasser & Zunin, 1979). The counselor works hard to develop a strong, warm, but confrontive relationship with the client; to emphasize what can be done in the present; to encourage the client to forget the past; and to seek alternatives to ineffectual client actions of the past, never giving up, and never accepting excuses for not trying to be different. Special effort is made to avoid punishing the client for past failures; the emphasis in sessions is on the planning of responsible actions.

Rational-Emotive Therapy

Albert Ellis, the founder of rational-emotive therapy (RET), has been one of the most prolific and energetic messengers of a therapeutic approach. He has maintained that the root source of human problems is irrational thoughts (mistaken ideas) learned by people early in life and maintained by a continual process of reindoctrination, willingly undertaken by those same people (Ellis, 1973). A counselor can help such clients by vigorously disputing those irrational thoughts and offering as a substitute a different set of ideas, based primarily on the tolerance of self and others.

RET epitomizes the view that sound thinking leads to emotional well-being; people feel bad because intervening between an unpleasant situation and strong negative feelings are thoughts that amplify the negative feelings. Two such thoughts have to do with believing that one must be loved and appreciated by everyone and that one must try to be perfect.

RET therapists teach clients how to intervene in this process by substituting more healthy thoughts for those that create strong negative feelings. When this substitution occurs, clients develop thought processes more consistent with the scientific method. Their mental health improves as a result of greater self-direction and acceptance of uncertainty. Their behavior changes; it becomes more flexible, and more risks are taken (Ellis, 1973). Behavior is not ignored in RET. Strong emphasis is placed on "homework" between sessions in order for the client to develop the skills needed to cope with life's situations, especially those of a social nature. Semantics also plays an important role in the teaching provided by the RET practitioner (Ellis & Abrahms, 1978). Words such as "terrible," "must," and "should" are replaced by words such as "unpleasant," "preferable," and "desirable." Such a vocabulary reminds the client of thought processes that are equally tolerant and flexible.

Behavior Therapy

Behavior therapy is a diverse and ever-expanding approach to helping that has its origins in academic psychology. In particular, it emphasizes the learning and unlearning of thoughts, behaviors, and associations between feelings and environmental stimuli. The principles governing this learning strive for scientific precision. At first behavior therapy was promoted as more or less an alternative to traditional therapy. While it directed attention to the treatment of anxiety and other common client complaints, it was developed as a specialized treatment for more select human problems (e.g., phobias). As it has matured, behavior therapy in actual practice has begun to resemble the more traditional "talk" therapies, with increased attention being paid to client variables other than observable behavior. In part this may be explained by looking at some of the historical developments within this approach.

Wolpe (1958) was one of the earliest to apply behavioral principles to the treatment of anxiety and other affective problems. Basic to his approach was the process of classical conditioning in which autonomic responses such as anxiety or fear became associated with the wrong stimuli. His approach, called reciprocal inhibition, was an attempt to reconnect more appropriate responses to those environmental stimuli.

Behavior modification, based on operant conditioning principles promoted by B. F. Skinner, emerged as the primary thrust behind the practice of behavioral counseling (Krumboltz & Thoresen, 1976). The 1960s were a time of much growth in behavioral treatments (Ullmann & Krasner, 1965). Emphasis was upon control of environmental factors influencing client behavior. In particular, the management of reinforcers, especially positive ones, was viewed as the way to change not only motor responses but verbal behavior as well. Together these behaviors were defined and categorized with particular relevance to social situations (social skills), a common area of concern for clients seeking counseling.

Learning such complex behaviors as those necessary to succeed in social situations expanded the repertoire of the behavior therapist through the use of modeling, a process in which one person learns complex responses by observing others and then imitating the actions that become reinforced (Bandura, 1977). When combined with sufficient practice, even that resulting from role playing (behavior rehearsal), the aquisition of a larger behavior repertoire is possible. Extended practice is also important in order for the client to be able to discriminate when one set of responses might or might not be appropriate. Depending on the situation, one set could be reinforced and another not.

As such learning principles were demonstrated as effective with observable behavior, greater attention was directed toward applying those same principles to unobservable behavior, especially to thoughts or cognitions (Mahoney, 1974; Meichenbaum, 1977). This evolution was reasonable for the practice of counseling or psychotherapy, in spite of the rigid emphasis in operant psychology on only observable behavior. One will recall the early emphasis in behavior therapy on the use of cognitive imagery to inhibit inappropriate emotional responses (Wolpe, 1958).

This expansion of behavior therapy has made it a far-reaching approach with some elements in its practice easily applied by counselors and other strategies left for future mastery. Cormier and Cormier (1985) describe many of the treatment strategies popular in contemporary behavior therapy. These include behavioral contracting (written agreements regarding rewards for achieving outcomes), behavior rehearsal (role playing), cognitive restructuring (similar to RET), the use of models (real and ones to be imagined), relaxation training (including biofeedback), and thought-stopping (aversive self-conditioning to break connections between cognition and response).

Common among the diverse strategies used in behavior therapy is an emphasis on specificity and the treatment of problem behavior as is, instead of as a "symptom" of some other problem. Specific behaviors become targeted first for observation, in order to specify the conditions under which the behaviors occur and the frequency in which they are emitted. The treatment goals are carefully set forth in light of the data gathered.

Treatment goals often have to do with both unlearning some behaviors and learning new ones. Reinforcement contingencies are at the core of most learning activities, whether they be observing a model, role playing, or real life practice. Self-reinforcement is very popular, since most contemporary behavior therapists rely heavily on self-management strategies. Modifying expectations regarding outcomes from negative to positive, in light of changed behavior, is also important.

Unlike other approaches, behavior therapy has paid special attention to consolidating gains by applying learning principles to prevention of relapse. Often clients make significant gains in counseling, only to see these gains disappear over time. It is like losing 10 pounds on a diet only to gradually regain the weight over a period of several months. The weight gain is a result of returning to old habits. Relapse prevention strategies strengthen new, more healthy habits, making return to old ones less probable.

Gestalt Therapy

Gestalt therapy is one of the earliest modern therapies (Perls, Hefferline, & Goodman, 1951) that remained largely unknown until the 1960s, when Frederick (Fritz) Perls' work at the Esalen Institute in California became well known. This approach is an imaginative marriage of concepts from existential philosophy and techniques from psychodrama (Moreno, 1946). Passons (1975) has taken elements of the approach, one best conducted in a controlled environment (e.g., a retreat-like, growth center), and reframed the procedures for application to a broader range of clientele seeking treatment at a variety of agencies. Earlier versions of Gestalt therapy often led to an intense expression of emotions that benefited from a more total integration into the client's personality, not efficiently achieved via once-a-week outpatient treatment.

According to Gestalt therapy, people strive for balance (homeostasis) in their interactions with the world and themselves (Perls, 1973). As one lives, one contacts the environment, deals with it for a time, then moves on to new experiences once old ones are complete. Unfinished situations inhibit the flow of experience, restricting the person, blurring boundaries, producing negative feelings of detachment and engulfment, creating rigidity in the person, and in general upsetting equilibrium. Awareness of self as an evolving entity with a unique identity with unique involvements becomes stalled.

To treat such problems, Gestalt counselors emphasize the expansion of awareness by focusing on the here-and-now experiences of the client. As unfinished experiences emerge, they are brought into the present, treated, and finished. To recapture meaning in life the client is continually challenged to assume responsibility for what is going on. The emphasis is extended even to language in which a statement like "I am sad" is changed to "I choose to be sad." The objective is to help the client assume greater self-responsibility and control over life.

The Gestalt-oriented counselor often uses a variety of confrontive strategies to help the client remove barriers to here-and-now experience. For example, the counselor may ask the client to live a fantasy, exaggerate a posture that represents something of meaning, stay in a feeling that the client often tries to flee, or act out a dream. Many of these strategies are quite dramatic.

Gestalt techniques are not applicable to the entire spectrum of clients seeking assistance (Shepherd, 1970). For this reason only a small percentage of practitioners are likely to identify with this approach (Smith, 1982). Gestalt therapy often is studied in counselor preparation programs as a means of enrichment and for its major contributions to treating client resistances.

Other Important Approaches

In addition to learning about the approaches briefly described above, counselors-in-training often are exposed to other therapy systems that will be discussed only briefly in this text. These include psychoanalytic therapy, transactional analysis, and trait and factor counseling.

Psychoanalytic theory, besides being the oldest conceptual framework, is one of the richest and most rapidly expanding of the dominant systems in use today. Its elegance and depth make it an approach best learned after considerable postdoctoral treatment experience and supervision.

In a master's degree program at best one can expect to review principal concepts developed by Freud and some of his contemporaries. Contemporary psychoanalytic theory is called by a number of titles. They include ego psychology, object relations theory, psychoanalytic developmental psychology, and possibly a few others. After Freud's death, psychoanalytic theory began to move away from an emphasis on instincts (primitive human impulses) to careful consideration of adaptive functions, called ego functions. While Freud contributed to such concepts to a degree, his daughter, Anna, and Hans Hartmann are considered to be the initial driving forces in the development of ego psychology (Blanck & Blanck, 1974).

With important contributions from Margaret Mahler (1979), Edith Jacobson (1971), Otto Kernberg (1984), and many others, ego psychology has made important advances in the treatment of depression, narcissism, and borderline conditions. The latter disorders are quite complicated to understand and treat, but worthy of study for the experienced practitioner or advanced student with prior counseling experience.

Transactional analysis (TA) is often studied in counselor preparation. It appears to have attracted few practitioners coming from graduate training programs (Smith, 1982), but is still used extensively by paraprofessionals, clergy, and other groups of help-givers.

Developed in the 1950s by Eric Berne, TA began as a system with primary use in groups, but has expanded to individual treatment as well. The unique contribution of TA has to do with understanding social interactions and how they influence mental health. Through his theory of interpersonal games, Berne (1964) offered the helping professions and the public as well a way of understanding subtle manipulations people use to both avoid intimacy and to control others.

At first TA relied on concepts represented by a vocabulary of terms intended to be easily understood by almost anyone entering a therapy group as a client. Today that vocabulary has expanded to include a complex array of terms to represent subtle features of personality and social interaction (Woollams & Brown, 1979). The essence of TA as a treatment approach is to do a lot of explaining of behavior using its vocabulary; then the goal becomes to help clients decide to redirect their lives. Once this decision is made, called a redecision (Goulding & Goulding, 1979), a process of reversing behavior or relearning takes place.

Trait and factor counseling is one of the few approaches that has it roots in differential psychology rather than psychiatry or clinical psychology. This approach is used extensively as a basis for career counseling and is discussed in Chapter 6.

Eclectic Approaches

Earlier in this chapter it was mentioned that Nisenholz (1983) has listed more than 100 different treatment approaches. The point was made that some approaches do not purport to be effective with all clients; rather, they have been developed with particular populations in mind. In addition, the reader was reminded that counseling theories are merely ideas developed to explain what happens in treatment. Rychlak (1985) describes his experiences in graduate school where he was supervised by three different, but equally renowned, professors, each of whom had developed therapy theories. At times he would have to discuss the same clients in a different way, depending on who was supervising him at that time. Of course, he noted that this was possible—the same client with the same behavior and problems was conceptualized to the satisfaction of each renowned professor and theoretician. Again the point is that there are many ways of understanding human situations, empirical data or "facts." In an earlier work Rychlak (1968) noted several forms of reasoning. Demonstrative reasoning essentially posits that there is only one correct answer to a question; however, dialectical reasoning proves that there is more than one correct answer. Rychlak (1968) argues that dialectics is more appropriate to conceptualizing issues in counseling and psychotherapy than demonstrative reasoning. If this is true, counseling practitioners may have to examine the utility of sticking firmly to only one theoretical system to explain what happens to clients.

Apparently this is precisely what people who practice counseling and psychotherapy have done. Surveys of theoretical preference among practicing psychologists (Garfield & Kurtz, 1976; Smith, 1982) show that the majority of those questioned identify themselves as eclectic, that is, not subscribing to only one theoretical approach. Rather, when faced with everyday treatment issues, practitioners seem to draw on several of the established systems.

There are pros and cons of eclecticism (Brabeck & Welfel, 1985; Hutchins, 1984; Ward, 1983). Eclecticism can be positive if it is simply drawing the largest variety of explanations and treatment techniques to become equipped to deal with the broadest range of issues. This position makes eclecticism seem an open and flexible way of both helping clients and advancing the profession. It does not seem so positive if it is viewed as a "shotgun" technique, of amassing concepts and techniques without much consideration of how they fit together and how they can be justified. In fact, using an approach to treat a client without a sound rationale for doing so is not only a hodgepodge way of doing things but is also unethical.

To avoid some of the problems noted, Hutchins (1984) and Brabeck and Welfel (1985) argue for the development of broader, more comprehensive models to synthesize current theories; such systems would provide the concepts to unify elements frequently combined in eclectic approaches. Rychlak (1985) cautions practitioners, reminding them that choosing a number of explanatory systems is more realistic than naively thinking that "facts" can eventually be explained by one "true" system.

Ward (1983) helps resolve some of the controversy by contending that the development of new theories is on the decline. Greater interest seems to exist in more fully developing current ones into more comprehensive systems. This brings attention to the fact that approaches to counseling and psychotherapy for the most part can be considered as still in their infancy. If the last 20 years is any indication of the momentum behind the development of counseling approaches, by the time today's counselors-in-training reach the midpoint in their careers, there will be major additions and revisions to the ways in which we understand how clients are helped.

SUMMARY

This chapter offered a brief overview of counseling theory, to be followed in the next chapter by a more detailed look at common elements in the counseling process. Counseling was compared to psychotherapy. A mental set was offered concerning how theoretical approaches to counseling might be used most effectively. The components of a counseling theory were identified, as were ways of classifying different theories. Finally, some of the dominant counseling/psychotherapy approaches were described briefly.

REVIEW QUESTIONS

1. Briefly describe some of the similarities and differences between counseling and psychotherapy.
2. Describe how the personality of the counselor might influence the selection and use of a counseling theory.
3. List and discuss the components of a counseling theory.
4. List two approaches that emphasize the importance of early childhood experience. How are these experiences explored during an interview?
5. List three approaches that emphasize here-and-now experience. How do they differ in the ways these experiences are utilized?
6. Explain why rational or cognitive approaches to counseling are so popular.

REFERENCES

Ansbacher, H. L., & Ansbacher, R. R. (Eds.) (1956). *The individual psychology of Alfred Adler: A systematic presentation in selections from his writings.* New York: Harper and Row.

Bandura, A. (1977). *Social learning theory.* Englewood Cliffs, NJ: Prentice-Hall.

Baruth, L. G., & Huber, C. H. (1985). *Counseling and psychotherapy: Theoretical analyses and skills applications.* Columbus, OH: Charles E. Merrill Publishing Co.

Belkin, G. S. (1980). *Contemporary psychotherapies.* Chicago: Rand McNally Publishing Co.

Belkin, G. S. (1984). *Introduction to counseling* (2nd ed.). Dubuque, IA: Wm. C. Brown Publishers.

Berne, E. (1964). *Games people play.* New York: Grove Press.

Blanck, R., & Blanck, G. (1974). *Ego psychology: Theory and practice.* New York: Columbia University Press.

Brabeck, M. M., & Welfel, E. R. (1985). Counseling theory: Understanding the trend toward eclecticism from a developmental perspective. *Journal of Counseling and Development, 63* (6), 343–348.

Cormier, W. H., & Cormier, L. S. (1985). *Interviewing strategies for helpers: A guide to assessment, intervention, and evaluation* (2nd ed.). Monterey, CA: Brooks/Cole.

Dinkmeyer, D. C., Pew, W. L., & Dinkmeyer, D. C., Jr. (1979). *Adlerian counseling and psychotherapy.* Monterey, CA: Brooks/Cole.

Dreikurs, R. (1953). *Fundamentals of Adlerian psychology.* Chicago: Alfred Adler Institute.

Dreikurs, R., & Soltz, V. (1964). *Children: The challenge.* New York: Hawthorn.

Ellis, A. (1973). *Humanistic psychotherapy: The rational-emotive approach.* New York: McGraw-Hill.

Ellis, A., & Abrahms, E. (1978). *Brief psychotherapy in medical and health practice.* New York: Springer.

Frank, J. D. (1973). *Persuasion and healing: A comparative study of psychotherapy* (2nd ed.). Baltimore: Johns Hopkins University Press.

Garfield, S. L., & Kurtz, R. (1976). Clinical psychologists in the 1970s. *American Psychologist, 31,* (1), 1–9.

Glasser, W. (1965). *Reality therapy.* New York: Harper and Row.

Glasser, W., & Zunin, L. M. (1979). Reality therapy. In R. J. Corsini (Ed.), *Current psychotherapies* (2nd ed.). Itasca, IL: F. E. Peacock.

Goulding, M., & Goulding, R. (1979). *Changing lives through redecision therapy.* New York: Brunner/Mazel.

Hutchins, D. E. (1984). Improving the counseling relationship. *Personnel and Guidance Journal, 62* (10), 572–575.

Jacobson, E. (1971). *Depression.* New York: International Universities Press.

Kernberg, O. F. (1984). *Severe personality disorders: Psychotherapeutic strategies.* New Haven: Yale University Press.

Krumboltz, J. D., & Thoresen, C. E. (Eds.). (1976). *Counseling methods.* New York: Holt, Rinehart and Winston.

Lazarus, R. S. (1984). On the primacy of cognition. *American Psychologist, 39* (2), 124–129.

Lichtenstein, E. (1980). *Psychotherapy: Approaches and applications.* Monterey, CA: Brooks/Cole.

Mahler, M. S. (1979). *The selected papers of Margaret S. Mahler,* Vols. I and II. New York: Jason Aronson.

Mahoney, M. J. (1974). *Cognition and behavior modification.* Cambridge, MA: Ballinger.

Meichenbaum, D. (1977). *Cognitive-behavior modification: An integrative approach.* New York: Plenum.

Moreno, J. L. (1946). *Psychodrama.* Beacon, NY: Beacon House.

Morse, S. J., & Watson, W. I., Jr. (1977). *Psychotherapies: A comparative casebook.* New York: Holt, Rinehart and Winston.

Mosak, H. H. (1972). Life style assessment: A demonstration based on family constellation. *Journal of Individual Psychology, 28,* 232–237.

Nisenholz, B. (1983). Solving the psychotherapy glut. *Personnel and Guidance Journal, 61*(9), 535–536.

Passons, W. R. (1975). *Gestalt approaches in counseling.* New York: Holt, Rinehart and Winston.

Perls, F. (1973). *The Gestalt approach and eyewitness to therapy.* New York: Bantam.

Perls, F., Hefferline, R., & Goodman, P. (1951). *Gestalt therapy: Excitement and growth in the human personality.* New York: Dell.

Rogers, C. R. (1942). *Counseling and psychotherapy.* Boston: Houghton Mifflin.

Rogers, C. R. (1951). *Client-centered therapy.* Boston: Houghton Mifflin.

Rogers, C. R. (1957). The necessary and sufficient conditions of therapeutic personality change. *Journal of Consulting Psychology, 21,* 95–103.

Rogers, C. R. (1977). *Carl Rogers on personal power: Inner strength and its revolutionary impact.* New York: Delacorte.

Rychlak, J. F. (1968). *A philosophy of science for personality theory.* Boston: Houghton Mifflin.

Rychlak, J. F. (1985). Eclecticism in psychological theorizing: Good and bad. *Journal of Counseling and Development, 63*(6), 351–353.

Shepherd, I. (1970). Limitations and cautions in the Gestalt approach. In J. Fagan & I. Shepherd (Eds.), *Gestalt therapy now.* New York: Harper and Row.

Smith, D. (1982). Trends in counseling and psychotherapy. *American Psychologist, 37*(7), 802–809.

Tremblay, J. M., Herron, W. G., & Schultz, C. L. (1986). Relationship between therapeutic orientation and personality in psychotherapists. *Professional Psychology: Research and Practice, 17*(2), 111–114.

Ullmann, L. P., & Krasner, L. (1965). *Case studies in behavior modification.* New York: Holt, Rinehart and Winston.

Ward, D. E. (1983). The trend toward eclecticism and the development of comprehensive models to guide counseling and psychotherapy. *Personnel and Guidance Journal, 62*(3), 154–157.

Wolberg, L. R. (1980). *Handbook of short-term psychotherapy.* New York: Thieme-Stratton.

Wolpe, J. (1958). *Psychotherapy by reciprocal inhibition.* Stanford: Stanford University Press.

Woollams, S., & Brown, M. (1979). *TA: The total handbook of transactional analysis.* Englewood Cliffs, NJ: Prentice-Hall.

Zajonc, R. B. (1984). On the primacy of affect. *American Psychologist, 39* (2), 117–123.

4

The Counseling Process

GOAL OF THE CHAPTER

The purpose of this chapter is to provide an overview of elements of the counseling process.

CHAPTER PREVIEW

1. The characteristics of clients will be explored.
2. The characteristics of effective counselors will be treated in detail.
3. The relationship between the counselor and client during counseling will be examined.
4. Stages in the counseling process will be summarized.
5. Group, couples, and family counseling will be discussed.

INTRODUCTION

The purpose of this chapter is to provide a synthesis of the diverse approaches to counseling surveyed in Chapter 3. The general motives of clients seeking counseling will be discussed, along with the characteristic ways effective counselors respond to clients. The relationship between the counselor and client will receive particular emphasis. Common goals established for the relationship will be discussed, as will how material and events tend to change as counseling continues. Finally, group, couples, and family counseling will be described.

CHARACTERISTICS OF CLIENTS

Counseling works best when clients enter it voluntarily. At some point even the most reticent clients gain more if they affirm the relevance of counseling and willingly participate in its process. At times this is difficult for the client to do, since the matter treated is often of a sensitive nature. Much of the technology underlying counseling has evolved to help clients join together with counselors in mutual problem-solving.

Whether a client was self-referred or referred by a third party, to remain motivated throughout counseling, the client must sense some improvement at least at various intervals during the process. Most often this means that clients have emotional pain upon entering counseling and begin to hurt less as it continues. Anxiety, depression and lesser forms of grief, and difficult-to-control hostility constitute types of emotional pain behind the client's quest for help.

In addition, clients may feel a loss of cognitive control over their behavior and the life events they must face. They are often confused and feel disorganized in their attempt to cope. Very seldom are clients so in control that they begin the first interview with a statement like this: "I have come to you with three issues in mind. The first is . . . ; the second is . . . ; finally, the third is . . . ." Rather, they will struggle to make sense out of their concerns, even if they have rehearsed what they planned to say. Certainly, this will vary across clients, but negative feelings and cognitive confusion are common client characteristics at the beginning of counseling.

Negative feelings and confusion reduce normal problem-solving ability. The resultant decline in problem-solving can lead to reduced self-esteem and the confidence necessary to persist at alternative solutions. If what has been described portrays short-term adjustment, the difficulty in helping the client will be less. On the other hand, if the client has a long history of struggling to cope with everyday challenges, the prospect of helping may be more long-term.

While most clients have difficult decisions to make, see a need to change themselves in some way, or find themselves not coping as well as they might with life, these and other problems are insufficient to prompt prospective clients to select counseling. Clients must be interested in understanding why these problems exist, their own personal responsibility for those problems, and how they can change to cope better with the same problems in the future. Heilbrun (1982) calls this set of attitudes "psychological-mindedness"; it becomes essential in order to complete the process of counseling. If one does not have it, other ways to solve problems are sought. For example, it is not unusual for someone to suggest that a friend seek counseling for some problem only to have the friend respond in disbelief, viewing the suggestion as inappropriate, perhaps preposterous. The friend would acknowledge the problem but not the proposed way to solve it.

Other desirable characteristics for clients include intelligence, flexibility, trustfulness and trustworthiness, and the ability to assume responsibility for personal actions. Goldstein (1971), in a classic description of preferred clients, proposed the acronym YAVIS (young, attractive, verbal, intelligent, and successful) to portray them. Such characteristics have importance, not because they are absolutely essential, but because they make the process more pleasant for the counselor. If a client can contact reality, attend appointed sessions, comprehend verbal communiction, and miminally bond with another human being, some benefit from counseling is possible.

CHARACTERISTICS OF EFFECTIVE COUNSELORS

While the use of counseling techniques influences positive outcomes in counseling (Brammer & Shostrom, 1982), there is widespread agreement that the personal characteristics of the counselor are largely responsible for the ultimate success or failure of counseling. Kurpius (1986) suggests that caring is the key ingredient in counseling and indicated that the source of caring is within the individual. Nearly 20 years earlier Combs (1969) put the same idea in somewhat different terms. He proposed that helpers, including counselors, have unique perceptual sets about themselves and the people they counsel. Specifically, they see themselves as identified with people, trustworthy, liked, accepted, accepting, nonauthoritarian, and valuing open communication. Combs also hypothesized that effective helpers would see others as capable, trustworthy, helpful, nonthreatening, respectable, and worthy.

Research has supported Combs' hypotheses (Carkhuff, 1969b; Ivey, 1983). Kanfer (1980) and Parloff, Waskow, and Wolfe (1978) regret that research has not been successful in identifying additional factors that would enable even more effective matches between specific counselors and clients. However, when one reviews the research literature on effective counselors, one is struck with the consensus that effective helpers have a definite set of traits. Brammer (1985) broke these down into eight categories: (1) self-awareness, (2) sensitivity to cultural differences, (3) ability to analyze one's own feelings, (4) ability to serve as a model, (5) altruism, (6) strong sense of ethics, (7) ability to assume responsibility for self and the person being helped, and (8) ability to assume the role of facilitator of personal growth.

It is obvious, when examining Brammer's list or the one posed earlier by Combs, that two sets of attitudes stand out: one set is related to self and the other is related to how the self treats another person, particularly one that is to be helped. Carkhuff and Berenson (1977) suggest that the latter grow out of the former. To combine much of the thinking on effective counselor characteristics, we will discuss six traits that seem to portray the effective counselor.

Personal Congruence

Hutchins and Cole (1986) depict the congruent individual by using three rings to represent thoughts, feelings, and actions. In their pictorial representation, these rings have considerable overlap. Historically, personal congruence among emotions, cognitions, and behaviors has been equated with good mental health as well.

    Congruent individuals are self-aware, that is, they understand their own values and motivations. They do not meet their own needs at the expense of others. They are open to feedback and act nondefensively and appropriately whenever they receive valid messages. Finally, congruent helpers are self-assured, not in the sense of being a "know-it-all," but they have confidence in their ability to be effective in human relationships.

Empathy/Understanding

In 1951 Carl Rogers wrote:

> It is the counselor's function to assume, in so far as he is able, the internal frame of reference of the client, to perceive the client himself as he is seen by himself, to lay aside all perceptions from the external frame of reference while doing so, and to communicate something of this empathic understanding to the client. (p. 29)

This definition of empathy has gone virtually unchanged (Carkhuff, 1983).

    Brammer and Shostrom (1982) point out that empathy can be equated with understanding. They divide understanding further into two categories: (1) therapeutic understanding, which is similar to Rogers' empathy, and (2) diagnostic understanding. The latter enables the counselor to describe the client in ways helpful to others, to plan meaningful interventions, and to predict client behavior under both current and future conditions. Brammer and Shostrom contend that both therapeutic and diagnostic understanding are important dimensions of effective counselors.

Cultural Sensitivity

In a very real sense empathy is a core ingredient in cultural sensitivity. But as Brammer (1985) points out, cultural awareness has a knowledge and experience base. Research has shown that cross-cultural counseling, conducted by culturally insensitive counselors, is likely to result in either premature termination by the client or unsatisfactory outcomes (Sue, 1981). Therefore, as Brammer suggests, counselors who expect to be effective with clients from different cultural backgrounds prize diversity and express an interest and commitment to learning about people with diverse traditions.

Genuineness

As early as 1967, Truax and Carkhuff (1967) pointed out that genuineness characterizes effective helping relationships. It is the capacity of all persons involved to emerge as real or authentic persons. Carkhuff and Berenson (1977) denote the absence of genuineness as not being fully aware of the here-and-now experience, hiding behind a role as a counselor, doing what one is "supposed" to do as though one were programed. Obviously, genuineness is correlated closely with congruence and empathy. Without the former, it would be difficult to supply the sensitivity necessary for congruence and empathy.

Respect/Positive Regard

Respect refers to the valuing of others, holding them in positive regard because they are human beings. Egan (1975) provides a more operational definition of respect. He indicates that being respectful involves being nonjudgmental, being "for" the individual, showing appreciation for the individual, and providing appreciative feedback for the efforts of the client. In its most basic sense, respect is communicating to one's clients that they are worthwhile, regardless of background, behaviors, or attitudes.

As Carkhuff and Berenson (1977) note, respect or holding the other person in positive regard has its basis in one's own self-respect. They also point out that there is evidence to suggest that respect is communicated through the warmth the individual conveys to the client. Spontaneity, commitment, and effort expended seem to be the basis for communicating warmth. Thus, while respect stems from our own feelings of self-worth, directing it outwardly to others requires energy, enthusiasm, and dedication.

Communication

Effective helpers must be effective communicators. In relating to others they make their intentions clear and concrete. They are able to communicate, both verbally and nonverbally, their empathy, genuineness, respect, and cultural sensitivity.

Communication is a skill that can be taught efficiently through carefully designed learning activities (Carkhuff, 1983; Egan, 1975; Hutchins & Cole,

1986). However, communication skills are not executed in a counselor's work without a commitment to helping, an attitude of caring, an optimism about the human condition, and a willingness to risk sharing one's self with another person.

Cormier and Cormier (1985) identify three potential problem areas, related to unresolved feelings and needs, that might inhibit this. First, issues related to perceived competence might result in "pollyanna" (overly positive) or overly self-critical interpersonal style. Unresolved are issues of incompetence and the fear of failure or success. The second potential problem area relates to the use of power to compensate for feelings of impotence, passivity, and dependence. Relationships may become difficult because the person acts too omnipotent (fearful of losing control) or too weak and unresourceful (fearful of assuming control). The third problem area has to do with being able to deal with intimacy and through it one's vulnerability for rejection.

STUDENT LEARNING EXERCISE

Rate yourself as a helper by responding as honestly as possible to the following items.

		Little	Some	A Lot
1.	I understand my values and motives.	1	2	3
2.	I understand other people.	1	2	3
3.	I can take another person's point of view.	1	2	3
4.	I appreciate views that are different from mine.	1	2	3
5.	I am aware of my prejudices and how they influence my interpersonal relationships.	1	2	3
6.	Lifestyles other than my own are acceptable to me.	1	2	3
7.	I try to understand the points of view of people from different racial and ethnic backgrounds.	1	2	3
8.	I can be myself with people.	1	2	3
9.	When put on a spot, I can respond nondefensively.	1	2	3
10.	I work toward equal rights and responsibilities for men and women.	1	2	3
11.	I believe that most human beings can solve their own problems if given the opportunity.	1	2	3
12.	I can communicate my thoughts and feelings clearly.	1	2	3
13.	People have told me that I am a warm person.	1	2	3
14.	I am aware of my faults.	1	2	3
15.	I am sought out by others as a helper.	1	2	3

THE COUNSELING RELATIONSHIP

The counselor behaviors described assist in building a unique relationship between counselor and client. Most interpersonal relationships have either formal or informal roles prescribed for the participants. For example, when one works for the Department of State, huge books on protocol govern relationships with members of the international community. In counseling there is a paradox; a role exists for counselors, but if they "play" that role, it is unlikely they will form a therapeutic relationship with clients. Naturalness and authenticity on the part of the counselor govern the favorable formation of a counseling relationship. To practice doing this, one practices approaching people as oneself.

Practically speaking, the counselor does not attempt to consciously rehearse how he or she is "supposed" to be. The counselor acts professionally, but does not put on a professional front, playacting some imaginary expert counselor. As one becomes trained as a counselor, one learns many skills, quite a few of which are taught specifically in the context of structured practice situations. But in the end counselors-in-training must take that repertoire of skills and personalize it, integrating it into the rest of their personality (Evans, Hearn, Uhlemann, & Ivey, 1984).

As this integration becomes increasingly more successful, counselors meet the clients' expectation of assistance from a professionally trained person, but soon learn from experiencing the humanness of the counselor that clients too can be free to be themselves, to be human, to reveal parts of themselves often hidden in other relationships. The natural, nonjudgmental style of the counselor makes it easier for clients to share parts of themselves. As the client becomes able to self-disclose, the relationship deepens (Jourard, 1964).

With these standards modeled by the counselor, both participants can begin to work together in a reciprocal manner, using the reactions to one another as important information. Effective counselors recognize that their greatest resource is the client.

Though such an open relationship exists, it is not without limits. Counseling is still a business relationship occurring in most instances on an "outpatient" basis. The relationship becomes structured within the context of a formal interview, usually lasting 45 to 50 minutes and scheduled weekly on the hour. For clients to be able to utilize such an arrangement, they must be able to function without professional assistance between interviews. If a client cannot do this, but must frequently telephone the counselor at home, demand frequent emergency sessions, and so forth, that client may need a more protective treatment (e.g., a residential placement).

Such limits demonstrate differences that exist in counseling versus close friendships or families. The American Psychological Association Ethical Standards warn psychologists of the hazards of dual relationships, when one serves a client in two different capacities (e.g., a therapist and a relative). Counselors too are wise to recognize how one relationship can contaminate the other. This is particularly important in counseling because of confidentiality. However, it is important to recognize that counselors also have a right to privacy as do clients. Often beginning counselors have difficulty limiting their availability to clients during nonwork hours. Poor boundary management between private and professional lives is linked to eventual burnout for counselors (Watkins, 1983).

STAGES IN THE COUNSELING PROCESS

Before we describe a common sequence of events in counseling, it is important to note that many clients, for one reason or another, will not complete all the stages of counseling. The process will be abandoned prematurely, not because something went wrong, but because of factors external to the counselor-client relationship. For example, the school year may end for a student client, or a client or counselor may move away to accept a new job. When counseling is in process and must abruptly end, the participants will feel the incompleteness and loss. For this reason counselors are encouraged to fit all the stages to be described into the time available, no matter how brief it may be. In accordance with this, accurately estimating the probable number of interviews available for working with a client becomes an important skill, especially for practitioners who will do a lot of time-limited counseling (e.g., school counselors).

The Beginning Phase

During the very early interviews the immediate goals become twofold: (1) to begin forming a good working relationship and (2) to explore the reasons the client sought counseling. In the latter problems and concerns will be uncovered, along with how they affect the client.

To achieve both immediate goals the counselor provides fundamental conditions that create an interpersonal atmosphere characterized by empathy, respect, and genuineness (Rogers, 1951; Carkhuff, 1969a; Carkhuff, 1969b). Central to providing the entire atmosphere is empathy. Briefly, empathy is the ability to understand the subjective experience of the client—to perceive the world as the client does while retaining one's own identity.

Empathy is important because the nature of a client's perceived world dictates how the client will behave. To understand the whys of a client's behavior requires empathetic understanding. In addition, the empathetic counselor becomes a more potent reinforcing agent—something that will become important throughout the rest of the process, but especially as the client acts upon the understanding gained in counseling (Corrigan, Dell, Lewis, & Schmidt, 1980).

To be able to empathize the counselor must be able to overcome self-consciousness and devote complete attention to what the client is trying to share. Often beginning counselors do not empathize well because they are trying to think of what they will say to the client, rather than listening to what the client is saying. Listening is the basis for being able to empathize.

In the early phase counselors do a lot of listening. If things go well, clients will realize that counselors appreciate and encourage their participation. It will become clear that there is a dual responsibility for progress in the relationship. The talk ratio early in counseling will be close to 50:50. In addition to listening, counselors will communicate their understanding through reflective statements ("You seem to be feeling . . ."), summaries ("Up to this point we have been talking about . . ."), and clarifications ("Am I hearing you correctly, you seem . . ."). This willingness on the part of the counselor to hear the client's story, rather than being too passive, seems to increase the attractiveness of the counselor, and may increase the counselor's ability to influence client change efforts later in the process (Heppner & Heesacker, 1982).

Counselors will also need to ask questions both to seek clarification and elaboration and to guide exploration into additional areas. However, the beginning phase of counseling is not an interrogation, and it should not seem so as a result of the counselor's asking too many questions. Repeated questions, especially closed-ended ones (questions that can be answered by a simple "yes" or "no"), tilt the responsibility too much toward the counselor. Before long the client will develop an increasingly passive stance in the interview, with the counselor increasingly feeling more pressure to make something happen.

When counselors-in-training attempt their first practice interviews, they often ask too many questions. They do this because they already know how to question, but must learn the skill of active listening in which they paraphrase client statements, reflect feelings, and summarize. A common exercise in counselor training is to prohibit the use of questions in a practice session in order to increase the use of other types of responses. It is like tying one's dominant arm behind the back in order to increase the facility of using the other arm. Later trainees are allowed to use questions after they are confident of their ability to use other responses. This results in counselors' becoming versatile interviewers, utilizing a variety of different verbal responses. Their early sessions have a conversational, rather than an interrogative, quality to them. Experienced interviewers may appear informal and relaxed, yet they are able to explore an extensive amount of material in a single interview.

Success in early interviews is judged by the degree to which the client self-discloses. Chit-chat becomes almost nonexistent as the client risks revealing information that could be embarrassing, socially disapproved, or even potentially damaging. Such disclosures will occur only if the counselor proves to be trustworthy.

Beginning counselors, however, should not expect the early phase to be all positive; clients will at times test and challenge, purposely deceive, and resist exploration into sensitive areas. Such negative behaviors may be connected with the very problems the client has come to solve. Thus, learning to relate better becomes a counseling goal for such clients, not a reason to reject or abandon them. That is why counselors are trained to deal with people others would find too troublesome.

With difficult and troublesome clients the counselor's patience may be tested. At times the counselor will feel abused and mistreated. Being able to handle such feelings without punishing the client is important. Because counselors have a genuine liking for people and can see beyond the immediate situation, they are able to respond therapeutically to these difficult situations.

At times a counselor may actually deserve a negative response from the client; often a counselor is mistreated not because of what she or he does, but because the client has projected onto the counselor traits associated with others in the client's life. This is called *transference*. If the client perceives the counselor as an authority figure, the counselor may be treated just as the client has treated other such figures. If the counselor is viewed as a nurturing person, he or she may be treated as the client treats other nurturing persons. On the same note, the counselor may respond emotionally to the client in some overly intense or otherwise unexplainable way, at least by virtue of what has transpired between the two of them. Here the counselor may have projected onto the client undeserved qualities. This is called *countertransference*. In both cases something unresolved from the past may have erupted. In the former, the client needs to work through transferences in counseling; in the latter the counselor needs to work through countertransferences with a supervisor.

Instead of such reactions, hopefully the counselor is able to display genuine caring for the client, even if times occur when scattered negative feelings must be restrained and evaluated. Understanding of clients is served by having counselors evaluate their reactions to them. Overall, the counselor strives in both verbal and nonverbal behavior to show spontaneity, congruence, and good humor. If this occurs with a reasonable degree of regularity during the beginning of helping, increasingly problems are identified and clarified along with unused opportunities to solve them (Egan, 1986). The client makes progress telling his or her story. Complex problems are reorganized into elements that allow one simpler solution to pave the way for other solutions (Egan, 1986). Blind spots inhibiting earlier problem-solving are uncovered along with new images and ideas that promote healing.

The Middle Phase

Problem exploration and relationship building, while characteristic of the early phase of counseling, reemerge in later stages as well. But once early exploration has resulted in the uncovering of a quantity of information useful in understanding and treating those problems, the tone of the interviews begins to change. Counselors become more active. They have intently listened to what the client has said, while they have also begun to assess the client's personality or repertoire of adaptive and not-so-adaptive attitudes and behaviors. The client's style of problem-solving, mistakes in logic, and faulty habits become more clear. In addition, environmental stressors, bad luck, and other external factors become more fully understood. The counselor must do something with this understanding.

Sharing this understanding may be a simple matter with a client who arrives at the same conclusions as the counselor at roughly the same time. In such situations the counselor could ask the client to draw an obvious conclusion (e.g., "What do you make out of what we have been talking about?"). A client with few blind spots and few rigid defenses can draw a conclusion with which the counselor can agree. Both can then explore what can be done with this new understanding.

Frequently the counselor sees something emerging out of early exploration that the client does not. Often this is connected to how the client contributes to the problems being explored. The counselor in this middle phase of helping must "personalize" the problem for the client (Carkhuff & Anthony, 1979).

Being given such information is often not very pleasant for the client. In fact at a subliminal level clients might be aware that there is something about them that is contributing to their difficulties, but are afraid to face it. It is like realizing over the winter that your clothes are fitting tighter; you know you have gained weight, but avoid stepping on a scale or looking at yourself naked in front of a mirror. The final confrontation of the reality is fearsome.

Part of the reason such confrontations with reality are so fearsome may lie in the fact that individuals in such situations already have lost so much self-esteem; to risk losing more might put them dangerously close to an amount of loss ultimately intolerable. When counselors confront clients with such information they expose clients to pain—pain often understood as necessary for a favorable, final outcome. Yet we know people avoid pain; people avoid going to the dentist, realizing they have decaying teeth, but unable to voluntarily submit themselves to pain. How pain is administered in a voluntary relationship, such as counseling, is crucial in the development of technical competence.

Well-trained counselors are careful and tactful in helping clients to personalize their problems in terms of how they contribute to what is bothering them. This tact pays special attention to timing things said to the client that will be difficult for the client to accept. This means that one waits for an appropriate time to deal with difficult confrontations, a time when the client is more ready to deal with them or when sufficient time exists for the matter to be fully treated. This can be achieved if input from the counselor about client problems points to solutions as well.

Egan (1986) describes the middle phase of helping as eventually constructing a new scenario—how things could be different and better. This can begin by understanding self-defeating behavior in a new, different light. The counselor is able to do this most often through the use of interpretations. Cormier and Cormier (1985) define an interpretation as "a counselor statement that makes an association or a causal connection among various client behaviors, events, or ideas or presents a possible explanation of a client's behavior (including the client's feelings, thoughts, and observable actions)." One language system replaces another. One set of ideas replaces another to explain the client's behavior and situation. The ideas come from the theories counselors study and use to organize their efforts. All counselors interpret; the interpretations change according to the theoretical orientation of the counselor.

With the new understanding gained from confronting and interpreting important client characteristics, the new scenario of how things could be better—how the client could change for the better—emerges. Early in counseling goals were discussed generally in terms of the elimination of various problems and symptoms. In this phase of counseling those goals are revised in terms of more clear, specific statements of how the client's attitudes and behaviors might change to achieve problem resolution.

At this point counselor and client must agree on these revised goals. If the way they were initially cast is not acceptable, they need to be revised until they are. Following this it is important that the client commit to those goals and to the actions required to attain them. Since much of what clients must commit to deals with their willingness to self-manage strategies requiring considerable effort and practice, commitment is especially crucial (Kanfer, 1980).

Achieving a commitment to work at changes based on a new understanding would not be possible were it not for the subtle achievements gained by the client in contact with the counselor. Cavanagh (1982) describes counseling as a new type of learning experience for most people. It is an intense curriculum in oneself. Emerging out of it is more than the recognition of internal conflicts, psychological imperatives ("musts" and "oughts" that govern life), and new insights into self. Clients, according to Cavanagh, experience something in the counseling relationship that offers them a chance for new psychological freedom. Because of this, they can begin to imagine themselves as different, and possibly for the first time in their lives, actually believe that they *can* be different. This is the launching pad for going out and trying to be what one imagines.

In preparing the client for the real-life attempts at change, the counselor has to work hard. In the middle phase the wisdom and experiences of the counselor pay off. More than likely the counselor in the middle phase, compared to the early phase, has initiated more and applied his or her own perspective to that of the client. In a sense the major contributions have been made; it is now up to the client to complete the process by working on permanent personal change that provides solutions to immediate problems and generalizes to other problems in the future.

The Late Phase

According to theoretical orientation, the later counseling sessions vary in content. Some counselors continue themes already developed; they continue to work on the new, emerging self-image of the client with the belief that the cognitive structure representing the self is the key to effective action-taking. Other counselors believe in more structured strategies aimed at action-taking. They emphasize the practice of concrete behaviors directly related to expressed problems and desired goals. Regardless of orientation, what has been talked about in the abstract can be solidified in real client change. Already, to get this far, the client feels better and has more self-confidence and optimism about the future; the client is energized and ready to try things that may have been too demanding prior to counseling. The client has more endurance and greater tolerance of frustration. If this were not true, neither structured, action-oriented approaches nor less structured, personal encounter approaches would work.

For some counselors a variety of techniques find their way into different sessions. Some of these are role playing, relaxation training, and exercises built around props or materials. Other sessions may be structured around review of diaries or logs the client was requested to keep. In still others readings assigned between sessions might be discussed (Hutchins & Cole, 1986).

All such adjuncts to simple counselor-client interactions are connected to the principal action point in the counseling process: the real, ongoing experience of the client as lived between counseling sessions. At times the counselor may desire to assume some control over this experience by assigning in consultation with the client "homework" to be completed between sessions. A sequential plan for such homework may develop to systematically approach the rehearsal of desired behaviors and roles.

In many instances later counseling sessions consist for the most part of the client reporting to the counselor what transpired over the past week, how difficult situations were managed, how successes could be explained. The counselor in such a situation is expected simply to comment on such experiences in light of what has occurred during counseling and as now a trusted, supportive consultant. Confusing or surprising events are mutually explored and analyzed for the purpose of fine-tuning the new, more effective stance the client has toward life experience.

In other instances there may be a need for the partners to cycle back to exploring or reunderstanding a particular problem, resulting in a need for the counselor to reinterpret a behavior or event. Eventually the client must encounter life on his or her own; that is a goal. As a parent learns to let go of a daughter or son, the counselor must let go of the client. As mentioned earlier, if the counselor has competence, power, or intimacy problems, this letting go will be difficult.

Toward the end of counseling, there is a tendency on the part of clients to forget what it was like prior to treatment. Review of problems and changes made remind clients of what they have achieved and serves as a precaution against their slipping back to less adaptive ways.

Eventually the counselor and client must confront the issue of termination. Ending an especially meaningful, ongoing relationship can be difficult; both members can experience considerable loss. Nevertheless, timing termination so it is neither too soon nor too late hopefully will occur. Ward (1984) lists the following as themes associated with termination: ending, growing up, autonomy, individuation, reviewing, summarizing, consolidating, and saying good-bye. If the client is ready to end, Ward notes that it will not be because of a complete cure; that rarely happens. However, presenting problems will be reduced; the client will feel better; there will be an increase in coping ability, marked also by greater playfulness and improved relationships with others.

STUDENT LEARNING EXERCISE

Read the following statements and indicate whether they suggest appropriate counselor behavior. Circle Y for yes or N for no.

1. A client appears very anxious during the first interview; the counselor interprets this as resistance.   Y   N

2. During one of the final sessions the client asks the counselor if her concerns were typical of someone her age. The counselor answers the question.   Y   N

3. A counselor has interpreted a client's behavior as a consequence of being sheltered as a child, not having the opportunity to learn needed social behaviors. The counselor uses the same interpretation in several later interviews for the same and other behaviors.   Y   N

4. A counselor, fearful of a client's becoming too uncomfortable during an interview, rarely confronts self-defeating actions and beliefs.   Y   N

5. A counselor spends considerable time with a client reviewing real-life experiences since the last interview.   Y   N

GROUP COUNSELING

Group counseling, like individual counseling, is represented by a vast array of differing orientations. This diversity expands when one considers the many different types of group treatments other than group counseling. For example, counselors lead guidance or psycho-educational groups. These groups tend to be more structured, with specific learning objectives. They deal, however, with personally relevant topics; thus, they are considered to be groups of a psychological nature. Encounter or sensitivity groups are also led by counselors. Such groups emphasize the development of interpersonal skills with the increased ability to deal with intimacy. Since such a varied involvement in group work is possible, developing group leadership skills is very important for the counselor-in-training. In part, skills relevant to group counseling apply to structured psycho-educational groups and vice versa.

Group Leadership Skills

While many of the skills used in individual counseling transfer to groups, additional issues confront the counselor in groups, requiring an increase in skills repertoire. Generally the counselor is seen as the group leader. In this capacity counselors are likely to do more than counsel individuals in a group context.

To get full benefit from the counseling group, the leader must learn how to maximize the therapeutic forces within each member and within the group as a whole.

How counselors actually lead groups varies according to theoretical orientation (Belkin, 1984). For example, a Gestaltist will design specific activities or exercises (games) to engage members in here-and-now awareness experiences. The rational therapy leader will spend time teaching members a view of healthy behavior. Following this, the rational counselor will attempt to enlist the aid of all in providing feedback to individual members concerning perceptions, thoughts, and behavior compatible or incompatible with the more healthy view. The behavioral counselor may take advantage of various group members as models and may use interactions within the group as a rehearsal of adaptive behavior.

Many such differences exist, but an effort has been made to identify those leadership behaviors common to all effective group leaders. Pearson (1981) divides these skills into teaching and group management. Teaching skills include being able to both explicitly and implicitly teach behaviors and observe group process. Group management skills include convening meetings, eliciting participation, channeling group effort in the direction of important topics or activities, limit-setting, and protecting members and the group from detrimental forces.

Gill and Barry (1982) also identify essential group leadership skills, putting them within a developmental framework according to stages specific to group counseling. Table 4.1 presents this framework.

Planning Counseling Groups

The selection of members for a counseling group is an important consideration. Strategies can vary according to treatment setting. For example, in a residential setting an ongoing group may exist in a ward or dormitory. New admittees automatically become part of this group. Members exit the group as they are released from the facility. In a school or outpatient clinic a group may be formed around common problems experienced by a number of clients. In this case the group becomes homogeneous with regard to problems and related objectives.

While similar concerns among group members are valuable in planning treatment, members tend to learn more from one another if their personalities and interpersonal styles are different. Where one member may be weak, another may be strong; this complementarity can be very useful as a means for members to learn from one another.

In many instances the counselor has a problem scheduling group sessions so that everyone can attend. For example, a school counselor often has difficulty taking a student out of the same class week after week. Sessions must be rotated across several different classes. With eight group members, scheduling becomes extremely difficult; more than likely several members will be in classes in which release for some other activity is seldom granted (e.g., physical education).

In some cases group counseling may supplement individual counseling rather than being a replacement for it. For example, a number of outpatient therapists at a mental health center may have been assigned battered women as individual clients. One of the therapists may propose the formation of a counseling group for battered women, recruiting some of the members of the group through referrals of clients already in individual therapy. As other outpatient therapists review the objectives of the group, they may encourage certain clients to join. The therapist's decision is based on the readiness of the client for such an experience. Depending on circumstances, some clients may continue in individual treatment along with the group, while others may not. The combination of both group and individual counseling can be especially effective in the later phases, when additional support and feedback help solidify changes made.

COUPLES AND FAMILY THERAPY

The number of convention programs and continuing education workshops offered in recent years indicates that couples therapy and family therapy are topics of great interest in the counseling profession. Such interventions are conjoint in nature; the counselor works with all or at least most of the members of the family during sessions. Couples therapy is a form of family therapy since each member is committed to the other, whether they are formally married or not. Ideally such social units have as goals the individual success of members and the preservation of the unit. Sometimes families become dysfunctional, working against themselves and the best interests of their members.

Working with families is considerably different from working with a typical counseling group. Before counseling, family members have been intimately involved with one another. The behavior of one family member has already affected the others. Families work to change some behaviors in members while they desperately attempt to maintain other behaviors. When a counselor holds a session with a family, alliances among different individuals already have been established. Factions within the family work in consort sometimes to support and sometimes to undermine the efforts of the counselor. Understanding and dealing with such interpersonal systems is an important part of treating individuals within the family. Besides helping members solve personal problems, family counseling strives to improve the way the family functions overall.

Such ideas become clearer to counselors as they work with an individual—for example, an adolescent in constant trouble. Over a period of time individual counseling seems to work—the client begins to improve. Then these initial gains are lost; the client seems to revert back to earlier actions. When the counselor investigates the situation, it seems that some members of the client's family intervened in some way to cause the regression of the client. In

Table 4.1 Classification System for Group-Focused Counseling Skills

Stage I	Stage II	Stage III
Group formation: Facilitating cooperation toward common goals through development of group identity.	*Group awareness*: Facilitating a shared understanding of the group's behavior.	*Group action*: Facilitating cooperative decision-making and problem-solving.
1. *Norming*: Stating explicitly the expected group behavior.	1. *Labeling group behavior*: Identifying and describing group feelings and performance.	1. *Identifying group needs*: Asking questions and making statements which clarify the want and needs of the group.
2. *Eliciting group responses*: Inquiries or invitations to members which encourage comments, questions, or observations.	2. *Implicit norming*: Describing behavior which has become typical of the group through common practice.	2. *Identifying group goals*: Asking questions and making statements which clarify group objectives.
3. *Eliciting sympathetic reactions*: Inquiries or invitations to members which encourage disclosure of experiences or feelings similar to those being expressed.	3. *Eliciting group observations*: Inquiries or invitations to members which encourage observations about group process.	3. *Attributing meaning*: Providing concepts for understanding group thought, feelings, and behavior.
4. *Identifying commonalities and differences*: Describing comparative characteristics of participants.	4. *Eliciting mutual feedback*: Inquiries or invitations to members which encourage sharing of perceptions about each other's behavior.	4. *Eliciting alternatives*: Providing descriptions of possible courses of action and inviting members to contribute alternatives.

5. *Eliciting empathic reactions:* Inquiries or invitations to members which encourage reflection of one member's expressed content or feeling.
6. *Task focusing:* Redirecting conversation to immediate objectives; restating themes being expressed by more than one member.

5. *Identifying conflict:* Labeling discordant elements of communication between members.
6. *Identifying nonverbal behavior:* Labeling unspoken communications between members (facial expression, posture, hand gestures, voice tone and intensity, etc.)
7. *Validating:* Requesting group confirmation of the accuracy of leader or members' perceptions.
8. *Transitioning:* Changing the group's focus on content or feelings being expressed.
9. *Connecting:* Relating material from group events at a particular time or session to what is happening currently.
10. *Extinguishing:* Ignoring, cutting-off, or diverting inappropriate talk or actions of members.

5. *Exploring consequences:* Inquiries or invitations to the group which evaluate actions and potential outcomes.
6. *Consensus testing:* Requesting group agreement on a decision or course of action.

Note. From "Group-focused Counseling: Classifying the Essential Skills" by S. J. Gill and R. A. Barry, 1982, *Personnel and Guidance Journal, 60,* p. 5. Reprinted by permission. No further reproduction authorized without further written permission of AACD.

another situation, a counselor may be working with an adult client. As he or she improves, the client's spouse becomes more troubled and in need of treatment. Making sense out of such situations has spawned new ideas concerning how to understand the influence of family members on one another and how to treat the family as a whole.

Important Family Therapy Approaches

While many individuals have contributed to family therapy practice, Ackerman (1958) and Satir (1964) were among the first to formulate general approaches to family work. In particular, Virginia Satir and Jay Haley (1976) were influenced by the seminal work of Don Jackson. Satir, Haley, and Jackson formed a circle of people from many different disciplines to begin understanding the family as a social system that affects the behavior of individual members in deceptive ways. This group, originally from Palo Alto, California, became known as the "communications" school because of their emphasis on treating dysfunctional families through improving the way members communicate with one another.

Jay Haley (1963, 1973) developed many different strategies to cope with the troublesome maneuvers of family members in treatment. Part of this resulted from his affiliation with Milton Erikson, an imaginative psychiatrist who also strongly influenced hypnotherapy. Haley's spouse, Cloé Madanes (1981), along with Haley, further refined the understanding of aspects of family interaction as maneuvers to usurp and retain power. Their approach has become known as Strategic Family Therapy.

Haley also worked with Minuchin (1974), who developed a system to understand the various interpersonal involvements among family members. These include different coalitions that attempt to isolate family members from one another. This approach has led to the notion of "structural" family therapy, in which maneuvers are planned on the basis of how the family is socially organized. From Minuchin have come very specific responses for the therapist in given situations. He too emphasizes the importance of communication; it is powerful feedback to members of the family from other members. If such feedback can change, so can the family and its ability to support positive changes in members.

These individuals and their associates have had a powerful impact on the practice of family therapy. Others, such as Bowen (1978), have offered additional theoretical aids in addition to synthesizing the work of still others. In particular, Bowen has eased the transition of many practitioners from understanding behavior as a consequence of individual personalities to effects of family influences. These different schools of thought have produced institutes dedicated to training family therapists. Thus family therapy has become a specialty practice, with its own definable body of knowledge and training standards. While other theoretical systems such as transactional analysis, Gestalt therapy, and behavior therapy also have ways of treating troubled families, certification standards for family therapy demand competence in the unique body of knowledge described earlier. The American Association for Marriage and Family Therapy (AAMFT) represents the many disciplines that have worked together to develop this practice and the certification standards attached to it.

SUMMARY

In this chapter a general overview of the counseling process was provided. Emphasis was on the behavior of the counselor as it influences the client immediately and also as it prepares the way for later change efforts. Note was taken on special issues arising during different phases of the process. Individual counseling was the principal topic covered, though special issues related to the practice of group and family counseling were discussed.

REVIEW QUESTIONS

1. Construct two lists of client characteristics—one that appears essential for favorable counseling outcome and another that simplifies the counseling process.
2. Write a profile of the effective counselor.
3. Describe characteristics of the counseling relationship that differentiate it from a friendship.
4. Describe early, middle, and late phases of counseling.
5. Describe how individual and group counseling can work together with certain types of clients.
6. List and briefly describe three important approaches to family therapy.

REFERENCES

Ackerman, N. W. (1958). *The psychodynamics of family life.* New York: Basic Books.
Belkin, G. S. (1984). *Introduction to counseling* (2nd ed.). Dubuque, IA: Wm. C. Brown.
Bowen, M. (1978). *Family therapy in clinical practice.* New York: Jason Aronson.
Brammer, L. (1985). *The helping relationship.* Englewood Cliffs, NJ: Prentice-Hall.
Brammer, L. M. & Shostrom, E. L. (1982). *Therapeutic psychology: Fundamentals of counseling and psychotherapy* (4th ed.). Englewood Cliffs, NJ: Prentice-Hall.
Carkhuff, R. R. (1969a). *Helping and human relations, Vol. I: Selection and training.* New York: Holt, Rinehart and Winston.
Carkhuff, R. R. (1969b.) *Helping and human relations, Vol. II: Practice and research.* New York: Holt, Rinehart and Winston.
Carkhuff, R. R. (1983). *The art of helping* (5th ed.). Amherst, MA: Human Resources Development Press.

Carkhuff, R. R., & Anthony, W. A. (1979). *The skills of helping.* Amherst, MA: Human Resource Development Press.

Carkhuff, R. R., & Berenson, B. G. (1977). *Beyond counseling and therapy* (2nd. ed.). New York: Holt, Rinehart and Winston.

Cavanagh, M. E. (1982). *The counseling experience.* Monterey, CA: Brooks/Cole.

Combs, A. W. (1969). *Florida studies in the helping professions.* Gainesville, FL: University of Florida Press.

Cormier, W. H., & Cormier, L. S. (1985). *Interviewing strategies for helpers: Fundamental skills and cognitive behavioral interventions* (2nd ed.). Monterey, CA: Brooks/Cole.

Corrigan, J. D., Dell, D. M., Lewis, K. N., & Schmidt, L. D. (1980). Counseling as a social influence process: A review. *Journal of Counseling Psychology, 27* (4), 395–441.

Egan, G. (1975). *Exercises in helping skills.* Monterey, CA: Brooks/Cole.

Egan, G. (1986). *The skilled helper: A systematic approach to effective helping* (3rd. ed.). Monterey, CA: Brooks/Cole.

Evans, D. R., Hearn, M. T., Uhlemann, M. R., & Ivey, A. E. (1984). *Essential interviewing: A programmed approach to effective communication* (2nd., ed.). Monterey, CA: Brooks/Cole.

Gill, S. J., & Barry, R. A. (1982). Group-focused counseling: Classifying the essential skills. *Personnel and Guidance Journal, 60* (5), 302–305.

Goldstein, A. P. (1971). *Psychotherapeutic attraction.* New York: Pergamon Press.

Haley, J. (1963). *Strategies for psychotherapy.* New York: Grune and Stratton.

Haley, J. (1973). *Uncommon therapy.* New York: W. W. Norton.

Haley, J. (1976). *Problem solving therapy.* San Francisco: Jossey-Bass.

Heilbrun, A. B., Jr. (1982). Cognitive factors in early counseling termination: Social insight and level of defensiveness. *Journal of Counseling Psychology, 29* (1), 29–38.

Heppner, P. P., & Heesacker, M. (1982). Interpersonal influence process in real-life counseling: Investigating client perceptions, counselor experience level, and counselor power over time. *Journal of Counseling Psychology, 29* (3), 215–223.

Hutchins, D. E., & Cole, C. G. (1986). *Helping relationships and strategies.* Monterey, CA: Brooks/Cole.

Ivey, A. E. (1983). *Intentional interviewing and counseling.* Monterey, CA: Brooks/Cole.

Jourard, S. M. (1964). *The transparent self.* Princeton: D. Van Nostrand.

Kanfer, F. H. (1980). Self-management methods. In F. H. Kanfer & A. P. Goldstein (Eds.), *Helping people change* (2nd. ed.). New York: Pergamon Press, 334–389.

Kurpius, D. J. (1986). The helping relationship. In M. D. Lewis, R. L. Hayes, & J. A. Lewis (Eds.), *An introduction to the counseling profession.* Itasca, IL: F. E. Peacock Publishers, 96–130.

Madanes, C. (1981). *Strategic family therapy.* San Francisco: Jossey-Bass.

Minuchin, S. (1974). *Families and family therapy.* Cambridge: Harvard University Press.

Parloff, M. B., Waskow, I. E., & Wolfe, B. E. (1978). Research on therapist variables in relationship to process and outcome. In S. L. Garfield and A. E. Bergin (Eds.), *Handbook of psychotherapy and behavior change: An empirical analysis.* New York: John Wiley and Sons, 233–282.

Pearson, R. E. (1981). Basic skills for leadership of counseling groups. *Counselor Education and Supervision, 21* (1), 30–37.

Rogers, C. R. (1951). *Client-centered therapy.* Boston: Houghton Mifflin Co.

Rogers, C. R. (1957). The necessary and sufficient conditions of therapeutic personality change. *Journal of Consulting Psychology, 21* (1), 95–103.

Satir, V. (1964). *Conjoint family therapy.* Palo Alto: Science and Behavior Books.

Sue, D. W. (1981). *Counseling the culturally different: Theory and practice.* New York: John Wiley and Sons.

Truax, C. B., & Carkhuff, R. R. (1967). *Toward effective counseling and psychotherapy.* Chicago: Aldine.

Ward, D. E. (1984). Termination of individual counseling: Concepts and strategies. *Journal of Counseling and Development, 63* (1), 21–25.

Watkins, C. E., Jr. (1983). Burnout in counseling practice: Some potential professional and personal hazards of becoming a counselor. *Personnel and Guidance Journal, 61* (5), 304–308.

5

Assessing Client Problems

GOALS OF THE CHAPTER

The purpose of this chapter is to provide an overview of the use of testing and interview assessment by counselors.

CHAPTER PREVIEW

1. The purpose of assessment will be explored.
2. The characteristics of standardized tests, their selection, and their use in counseling will be examined.
3. The use of computer technology in assessment will be described.
4. Nonstandardized or interview assessment will be discussed and exemplified.

INTRODUCTION

This chapter will survey the purpose of assessment—its use and value in the counseling profession. Types of assessment procedures will be differentiated. Standardized tests and inventories commonly used by counselors will be discussed. At the end of the chapter the diagnostic interview as a means of assessing clients will be highlighted.

THE PURPOSE OF ASSESSMENT

Assessment is used to diagnose client problems, to make predictions about clients, and to develop client self-awareness. It is a process not restricted to the client-counselor relationship; organizations such as schools and corporations can follow some of the same assessment practices.

Counselors are constantly processing information related to the welfare of clients. This information is linked to decisions that clients must make, that organizations dealing with clients (e.g., schools and employers) must make, and that counselors must make when treating their clients. Important questions emerge related to such decisions:

- *From clients.* What are the chances that I can be successful in a particular training program? What occupations fit with my talents and interests? Why am I so discouraged about life and my future? What can I do to feel better?
- *From family members.* Is it a good idea to transfer our child to a private boarding school with very high academic standards? Is my spouse just as dissatisfied with our marriage as I am?
- *From schools.* What students should be placed in special classes? Which applicants can succeed in a highly competitive academic program?
- *From employers.* Will your client's past difficulties prevent him or her from fitting into our organization? Which employees have the most advancement potential—the greatest potential to handle top-level positions?
- *From counselors.* Is this client potentially dangerous to himself or to others? Might he kill himself or harm others within the next few days? Why is it that this seemingly bright student is having difficulty in certain of her classes? What goals should I discuss with this client for our counseling relationship?

The parameters of these various questions differ. Some of them demand quick decisions; others can be entertained over time. Some can be made by the counselor alone; others are best handled in consultation with others, including the client. Some allow considerable room for error; others must be made carefully or the client might be put in danger.

The questions posed above are difficult ones to answer. They demonstrate how counselors work with clients and organizations to deal with important issues. In helping to answer such questions, counselors have earned the respect of both their clients and other helping professionals.

Assessment Defined

Assessment is the process by which counselors systematically collect data about clients that can be used to make vital decisions. Assessment can be formal, where carefully developed tests and inventories are administered under carefully controlled conditions. It can also be informal, where the counselor draws conclusions from observing clients both during and outside of interviews.

In counselor-related activities assessment is aimed first at description, then at prediction of client behavior. For example, a high school student might want to learn how her mathematical reasoning compares to other students (description). Based on this information, she may solicit an estimate concerning her chances for admission into a college of engineering (prediction).

In using assessment to help clients make decisions, counselors strive for precision. They want to gather accurate information to predict the future. Prediction of the future is always less than perfect. This is especially true with an individual. For example, when using SAT scores to predict grade point average in college, we can be more accurate for a group of students than for an individual.

Types of Assessment

Standardized Tests.   Standardized testing is perhaps the most important approach to assessment used by counselors. Standardized tests provide a sample of behavior, drawn by an examiner in a fixed way, so that results collected at different times and places will be fully comparable (Cronbach, 1984). Hopefully, a standardized test also will be objective in that every observer of the test-taker's performance would report the very same results. In addition, the test will be reliable and valid; that is, it will consistently measure what it is supposed to measure and will truly measure what it says it measures, not something else. If an instrument says it measures trustworthiness, but respondents answer questions primarily to meet socially approved standards, the instrument is not very valid, because it does not measure what it says it measures. If an intelligence test is administered three times at monthly intervals, and it generates discrepant scores, it is not very reliable.

For decades psychologists have been developing standardized tests to sample many different human traits and behaviors. These tests are particularly useful in comparing individuals to larger groups because results are normed. That is, outcomes from using those instruments with different groups of people are described in mathematical terms (statistics), so a counselor can help a client size up her or his performance compared to those norms. This brief review of important assessment concepts demonstrates the existence of a special vocabulary. Table 5.1 provides a glossary of some frequently used assessment terms.

Table 5.1 Glossary of Selected Assessment Terms

Academic aptitude: A combination of inherited and learned abilities necessary for school work.

Aptitude: A combination of inherited and learned abilities that are known to be predictive of success in a given area of performance (e.g., music).

Battery: A group of several tests usually administered at one time.

Diagnostic test: A test used to locate the particular nature of a strength or weakness—for example, to assess reading or mathematics difficulties.

Norms: Statistics (mean, standard deviations, etc.) used to describe the performance of various groups on a test (e.g., grade, gender, age norms).

Objective test: A test for which the outcome will be exactly the same no matter who scores the test.

Performance test: A test requiring manual responses, such as the manipulation of equipment.

Profile: The results of a series of tests or subtests within a test presented in graphic form.

Reliability: The stability of a test to consistently measure what it is supposed to measure. The freedom of a test from error.

Standardized test: The use of systematic procedures or rules to ensure that the test will be administered in the same way regardless of who is administering the test.

Validity: The extent to which a test truly measures what it is supposed to measure. Valid tests measuring the same trait will achieve the same result.

Statistics and Standardized Assessment. Statistics are wonderful tools for accurately describing things. For example, a person could say, "I had a wonderful day," and we would know very little about that day, especially compared to other days. However, if the person says, "On a scale from 1 to 10, it was a 10 day," we would have a more precise representation of her experiences for that day. Statistics do this for us in even more graphic ways; they help achieve greater clarity in description and prediction. It is often unfortunate that many counselors-in-training are afraid of mathematics and subsequently fail to use numbers to full advantage as a way to effectively communicate.

In general, tests are a way of communicating information about both how well a person can do something and what that person thinks or believes, depending on the type of test. Counselors use both tests and inventories. Items on tests usually have right and wrong answers and attempt to measure maximum performance. Items on inventories usually do not have right or wrong answers; they are opinions or judgments, and they sample typical performance.

In most cases standardized tests and inventories are developed to measure lasting characteristics, that is, characteristics that influence long-term adjustment. Clients come to counselors to make long-term plans. Helping clients assess stable characteristics provides information about the personal assets that will be invested in those plans.

Nonstandardized Assessment. Not all important decisions counselors make are related to long-term conditions. For example, when a student comes to a counselor complaining about the erratic behavior of her mother and the potential threat of injury to the student or her siblings, the mother often cannot be assessed through the administration of standardized instruments. There is neither time nor opportunity to do so. Whether a person is actually going to commit homicide has never been effectively measured by an inventory.

Nonstandardized assessment, or what has been called clinical assessment, continually filters through much of what counselors do. Often this assessment is immediate. It is data gathering face-to-face with people. Norms are irrelevant or do not exist for the behavior in question. A computer will not help in making the decision on what to do. However, by training and experience, counselors are able to assess the nature of the situation and decide what to do. The ability to deal with emergencies or one-of-a-kind situations comes from sharpening one's skills in nonstandardized assessment. Both standardized and nonstandardized assessment skills enable counselors to do their job.

TYPES OF STANDARDIZED TESTS AND INVENTORIES

The types of instruments frequently used by counselors include tests of intelligence, aptitude, and achievement. Inventories measuring personality factors, career interests, and attitudes are also common to the assessment repertoire of the counselor.

Intelligence Tests

Anastasi (1982) notes that intelligence tests are most often validated against measures of academic achievement and thus often are designed as tests of scholastic aptitude. Some prefer to call intelligence tests measures of cognitive development. Most intelligence tests emphasize a single numeric score (e.g., IQ) as the outcome. Intelligence tests do not measure the size of one's intellectual capacity. They measure one's potential to do well in life situations valued by our dominant culture, requiring in the majority of cases verbal and mathematical skills. Such skills are developed through opportunity. This is why people continue to argue about whether intelligence tests are measures of aptitude or achievement.

The standards for the measurement of intelligence are found in the individually administered tests of intelligence, such as the Stanford-Binet and the scales developed by David Wechsler (Anastasi, 1982). School and clinical psychologists spend more time administering and interpreting individually administered tests of intelligence than do counselors.

Counselors more often use group-administered tests of intelligence. The Otis-Lennon School Ability Test is an example of such an instrument. Tests developed to screen college students are considered measures of intelligence (Anastasi, 1982). A good example is the Scholastic Aptitude Test (SAT) of the

College Entrance Examination Board. It is one of the most researched, technically perfect assessment tools (Anastasi, 1982). Because of the link between intelligence testing and academic achievement, such instruments are most often used to make educational decisions for school-age individuals. Examples of uses include placement into special education, honors programs, and other curricular offerings.

Aptitude Tests

Aptitude tests also are measures of special abilities. They focus on some future behavior that a person is capable of learning with appropriate training (Aiken, 1985). The most frequently used aptitude tests measure multiple factors; that is, they include numerous subtests that assess specialized aptitudes. Results of all subtests form a profile of the multiple factors that can be graphically represented and associated with such important issues as occupational success. An example of a measure of multiple aptitudes is the Generalized Aptitude Test Battery (GATB) developed by the U.S. Employment Service. The GATB measures the following:

1. Intelligence (General learning ability)
2. Verbal aptitude
3. Numerical aptitude
4. Spatial aptitude
5. Perception of geometric forms (form perception)
6. Clerical perception
7. Motor coordination
8. Finger dexterity
9. Manual dexterity

Extensive work has been done associating GATB profiles with success in various occupations. Thus they are useful in making career decisions both in school and work settings.

Industry and vocational rehabilitation often use more specialized instruments to help in job placement. There are many different measures of manual dexterity, eye/hand coordination, clerical ability, and so forth. Some of these tests are paper-and-pencil tests, especially those that measure verbal aptitudes. Others rely on a piece of apparatus to measure motor skills. The device may be as simple as a metal box with holes of different sizes in which the test-taker inserts and tightens nuts and bolts. These tasks are timed and the results compared with norms for employees in various occupations.

Work samples can be used to assess managerial ability. Corporate decision-making has been simulated via what is called an "in-basket" technique in which problem situations are presented as if they have just arisen in a worklike situation. This strategy, often not very standardized, is used in corporate assessment centers described in Chapter 14.

Achievement Tests

Tests of achievement for the most part are intended to be used in education to assess the outcome of various learning activities. Entire school districts in cooperation with state departments of education assess general academic achievement at regular intervals. School counselors usually are involved in this process.

Standardized achievement testing is a big business, with large corporations marketing dozens of achievement test batteries and hundreds of different subject matter tests. Achievement test batteries are supposed to meaure what is called general educational development, what we consider to be the basic skills in reading, language usage, mathematics, and general knowledge in science and social studies. The results are used for curriculum evaluation and identification of students for remediation and advanced placement. The Stanford Achievement Tests and the Iowa Tests of Basic Skills are examples of these instruments. The American College Testing Program (ACT) examines college applicants on English usage, mathematics, social studies reading, and natural sciences reading.

Achievement test results can play a role in academic advising, but are of limited use in personal counseling. Some exceptions may be with students who have discrepancies between the grades they receive and the scores they achieve on standardized tests. Sending home a student's test results informs parents of a student's standing but can intensify conflicts between parent and child on school and future planning issues. Often parents take an interest in the test results and change their attitudes toward counseling.

Career-Related Inventories

The administration and interpretation of occupational interest inventories is a key factor in career planning. Through their usage counselors help clients to crystallize their interests, which then become the guide used to explore relevant opportunities in the immense world of work. If one recognizes that *The Dictionary of Occupational Titles* lists more than 24,000 different occupational titles, one begins to visualize the impossibility of exploring all conceivable opportunities for employment. More realistic is the tactic of narrowing down occupations for consideration according to a client's interests.

Popular interest inventories include the Strong-Campbell Interest Inventory, The Self-Directed Search, The Harrington/O'Shea System for Career Decision-Making, and the Ohio Vocational Interest Survey (OVIS). These inventories generally list household and work tasks, hobbies, school subjects, and various occupations. The person taking the inventory then indicates whether he or she likes, dislikes, or is neutral to the activity. Responses are then normed to various groups. For example, the Strong-Campbell compares the responses of the person completing the inventory to norm groups in 162 different occupations. These and other results are profiled for use in career decision-making. Figure 5.1 shows a sample Strong-Campbell Profile.

The interest profile serves many purposes. One is to guide career exploration; another is to diagnose the client's readiness to make a career choice. A "flat" or undifferentiated (no low- or high-interest areas) profile represents people who as yet do not know what they like or dislike. With more life experience they may clarify their preferences. In a sense they need to grow a little more before they are ready to make an important career choice.

Many other factors are related to a person's readiness to make career decisions. To assess many of these, measures of career maturity or career development have been developed. One such instrument is the Career Maturity Inventory (CMI), developed by John Crites (1973) to measure attitudes and competencies needed to make effective career decisions. The CMI can measure both attitudes and self-reported competencies. Career development competencies assessed include self-appraisal, occupational information, goal selection, planning, and problem-solving. In addition to use in individual and group counseling, measures of career development are useful in assessing needs of client populations as well as outcomes of career guidance programs.

Personality Inventories

Because their reliability and validity tend to be lower than other types of standardized instruments, personality inventories have been a little more suspect than other standardized instruments. Nevertheless, every year dozens of new measures of personality appear. However, most of these are intended for use in research in which they will be administered to groups of subjects for the purpose of norming human factors and for drawing general conclusions about populations of people. When a counselor uses such instruments to draw conclusions about an individual client, the inventory results should conform closely to other information about the client. As part of an overall evaluation, personality inventories have their place. They can stimulate useful inquiry into dimensions of the client that might otherwise have been avoided.

Some of the most frequently used personality inventories are those that assess psychopathology. The Minnesota Multiphasic Personality Inventory (MMPI) is used for this purpose; extensive, specialized training is required for its use, and considerable experience is needed for its interpretation.

Traditionally counselors have served normal populations facing regular developmental challenges. Thus instruments intended for these populations have been of greater interest for counselors. For example, the California Psychological

STRONG-CAMPBELL INTEREST INVENTORY OF THE

STRONG VOCATIONAL INTEREST BLANK

PROFILE REPORT FOR:

DATE TESTED:

ID:

SEX:

DATE SCORED:

AGE:

SPECIAL SCALES: ACADEMIC COMFORT
INTROVERSION-EXTROVERSION

TOTAL RESPONSES: **INFREQUENT RESPONSES:**

OCCUPATIONAL SCALES

			STANDARD SCORES		VERY DISSIMILAR	DISSIMILAR	MODERATELY DISSIMILAR	MID-RANGE	MODERATELY SIMILAR	SIMILAR	VERY SIMILAR
			F	M	15	25	30		40 45	45 55	55
F	M										
(CRS)	RC	Marine Corps enlisted personnel	(CRS)								
RC	RC	Navy enlisted personnel									
RC	RC	Army officer									
RI	RIC	Navy officer									
R	R	Air Force officer									
(C)	R	Air Force enlisted personnel	(C)								
R	R	Police officer									
R	R	Bus driver									
R	R	Horticultural worker									
RC	R	Farmer									
R	RCS	Vocational agriculture teacher									
RI	R	Forester									
(IR)	RI	Veterinarian	(IR)								
RIS	(SRI)	Athletic trainer	(SRI)								
RIS	R	Emergency medical technician									
RI	RI	Radiologic technologist									
RI	R	Carpenter									
RI	RI	Electrician									
RIA	(ARI)	Architect	(ARI)								
RI	RI	Engineer									

REALISTIC

GENERAL OCCUPATIONAL THEME - R

30   40   50   60   70

F

M

BASIC INTEREST SCALES

(STANDARD SCORE)

AGRICULTURE
F
M

NATURE
F
M

ADVENTURE
F
M

MILITARY ACTIVITIES
F
M

MECHANICAL ACTIVITIES
F
M

INVESTIGATIVE

GENERAL OCCUPATIONAL THEME - I 30 40 50 60 70

BASIC INTEREST SCALES (STANDARD SCORE)

SCIENCE

MATHEMATICS

MEDICAL SCIENCE

MEDICAL SERVICE

F	M		15	25	30	40	45	55
IRC	IRC	Computer programmer						
IRC	IRC	Systems analyst						
IRC	IR	Medical technologist						
IR	IR	R & D manager						
IR	IR	Geologist						
IR	[I]	Biologist	(I)					
IR	IR	Chemist						
IR	IR	Physicist						
IR	[RI]	Veterinarian	(RI)					
IRS	IR	Science teacher						
IRS	IRS	Physical therapist						
IR	IRS	Respiratory therapist						
IC	IR	Medical technician						
IC	IE	Pharmacist						
ISR	[CSE]	Dietitian	(CSE)					
[SI]	ISR	Nurse, RN	(SI)					
IR	I	Chiropractor						
IR	IR	Optometrist						
IR	IR	Dentist						
I	IA	Physician						
[IR]	I	Biologist	(IR)					
	I	Mathematician						
	IR	Geographer						
	I	College professor						
I	IA	Psychologist						
IA	IA	Sociologist						

ARTISTIC

GENERAL OCCUPATIONAL THEME - A 30 40 50 60 70

BASIC INTEREST SCALES (STANDARD SCORE)

MUSIC/DRAMATICS

ART

WRITING

F	M		15	25	30	40	45	55
AI	AI	Medical illustrator						
A		Art teacher						
A		Artist, fine						
A		Artist, commercial						
AE	A	Interior decorator						
[RIA]	ARI	Architect	(RIA)					
A		Photographer						
A		Musician						
AR	[EA]	Chef	(EA)					
[E]	AE	Beautician	(E)					
AE	A	Flight attendant						
A		Advertising executive						
A		Broadcaster						
A		Public relations director						
A		Lawyer						
AS	AS	Public administrator						
A		Reporter						
A		Librarian						
AS	AS	English teacher						
[SA]	AS	Foreign language teacher	(SA)					

CONSULTING PSYCHOLOGISTS PRESS
577 COLLEGE AVENUE
PALO ALTO, CA 94306

(Continued)

93

STRONG-CAMPBELL INTEREST INVENTORY OF THE
STRONG VOCATIONAL INTEREST BLANK

PROFILE REPORT FOR: **DATE TESTED:**

ID:

AGE: **SEX:**   **DATE SCORED:**

OCCUPATIONAL SCALES

		STANDARD SCORES			VERY DISSIMILAR	DISSIMILAR	MODERATELY DISSIMILAR	MID-RANGE	MODERATELY SIMILAR	SIMILAR	VERY SIMILAR
			F	M	15	25	30	40	45	55	
SA	**(AS)**	Foreign language teacher		(AS)							
SA	**SA**	Minister									
SA	**SA**	Social worker									
S	**S**	Guidance counselor									
S	**S**	Social science teacher									
S	**S**	Elementary teacher									
SRI	**SAR**	Special education teacher									
SIA	**SAI**	Occupational therapist									
SI	**(ISR)**	Speech pathologist									
SI	**(ISR)**	Nurse, RN		(ISR)							
SCI	**N/A**	Dental hygienist		N/A							
SC	**SC**	Nurse, LPN									
[RIS]	**SR**	Athletic trainer	(RIS)								
SR	**SR**	Physical education teacher									
SRE	**SE**	Recreation leader									
SE	**SE**	YWCA/YMCA director									
SEC	**SCE**	School administrator									
SCE	**N/A**	Home economics teacher		N/A							

SOCIAL

	30	40	50	60	70	
GENERAL OCCUPATIONAL THEME - S						F
						M

BASIC INTEREST SCALES   (STANDARD SCORE)

TEACHING						F
						M
SOCIAL SERVICE						F
						M
ATHLETICS						F
						M
DOMESTIC ARTS						F
						M
RELIGIOUS ACTIVITIES						F
						M

94

ENTERPRISING

GENERAL OCCUPATIONAL THEME - E

30 40 50 60 70

(STANDARD SCORE)

15 25 30 40 45 55

BASIC INTEREST SCALES

PUBLIC SPEAKING

LAW/POLITICS

MERCHANDISING

SALES

BUSINESS MANAGEMENT

	F	M		
	E	ES	Personnel director	
	ES	E	Elected public official	
	ES	ES	Life insurance agent	
	EC	E	Chamber of Commerce executive	
	EC	EC	Store manager	
	N/A	ECR	Agribusiness manager	N/A
	EC	EC	Purchasing agent	
	EC	E	Restaurant manager	
	[AR]	EA	Chef	(AR)
	EC	E	Travel agent	
	ECS	E	Funeral director	
	[CSE]	ESC	Nursing home administrator	(CSE)
	EC	ER	Optician	
	E	[AE]	Beautician	(AE)
	E	E	Florist	
	EC	E	Buyer	
	EI	EI	Marketing executive	
	EIC	ECI	Investments manager	

CONVENTIONAL

GENERAL OCCUPATIONAL THEME - C

30 40 50 60 70

(STANDARD SCORE)

15 25 30 40 45 55

BASIC INTEREST SCALES

OFFICE PRACTICES

	F	M		
	C	C	Accountant	
	C	C	Banker	
	CE	CE	IRS agent	
	CES	CES	Credit manager	
	CES	CES	Business education teacher	
	[CS]	CES	Food service manager	(CS)
	[ISR]	CSE	Dietitian	(ISR)
	CSE	[ESC]	Nursing home administrator	(ESC)
	CSE	CSE	Executive housekeeper	
	CS	[CES]	Food service manager	(CES)
	CS	N/A	Dental assistant	N/A
	C	N/A	Secretary	N/A
	C	[R]	Air Force enlisted personnel	(R)
	CES	[RC]	Marine Corps enlisted personnel	(RC)
	CES	CR	Army enlisted personnel	
	CIR	CIR	Mathematics teacher	

ADMINISTRATIVE INDEXES (RESPONSE %)

OCCUPATIONS	%
SCHOOL SUBJECTS	%
ACTIVITIES	%
LEISURE ACTIVITIES	%
TYPES OF PEOPLE	%
PREFERENCES	%
CHARACTERISTICS	%
ALL PARTS	%

Inventory (CPI) uses some items from the MMPI, but assesses personality dimensions of interest in everyday interpersonal relationships and work/school situations.

The counseling profession has been able to overcome many concerns about the reliability and validity of personality inventories by the way it uses them as part of an ongoing, interactive relationship with a client. The most common abuse of these inventories results when counselors make judgments about clients in isolation from other information. A counselor who uses a personality inventory as a point of departure for discussion of issues with the client probably will avoid these mistakes. The inventory leads to additional subjective data from the client. Together counselor and client find their efforts enriched by the way the inventory may have stimulated additional questions and answers.

An example of this would be the use of the Myers-Briggs Type Indicator in counseling. Based on Jungian personality theory, this inventory helps clients arrive at hypotheses about their personality, the kind of cognitive style they might have, and the types of people they might enjoy and complement. At the same time clients learn to appreciate diverse characteristics among people, coming to see the complementarity of these traits and how they enrich social interactions. They learn about themselves through the personality inventory, but they also learn a lesson in tolerance of individual differences. This lesson may be integral to the overall objective of the counseling relationship, especially if intolerance of others is at the heart of the client's difficulties. A profile for reporting the Myers-Briggs is presented in Figure 5.2.

SELECTING AND INTERPRETING TESTS
AND INVENTORIES

With all the possibilities available, the selection of standardized tests and inventories becomes quite a challenge. Standardized assessment requires in-depth, comprehensive knowledge if its use is to help clients. Continual study is necessary. Counselors using tests are wise to receive current catalogues from the test publishers, tour test-related exhibits at conferences, and regularly review tests by reading the *Mental Measurements Yearbook* (Buros, 1978) and test reviews in professional journals such as *Measurement and Evaluation in Counseling and Development.*

Controversies frequently occur concerning the use of tests. Thus counselors at times are faced with angry parents, employees, and students who wish to contest decisions that were based on test data. Anxieties over ensuring confidentiality of results is also common. Test results are invalid when instruments have not been administered under conditions specified by the publisher; thus counselors must worry about the administration process. Tyler (1984) notes a common myth that assumes that test performance results from innate ability when in fact it results more from background and experience. Minorities at times have been deprived of this background and experience. Their familites often do not have the economic means needed to supplement classroom learning with learning that occurs during a vacation, summer camp, a house full of stimulating toys and games, and so forth. Such lack of opportunity among racial and ethnic minorities may influence results from standardized assessment (Gregory & Lee, 1986).

In spite of the precautions that must be taken when standardized tests are used, millions of individuals, especially students, are given such tests every year. In a national survey of educational testing (Engen, Lamb, & Prediger, 1982, p. 289), data indicated "that nine out of ten schools provide career guidance tests, three out of four administer achievement tests, and two out of three use aptitude tests." The wide use of standardized testing is in part a reaction to the capricious practices used before its arrival. Standardized assessment techniques, while imperfect, represent an effort to supply objective data for use in equitable decision-making.

Because of some of the historic abuse of test results, many counselors and educators have proposed that limitations be placed on the use of tests (Engen, Lamb, & Prediger, 1982). Tinsley and Bradley (1986) argue that some of the pessimism about the use of tests, especially among counselors, results from the underemphasis on test interpretation in counselor education and an overemphasis on the technical aspects of testing (e.g., reliability and validity). Test results are not damaging, but how those results are communicated and understood determines their value. Greater integration of test results into the counseling process is possible.

One major problem in using information from tests is the tendency of counselors to process it in isolation from other information. Often counselors seem to interrupt what they are doing with clients to interpret tests, rather than integrating them with other aspects of their work with clients. In career counseling, where test information is often used, clients seem to become overloaded with information (Crites, 1976). For example, in one hour an inexperienced counselor might interpret a battery of three or four instruments. As a result there is a tendency for clients either to forget much of what was interpreted or to remember it inaccurately. Crites (1976) proposed the avoidance of a formal test interpretation session in favor of the strategic introduction of test information when other circumstances in counseling call for it. For instance, a client may have considered dropping out of school because of failing grades. Interpreting intelligence and aptitude test results may increase the student's understanding of the situation.

In summary, the effective interpretation of test results is the only way to take advantage of the information offered by these instruments. The following are some suggestions for the interpretation of tests.

1. Always prepare in advance for a test interpretation session by reviewing results for the purpose of arriving at a synthesis of their meaning. Integrate this synthesis with other information (Tinsley & Bradley, 1986).

Report Form for Myers-Briggs Type Indicator

Name _____ Sex: M ☐ F ☐ Age _____ Other _____ Date _____

PREFERENCE STRENGTHS

POINTS FOR

E EXTRAVERSION

S SENSING

T THINKING

J JUDGING

60   40   20   0   20   40   60

POINTS FOR

I INTROVERSION

iN INTUITION

F FEELING

P PERCEPTIVE

TYPE

Indicator questions deal with the way you like to use your perception and judgment, that is, the way you like to look at things and the way you like to go about deciding things. The answers given reflect four separate preferences called EI, SN, TF and JP. The profile above shows your score on each preference. The four letters of your "type" tell how you came out on all four preferences. What each preference means is shown below.

E An E for extraversion probably means you relate more easily to the outer world of people and things than to the inner world of ideas.

S An S for sensing probably means you would rather work with known facts than look for possibilities and relationships.

T A T for thinking probably means you base your judgments more on impersonal analysis and logic than on personal values.

J A J for the judging attitude probably means you like a planned, decided, orderly way of life better than a flexible, spontaneous way.

I An I for introversion probably means you relate more easily to the inner world of ideas than to the outer world of people and things.

N An N for intuition probably means you would rather look for possibilities and relationships than work with known facts.

F An F for feeling probably means you base your judgments more on personal values than on impersonal analysis and logic.

P A P for the perceptive attitude probably means you like a flexible, spontaneous way of life better than a planned, decided, orderly way.

Each combination of preferences tends to be characterized by its own set of interests, values and skills. On the back of this page are very brief descriptions of each type. Find the one matching your four letters and see whether or not it fits you. If it doesn't, try to find one that does. Whatever your preferences, of course, you may still use some behaviors characteristic of contrasting preferences, but not with equal liking or skill. This tendency may be greater if preference strength on a scale is low (under 15). For a more complete discussion of the types and their vocational and personal implications, see *Introduction to Type* by Isabel Briggs Myers, or consult your counselor.

CONSULTING PSYCHOLOGISTS PRESS, INC., 577 COLLEGE AVENUE, PALO ALTO, CALIFORNIA 94306

CHARACTERISTICS FREQUENTLY ASSOCIATED WITH EACH TYPE

SENSING TYPES		INTUITIVE TYPES	
ISTJ Serious, quiet, earn success by concentration and thoroughness. Practical, orderly, matter-of-fact, logical, realistic and dependable. See to it that everything is well organized. Take responsibility. Make up their own minds as to what should be accomplished and work toward it steadily, regardless of protests or distractions.	**ISFJ** Quiet, friendly, responsible and conscientious. Work devotedly to meet their obligations and serve their friends and school. Thorough, painstaking, accurate. May need time to master technical subjects, as their interests are usually not technical. Patient with detail and routine. Loyal, considerate, concerned with how other people feel.	**INFJ** Succeed by perseverance, originality and desire to do whatever is needed or wanted. Put their best efforts into their work. Quietly forceful, conscientious, concerned for others. Respected for their firm principles. Likely to be honored and followed for their clear convictions as to how best to serve the common good.	**INTJ** Usually have original minds and great drive for their own ideas and purposes. In fields that appeal to them, they have a fine power to organize a job and carry it through with or without help. Skeptical, critical, independent, determined, often stubborn. Must learn to yield less important points in order to win the most important.
ISTP Cool onlookers—quiet, reserved, observing and analyzing life with detached curiosity and unexpected flashes of original humor. Usually interested in impersonal principles, cause and effect, how and why mechanical things work. Exert themselves no more than they think necessary, because any waste of energy would be inefficient.	**ISFP** Retiring, quietly friendly, sensitive, kind, modest about their abilities. Shun disagreements, do not force their opinions or values on others. Usually do not care to lead but are often loyal followers. Often relaxed about getting things done, because they enjoy the present moment and do not want to spoil it by undue haste or exertion.	**INFP** Full of enthusiasms and loyalties, but seldom talk of these until they know you well. Care about learning, ideas, language, and independent projects of their own. Tend to undertake too much, then somehow get it done. Friendly, but often too absorbed in what they are doing to be sociable. Little concerned with possessions or physical surroundings.	**INTP** Quiet, reserved, brilliant in exams, especially in theoretical or scientific subjects. Logical to the point of hair-splitting. Usually interested mainly in ideas, with little liking for parties or small talk. Tend to have sharply defined interests. Need to choose careers where some strong interest can be used and useful.
ESTP Matter-of-fact, do not worry or hurry, enjoy whatever comes along. Tend to like mechanical things and sports, with friends on the side. May be a bit blunt or insensitive. Can do math or science when they see the need. Dislike long explanations. Are best with real things that can be worked, handled, taken apart or put together.	**ESFP** Outgoing, easygoing, accepting, friendly, enjoy everything and make things more fun for others by their enjoyment. Like sports and making things. Know what's going on and join in eagerly. Find remembering facts easier than mastering theories. Are best in situations that need sound common sense and practical ability with people as well as with things.	**ENFP** Warmly enthusiastic, high-spirited, ingenious, imaginative. Able to do almost anything that interests them. Quick with a solution for any difficulty and ready to help anyone with a problem. Often rely on their ability to improvise instead of preparing in advance. Can usually find compelling reasons for whatever they want.	**ENTP** Quick, ingenious, good at many things. Stimulating company, alert and outspoken. May argue for fun on either side of a question. Resourceful in solving new and challenging problems, but may neglect routine assignments. Apt to turn to one new interest after another. Skillful in finding logical reasons for what they want.
ESTJ Practical, realistic, matter-of-fact, with a natural head for business or mechanics. Not interested in subjects they see no use for, but can apply themselves when necessary. Like to organize and run activities. May make good administrators, especially if they remember to consider others' feelings and points of view.	**ESFJ** Warm-hearted, talkative, popular, conscientious, born cooperators, active committee members. Need harmony and may be good at creating it. Always doing something nice for someone. Work best with encouragement and praise. Little interest in abstract thinking or technical subjects. Main interest is in things that directly and visibly affect people's lives.	**ENFJ** Responsive and responsible. Generally feel real concern for what others think or want, and try to handle things with due regard for other people's feelings. Can present a proposal or lead a group discussion with ease and tact. Sociable, popular, active in school affairs, but put time enough on their studies to do good work.	**ENTJ** Hearty, frank, able in studies, leaders in activities. Usually good in anything that requires reasoning and intelligent talk, such as public speaking. Are usually well-informed and enjoy adding to their fund of knowledge. May sometimes be more positive and confident than their experience in an area warrants.

INTROVERTS   EXTRAVERTS

Figure 5.2 *A Sample Myers-Briggs Type Indicator Profile. Note.* Copyright © 1976 by Isabel Briggs Myers. Reprinted by permission from the publisher, Consulting Psychologists Press.

2. Prepare materials or teaching aides (e.g., miniposters), such as those used by door-to-door salespersons, to assist you in explaining material you will repeatedly need to review (Srebalus, Marinelli, & Messing, 1982). Visual as well as verbal explanations increase the likelihood of the client's remembering the information.

3. Help the client remember the instruments being discussed by showing copies of the test booklets along with sample items.

4. Solicit client recollections of the testing situation to determine whether conditions might have existed that would invalidate the results.

5. Invite client self-estimates of performance on different instruments and subtests. Be alert to discrepancies between self-estimates and actual results. Process them in detail.

6. If time runs short, schedule another interpretive session instead of rushing through the remainder of the results.

7. Before ending, ask the client to summarize the information discussed. This is an important check on the client's comprehension of the material.

8. Plan to follow up the session in the future to check on the client's retention of the material.

Using tests in counseling has been viewed historically (Goldman, 1972) as a "marriage that failed." However, with greater attention to the integration of test information, clients can benefit from testing by virtue of its ability to supply data useful in the making of important personal decisions.

STUDENT LEARNING EXERCISE

Read the following statements and indicate whether they reflect an appropriate use of assessment. Circle Y for yes or N for no.

1. A counselor who is uncertain how to handle a client having marital problems administers a marital adjustment inventory.   Y   N

2. A counselor meets with the school's curriculum committee to review the results of achievement tests administered to the sixth grade.   Y   N

3. A counselor working with a group of nondating college males administers a social skills inventory with the plan to interpret the results during the next group meeting.   Y   N

4. A counselor disregards the results of a client's aptitude test results when it is learned that the test administrator was not certified to give the test.   Y   N

ASSESSMENT REFERRALS

There are situations in which the type of assessment needed for a client is not within the job description or the expertise of a counselor, and referral for testing may be made to a school or clinical psychologist. For example, in many states the identification of a student for placement in a special education class must be based on testing conducted by a school or licensed psychologist.

Neuropsychological assessment is another reason for referral. This activity evaluates general changes as well as specific intellectual and emotional functioning of patients suffering from traumatic brain injury, disease, epilepsy, or drug reactions. Tests often used for neuropsychological assessment include the Wechsler scales, portions of the Reitan-Halstead battery, the Wide Range Achievement Test, the Bender-Gestalt, and the Luria-Nebraska Test (Korchin & Schuldberg, 1981). Reitan (1975) presents a clear description of neuropsychological assessment with examples from many of these instruments.

Testing and Computer Technology

Since the 1950s business computers have been used to assist in the scoring of tests and in the compilation and profiling of their results. Testing corporations, such as the Educational Testing Service and Houghton Mifflin, have needed large mainframe computers in order to score and profile instruments from school districts and national testing programs. With the introduction of microcomputers in the 1970s, computer technology has offered yet another dimension in test utilization.

The Effects of Computers on Testing.   In general, experts are very optimistic about the potential benefits of computer technology for standardized assessment (Sampson & Loesch, 1985; Matarazzo, 1986; Skinner & Pakula, 1986). The introduction of microcomputers, however, has raised some serious questions in reference to new uses of computers in testing. Micros are used both to administer and to interpret tests in addition to scoring and profiling their results. More and more programs are being marketed by firms other than the established, reputable test publishers. In a sense there is now a "cottage industry" producing software that interprets the significance of test scores. In most cases counselors and psychologists cannot inspect the programs to determine the validity of the judgments made by the programs. It is precisely because computers are now being used to make clinical judgments that concern about them exists (Skinner & Pakula, 1986). Also, there is fear that unqualified practitioners will purchase or illegally copy test interpretation programs and present themselves as competent to use various instruments without real expertise.

The use of test interpretation programs can have some benefits. First, such programs can reduce the cost of test utilization through reduction in professional time needed to interpret, profile, and write test reports. Korchin and Schuldberg (1981) have noted that the cost of thorough assessment has become difficult to justify in relation to the increasing use of briefer therapies. Thus extensive clinical assessment has been on the decline. In national surveys clinical psychologists reported in 1959 that 44% of their time was spent in testing, but by 1969 that portion of time was reduced to 28% (Korchin & Schuldberg, 1981). This trend has probably continued to the present.

Second, many test interpretation programs supply graphics as part of the package, and this can increase the effectiveness of feedback to the client by creating a visual dimension. Third, administration of an instrument through the console of a microcomputer (keyboard and monitor) has much greater potential than paper-and-pencil to present more varied stimuli. For example, perception and artistic aptitude can be assessed through the presentation of computer-driven images (high resolution graphics) that would be impossible with paper-and-pencil. Where microcomputer and paper-and-pencil versions of instruments exist (e.g., the Ohio Vocational Interest Inventory), the microcomputer version compares favorably to the other versions (Hoyt, 1986). While greater supervision of the use of software may be needed, no one questions the use of computer hardware by the helping professions. Both the use of software and hardware in interpretation of such popular instruments as the MMPI show general customer satisfaction (Green, 1982). Computer technology in testing is here to stay.

ASSESSING CLIENTS THROUGH INTERVIEWS

Earlier in this chapter it was noted that questions regarding clients often dictate informal assessment through an interview. Interactions with clients provide a rich source of relevant data that, if utilized properly, can allow the counselor to draw meaningful conclusions about both immediate crisis situations and the long-term well-being of clients.

Before entering a discussion of informal assessment certain cautions should be noted. First, a counselor's judgment is no better than his or her training and experience. Thus, without a background in mental health problems, it is inappropriate for a counselor to draw conclusions about them. Second, in crisis situations sensitivity to all relevant factors is ensured through consultation with others, if time permits. Third, guidelines offered to assist in making judgments in crisis situations are only guidelines, not recipes that can be followed blindly.

The Intake Interview

Assessment through face-to-face interviewing can occur as part of ongoing treatment or as a function of an interview formally structured for assessment purposes. The most common example of the latter is the "intake" interview. Intakes are used in many treatment settings to assess both client problems and resources in preparation for treatment or referral. Traditionally the intake interview has attempted to generate a comprehensive picture of clients, their current functioning and situation, and a history of their development and adjustment. For this reason the intake is also called the "history-taking interview." Outlines for the intake interview appear in dozens of psychiatric and counseling texts. The most common elements listed for the intake are:

1. The client's presenting problem (complaint)
2. The history of the presenting problem, including efforts to treat or manage the problem
3. Other complaints and problems and previous treatment of those problems
4. Educational, social, and occupational history
5. Family and marital background
6. Medical history
7. The current ability and resources to manage the problems presented

The use of intake interviewing in community mental health is described in Chapter 13.

Historically, the outcome of the intake interview was a diagnosis. The diagnosis was supposed to point the way to treatment. Diagnosis is usually based on some kind of classification system. The most popular system used worldwide in psychiatry, psychology, and mental health counseling is the one presented in the revised version of the *Diagnostic and Statistical Manual,* Third Edition, of The American Psychiatric Association (1980, 1987). The *DSM-III* is described for counselors with little psychiatric or mental health experience by Seligman (1983). Many of the pros and cons of the *DSM-III* are examined in the July 1983 issue of the *American Psychologist.* The *DSM-III* attempts a more comprehensive diagnosis than its predecessors by using a multiaxial system to identify presenting problem (Axis I), long-term personality orientation (Axis II), physical/medical condition (Axis III), presence and severity of psychosocial stressors (Axis IV), and highest level of adaptive functioning during the past year (Axis V). The principal diagnosis (Axis I) identifies a condition from a list of disorders that have been divided into 17 broad categories. Examples are substance abuse disorders, schizophrenic disorders, anxiety disorders, psychosexual disorders, adjustment disorders, and so forth.

In response to Seligman's (1983) article, Dattilio (1984) argued that counselors need to be cautious when they use the *DSM-III.* It is a complicated system to use accurately. Understanding some of the disorders may require exposure to behavioral disorders and clinical assessment beyond the training of most counselors. In a reply Seligman (1984) noted that the American Mental Health Counselors Association (AMHCA) has taken steps to upgrade counselor background in clinical assessment by recommending increased coursework and experience in the assessment of psychopathology. This text makes a similar

Table 5.2   Signs of People in Active Crisis

Disorganized thinking
Impulsivity
Hostility and emotional distance
Acute anxiety
Immobilization
Feelings of helplessness
Loss of behavior control
Panic
Conflict and indecision
Escape through substance abuse

---

recommendation for mental health counselors in Chapter 14. Thus the setting in which one works (e.g., educational versus mental health) may dictate greater or lesser involvement in diagnosis, intake interviewing, and the *DSM-III*.

ASSESSING EMERGENCY CONDITIONS[1]

Regardless of where counselors work, chances are high that they will encounter people in crisis. In times of crisis individuals find that their normal means for dealing with situations do not work. They cannot cope, and some will turn to counselors for help. Two such situations that challenge the ability of the counselor to assess a crisis situation are dangerousness and suicide. Signs of active crisis are listed in Table 5.2.

The Assessment of Dangerousness

People run the risk of being endangered through the prospect of encountering someone who may inflict bodily injury or death. Certain individuals have a history of acting out aggression. According to Gutheil and Applebaum (1982), potentially dangerous persons themselves show a history of being victimized both as a child and as an adult. Poor impulse control is compounded through the use of alcohol and drugs. Dangerous persons tend to harbor persecutory thoughts, lasting grudges, and images of revenge or retribution. Often they have made written or mental lists of people who have harmed them, people they would like to see dead. Investigation often will show a criminal record documenting charges of assault and battery, drunk driving, and property damage. Such people are likely to own weapons, including a degree in the martial arts. Table 5.3 identifies factors to observe in an assessment interview. Chapter 13 describes some issues in the management of potentially dangerous individuals.

[1]The authors are grateful to Dr. Rosemary Srebalus for her assistance with this section.

Table 5.3 Assessment of Dangerousness

Appearance: Psychical tension (grimacing, clenching of fists, tightening of jaw, etc.), preoccupation, pacing, presence of real or potential weapons (knife, length of pipe, etc.)

Mood and speech: Angry, threatening, glaring or hostile looks, words, or threats. Answers positively to the question, "Have you ever for any reason, accidentally or otherwise, caused the death of or severe injury to another human being?"

Thought content: Persecutory delusions, command hallucinations directing violent acts, obsessive thoughts, fantasies, and ruminations of assault, loss of control, revenge motives.

Circumstances: Brought to interview in handcuffs, shackles, or by law enforcement officials, or seen raving in restraints.

Note. Adapted from *Clinical Handbook of Psychiatry and the Law* by T. G. Gutheil and P. S. Applebaum, 1982, New York: McGraw-Hill. Reprinted by permission.

The Assessment of Suicide

The incidence of suicide is discussed in Chapter 13. Inspection of that chapter shows that suicide and attempted suicide are serious risks to most client populations, in particular to adolescents, young adults, and the elderly.

According to Gutheil and Applebaum (1982), factors to consider in the assessment of suicide, besides those in Table 5.4 are the following:

1. The presence of severe depression or the lifting of such a depression, making available the energy needed to take one's life. Adding risk are other disphoric feeling states such as rage or panic.
2. The presence of a psychosis, especially with command hallucinations to commit suicide.
3. A history of substance abuse, which increases a history of poor impulse control, especially toward violence.
4. The loss of a loved person, job, residence, academic or social standing.
5. A history of marginal adaptation with few accomplishments.

Table 5.4 Assessment of Suicide Potential

Suicidal intent (decision to die) with decreased tension
Presence of a specific plan
Availability of means to kill oneself
Previous attempts to commit suicide

---

6. Lacking support and living in a hostile environment (e. g. a teenager who is shy or withdrawn and subject to harassment from neighborhood gangs).
7. Thoughts and fantasies with destructive content, including revenge and "resting in peace."

Assessing a Client's Coping Abilities

Face-to-face interviewing not only can be potent in identifying problems but can also assess client personal and evnironmental resources. Problem-solving style comes across during an interview. Can the client be decisive? Will he or she respond impulsively to pressure? How will the client enlist help from others? Will he or she be able to sustain involvement in executing a long-term solution?

In addition to helping the counselor learn what the client might do, data processed during an interview might hint at the response others might make toward the client's attempt to change. For example, will an adolescent's attempt to lose weight be supported by her family? Will a distressed worker who wants to change occupations get support from his or her spouse?

Few standardized instruments measure such situations. During an interview client and counselor can become very concrete, naming people, places, and events related to counseling objectives. Alternative solutions already attempted or considered can be explored on the spot. Concrete evidence about previous successes and failures can be provided.

Assessment and treatment both rest on the degree to which a counselor has become skilled in interviewing, in dealing face-to-face with people. When those skills are combined with testing and new forms of assessment emerging from computer technology, the counseling profession can increase its responsiveness to human concerns.

SUMMARY

This chapter explored the nature and purpose of assessment, with emphasis on the use of standardized tests and inventories. Nonstandardized assessment through the intake interview was also discussed. Suggestions were made regarding counselor selection, use, and interpretation of tests. Computer applications in assessment were also surveyed.

REVIEW QUESTIONS

1. Describe the characteristics of a well-developed test.
2. List the types of standardized tests and inventories commonly used by counselors.

3. What are the advantages and disadvantages of using informal or interview assessment?
4. What issues should be considered in the selection, administration, and interpretation of standardized tests?
5. Give two examples of circumstances in which a counselor might refer a client for testing by a school or clinical psychologist.
6. What are some of the issues in the use of microcomputers for test administration, scoring, and interpretation?
7. List criteria for the assessment of people in active crisis.
8. List criteria for the assessment of dangerousness and suicide.

REFERENCES

Aiken, L. R. (1985). *Psychological testing and assessment* (5th ed.). Boston: Allyn and Bacon.

American Psychiatric Association. (1980). *Diagnostic and statistical manual of mental disorders* (3rd ed.). Washington, DC: Author.

American Psychiatric Association. (1987). *Diagnostic and statistical manual of mental disorders* (3rd ed. revised). Washington, DC: Author.

Anastasi, A. (1982). *Psychological testing* (5th ed.). New York: Macmillan.

Buros, O. K. (1978). *The mental measurements yearbook.* Highland Park, NJ: Gryphon Press.

Crites, J. O. (1973). *Career maturity inventory: Administration and use manual.* Monterey, CA: CBT/McGraw-Hill.

Crites, J. O. (1976). Career counseling: A comprehensive approach. *The Counseling Psychologist, 6,* 2–11.

Cronbach, L. J. (1984). *Essentials of psychological testing.* New York: Harper and Row.

Dattilio, F. M. (1984). Comment. *The Personnel and Guidance Journal, 62*(5), 306.

Engen, H. B., Lamb, R. R., & Prediger, D. J. (1982). Are secondary schools still using standardized tests? *The Personnel and Guidance Journal, 60*(5), 287–293.

Goldman, L. (1972). Tests and counseling: The marriage that failed. *Measurement and Evaluation in Guidance, 4*(2), 213–220.

Gregory, S., & Lee, S. (1986). Psychoeducational assessment of racial and ethnic minority groups: Professional implications. *Journal of Counseling and Development, 64*(10), 635–637.

Green, C. J. (1982). The diagnostic accuracy and utility of MMPI and MCMI computer-interpretive reports. *Journal of Personality Assessment, 46*(3), 359–365.

Gutheil, T. G., & Applebaum, P. S. (1982). *Clinical handbook of psychiatry and the law.* New York: McGraw-Hill.

Hoyt, K. B. (1986). Ohio Vocational Interest Survey (OVIS II), Microcomputer version. *Journal of Counseling and Development, 64*(10), 655–657.

Korchin, S. J., & Schuldberg, D. (1981). The future of clinical assessment. *American Psychologist, 36*(10), 1147–1158.

Matarazzo, J. D. (1986). Computerized clinical psychological test interpretations: Unvalidated plus all mean and no sigma. *American Psychologist, 41*(1), 14–24.

Reitan, R. M. (1975). Assessment of brain-behavior relationships. In P. McReynolds, *Advances in psychological assessment* (Vol. 3). San Francisco: Jossey-Bass.

Reschly, D. J. (1981). Psychological testing in educational classification and placement. *American Psychologist, 36*(10), 1094–1102.

Sampson, J. P. Jr., & Loesch, L. C. (1985). Computer preparation standards for counselors and human development specialists. *Journal of Counseling and Development, 64*(1), 31–33.

Seligman, L. (1983). An introduction to the new DSM-III. *The Personnel and Guidance Journal, 61*(10), 601–605.

Seligman, L. (1984). Comment. *Journal of Counseling and Development, 63*(1), 55–56.

Skinner, H. A., & Pakula, A. (1986). Challenge of computers in psychological assessment. *Professional Psychology: Research and Practice, 17*(1), 44–50.

Srebalus, D., Marinelli, R., & Messing, J. (1982). *Career development: Concepts and Procedures.* Monterey, CA: Brooks/Cole.

Tinsley, H., & Bradley, R. W. (1986). Test interpretation. *Journal of Counseling and Development, 64*(7), 462–466.

Tyler, L. E. (1984). What tests don't measure. *Journal of Counseling and Development, 63*(1), 48–50.

6

Life Career Development and Counseling

GOALS OF THE CHAPTER

The goals of the chapter are threefold; first, to provide an overview of career and life development; second, to familiarize the reader with work in America; and third, to acquaint the reader with some of the approaches that can be used to facilitate career choice and adjustment.

CHAPTER PREVIEW

1. Definitions of the terms associated with life career development will be provided.
2. A brief view of the current status of work in America will be provided.
3. Career information and assistance programs for various age groups will be illustrated along with a discussion of the career development problems of groups such as women and minorities.
4. The processes of life career and career counseling will be surveyed.
5. A brief summary of computerized information and career assistance programs will be provided.

INTRODUCTION

In the past, the counseling profession has only tacitly recognized the interrelationships of various life roles. Within the past 10 to 15 years, this has begun to change, partly because of new theories, and partly because research on areas such as job stress and family relationships has clearly pointed to interrelationships among life roles and their influences on the functioning of individuals.

A number of terms have been presented that were aimed at illustrating the dynamic relationship among life roles. Herr (1986a), along with McDaniels (1978) and Super (1976), have argued that the term "career" actually has a

Figure 6.1   Life system and subsystems. *Note.* From *Working with Adults: Individual, Family & Career Development* (p. 32) by B. F. Cole, 1984, Monterey, CA: Brooks/Cole. Reprinted by permission.

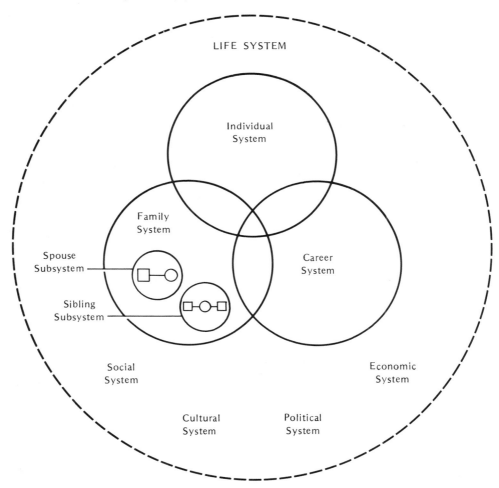

broader connotation than just the jobs that one holds; it can be used to depict the interrelationship of life roles. Zunker (1986) notes that lifestyle is also a concept that denotes the individual's overall orientation to life roles. However, the term *life career* was chosen here to depict the interrelationship between career and other life roles because it more clearly denotes that career cannot be considered separately from the rest of one's existence (Gysbers & Moore, 1981; Okun, 1984).

While many individuals have discussed not only the concept of life career development but also how it can be facilitated, Okun (1984) has provided a visual illustration of this relationship. Her model is shown in Figure 6.1. As can be seen, the individual, his or her career, and the family are part of a broader life system, and they are influenced by the social, cultural, political, and economic aspects of that system. It is important to note that the individual, career, and family subsystems are portrayed in dynamic interaction with each other.

Super (1984) has also provided us with a visual image of the interaction of various life roles in his Life-Career Rainbow (Figure 6.2). He suggests that at various stages of our lives, we fill all the following roles: child, student, leisurite, citizen, worker, spouse, homemaker, parent, and pensioner. He also suggests that at any of the various stages of development, each of us fills a number of these roles. For example, during our middle years, it is likely that a parent, spouse, worker, and citizen are the dominant roles in our lives, but this does not suggest that we are not involved in the roles of child, student, and leisurite. Factors such as age, gender, race, personal characteristics, and economic conditions will influence the extent to which we fill various roles at any given time.

The recognition that life roles are interconnected has slowly begun to change the nature of career and life planning. However, for many individuals, work is still the dominant life role, and some counselors, particularly those working in employment agencies, focus almost exclusively on this role. It would, therefore, be an oversight not to highlight in this chapter the importance of work and the problems involved in career choice and work adjustment.

SOME DEFINITIONS

A number of terms and concepts have already been introduced. Before proceeding, it seems prudent to define both the terms that have been introduced to this point and those that will be used later.

- *Work:* A paid or unpaid systematic activity aimed at producing something of value for one's self, others, or a combination thereof.
- *Occupation:* A formally classified work activity that involves a group of people working in different situations. School counseling and social work are occupations.

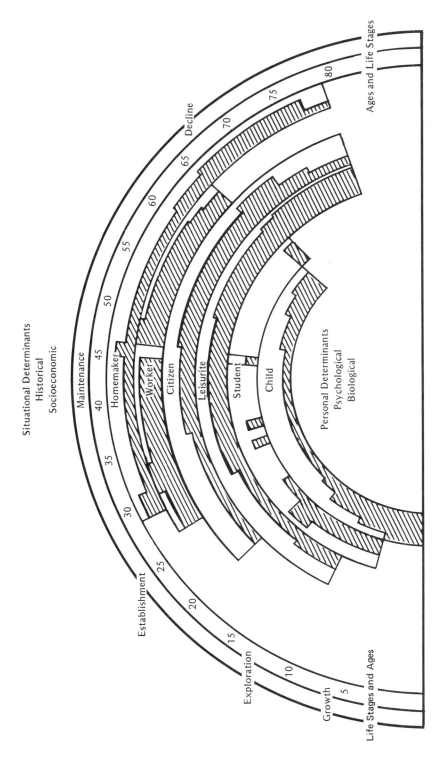

Figure 6.2 The life-career rainbow: nine life roles in schematic life space. *Note.* From "A Life-span, Life-space Approach to Career Development" by D. E. Super, 1980, *Journal of Vocational Behavior, 16,* pp. 282–298. Reprinted by permission.

- *Job:* A specific occupation held by an individual at any given time. Usually used synonymously with occupation.
- *Career:* The totality of work and related experiences held by an individual over her or his life span.
- *Career development:* The sum total of changes that occur in the individual as a result of physiological, psychological, sociological, and economic forces that influence entry into and progression in those occupations that make up the career over the life span.
- *Life-career development:* The totality of the changes that occur as a result of physiological, psychological, sociological, and economic forces that influence individual, family, career, and other life role development and the interaction of these subsystems over the life span.
- *Leisure:* Planned or spontaneous events, usually relatively short-term in nature, aimed at enlightening, entertaining, relaxing, or stimulating the individual.
- *Occupational information:* Materials ranging from single printed pages and extensive directories to computer programs designed to impart data about specific occupations, including descriptions of the work done, rewards, training requirements, and employment trends.

WORK IN AMERICA

There has been considerable conjecture regarding work and working in American society. Some researchers, pointing to the decline in productivity in this country when compared to the Japanese or most West European countries, have concluded that the importance attached to work in America is eroding. However, Neff (1985) points out that it is difficult to reach this conclusion objectively since productivity is tied to so many factors. But most authorities on work do agree that the importance placed on work may be lessening.

No one seems to doubt that the work we perform in our jobs influences our economic, psychological, and sociological functioning. Herr (1986b) suggests that the nature of our occupation is a primary determiner of our lifestyle. Whether or not "work responds to something profound and basic in human nature" (Report of Special Task Force, 1973, p. 1), as was suggested a decade and a half ago, is open to question. What is not open to question is that most Americans will spend a large part of their waking adult hours involved in some form of paid or unpaid work. Because of this, work will remain a topic of considerable study and concern for psychologists, counselors, and others.

Of particular concern to career counselors and others is the nature of the workplace in the future and the impact it will have upon the worker. The workplace is already having profound effects on American workers. For example, job stress is recognized as a major source of physiological problems (e.g., heart attacks), as well as mental health problems in this country (Brown &

Brooks, 1985; Neff, 1985). Naisbitt (1984) has forecast that technology will continue to make significant changes in the nature of work as microprocessors and robots become increasingly sophisticated. According to Naisbitt, "The introduction of technology into the industrial workplace is on a collision course with much of the workforce (p. 23)." It may very well be that technology will alleviate the stress induced by the workplace, but it is more likely that technology will reduce the skill level and personal involvement in a wide variety of occupations (Naisbitt, 1984; National Alliance of Business, 1986) and thus create more stress and job dissatisfaction.

Research supports a long-standing trend of relatively high worker satisfaction. For example, in a Bureau of the Census (1981) survey, workers were asked, "How satisfied are you with your job or your work?" The data are summarized in Table 6.1. As can be seen, at least 80% of all groups surveyed in 1987 indicated that they were fairly, somewhat, or very satisfied with their jobs. What is not clear from these data is what workers mean when they say when they are fairly or somewhat satisfied with their jobs.

McDaniels (1986) has examined the literature regarding the future of work in American society and has painted three scenarios: green, yellow, and red. In the green scenario, robots and computers will assume many of the roles now filled by people, new careers will replace old ones, entrepreneurial enterprises will flourish, and the Informal Age will replace the Industrial Age. The green scenario is essentially a positive view of the world of work, although only those individuals who are properly prepared will be successful in this dynamic situation.

The yellow scenario can be characterized as a steady-state view. Change is expected, but it will be orderly, and the future will look very much like the

Table 6.1 Percentages of Workers Indicating That They Were Satisfied, Somewhat Satisfied, or Fairly Satisfied with Their Jobs

Worker characteristics	1962	1972	1980
Men	84	86	85
Women	81	86	83
21–29-year-olds	74	76	78
30–39-year-olds	82	88	82
40–49-year-olds	84	89	88
50–59-year-olds	Not available	91	86
60+ -year-olds	Not available	95	90
Minorities	76 (Black only)	78	81
Grade school	83	86	87
High school	81	86	81
College degree	90	85	88
Graduate work	84	95	90

Note. From Statistical Abstracts of the United States (p. 387) Bureau of the Census, 1981; Washington, DC: Department of Commerce.

present. In this future, not only will occupations appear much as they do today, but they will continue to be open to people of all backgrounds, not just to highly trained individuals. The only negative aspect of this scenario is that new jobs will not be created, and thus opportunity will stem from the replacement of current jobs.

The red scenario projects a bleak future for the world of work. This scenario draws upon the spiraling unemployment in this country, the cheap cost of foreign labor, and the negative balance of payments, among other things, to forecast the belief that 10 to 20 million members of our future workforce will be chronically underemployed or unemployed, creating an underclass in our society.

Whether or not the trend of apparent job satisfaction among workers will maintain itself in the face of changing work values and changes in the workplace itself remains to be seen. What is clear is that career and life planning are increasingly important in our society. Career planning is increasingly needed so that young adolescents, young adults, and career changers of all ages can anticipate the nature of the workplace and prepare for it (National Alliance of Business, 1986). Life planning is becoming more crucial so that the interaction of work and other life roles can be anticipated and accommodated. In addition, if some of the worst concerns about the nature of work are realized, life planning may assume even more important dimensions because much of life satisfaction may have to be derived from family, leisure, or life roles rather than from work.

CAREER DEVELOPMENT

Theorists such as Roe (1984), Super (1984), Bordin (1984) and others trace occupational choice and ultimately career development back to the earliest developmental stages of the individual. Donald Super has been particularly influential as an advocate of career development as a life-long process. He believes that from birth to adolescence, children develop many of the attitudes and values that lead to occupational choice. During childhood, fantasies about the world of work and unbridled interests serve as the bases for thinking about careers.

During adolescence, interests and fantasies are still important, but capacities or abilities also begin to play a major role in the thinking of the adolescent as he or she moves through a succession of reality-testing experiences. The result of this reality testing is a series of tentative choices which lead in turn to a number of trial jobs.

As the young adult gains more experience in the world of work, establishment in a relatively stable work pattern occurs. Establishment is followed by stabilization in the occupation and then advancement.

The middle and later years of life, according to Super (1984), are followed typically by maintenance of one's occupational position. Ultimately, aging produces a period marked by declining interest and involvement in work in most people. These stages are depicted in Figure 6.3.

Super (1984), along with Levinson (1978), Lowenthal and Weiss (1976), Neugarten (1976), Gould (1978), as well as others, realize that many, and perhaps most, people do not enter a single career and move through it in linear fashion. As can be seen in Figure 6.3, Super (1984) postulates that transition points in the development of the individual, such as moving from tentative choices to tryouts (trial occupations) are characterized by a minicycle involving some or all of the developmental stages. For example, an adolescent preparing to assume a trial occupation probably passes through the growth stage in which he or she fantasizes about occupations, searches his or her interests, examines his or her capacities, and selects from the options available. Similarly, adults dissatisfied with their jobs may very well recycle through the growth, exploration, establishment, and maintenance stages again. They have already experienced decline and withdrawal from their previous occupation.

As can be seen, career development is a process that occurs throughout life. Counselors working with all age groups and populations ultimately become involved with the process.

Figure 6.3   Life stages and substages based on the typical developmental tasks, with focus on the maxicycle. *Note.* Each transition, whether psychogenic, sociogenic, econogenic, or all of these, has its own minicycle of growth, exploration, establishment, maintenance, and decline: its recycling. From "Career and Life Development" (p. 201) by D. E. Super. In *Career Choice and Development* by D. Brown and L. Brooks, eds., 1984, San Francisco: Jossey-Bass. Reprinted by permission.

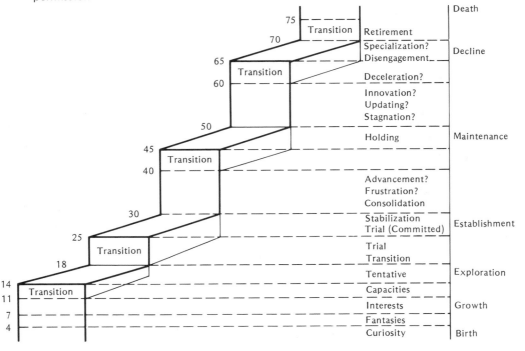

Career Development at Different Developmental Stages

Elementary school counselors are, of course, dealing with children in Super's (1984) growth stage. In some school districts, extensive career education programs have been implemented in which children are systematically exposed to various facets of the world of work in the form of self-awareness activities designed to clarify interests and values. Awareness activities are also aimed at clarifying a vocational self-concept (Super, 1984), that is, having the child project himself or herself into a variety of work roles. The following are illustrations of some of these ideas.

- Children in one school were exposed to increasing numbers of careers in relationship to their social studies curriculum. First graders explored their parents' careers and those of people in their neighborhoods. Second graders studied occupations in their county, while third graders studied careers in their state. Fourth, fifth, and sixth graders studied careers in their geographic region, the nation, and the world, respectively.
- Tools were brought into one classroom, and students took turns using hammers, saws, chisels, and other hand tools to build various projects. Follow-up activities involved discussing types of workers that used the various tools and how the children felt about performing the tasks.
- Counselors in one district conducted extensive field trips designed to show children occupations that were related to each of their subject matter areas.

During the early 1970s career education programs flourished in American education, due to the leadership of then Secretary of Education Sydney Marland. Recently, these programs have been on the decline, primarily because of the "Back to Basics" movement aimed at enhancing academic achievement. However, many of the activities engaged in by elementary school counselors enhance career development, even if they do so less deliberately than those mentioned above.

Junior high school and high school counselors are dealing with students in Super's (1984) exploration phase, where capacities become more important. As a result, many counseling programs at these levels include the administration of tests that provide feedback on interests, aptitudes, and experiences that will enable students to assess how their aptitudes, interests, and values can be realistically utilized in the world of work. In a few school situations, students are exposed to simulated work environments. Most approaches involve discussion with workers, job shadowing experiences, where students literally follow workers around, and internship programs, where students can get "hands on" experiences. Computerized systems and other informational approaches can also assist students in assessing their characteristics relative to various occupations.

Counselors working with young adults in college and vocational technical schools often offer programs quite similar in nature to those described for counselors working with adolescents. Counselors working with adults in continuing education centers, employee assistance programs, business and industry, and other settings may also provide career exploration and personal development programs aimed at helping individuals make career choices. They may also be involved in assisting workers cope with job stress and in outplacement counseling. Outplacement counseling, a relatively new activity, is the assistance provided by some employers when an employee is terminated; it helps the employee in the transition from the job he's leaving to another one.

Services to adults involve career exploration and choice making, as well as adjustment to the current work setting (Brooks & Brown, 1986; Brown & Brooks, 1985). When helping adults adjust to a work setting, life planning comes strongly to the fore, since work and other life roles (parent and worker) may be interacting to negatively influence work adjustment. For those stuck in an unrewarding occupation, review of more personally satisfying alternatives may be emphasized.

The final transition in career development is withdrawal from the world of work. For nearly two-thirds of retirees, this occurs before age 65 (Harris & Associates, 1979). In one sense, planning for retirement is the ultimate in life planning, since a major life role, work, is often being abandoned. Not surprisingly, readiness for retirement seems to be a key factor in making this change (Johnson & Riker, 1981; Kingson, 1981; Meier, 1975), as are income (Schmitt & McCune, 1981; U.S. Senate Special Committee on Aging, 1985–86) and planning for retirement (Graney & Zimmerman, 1981).

OCCUPATIONAL CHOICE MAKING

Career development is a dynamic, life-long process involving a series of occupational choices. Just as there are theories of career development, so too there are theories of occupational choice making. One of the earliest of these was presented by Parsons (1909). His conceptualization of career choice involved three steps: (1) self-analysis, (2) analysis of the world of work, and (3) matching of one's personal characteristics to those required by occupations through "true reasoning." Parson's tripartite model became the foundation for the trait-and-factor model of occupational choice. E. G. Williamson (1939, 1965) became the best known of the early advocates of this model. He and others who came after Parsons followed the three-step model but had the advantage of aptitude and ability tests, interest and personality inventories to measure traits, and sophisticated occupational information based on a systematic analysis of the skills and personal qualities demanded in a particular occupation.

More recently, John Holland (1985) has presented an elaborate trait-and-factor model of occupational choice. Holland believes that the essence of occupational choice is matching one's personality to a congruent occupational environment. He believes that personalities are comprised of six different types:

realistic, investigative, artistic, social, enterprising, and conventional. But an individual is rarely a pure type, and thus the personality is made up of different components of the six types.

Realistic types prefer orderly activities, often involving tools and machines, and have aversions to educational and therapeutic activities. Investigative types also prefer systematic activities, but differ from realistic types in that their preferences are for symbolic activities that lead to the investigation of various social and scientific phenomena. Investigative types have aversions to persuasive, social, and repetitive activities. Artistic types diverge substantially from realistic and investigative types in that they have aversions to systematic and ordered activities. They have preferences for free-flowing, ambiguous activities that involve various art forms.

Social types have deficits in the manual arts and prefer interactions with people aimed at leading, informing, or curing them. They also have aversions to systemic, ordered activities. Preferences for leadership and the development of interpersonal and persuasive skills characterize enterprising types. Conventional types, like realistic and investigative types, prefer activities that involve order and system, particularly those that involve maintaining, reordering, or filing data or materials. Conventional types have aversions to the ambiguous and unsystematic.

Holland (1985) also believes that there are six work environments that correspond to the six personality types, that is, realistic, investigative, artistic, social, enterprising, and conventional. These environments can be so characterized because they are made up of workers with similar personality types. Realistic work environments would be made up of people with realistic personalities, a social environment of people with social personalities, and so forth.

Job satisfaction, career stability, achievement, and reduction of job stress are likely to be enhanced if the individual matches his or her personality to a similar work environment (Holland, 1985).

There are, of course, other ideas about career decision-making, most of which use some form of the scientific method as their basis. They hold that good decision-making involves a process of (1) identifying the problem, (2) generating alternative solutions, (3) systematically collecting data about the alternatives generated, (4) selecting from among the alternatives, (5) implementing the solution, (6) evaluating the solution, and (7) recycling as necessary. These decision-making models point to the process that one might follow, but do not suggest what factors should be employed in reaching the decision.

Problems in Decision-Making

A number of occupational decision-making approaches have suggested that values are a key factor (Gelatt, Varenhorst, & Carey, 1972; Gelatt, Varenhorst, Carey, & Miller, 1973; Katz, 1980), although Harren (1979) has posed that self-esteem and personal identity are key factors in the process. It is unquestionably the case that a variety of factors enter into the occupational decision-making

Table 6.2 Forty Occupations with Largest Job Growth, 1982–1995

Occupation	Change in total employment (in thousands)	Percentage of total job growth	Percentage change
Building custodians	779	3.0	27.5
Cashiers	744	2.9	47.4
Secretaries	719	2.8	29.5
General clerks, office	696	2.7	29.6
Salesclerks	685	2.7	23.5
Nurses, registered	642	2.5	48.9
Waiters and waitresses	562	2.2	33.8
Teachers, kindergarten and elementary	511	2.0	37.4
Truckdrivers	425	1.7	26.5
Nursing aides and orderlies	423	1.7	34.8
Sales representatives, technical	386	1.5	29.3
Accountants and auditors	344	1.3	40.2
Automotive mechanics	324	1.3	38.3
Supervisors of blue-collar workers	319	1.2	26.6
Kitchen helpers	305	1.2	35.9
Guards and doorkeepers	300	1.2	47.3
Food preparation and service workers, fast food restaurants	297	1.2	36.7
Managers, store	292	1.1	0.1
Carpenters	247	1.0	28.6
Electrical and electronic technicians	222	.9	60.7
Licensed practical nurses	20	.9	37.1
Computer systems analysts	217	.8	85.3
Electrical engineers	209	.8	65.3
Computer programmers	205	.8	76.9
Maintenance repairers, general utility	193	.8	27.8
Helpers, trades	190	.7	31.2
Receptionists	189	.7	48.8
Electricians	173	.7	31.8
Physicians	163	.7	34.0
Clerical supervisors	162	.6	34.6
Computer operators	160	.6	75.8
Sales representatives, nontechnical	160	.6	27.4
Lawyers	159	.6	34.3
Stock clerks, stockroom and warehouse	156	.6	18.8
Typists	155	.6	15.7
Delivery and route workers	153	.6	19.2
Bookkeepers, hand	152	.6	15.9
Cooks, restaurants	149	.6	42.3
Bank tellers	142	.6	30.0
Cooks, short order, specialty, and fast food	141	.6	32.2

Note. Includes only detailed occupations with 1982 employment of 25,000 or more. Data for 1995 are based on moderate-trend projections. From Occupational Outlook Handbook (1984–85), Washington, DC: Bureau of Labor Statistics.

Table 6.3   Twenty Fastest Growing Occupations, 1982–1995

Occupation	Percentage growth in employment
Computer service technicians	96.8
Legal assistants	94.3
Computer systems analysts	85.3
Computer programmers	76.9
Computer operators	75.8
Office machine repairers	71.7
Physical therapy assistants	67.8
Electrical engineers	65.3
Civil engineering technicians	63.9
Peripheral EDP equipment operators	63.5
Insurance clerks, medical	62.2
Electrical and electronic technicians	60.7
Occupational therapists	59.8
Surveyor helpers	58.6
Credit clerks, banking and insurance	54.1
Physical therapists	53.6
Employment interviewers	52.5
Mechanical engineers	52.1
Mechanical engineering technicians	51.6
Compression and injection mold machine operators, plastics	50.3

Note. Includes only detailed occupations with 1982 employment of 25,000 or more. Data for 1995 are based on moderate-trend projections. From Occupational Outlook Handbook (1984–85), Washington, DC: Bureau of Labor Statistics.

process, including personality, self-esteem, and values. It is also the case that neither the factors nor the process are well understood. Increasingly, we understand the inoperative nature of Parson's (1909) idea of using true logic to match one's personal characteristics to corresponding jobs.

For example, it is increasingly recognized that persons without career goals can be classified as undecided and indecisive. Undecided individuals can make an adequate career choice given the proper information. Crites (1969), who may have been the first to recognize the difference between these groups, postulated that some undecided individuals may have difficulty choosing from available alternatives by virtue of not having a well-developed set of interests. Indecisive individuals are unable to commit to a career decision because of personal problems (Crites, 1969). Recent research has suggested that indecisive individuals may be subdivided into two groups; those with low self-confidence in their ability to select an occupation, and those for whom making an occupational choice raises a high level of anxiety (Kaplan & Brown, 1986). Both groups avoid the occupational decision-making process, but for different reasons.

Earlier it was suggested that the preferred decision-making approach is one approximating the scientific method. However, it is also increasingly recognized that not all persons choosing a career follow this method. Arroba (1977) has posed that individuals employ the following six decision-making styles:

- *Logical:* The step-by-step approach of identifying the problem, generating alternatives, and so forth is followed. This style has also been called a rational style (Harren, 1979).
- *No thought:* No objective consideration is given to the decision at hand.
- *Hesitant:* In this style, the decision is postponed and the individual is unable to commit.
- *Emotional:* Subjective "wants" as opposed to objective data are considered.
- *Compliant:* The expectations of others or the demands of the situation are the dominant factors in the decision-making. Harren (1979) called this a dependent style.
- *Intuitive:* Data generated internally. Harren (1979) characterized this as one involving emotional self-awareness and fantasy.

All of the foregoing decision-making styles can lead to faulty decisions, although it is presumed that the logical style is less likely to do so.

OTHER FACTORS IN OCCUPATIONAL CHOICE

Personality, values, and other psychological aspects of the individual play an important role in the choice of occupation. The process followed can also be a major determinant of the outcome. But psychological characteristics and the decision-making process are not the only concern of the career counselor.

Occupational Outlook

The U.S. Department of Labor's Bureau of Labor Statistics publishes a wide range of materials that attempt to forecast the future of various occupations, such as the widely used *Occupational Outlook Handbook.* For example, a Bureau of Labor Statistics looked at the 40 occupations with the largest expected job growth during the 1982–1995 period. The projections can be seen in Table 6.2. That same publication also looked at those occupations growing the fastest, and these data are presented in Table 6.3. These types of data give the decision-maker valuable information about areas in which jobs are developing, and similar information is available about jobs that are declining. What is also important is a supply profile, that is, the numbers of workers that are going to be available to fill certain types of jobs. The *Occupational Outlook Handbook* provides these data, as do special publications such as *Occupational Projections and Training Data.* For example, the following information about counselors appeared in the 1984 version of the latter document.

Counselors

Employment Profile
Total employment, 1982   148,000

Selected characteristics of workers, 1982:
  Percent female   51.8
  Percent black   12.8
  Percent employed part time   13.6

Unemployment rate—About average

Industry concentration of employment (wage and salary workers), 1982 (in percent):
  Educational Services   61.7
  Social services   17.9
  State government   12.5

Projected employment, 1982–1995:

	Low	Moderate	High
1995 employment	159,000	163,000	167,000
Percent change	7.4	9.8	12.4

Employment change   Slower than average

Annual replacement rate   13.5 percent

Supply Profile

Usual entry level requirements. A master's degree in some area of counseling or psychology generally is required. In some cases, individuals with a bachelor's degree in psychology, sociology, counseling, and rehabilitation services are qualified, particularly if they have appropriate work experience. Many states require public school counselors to have both counseling and teaching certificates. Counselors in most state vocational rehabilitation agencies must pass a written exam and be evaluated by a board of examiners.

Training completions:
Earned degrees, baccalaureate and above, 1982:[1]
  Bachelor's   568
  Master's   16,263
  Ph.D.   1,468

Characteristics of entrants. Most entrants are college graduates who transfer from related fields such as social work, teaching, interviewing, job placement, psychology, or personnel work. Others are recent college graduates,

---

[1]Includes educational psychology, student personnel, and psychology for counseling.

some of whom have held part time jobs while in school. Some have been tending to family responsibilities. Because prior work experience is usual for counselors, entrants tend to be somewhat older than entrants to other occupations.

Other data about salaries, working conditions, and training requirements are also included in various forms of occupational information.

Gender undoubtedly influences occupational choice and therefore must be considered as a special factor. Brooks (1986) indicates that women typically engage in career, marriage, and family planning simultaneously and thus may restrict themselves since they do not always anticipate events such as divorce, widowhood, childlessness, and other family events that have an impact on career planning. Brooks also suggests that because of the unique socialization of women, they may not consider a number of careers that have traditionally been viewed as primarily for men. This latter contention is borne out by a Labor Publication (1982), *20 Facts on Women Workers*, that indicates that 80% of all clerical workers, 63% of retail sales workers, and 62% of all service workers are women, while only about 6% of occupations such as plumbers and electricians and 45% of professional and technical workers are women, though in the latter group women are concentrated in teaching, nursing, and similar occupations.

Minority Status

Some research (Brown, Fulkerson, Vedder, & Ware, 1983; Lawrence & Brown, 1976; McNair & Brown, 1983) has shown that black minorities have deficits with regard to estimating abilities and interests, but generally the differences between blacks and their white counterparts have not been startling. However, as Dillard (1980) notes, there are a number of barriers to the career development of blacks. These include poverty, quality of educational opportunities, and family conditions. Whether other minorities are faced with these same barriers is not clear, but the dropout rate for Hispanic students seems to exceed that of their white counterparts (Bureau of the Census, 1985). Unemployment figures also support the idea that Hispanic and black minorities, in particular, are less able than whites to negotiate the occupational structure of this country (Bureau of the Census, 1985).

Because of the barriers of poverty, lack of family support, decreased educational opportunity and continued discrimination in the work force, some minorities may be apathetic. They may avoid the occupational decision-making process or, at least, not give the process the attention it deserves. They may select occupations stereotypically and may not consider the numerous conditions that influence their lives as workers.

STUDENT LEARNING EXERCISE
True or False

1. The personality types realistic, artistic, investigative, social, and enterprising are a part of Holland's theory of occupational choice.   T   F

2. One major difference between career developmental and occupational choice is the time frame in which they occur.   T   F

3. There is a resurgence of interest in career education in this country.   T   F

4. Work and occupation are interchangeable terms.   T   F

5. Job stress can cause physiological as well as psychological problems.   T   F

6. Technology appears to be the long-term solution for the problems experienced by people in the work environment.   T   F

7. For Super, the vocational concept is the key variable in career decision-making.   T   F

8. Realistic types have aversions to education.   T   F

9. Career indecisiveness is caused by lack of information.   T   F

LIFE CAREER COUNSELING

It was suggested at the beginning of this chapter that life career development is a phrase meant to denote the interrelationship of various life roles. Gysbers and Moore (1975, 1981) have taken this one step further. More recently they state, "life career development is advocated as an organizing and integrating concept for understanding and facilitating human growth and development" (Gysbers and Moore, 1986, p. 4). Thus far, the emphasis of this chapter has been on the use of the concept as an organizing and integrating concept. This section will focus on life career counseling as a means for facilitating human growth and development.

Recently a number of articles and books have appeared that focus on various aspects of life career counseling. For example, Brown (1985) argued that many problems may appear to be psychological in nature but in fact are work related. He noted that job stress can cause depression, headaches, lower back pain, loss of motivation, and a variety of other problems. Thus career counseling may be a viable form of therapy for many distressed clients. Brown and Brooks (1985) provided a schema for assessing the primary locus of a problem, along with suggesting some interventions for dealing with psychological, career, and interrelated problems. Finally, Brooks and Brown (1986), writing about the career counseling of adults, posed the following definition of career counseling which reflects a life career development perspective.

Career counseling is an interpersonal process designed to assist individuals with career development problems. Career development is that process of choosing, enjoying, adjusting to, and advancing in an occupation or occupations. It is a lifelong psychological process that interacts dynamically with other life roles. Career development problems include, but are not limited to, career indecision and undecidedness, work performance, stress and adjustment, incongruence of the person and the work environment, inadequate or unsatisfactory integration of life roles with other life roles (e.g., parent, friend, citizen). (p. 98.)

In the above definition, the focus of counseling is on careers, whether it be choosing a first or a new career, or adjusting to one already chosen. Other life roles become important only when they impinge upon the individual's work role which, it should be added, they invariably do. However, life career counseling has a somewhat different emphasis. It has as its primary focus the most salient and troublesome life role while focusing on the interaction of other life roles with the problematic one. The assumptions of life career counseling are as follows:

1. All life roles are interconnected.
2. Individuals strive to attain homeostatis among their life roles.
3. Difficulty in one life role (e.g., career) will have a negative impact on other life roles.
4. Harmony and congruence in one life role will positively affect other life roles.
5. Positive functioning in one life role can attenuate stress brought about by negative aspects of another life role.
6. All life roles offer the possibility of satisfaction and dissatisfaction, although they do not hold the same potential at any given time.
7. Personal perceptions of the importance of a particular life role will be directly related to its potential for satisfaction or dissatisfaction.
8. Intervention in one life role may be made directly in that life role, or indirectly in other life roles. Thus, all problems have multiple solutions.
9. Interventions that bring positive changes in one life role may break the dynamic homeostasis that has developed among various life roles and thus have a negative impact on another.

THE PROCESS OF LIFE CAREER COUNSELING

As has been noted by a number of authors (e.g., Brooks & Brown, 1986; Brown & Brooks, 1985; Herr & Cramer, 1984), and as will be pointed out directly later in this book, all counseling—career, life career, or personal—begins with establishment of a therapeutic relationship. This relationship will be discussed in Chapter 8.

Assessment or diagnosis of the client's problems begins simultaneously with relationship development and follows after the relationship has been built. Assessment involves identifying the nature of the problem and those causal factors that are contributing to it. Gysbers and Moore (1986), while writing about career counseling, have presented an approach to assessment in life career counseling. They call the approach Life Career Assessment (LCA), and describe it as follows: "The LCA is designed to cover your client's level of functioning in various life roles including the worker, learner, and personal roles as well as yielding information on how they negotiate with their environment" (p. 89). An outline of Gysbers and Moore's LCA can be seen in Table 6.4.

As the table shows, life career assessment begins with an assessment of the personal characteristics of the individual. Any of the major theories described later in this book can be used as the basis for the personal analysis phase of life career counseling. However, as Brown and Brooks (1985) have suggested, one of the basic thrusts in this assessment is to determine the perceptual clarity of the individual. Does the person possess the ability to objectively assess his own characteristics (self-awareness), the various aspects of his life (environmental awareness), and how they "fit" into those situations (interactional awareness)?

Once perceptual clarity is ascertained, the counselor must decide whether to proceed to life career planning and adjustment or to deal with the perceptual problems that have been discovered. Mild perceptual problems, such

Table 6.4   Life Career Assessment Interview(s)

1. Personal assessment
     Inter- and intrapersonal functioning examined
2. Career assessment (life role = work)
     Totality of work experience examined including likes, dislikes, etc.
3. Education (life role = student)
     Educational and training experiences examined as they relate to work and other life roles
4. Recreation (life role = leisurite)
     Leisure activities including time spent in recreational and social activities
5. Significant others (life roles = child, parent, spouse, friend)
     Spouse and/or significant others examined
6. Community involvement (life role = citizen)
     Examination of citizenship roles pursued
7. Interaction
     The interaction of all life roles examined for positive and negative aspects

Note. Adapted from *Career Counseling: Skills and Techniques for Practitioners* by N. C. Gysbers and E. J. Moore, 1986, Englewood Cliffs, NJ: Prentice-Hall.

as stereotypical thinking, can probably be dealt with routinely in the role assessment and planning process. Severe problems will need to become the major agenda item in the counseling process and should supercede life career role planning and adjustment work.

If the decision is to proceed with life career planning and adjustment, inventories such as *The Salience Inventory* (Super & Nevill, 1985) that give indications of the relative importance of life roles will be helpful. So can logs that focus on how time is spent, which is one indicator of role salience. Some of the techniques discussed in the next section can also be used individually.

The outcomes of life career counseling will quite obviously depend on a variety of factors. An adolescent may simply want to make some tentative plans about various aspects of his or her life, usually beginning with education and work roles, but ultimately including roles involving leisure and significant others. Young adults may be interested in developing some balance among their life roles (adjustment) after being preoccupied with education and work. Older adults may be interested in making a change in a single life role (e.g., leisurite or worker), changing the emphasis among the life roles, or planning to totally deemphasize a life role such as work. Retirees, faced with the loss of the role of worker, may be seeking ways to derive meaning and satisfaction from other life roles, and the aged, faced with the loss of the role of spouse, may have similar concerns.

LIFE CAREER PLANNING WORKSHOPS

Zunker (1986) suggests that workshops designed to help adults have been around since the mid-1960s, and that life career planning on some college campuses began soon after. Zunker indicates that some of these workshops are as brief as a single day and involve participants in developing a future orientation, examining life roles in detail, establishing some new life career goals, and developing strategies for pursuing those goals.

Rozzelle and McCoy (1977), at the University of Kansas, have developed a life career workshop that would take approximately 18 hours to complete. The outline for the workshop follows:

1. Looking at who you are and what you want (Life Roles Analysis)
2. Examining your values
3. Your personality and your work
4. Researching an occupation
5. Goal achievement strategies
6. School and work

As can be seen, the Rozzelle-McCoy outline is very work-centered.

Brown (1980) developed a life career planning program for adolescents that was designed to develop life planning skills. The components involved:

1. Why people behave as they do (understanding motivation)
2. Winners and losers (positive thinking and planning emphasized)
3. Your fantasy life
4. Your real life (relationship of fantasy and reality emphasized)
5. Setting life goals
6. Short-term planning—high school graduation
7–10. Long-term planning—education, career, close relationships, leisure, and community involvement

CAREER COUNSELING

The discussion to this point has focused on a counseling process that considers and deals with multiple life roles. Career counseling was defined as a process of choosing or adjusting to an occupation with consideration given to other life roles in the process (Brooks & Brown, 1986). Career counseling varies from life career counseling in that in the former the client's role of worker receives the primary emphasis, and in crisis situations such as those that occur when a client loses his source of livelihood, regaining the work role may be the only emphasis.

STUDENT LEARNING EXERCISE

List five potential explanations for the following presenting problems and think of some possible solutions.

Carlos is a 35-year-old Hispanic laborer who was recently granted citizenship. His wife works as a waitress. They have three children. Lately, Carlos has had difficulty getting himself motivated to go to work. As a result, he has been late on numerous occasions, and has missed five days of work. His supervisor told him three days ago that unless he "shapes up," he is going to be fired.

1.
2.
3.
4.
5.

Computers in Career Counseling

The process of career counseling varies little from that already described for life career counseling except for its narrower focus. However, a number of adjuncts, which include the use of aptitude tests, interest and personality inventories, as well as occupational information and computerized assistance systems have been developed. Tests and inventories will be discussed later but computerized adjuncts to career counseling will be discussed here briefly.

One of the first computerized systems was developed under the direction of David Tiedeman and Robert O'Hara (1930). This system, *Information System* for *Vocational Decisions (ISVD)*, was interactive in nature and assisted students to relate information about themselves to various types of educational career data including those in the military. Students who used *ISVD* were presented interactive scripts in which they were asked to relate data about themselves to educational, career, and military information, with the expected result being that they would develop personalized decisions.

A more current computerized system is the *System of Interactive Guidance (SIGI)*, plus *The Next Generation on Computerized Guidance*, which was developed under the leadership of Martin Katz at the Educational Testing Service. *SIGI* was developed for use by college students (Norris, Shatkin, Schott, & Bennett, 1986). It includes the following nine sections:

- *Introduction* gives an overview and helps a user decide how best to use the eight remaining sections.
- *Self-assessment* has a user rate 15 work-related values, including such specific job-related values as "Staying Put," "Easy Commute," and "Challenge." Interests are examined on two dimensions—fields of knowledge and types of activities. Thus a user can combine an interest in remaining in a particular field with an interest in engaging in different kinds of activities (for example, combining engineering and sales); users can look at classified lists of activities and decide which ones they are good at.
- *Search* allows a user to retrieve occupations from a database of about 230 on the basis of values, interests, skills, and educational requirements. An additional search is available to avoid certain attributes of activities (e.g., doing math, poor outlook).
- *Information* allows a user to ask up to 27 questions about occupations and, in response, to receive national information. If the system has been tailored, local information is also given (e.g., salary figures for jobs within a company might be given along with national estimates for the occupation as a whole).
- *Skills* provides information about the skills required to perform important work tasks and has users assess themselves on these skills. Managerial skills are also described and assessed.
- *Preparing* offers a detailed look at preparation for entry into an occupation. It shows educational and training requirements, plus work tasks that must be mastered. Users then evaluate their readiness to enter.
- *Coping* examines a number of practical considerations (e.g., money, child care, college credit for life experiences) related to career change.

- *Deciding* helps users reach decisions by evaluating and combining (a) the desirability of each occupation they are considering (including their present job) and (b) their chances of success in entering it.
- *Next steps* helps users plan a course of action to meet their objectives.

SIGI's subsystems illustrate the two uses to which computers can be put in the career planning process. The planning subsystem simply presents and sorts information on demand. The strategy subsystem interacts with the user to assist in the choice-making process. One criticism of the strategy subsystems, and others like it, is that the computer has only so many alternatives available and thus acts as a limiting force in the choice-making process.

Discover was developed by the American College Testing Program, and like *SIGI* and *ISVD*, is an interactive program. In the first part of the program, for adolescents and young adults, users can complete interest and values inventories, and these in turn can be used to generate a list of related occupations. However, it is not necessary to take these inventories if the results of a number of popular interests inventories and aptitude batteries are available, because the results of these can be entered and lists of occupations can be generated with these results. The user has the option of taking the tests and inventories included in *Discover* and entering the results of others.

Once occupational interests are listed, the user of *Discover* may consult the occupational information file and ask up to 14 questions about each occupation. This exercise can be followed by using a file that contains information on more than 30,000 two- and four-year institutions that may offer courses or programs of study related to occupations users have identified. These files contain data regarding cost, size, admissions policies, minority representation, male-to-female ratios, and so forth.

The *Discover* program for adults varies from the one for young adults in that it contains a section on weathering life transitions. It also allows the adult learner to engage in self-analysis by taking interest inventories, rating his or her skills and experiences, and surveying his or her values. Once this is completed, the adult can obtain a list of occupations related to his or her self-analysis, along with suggestions regarding the training needed. The user can also get detailed descriptions of occupations of interest, training in occupational decision-making, assistance with educational planning, and such job-seeking strategies as preparing resumes and job interviews.

Computerized Vocational Information System (CVIS), like *ISVD*, was one of the early computerized systems. It was developed for use by the College of DuPage (Glenellyn, Illinois) and Willowbrook High School (suburban Chicago) (Zunker, 1986). It contains three files: a career guidance system, a counseling-administrator support system, and one that enables the development of local computerized guidance information. At this time, there are three separate programs available, one each for junior high schools, senior high schools, and community colleges.

Choices was developed by the Employment and Immigration Commission in Canada. The user begins by interacting with the system to determine whether or not he or she can benefit from the system. If the user determines that he or she can benefit, self-assessment is pursued. This involves either making self-estimates of various traits or actually taking tests. The user is also asked to complete a "data sheet" that includes information about education and preferences regarding the world of work, such as expected salary, training requirements, and working conditions.

Once all information about the user is placed into the program, the user elects one of four "routes" to complete the career exploration process. The Specific Route simply provides brief informational descriptions of various occupations. The Compare Route allows the user to actually compare various aspects of various occupations, such as training requirements. The Related Route provides a listing of occupations that are similar in nature to those previously explained in the Specific and Compare Routes. The Explore Route is used by the relatively naive user who needs rather extensive career exploration experience.

The foregoing list of computerized systems is not meant to be exhaustive, only illustrative. Other, more sophisticated, computerized systems of career exploration that will soon replace these systems with faster, more creative programs are now being developed. When the *ISVD* was developed, a large mainframe computer was required to handle the system. For the most part, current computerized systems are available on microcomputers. In 1973, Harris estimated that the annual cost of operating *CVIS* was $18,000. While current systems are still expensive, the microcomputer and program can be purchased for about one-third of that cost currently, and it is expected that costs will continue to come down. The result will be that computerized systems of career exploration and decision-making will be readily available throughout the United States in a very short time.

COMPUTERS AND COUNSELORS

Will computers replace counselors in the career counseling process? In some instances with some clients, probably yes. Undecided clients who simply need information can certainly benefit from direct interaction with computers. Indecisive clients who have personal deficits are unlikely to benefit to the same degree or, in some instances, not at all. Computers must, therefore, be viewed as one means of expanding counseling services, not as a threat.

SELECTING A COMPUTERIZED SYSTEM

Maze (1984) suggests seven steps that should be followed in selecting a computerized system. To a certain extent, the following list is based on his recommendations along with the recommendations of Zunker (1986) and Harris-Bowlsby (1984).

First, determine the characteristics of the users. Some systems are geared toward adults, others toward adolescents. Some systems require that each user complete the entire program, while others allow users to access only those aspects of the program that user deems appropriate. In the latter case, time may be saved, but thoroughness may be sacrificed.

Second, determine what the counseling staff wants to accomplish? Should the program be primarily informationally oriented, or is it important to produce high levels of personal self-awareness?

Third, what is the cost? Terminals, microcomputers, programs, computer paper, telephone time if the computer is on-line, costs of updating the program, etc., are all important considerations. Those considering these programs should get a "bottom line figure" before proceeding.

Fourth, how fast is the program? Some computerized systems, particularly those on microcomputers, may operate somewhat slowly, and thus user motivation may wane. Also, and importantly, more systems may be required if the time on machine per user is too long.

Fifth—a consideration related to the fourth point—will the program maintain user motivation? Not all the computerized systems available have the same ability to involve the user. Only "hands-on" experience by users can provide this type of information.

Sixth, does the theoretical rationale of the program correspond to that of the staff? It may come as a surprise to some that theory would enter into computer programs, but in fact most career exploration programs have well-defined theoretical rationales. For example, *SIGI* is predicated on the idea that values are the most salient variable in career decision-making. *ISVD* was based on O'Hara and Tiedeman's theory of career decision-making. Each counselor and counseling staff needs to examine their own beliefs about this process before proceeding to purchase a system.

Seventh, and finally, is there a good technical support system for the program? All computer programs have "glitches" and "bugs." Unless adequate techincal support is available, these problems that plague most systems may result in total failure.

SUMMARY

The increasing recognition that work and other life roles are interrelated has been emphasized in this chapter. Various approaches to life career planning and adjustment have been presented, along with some information about career planning.

The fact that work is still the most important life role has been recognized, the importance of job satisfaction has been emphasized, and the processes involved in career development and occupational choices discussed. The importance of occupational information was also touched on.

In the final section of the chapter, a number of computerized and occupational information and career planning systems were outlined, and the relationship of counselors and computers discussed.

REVIEW QUESTIONS

1. Discuss the pro's and con's of life career versus career planning.
2. How do career and life career counseling differ from personal counseling? Which takes precedence?
3. Discuss the possible advantages and disadvantages of using computers in the career planning process.
4. What are the factors related to job satisfaction? What individual characteristics might influence job satisfaction?
5. On the basis of the information that you learned about trends in the world of work, what personal ideas that you held had to be changed?
6. Will women and minorities need any unusual or different assistance in career planning? If so, specify these differences.
7. Distinguish between Super's minicycle and maxicycle.

REFERENCES

Arroba, T. (1977). Styles of decision making and their use: An empirical study. *British Journal of Guidance and Counseling, 5,* 149–158.

Bordin, E. J. (1984). Psychodynamic model of career choice and satisfaction. In D. Brown & L. Brooks (Eds.), *Career choice and development* (pp. 94–136). San Francisco: Jossey-Bass.

Brooks, L. (1986). Counseling women. Presentation at the University of North Carolina, Chapel Hill.

Brooks, L., & Brown, D. (1986). Career counseling for adults: Implications for mental health counselors. In A. J. Palmo & W. J. Weikel (Eds.), *Foundations of mental health counseling* (pp. 95–114). Springfield, IL: Charles C Thomas.

Brown, D. (1980). A life-planning workshop for high school students. *Vocational Guidance Quarterly, 29,* 77–83.

Brown, D. (1985). Career counseling: Before, after, or instead of personal counseling? *Vocational Guidance Quarterly, 33,* 197–201.

Brown, D., & Brooks, L. (1985). Career counseling as a mental health intervention. *Professional Psychology: Research and Practice, 16,* 860–867.

Brown, D., Fulkerson, K. F., Vedder, M., & Ware, W. B. (1983). Self-estimate ability in black and white 8th-, 10th-, and 12th-grade males and females. *Vocational Guidance Quarterly, 32,* 21–28.

Bureau of the Census. (1981). *Statistical abstracts of the United States, 1980.* Washington, DC: U.S. Department of Commerce.

Bureau of the Census. (1985). *Statistical abstracts of the United States, 1985.* Washington, DC: Bureau of the Census.

Crites, J. O. (1969). *Vocational psychology.* New York: McGraw-Hill.

Dillard, J. M. (1980). Some unique career behavior characteristics of blacks. Career theories, counseling practice, and research. *Journal of Employment Counseling, 17,* 288–298.

Gelatt, H. B., Varenhorst, B., & Carey, R. (1972). *Deciding.* New York: College Entrance Examination Board.

Gelatt, H. B., Varenhorst, B., Carey, R., & Miller, G. P. (1973). *Decisions and outcomes.* New York: College Entrance Examination Board.

Gould, R. (1978). *Transformations: Growth and change in adult life.* New York: Simon and Schuster.

Graney, J. J., & Zimmerman, R. M. (1981). Causes and consequences of health self-report variations among older people. *Interactional Journal of Aging and Human Development, 12,* 291–300.

Gysbers, N. C., & Moore, E. J. (1975). Beyond career development—life career development. *The Personnel and Guidance Journal, 53,* 647–652.

Gysbers, N. C., & Moore, E. J. (1981). *Improving guidance programs.* Englewood Cliffs, NJ: Prentice-Hall.

Gysbers, N. C., & Moore, E. J. (1986). *Career counseling: Skills and techniques for practitioners.* Englewood Cliffs, NJ: Prentice-Hall.

Harren, V. (1979). A model of career decision-making for college students. *Journal of Vocational Behavior, 14,* 119–133.

Harris, J. (1974). The computer: Guidance tool of the future. *Journal of Counseling Psychology, 21,* 331–339.

Harris, L., & Associates. (1979). *A nationwide survey of employees, retirees and business leaders.* Washington, DC: Harris and Associates.

Harris-Bowlsby, J. (1984). The computer and career development. *Journal of Counseling and Development, 63,* 145–149.

Herr, E. L. & Cramec, S. H. (1984). *Career guidance and counseling through the life span* (2nd ed.). Boston: Little, Brown.

Herr, E. L. (1986a). Career development theory: An overview. In R. L. Frank (Ed.), *Proceedings of statewide conference on career guidance theory.* Cedar Falls, IA: University of Northern Iowa.

Herr, E. L. (1986b). Life-style and career development. In M. D. Lewis, R. L. Hayes & J. A. Lewis (Eds.), *An introduction to the counseling profession* (pp. 167–214). Itasca, IL: F. E. Peacock.

Holland, J. L. (1985). *Making vocational choices: A theory of vocational personalities and work environments* (2nd ed.). Englewood Cliffs, NJ: Prentice-Hall.

Isaacson, L. E. (1977). *Career information in counseling and teaching.* Boston: Allyn and Bacon.

Johnson, R. P., & Riker, H. C. (1981). Retirement maturity: A valuable concept for pre-retirement counselors. *Personnel and Guidance Journal, 59,* 291–295.

Kaplan, D., & Brown, D. (1986). Self-efficacy, anxiety, and career indecisiveness. Unpublished manuscript. Chapel Hill, NC: University of North Carolina.

Katz, (1980). SIGI: An interactive aid to career decision-making. *Journal of College Student Personnel, 21,* 34–40.

Kingson, E. R. (1981). Retirement circumstances of very early retirees: A life cycle perspective. *Aging and Work, 4,* 161–174.

Lawrence, W., & Brown, D. (1976). An investigation of intelligence, self-concept, socioeconomic status, race, and sex as predictors of career maturity. *Journal of Vocational Behavior, 9,* 43–52.

Levinson, D. (1978). *The seasons of a man's life.* New York: Knopf. Lowenthal, M., & Weiss, L. (1976). Intimacy and crises in adulthood. *The Counseling Psychologist, 6,* 10–16.

McDaniels, D. (1978). The practice of career guidance and counseling. *Inform, 7,* 1–2, 7–8.

McDaniels, C. (1986). Three of the many future occupational scenarios for the 1900s. *The Journal of Cooperative Education, 22,* 6–15.

McNair, D., & Brown, D. (1983). Predicting the occupational aspirations, occupational expectations and career maturity of black and white male and female 10th graders. *Vocational Guidance Quarterly, 32,* 29–36.

Maze, M. (1984). How to select a computerized guidance system. *Journal of Counseling and Development, 63,* 158–162.

Meier, E. L. (1975). Over 65: Expectations and realities of work and retirement. *Industrial Gerontology, 2,* 95–109.

Naisbitt, J. (1984). *Megatrends: Ten new directions transforming our lives.* New York: Warner Books.

National Alliance of Business. (1986). *Employment policies: Looking to the year 2000.* Washington, DC: National Alliance of Business.

Neff, W. S. (1985). *Work and human behavior.* New York: Aldine.

Neugarten, B. (1976). Adaptation and the life cycle. *The Counseling Psychologist, 6,* 16–21.

Norris, L., Shatkin, L., Schott, P. S., & Bennett, M. F. (1986). The field test of the SIGI PLUS, the computer-based system of interactive guidance—plus more. Unpublished study. Princeton, NJ: ETS.

Okun, B. F. (1984). *Working with adults: Individual, family, & career development.* Monterey, CA: Brooks/Cole.

Parsons, F. (1909). *Choosing a vocation.* Boston: Houghton Mifflin.

Rabinowitz, W., Falkenbach, K., Travers, J. R., Valentine, C. G., & Weener, P. (1983). Worker motivation: Unsolved problems or untapped resources? *California Monograph Review, 25,* 45–56.

Report of a Special Task Force to the Secretary of Health, Education and Welfare. (1973). *Work in America.* Cambridge, MA: MIT Press.

Roe, A. (1984). Personality development and career choice. In D. Brown & L. Brooks (Eds.), *Career choice and development* (pp. 31–53). San Francisco: Jossey-Bass.

Rozzelle, R. W., & McCoy, V. R. (1977). *Life/career manual.* Lawrence, KS: University of Kansas.

Schmitt, N., & McCune, J. T. (1981). The relationship between job attitudes and the decision to retire. *Academy of Management Journal, 24,* 795–802.

Super, D. E. (1976). *Career education and the meaning of work.* Washington, DC: U.S. Office of Education.

Super, D. E. (1984). Career and life development. In D. Brown & L. Brooks (Eds.), *Career choice and development* (pp. 192–234). San Francisco: Jossey-Bass.

Super, D. E., & Nevill, D. D. (1985). *The salience inventory.* Palo Alto, CA: Consulting Psychologists Press.

Tiedeman, D. V., & O'Hara, R. P. (1963). *Career development: Choice and adjustment.* New York: College Examination Board.

U.S. Senate Special Committee on Aging. (1985–86). *Aging America: Trends and projections.* Washington, DC: U.S. Department of Health and Human Services.

Women's Bureau. (1982). *20 facts on women workers.* Washington, DC: U.S. Department of Labor.

Williamson, E. G. (1939). *How to counsel students.* New York: McGraw-Hill.

Williamson, E. G. (1965). *Vocational counseling.* New York: McGraw-Hill.

Zunker, V. G. (1986). *Career counseling: Applied concepts of life planning* (2nd ed.). Monterey, CA: Brooks/Cole.

7

Client Groups That Require Specialized Skills and Sensitivities

GOAL OF THE CHAPTER

The aim of this chapter is to survey cultural issues and their impact on the practice of counseling.

CHAPTER PREVIEW

1. The concept of culture will be defined.
2. Cross-cultural counseling will be described.
3. Barriers to cross-cultural counseling will be examined.
4. Counseling of minorities will be examined.
5. Particular attention will be given to the counseling of women and the physically disabled.

INTRODUCTION

Much of the counseling literature focuses on the YAVIS client, that is, the young, attractive, verbal, intelligent, and successful individual. Most counselors freely admit that some of their most difficult clients are those that fall outside this group, including the physically and mentally handicapped, clients mired in poverty, and individuals who have not, for whatever reasons, been able to be successful in our society.

It is also true that historically much of the counseling literature has focused on white males to the detriment of the counseling of women and ethnic and racial minorities. Research and practitioners' observations have shown that theories and practices developed for white males and YAVIS clients do not necessarily generalize to the many client groups that exist in our culture. It is the purpose of this chapter to discuss some of the counseling issues that must be addressed if one is successfully to provide services to clients who belong to ethnic and racial minorities, or who are women, homosexuals, aged, or disabled.

CULTURAL DIFFERENCES AND COUNSELING

The Concept of Culture

Defining culture is no easy task, as Copeland (1983) notes. As early as 1952, Kroeber and Kluckhohn identified more than 150 different definitions of culture. However, as Copeland (1983) did, so did Herskovits (1955) define culture as the human made part of the environment. Cultures form when people share common experiences, history, language, and geographic location, although national boundaries often contain more than one culture. Common experiences and social tools such as language used to describe experience affect the perceptions of the people in a culture, and thus culture contains many subjective elements.

Ibrahim (1985) describes culture-building as a process in which a group of people form a world view, a philosophy of life. Important elements in this philosophy are (1) a characterization of human nature, (2) a definition of the goals of human relationships, (3) the relationship of people to nature, (4) the relationship of people to time, and (5) the goals and implications of human action.

Table 7.1 lists the differences that exist among various cultural groups in this country. One can see from the table that cultural influences on an individual affect basic values and beliefs. When individuals from different cultures attempt to relate to one another, they may begin with very different perceptions about the nature of people, what people need, how people succeed, and the relationship of people to nature.

Cross-Cultural Counseling

Locke (1986) has defined cross-cultural counseling as a practical area that (1) emphasizes the importance and uniqueness of the individual, (2) recognizes that counselors bring to the counseling setting a set of values that stem from their

Table 7.1 Cultural Differences That May Influence Cross-Cultural Counselors

Clients	Language	Views of Human Nature	Goals of Human Relationships	Time Orientation	Relationship with Nature	Action Orientation
White Americans	Standard English	Individual has primary responsibility	Competition; dominance	Adhere to rigid time schedule	Must dominate	Action-oriented
Black Americans	Nonstandard English; nonverbal communication important	Affiliation with others valued	Support	Schedules less important	Accept nature	Action-oriented; meet immediate short-term goals
Hispanics	Bilingual or Spanish speaking	Group-centered	Cooperation; comaraderie	Schedules less important	Accept nature	Action-oriented; short-term goals
American Indians	Bilingual; nonstandard English	Advancement through group	Cooperation not competition	Time Unimportant	Unite with nature	Action-oriented to meet present needs
Asian Americans	Nonstandard English for some; standard English for others; Asian language for others	Emphasis on group, particularly family	Cooperation stressed but can be competitive; respect for authority stressed	Schedules less important	Appreciation for nature	Action-oriented to meet short- and long-term goals

Note. Adapted from *Counseling the Culturally Different* (pp. 30–31) by D. W. Sue, 1981, New York: John Wiley and Sons; and "The Sociopolitical Nature of Counseling," by J. H. Katz, 1985, *The Counseling Psychologist, 13,* p. 618. Reprinted by permission.

culture, and (3) further recognizes that clients from ethnic or racial minority groups come with a set of values and attitudes that reflect their cultural background. Locke goes on to note that in cross-cultural counseling it is important for the counselor to remember and value different learning styles, career goals, and overall philosophies of life that may emerge from different groups in a pluralistic society.

Locke (1986) suggests that there is a cross-cultural counseling awareness continuum (Figure 7.1) through which a counselor should pass before engaging in cross-cultural counseling. This development begins with self-awareness, including, one presumes, an awareness of prejudices that one holds. Self-awareness should be followed by the development of an awareness of one's own culture; increased sensitivity to the presence of racism, sexism, and poverty in our society; awareness of individual differences; awareness of other cultural groups and the diversity within those cultures; and, finally, the development of counseling techniques that will enable the counselor to bridge the gaps that exist between self and culturally different clients.

Sue (1981) has elaborated extensively on the counseling skills that are needed in cross-cultural counseling. He stresses that the culturally skilled counselor must have a basic understanding of counseling techniques and must be culturally sensitive enough to apply those techniques appropriately. For example, most counseling techniques are oriented toward inducing increasing self-disclosure on the part of the client. But according to Sue (1981), "Self-disclosure may be incompatible with the cultural values of Asian Americans, Chicanos, and Native Americans" (p. 107).

It is also worth noting that traditional insight-oriented therapy, such as that emphasized in the traditional therapies, may be inappropriate for certain cultural groups since economically and educationally disadvantaged clients may be uncomfortable in a role that requires extensive verbalization. Also, many minority clients prefer the more action-oriented approaches characterized by the behavior and cognitive therapies, as opposed to the longer, more deliberate approaches (Sue, 1981).

Sue (1981) suggests that there are four scenarios that may evolve from cross-cultural counseling, only one of which is positive. In that positive scenario,

Figure 7.1: Cross-Cultural Awareness Continuum. *Note.* "Cross-cultural Counseling Issues" (p. 122) by D. C. Locke. In *Foundations of Mental Health Counseling* (pp. 119–137) by A. J. Palmo and W. J. Weikel, eds., 1986, Springfield, IL: Charles C Thomas. Reprinted by courtesy of Charles C Thomas, Publisher, Springfield, Illinois.

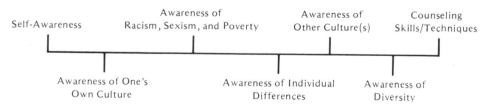

the process engaged in by the counselor is appropriate with regard to the cultural background of the client, and the goals pursued are also in keeping with the cultural situation and sociopolitical realities of the client's existence. The other outcomes of cross-cultural counseling described by Sue are (1) appropriate process, inappropriate goals, (2) inappropriate process, appropriate goals, and (3) inappropriate process, inappropriate goals.

In the first of these negative situations, a cross-cultural counselor might engage in a more active process with a Native American client and help him or her pursue counseling goals that are compatible with his or her view of the relationship of humans to nature and time. One community college counselor reported trying to help Native Americans reconcile a desire to achieve in academic arenas that required punctuality and attendance with beliefs that the annual salmon runs also demanded their attention and, of course, absence from the academic setting.

An appropriate process coupled with an inappropriate goal is illustrated by an active counseling process engaged in by a middle-class white counselor with a poor white fourth-grade boy in which she attempts to teach him to stop fighting. In this situation, fighting skills are necessary if the child is to get to school with his lunch. An appropriate goal for the counselor would be for her to help the child discriminate between appropriate and inappropriate fighting. However, the middle-class white counselor may still use an inappropriate process by attempting to justify not fighting as a civilized means for solving problems.

Sue (1981) believes that premature termination of counseling is likely to occur when the process is inappropriate, even though the goals of the counseling situation are appropriate. A nondirective counselor working with clients who are black and poor, regardless of the goal being pursued, is likely to be ineffective, as is the counselor who chooses the wrong counseling process as well as an inappropriate goal.

BARRIERS TO CROSS-CULTURAL COUNSELING

Language

Conversation is the most fundamental tool utilized by counselors. In cross-cultural counseling, a major obstacle to be overcome is often a language difference. Even though this country is understood to be an English-speaking nation, millions of its citizens regularly use other languages. In fact, many individuals are far more fluent in a language other than English and are therefore handicapped in their ability to take advantage of opportunities available to those who are fluent in English. Among those who do speak English, many use a nonstandard form with word connotations and slang phrases that are quite different from those in standard English. Language barriers must be overcome if counseling is to be successful.

Minorities have been underrepresented in the counseling profession. At present only a few counseling practitioners are bilingual, even though we are becoming a bilingual nation (Arrendondo-Dowd & Gonsalves, 1980). Legislation has recognized this situation, including a need to provide counseling services to non-English-speaking clients. The amended Bilingual Education Act of 1978 specifically named counselors as recipients of federal funds to develop better bilingual programs, including programs to train bilingual counselors. However, providing bilingual counseling will not solve the problem that exists between a counselor who speaks standard English and a client who speaks a nonstandard form. Only cultural sensitivity and hard work can bridge this gap.

Values

As has already been noted, culture-bound values are an important impediment to cross-cultural counseling. Belkin (1984) highlights several examples in which counselors unconsciously impose their values on minority clients. As was also noted, one of the most valued behaviors related to the counseling process is self-disclosure. Therapists believe clients benefit more from counseling if they are willing to share hidden thoughts and feelings, but clients may not share this value.

Sue and Sue (1977) note how threatening the expectation of self-disclosure is to Chinese American clients who have been raised to minimize the expression of feelings. More recently, Sue (1983) compared the typical American therapist with the typical Chinese American. The former often prizes being open, competitive, verbally direct, and independent minded; the latter learns through cultural conditioning to revere solidarity, adherence to roles, conformity, and continuity within a kinship system. As an example, Sue presented the conflict of diverse values at a conference in which professional papers are read. Typically, the work of even a revered scholar will receive direct, open criticism by a reactor. This is completely contrary to Asian tradition.

Even the most conscientious counselors from the dominant culture may unknowingly alienate a minority client. They fail to see that what they take for granted as the clearly superior standard is nothing more than one of many options. For example, the counselor may value competition in the classroom, while his Native American client values cooperation and thus sees direct competition as inappropriate. Unless the counselor perceives the client's point of view, the result of counseling is likely to be less than satisfactory.

Stereotypes

Much has been written about the potential dangers of stereotypes. Usually defined as generalizations one group of people make about another group, stereotypes at first do not seem so negative. However, stereotypes are oversimplified opinions that do not receive critical examination. Thus, stereotypes misrepresent individuals from the group being typed.

When counselors use stereotypes, they lose flexibility in responding to the needs of their clients. Noted throughout this text are the efforts of the American Association for Counseling and Development (AACD) and the American Psychological Association (APA) to establish commissions and task forces to minimize the damage of cultural stereotypes. While this effort has been successful to some degree, it also seems likely that counselors now more effectively conceal their stereotypes. Paradis (1981) documents the reluctance of counselor/therapists to admit to stereotypes. In his study, many reflect repressed hostility toward other cultural groups. However, problematic overgeneralization in the profession is probably a two-way street. White middle-class counselors should be aware that their clients hold stereotypes of them, and counselors must be prepared to deal with these views.

STUDENT LEARNING EXERCISE

Read the following descriptions and indicate whether you think the counseling profession has been successful in dealing with the issue identified. Circle Y for yes or N for no.

1. There is an emerging definition of what constitutes effective cross-cultural counseling.   Y   N
2. Self-disclosure is not a problem in cross-cultural counseling.   Y   N
3. There are adequate numbers of bilingual counselors today.   Y   N
4. Counselors are rarely affected by cultural stereotypes.   Y   N
5. Differences in cultural background between counselor and client often lead to premature termination of counseling.   Y   N

Social Class

Low social class or poverty appears to affect both the rate of diagnosed mental health problems and access to treatment. Studies tend to show an inverse relationship between social class and such disorders as schizophrenia, alcoholism, drug abuse, and antisocial behavior (Dohrenwend & Dohrenwend, 1974). In part, this has been explained as a function of the stressors related to poverty.

In the counseling process, the different experience levels of the client and counselor, and thus their perceptions or world views, may pose the greatest barriers. The middle-class counselor may not have learned that deciding to delay gratification is of doubtful value to the poor because experience has taught them that promises of future rewards never materialize. These differences, when encountered, must be processed.

Race and Ethnicity

Much attention has been given to the cultural differences of racial minorities and the effect of these differences on counseling-related issues (Atkinson, Morten, & Sue, 1979; Marsella & Pedersen, 1981). Evidence does show that minority clients are more likely to drop out of therapy early, miss scheduled appointments, and verbalize greater dissatisfaction with the treatment process (Raynes & Warren, 1969; Sue, 1977; Acosta, 1980). In addition, they are likely to be assigned lower level staff as therapists and are more often assigned inpatient treatment. This suggests that in the past minorities have felt undervalued and mistreated when seeking mental health services (Korchin, 1980).

The process of counseling itself may be problematic to minority clients. Most therapy systems emphasize introspection, assuming responsibility for life's consequences, and the necessity for arriving at personal decisions and solutions. Minority clients, on the other hand, recognize well their identity as an oppressed people. They can point to a social environment outside themselves as the source for much of their hardship. Thus much of the theory underlying client involvement in therapy is at odds with core elements of minority group identity.

Minority individuals often want more from their therapists than is given. In part this includes more direct intervention—more explicit advice, financial counseling, and vocational help (Korchin, 1980). Most counselors, since they do not really understand the stressors affecting minority clients, find it difficult to provide such direct assistance.

Such issues point out again the need for cross-cultural counselors. As Locke (1986) noted, fundamental to cross-cultural involvement is the recognition of group identity as well as individual differences. Tolerance of both represents an ethical necessity for counselors (Pedersen & Marsella, 1982). To the credit of our dominant cultural values is the prizing of diversity that strengthens the culture, just as hybridizing improves the strength of plants. The counseling profession itself has sought to become a hybrid science by incorporating diverse viewpoints and strategies for helping people. Continuation of this process should ensure an adequate supply of cross-cultural counselors.

Gender

One of the most powerful influences on our culture and our profession in the last two decades has been the women's movement. Feminist counselors and psychologists have been extremely important in mobilizing the helping professions to respond to sexist practices.

In 1970 therapists were shocked into the reality of sexist attitudes in the helping professions by the historic study by Broverman and co-workers (Broverman, Broverman, Clarkson, Rosenkrantz, & Vogel, 1970). This investigation documented not only the presence of gender stereotypes among therapists, but also the devalued nature of the female stereotypes. In this study counselors viewed healthy adults as different from healthy females but not from healthy males; by implication counselors viewed women as less psychologically healthy than men. Women in the minds of therapists at that time were less independent and adventurous than men; they were seen as easily influenced and overly emotional. Additional studies in the mid-1970s supported the continuation of these gender-related stereotypes among counselors (Moore & Strickler, 1980).

While the presence of such stereotypes became a source of concern in itself, the helping professions were faced with the question of whether or not their presence led to negative outcomes for women who had undergone counseling or psychotherapy. Over the past decade and a half this issue has been hotly contested and examined. It seems that a review of the evidence (Whitley, 1979; Smith, 1980) does not support the view that therapy is unhealthy for women. On the other hand, many issues remain regarding the ability of the therapy professions to respond to the unique needs and aspirations of female clients.

The alarm set off regarding sexist practices in the helping professions has been responded to vigorously by our professional associations and the federal government. The Education Amendments Act of 1972 opened up many new opportunities for women. Early in the sexism debate the American Association for Counseling and Development (then the American Personnel and Guidance Association) published the following strong position papers on sex-fair counseling practices: "Standards for the Preparation of Counselors and Other Personnel Services Specialists" (ACES, 1973); "Career Guidance: Role and Function of Counseling and Guidance Personnel Practitioners in Career Education" (APGA, 1974); and "Position Paper on Counselor Preparation for Career Development/Career Education" (ACES, 1978).

The American Psychological Association in turn has addressed sexism with the following: the report from the National Conference on Levels and Patterns of Professional Training in Psychology (APA, 1973); the report of the Task Force on Issues of Sex Bias in Graduate Education (APA, 1975a); the report of the Task Force on Sex Bias and Sex Role Stereotyping in Psychotherapeutic Practice (APA, 1975b); and APA Division 17's "Principles Concerning the Counseling and Therapy of Women" (see Exhibit 7.1).

In addition, these professional associations attempted to promote sex-fair practices through the use of nonsexist language in their publications and in efforts to revise ethical standards in accord with nonsexist principles. Moore and Strickler (1980) document numerous other professional efforts to eliminate sex bias from the helping professions.

In 1980 Worell reviewed more than 500 articles dealing with ideologies, goals, needs, rationales, strategies, and research findings related to counseling women. Johnson (1979) notes this explosion of literature as a true beginning of a feminine psychology and outlines the topics such a psychology can explore with direct attention to treatment.

Much of this effort appears necessary in the helping professions in light of the fact that historically most therapy approaches emerge out of the study of males (Hare-Mustin, 1983), leaving many feminine lifestyle issues still under-

Exhibit 7.1   Principles Concerning the Counseling and Therapy of Women

Preamble

Although competent counseling/therapy processes are essentially the same for all counselor/therapist interactions, special subgroups require specialized skills, attitudes and knowledge. Women constitute a special subgroup.

Competent counseling-therapy requires recognition and appreciation that contemporary society is not sex fair. Many institutions, test standards and attitudes of mental health professionals limit the options of women clients. Counselors/therapists should sensitize women clients to these real-world limitations, confront them with both the external and their own internalized limitations and explore with them their reactions to these constraints.

The principles presented here are considered essential for the competent counseling/therapy of women.

1. Counselors/therapists are knowledgeable about women, particularly with regard to biological, psychological and social issues which have impact on women in general or on particular groups of women in our society.
2. Counselors/therapists are aware that the assumptions and precepts of theories relevant to their practice may apply differently to men and women. Counselors/therapists are aware of those theories and models that proscribe or limit the potential of women clients, as well as those that may have particular usefulness for women clients.
3. After formal training, counselors/therapists continue to explore and learn of issues related to women, including the special problems of female subgroups, throughout their professional careers.
4. Counselors/therapists recognize and are aware of all forms of oppression and how these interact with sexism.
5. Counselors/therapists are knowledgeable and aware of verbal and nonverbal process variables (particularly with regard to power in the relationship) as these affect women in counseling/therapy so that the counselor/therapist-client interactions are not adversely affected. The need for shared responsibility between clients and counselors/therapists is acknowledged and implemented.
6. Counselors/therapists have the capability of utilizing skills that are particularly facilitative to women in general and to particular subgroups of women.

(continued)

7. Counselors/therapists ascribe no pre-conceived limitations on the direction or nature of potential changes or goals in counseling/therapy for women.

8. Counselors/therapists are sensitive to circumstances where it is more desirable for a woman client to be seen by a female or male counselor/therapist.

9. Counselors/therapists use nonsexist language in counseling/therapy, supervision, teaching and journal publications.

10. Counselors/therapists do not engage in sexual activity with their women clients under any circumstances.

11. Counselors/therapists are aware of and continually review their own values and biases and the effects of these on their women clients. Counselors/therapists understand the effects of sex-role socialization upon their own development and functioning and the consequent values and attitudes they hold for themselves and others. They recognize that behaviors and roles need not be sex based.

12. Counselors/therapists are aware of how their personal functioning may influence their effectiveness in counseling/therapy with women clients. They monitor their functioning through consultation, supervision or therapy so that it does not adversely affect their work with women clients.

13. Counselors/therapists support the elimination of sex bias with institutions and individuals.

These principles were endorsed unanimously by the Division 17 Ad Hoc Committee on Women, the Executive Committee of Division 17, and the entire membership of Division 17 during the August 1978 meeting of APA in Toronto as necessary for responsible professional practice in the counseling and therapy of women. Reprinted with permission of the American Psychological Association.

treated. This applies especially to career development and counseling, where sex-bias may have had its most significant impact (Fitzgerald & Crites, 1980). Female theories of career development have begun to emerge (e.g., Astin, 1984), but are viewed as still rudimentary; the need exists to synthesize this growing body of literature on feminine psychology (Fitzgerald & Betz, 1984).

Areas of high relevance to women include marital and family relations, reproductive problems, physical and sexual abuse, depression, diagnosis based on sexist tenets, and problems associated with eating (Hare-Mustin, 1983). Fitzgerald and Crites (1980) note that women may follow a wider variety of lifestyle patterns, making adaptation more of a challenge. A key issue for women is the merging of career and family. Gray's (1980) review of the literature shows that working women still shoulder most of the burden of managing a household. Women are often put in a position of multiple-role involvements, with high expectations from themselves and others for each separate role. Helping women, then, often involves working not only with the women themselves but also with their families, friends, or associates.

Much has been accomplished in the almost two decades since the study by Broverman and co-workers. Through the efforts of mostly women, there has been a moderating of gender stereotypes in the helping professions (Brodsky & Hare-Mustin, 1980). O'Malley and Richardson (1985), in a replication of the Broverman study, found that many therapists still hold gender stereotypes, as they did in 1970. However, such stereotypes no longer cast women as less psychologically healthy. The achievements noted raise hope for other special groups in their contact with help-givers.

Sexual Preference

Coming to grips with one's sexuality is an issue commonly explored in counseling. It concerns recognizing sexual feelings, assimulating them into one's self-image, and making decisions on how to act on one's feelings and identity. This process is difficult enough when one receives considerable support from others; it can be overwhelming when the direction taken runs counter to carefully guarded norms.

Homosexuality runs counter to current societal norms. The individual grappling with a homosexual identity often finds little support. The penalties for this sexual preference have been severe. Evolving out of this has been what Weinberg (1973) coined as *homophobia:* a strong, irrational fear of homosexuality and homosexuals. Advanced by the dominant culture, it is an attempt to establish control over the incidence of homosexuality. Beane (1981) describes how both clients and counselors can bring a homophobic presence into the counseling process.

While the evidence shows that many well-adjusted gay persons follow diverse lifestyles consistent with their varied personalities (Bell & Weinberg, 1978), accepting and maintaining a gay identity and lifestyle are particularly troublesome because of the negative pressures already cited. It has been the experience of gay men and women (Groves & Ventura, 1983) that little help will result from counseling with someone other than a gay therapist; this is because of the homophobic issue. This challenges nongay counselors to evaluate themselves regarding this factor. It also demonstrates the expanse of cross-cultural counseling; cultural differences between counselor and client may result from sexual preference as well as from racial or ethnic background.

Helping with the Coming Out Process. The process of gay self-identification (coming out), compared to other gay issues, has received the most attention in the counseling literature (Beane, 1982; Sophie, 1982; Groves & Ventura, 1983). Coming out often begins with anxiety and self-rebuke as attraction toward friends of the same sex can no longer be denied. With the pressure to conceal such feelings, adolescents especially remain isolated and lack the opportunity to discover the varied nature of the gay community. Often they retain the negative stereotypes they learned earlier about that community.

When a person who is coming out turns to a counselor for help, several precautions must be mentioned. Like other important parts of one's identity, sexual preference deserves extended deliberation. Young people often have so little experience in sexual matters that they cannot establish a position on the matter. Thus, the counselor, especially the nongay counselor, needs to be gentle, accepting, nonhomophobic, and *informed*. Clients can directly benefit from some straightforward information; in some instances information regarding how to contact the gay community to learn more about it is sufficient.

A gentle, caring counselor, dealing with the issue of coming out, shows the same sensitivity as in other situations. This includes avoidance of vocabulary likely to raise anxiety, avoidance of premature labeling, recognition of the oppression of gay men and women, and the realization that the establishment of a sexual preference is just one small part of each person's existence. For the nongay therapist, helping with the coming out process requires much self-reflection and reading and some contact with the gay community.

Helping Gay Couples. Winkelpleck and Westfeld's (1982) review of the literature indicates that the majority of gay people eventually enter into a relationship with the thought of making it work and last. Yet many factors mitigate against that outcome. Besides dealing with prevailing prejudice in society, gay couples often find that they lack role models from whom to learn relationship coping skills. Gay people have no terminology (e.g., "engaged," "premarital," "marriage") to express the nature of their relationships.

The patterns of forming relationships vary. Groves and Ventura (1983) cite literature that shows that gay men enter committed relationships after establishing a gay identity; women, on the other hand, often enter into a committed relationship with another woman before accepting themselves as lesbians. While heterosexual partners have available many sources of assistance with such problems as sexual dysfunction, gay couples do not. Gerontological counseling for gay couples is another area not being addressed (Winkelpleck & Westfeld, 1982).

Alternative Lifestyles

It seems that the counseling profession has taken the position that the overall interests of individuals and society are served more effectively in a pluralistic culture that recognizes the validity of multiple lifestyles than in a culture that has a narrow view of acceptable lifestyles. Patterns of living or lifestyles can be divided into traditional ones, supported openly by the majority, and alternative ones, occurring less often and usually not endorsed by society at large.

If marriage and children represent the core of a traditional lifestyle, some alternatives include communal living, single living, and child-free marriages. To any of these can be added such conditions as celibacy, living together without formal marriage, or simple nonmaterialistic living—lifestyles that have been difficult to understand and accept not only by society in general, but by some counselors as well.

It is important to recognize that many social institutions support and actively assist persons leading traditional lives, but few do the same for those adopting alternative patterns. It makes sense to see that counselors are needed to fill the gap.

To meet this need counselors must accept any lifestyle in itself that is not better or worse than any other, except for those that violate the rights of others (e.g., survivalists). Yet a particular lifestyle, including a traditional one, can be better or worse for a given individual than another lifestyle. A person's potential may be advanced by access to an alternative lifestyle that provides personal meaning and fulfills social needs.

The Single, Never-Married Lifestyle.   This lifestyle is an example of an alternative lifestyle that is often misunderstood in the helping professions. It is commonly held that married persons are better adjusted, more happy, and more well-rounded. Single, never-married individuals are supposed to be lonely, conflicted, narcissistic, and possibly schizoid. In reality, single people are a diverse group, coming from a variety of backgrounds, and manifesting heterogeneous demographic characteristics (Stein, 1978). Johnston and Eklund (1984), in their careful review of the literature on the life-adjustment of never-marrieds and marrieds, show no clear support for the above stereotype. While the research tends to support single males as less well-adjusted than married males, non-married females seem to be better adjusted than married females.

Counseling single individuals should have the same goal as all counseling; helping the client more fully develop within the context of a valid chosen lifestyle. Assumptions about the lifestyle by the counselors need to be examined carefully. Like all lifestyles, being single has its advantages and disadvantages (Edwards & Hoover, 1974).

Johnston and Eklund (1984) note that social support and satisfaction of intimacy needs are key issues in working with singles. In an adult society dominated by couples and extended family contacts, singles often need creative methods for ensuring contact with others. Such contacts need to be planned and regularly scheduled, especially if one is out of school or away from settings in which many other singles are present. Diversified friendship networks that allow for intimate sharing might even be something counselors actively promote as part of their service to singles.

Using single persons as an example of an alternative lifestyle makes the point that social roles are often a veneer under which lie universal strivings for meaning. Cross-cultural counselors are good at seeing those strivings.

STUDENT LEARNING EXERCISE
Read the following descriptions of situations and indicate whether you think the counselor responded effectively. Circle Y for yes or N for no.

1. The counselor working in a women's center specializes in such issues as marital/family relations, eating disorders, sexual abuse, and depression.   Y   N

2. A counselor generalizes characteristics of relationships of gay men to gay women.   Y   N

3. A counselor interprets a celibate lifestyle as indicative of sexual problems.   Y   N

4. A group of college counselors hold a discussion group with minority students to broaden the counselors' understanding of cross-cultural issues in hopes of being more help to the students.   Y   N

Old Age

The historic roots of counseling lie in the service of adolescents and young adults making key decisions about their lives. As the profession has grown, new populations have been added so that now clients of all ages are served. In the future aged clients will likely make up a large part of a counselor's caseload. This will be true especially because of the increasing lifespan of people as a result of medical breakthroughs in the treatment of cancer and heart disease.

Counselor stereotypes of the aged are likely to be the most challenged stereotypes in the future. The Social Security Administration (Irelan, Motley, Schwab, Sherman, & Murray, 1976) found that major differences occurred every six years among groups of retirees seeking benefits. This evidence may well challenge the validity of most theories on old age. At a minimum, what we have considered the problems of the aged will likely apply to increasingly older individuals.

Glass and Grant (1983) attend specifically to some of the issues affecting persons beyond 75 years of age. While chronological age is often not a reliable index of the issues associated with the last stage of human development, the likelihood for such clients experiencing significant physical and social loss are greater than for younger clients. Institutionalization of this age group is often done inappropriately, without consideration of less restrictive but effective services (Subcommittee on Human Services of the Select Committee on Aging, 1980). Counselors can ally themselves with other professionals to increase their knowledge of gerontology (i.e., the study of the aging process) to further ensure the meaningfulness of this life stage. In part this may mean the support of the continued independence of clients in advanced age. This support can be operationalized in terms of adequate income, quality health care, social involvement, a variety of housing arrangements, and reinforcement of coping skills associated with younger groups.

Handicapping Conditions

With the implementation of The Rehabilitation Act of 1973 (P.L. 93–112) and the Education for All Handicapped Children Act of 1975 (P.L. 94–142), the legal mechanisms to more fully integrate disabled adults and children have been established. The counseling profession needs to continue its efforts to maximize the intents of these laws.

Nathanson (1979) reviews some of the literature on the attitudes of professionals who deal with individuals with disabilities or handicaps. Not immune to bias, counselors often unconsciously reveal their problems with such conditions. Nathanson identifies the following as common counselor violations of the integrity of disabled persons:

1. To perceive one handicapping condition as spreading to other aspects of the person so that the whole individual is evaluated by a single physical characteristic.
2. To falsely pity the individual by seeing him or her as fragile, hopeless, suffering, frustrated, and rejected.
3. To damage the individual's opportunity for accountability and self-reliance by too readily encouraging others to give the disabled person "a break."
4. To dampen the enthusiasm and optimism of the client by too quickly setting limits on action in hopes of avoiding failure.
5. To reject the client by being unable to cope with the client's physical deformity without displaying revulsion and disgust.
6. To overvalue the achievements of a client as "amazing" or "outstanding," with the implication that most disabled persons are inferior.

To effectively deal with disabled populations, counselors need considerable background knowledge and a variety of skills, in addition to an examination of their own attitudes and their use of language. Exhibit 7.2 provides guidelines regarding the latter. With an emphasis on the younger client, Hosie (1979) lists the following areas of emphasis in pre- and in-service training:

1. Federal and state legislation, guidelines, and local policies relating to programs and services for the handicapped.
2. Rights of handicapped children and their parents, and the skills necessary to advise parents and enable them to exercise their rights.
3. State guidelines for classification, diagnostic tools and their limitations, and the skills necessary to relate these to learning characteristics and the common elements of correction.

4. Informal assessment procedures and the skills necessary to relate these to the special learning strategies of the handicapped.

5. Growth and development process, characteristics, and the impediments of the handicapped, and the skills necessary to relate this knowledge to developmental learning tasks and strategies.

6. Characteristics and development of the learning disabled and the skills necessary to diagnose why the individual is failing tasks and to change methods and objectives when necessary.

7. Sensory impairments, speech disorders, and communication deficits, their effect on diagnosis and remediation, and the skills necessary to overcome or lessen their effect in learning and counseling settings.

8. Input, structure, and potential outcomes of the Individual Educational Program (IEP), and the skills necessary to consult and assist in the construction of such a program for the mainstreamed student.

9. Ability, learning rates, and modes of learning of the handicapped, and the skills necessary to utilize these factors in recommending educational placements and environments.

10. Attitudinal biases of teachers and others and the skills necessary to teach and consult with regular and special educators to produce a facilitative learning environment.

11. Learning disorders, the social and emotional behavior problems of handicapped students, and the skills necessary to instruct and consult with teachers, using behavior modification and management principles to enhance academic learning and social behavior.

12. Potential growth and development of the handicapped child; fears, concerns, and needs of the parents; and the skills necessary to consult, counsel, and teach parents regarding methods to facilitate their child's academic and social development.

13. Characteristics of the handicapped related to employment skills, training programs, and potential occupational and educational opportunities, and the skills necessary to assist the individual in career decision-making and development.

14. Roles and skills of other personnel within and outside the institution and the skills necessary to refer them or work with them to enhance the learning and development of the handicapped individual.

Exhibit 7.2   Guidelines for Reporting and Writing About People with Disabilities

Introduction

Media professionals are in a unique position to shape the public image of persons with disabilities. The words and images they use can create an insensitive, negative portrayal or a straightforward, positive view of persons with disabilities.

There has never been a clear set of guidelines to help media professionals make the right choices in terms of language and portrayal. The guidelines presented here offfer suggestions for appropriate descriptions and preferred terminology. They reflect input from over 50 national disability organizations and have been reviewed and endorsed by media and disability experts. These guidelines are currently being considered for inclusion in the Associated Press' 1985 Stylebook. Although opinions may differ on some terms, these guidelines represent the current consensus.

Please read through the guidelines and consult them when writing about persons with disabilities. If you have questions or would like additional information, contact your local independent living center, or write: Media Project, Research and Training Center on Independent Living, 348 Haworth Hall, University of Kansas, Lawrence, Kansas 66045.

Portrayal Issues

Please consider the following when writing about persons with disabilities.

1. Do not refer to a disability unless it is crucial to a story.
2. Avoid portraying persons with disabilities who succeed as superhuman. This implies that persons who are disabled have no talents or unusual gifts.
3. Do not sensationalize a disability by saying afflicted with, victim of, and so on. Instead, say *person who has multiple sclerosis, person who had polio.*
4. Avoid labeling persons into groups, as in the disabled, the deaf, a retardate, an arthritic. Instead, say *people who are deaf, person with arthritis, persons with disabilities.*
5. Where possible, emphasize an individual, not a disability. Say *people* or *persons with disabilities* or *person who is blind* rather than disabled persons or blind person.
6. Avoid using emotional descriptors such as unfortunate, pitiful, and so on. Emphasize abilities, such as *uses a wheelchair/braces* rather than confined to a wheelchair, *walks with crutches/braces* rather than is crippled, is *partially sighted* rather than partially blind.
7. Avoid implying disease when discussing disabilities. A disability such as Parkinson's disease may be caused by a sickness, but it is not a disease itself, nor is the person necessarily chronically ill. Persons with disabilities should not be referred to as patients or cases unless they are under medical care.

Appropriate Terminology for Specific Disabilities

Listed below are preferred words that reflect a positive attitude in portraying disabilities. The general terms disability and handicap are described first, but remaining terms are listed alphabetically.

Disability (disabled, physically disabled). General term used for a (semi)permanent condition that interferes with a person's ability to do something independently—walk, see, hear, learn, lift. It may refer to a physical, mental, or sensory condition. Preferred usage is as a descriptive noun or adjective, as in *persons who are disabled, people with disabilities,* or *disabled persons.* Terms such as the disabled, crippled, deformed, or invalid are inappropriate.

Handicap. Often used as a synonym for disability. However, usage has become less acceptable (one origin is from "cap in hand," as in begging). Except when citing laws or regulations, handicap should not be used to describe a disability. Say, "The stairs are a *handicap* for her," but not, "The handicapped child could not use the stairs."

Blind. Describes a person with total loss of vision. Not appropriate for persons with partial vision. Use *partially sighted, with partial vision, visually impaired.*

Congenital disability. Describes a disability that has existed since birth. The term birth defect is not appropriate.

Deaf. Describes a person with a total hearing loss. Not appropriate for persons with partial hearing. Use *with a partial hearing loss,* or *hearing impairment,* or *hearing impaired.*

Developmental disability. Any mental and/or physical disability incurred before the age of 22 that may continue indefinitely. The disability may substantially limit major activities and require lifelong support. Term includes individuals with mental retardation, cerebral palsy, autism, epilepsy, sensory impairments, congenital disabilities, traumatic accidents, or other disease processes.

Down's syndrome. Preferred over mongoloid to describe a form of mental retardation caused by improper chromosomal division during gestation.

Mentally ill/mental disorder. Describes a person who has lost the social and/or vocational skills necessary to function independently. Terms such as mentally deranged, deviant, and crazy are inappropriate. *Mental disorder* is a more comprehensive term that describes any of the recognized forms of mental illness, severe emotional disorder, or mental retardation. Terms such as neurotic, psychotic, psychopathic, and schizophrenic should be reserved for technical medical writing.

Mental retardation. Describes a person with significantly below-average general intellectual functioning. Terms such as moron, mentally deficient/defective, and feeble-minded are inappropriate.

Mute/Person who cannot speak. Preferred terms to describe persons who cannot speak. Terms such as deaf/mute and deaf and dumb are inappropriate. They imply that persons without speech are always deaf.

Nondisabled. In a media portrayal of persons with and without disabilities, nondisabled is the appropriate term. Able-bodied should not be used, since it implies that persons with disabilities are less able. Normal is only appropriate in reference to statistical norms.

Seizure. Describes an involuntary muscular contraction symptomatic of the brain disorder, epilepsy. Rather than saying epileptic, say *a person with epilepsy* or *person with a seizure disorder*. The term convulsion should be reserved for seizures involving contractions of the entire body. The term *fit* is used by the medical profession in England, but it has strong negative connotations.

Spastic. Describes a muscle with sudden, abnormal involuntary spasms. It is not appropriate for describing a person with cerebral palsy. Muscles are spastic, not people.

Special. Describes that which is different or uncommon about *any* person. Except when citing laws or regulations, it is not an appropriate term to describe persons with disabilities in general.

Specific learning disability (S.L.D.). Describes a disorder in the ability to learn effectively in a regular educational environment. Does not include persons with vision, hearing, or motor impairment, those who are mentally retarded or emotionally disturbed, or persons who are environmentally, culturally, or economically disadvantaged. The term *specific* learning disability is preferred, because it emphasizes that the disability affects only certain learning processes.

Speech impaired. Describes persons with limited or difficult speech patterns.

Used with permission from the Research and Training Center on Independent Living, 348 Haworth Hall, University of Kansas, Lawrence, Kansas 66045.

PREPARING COUNSELORS TO WORK WITH SPECIAL POPULATIONS

Whether one is preparing to enter the counseling profession or a veteran striving to develop further as a cross-cultural counselor, there are a number of general strategies that augment practice with diverse client populations. First and foremost is a journey inward for the examination of hidden prejudices and misconceptions. There exists a wealth of literature to bombard those beliefs.

Second, contact with minority members of minority groups and the development of close friendships can provide personal "interpreters" for various subcultural issues. Preparation programs can assist by working actively to recruit minority candidates. Friends can warmly challenge one another and provide access to broadly based experiences with numerous subcultures.

Third, with greater experience as a transcultural person comes the need to analyze and synthesize those adventures. Important questions need to be answered: How far do cultural differences go in actual work with clients? What about common human traits that transcend culture? Where are we in history regarding the rapprochement of cultures? In the future, how much further will we advance toward such things as androgeny, transnationalism, and so forth? What is the formula for maintaining unique background and heritage and universal humanness in one's identity?

The ending has not been written for the counseling profession in its effort to serve special populations. However, the beginning, the ideal, and the direction are clear. Counselors as human beings *are* striving to achieve more fully what has begun.

SUMMARY

This chapter explored the evolution of the counseling profession in its attempts to meet the needs of special client populations. Cross-cultural counseling was described. Barriers that can affect clients and counselors from different cultural backgrounds were examined.

REVIEW QUESTIONS

1. Define cross-cultural counseling and contrast it to counseling lacking sensitivity to cultural issues.
2. List and briefly describe barriers to cross-cultural counseling.
3. Describe some of the issues related to gender that have influenced the counseling profession and other helping professions.
4. How does sexual preference of the client influence the delivery of counseling profession?
5. What special sensitivities are important for counselors working with physically disabled clients?
6. How might a counselor-in-training prepare to meet cross-cultural issues?

REFERENCES

Acosta, G. (1980). Self-described reasons for premature termination of psychotherapy by Mexican-American, Black American, and Anglo-American patients. *Psychological Reports, 47*(3), 435–443.

American Personnel and Guidance Association. (1974). "Career guidance: Role and function of counseling and guidance personnel practitioners in career education." Washington, DC: Author.

American Psychological Association. (1975). Report of the task force on sex bias and sex-role stereotyping in psychotherapeutic practice. *American Psychologist, 30*(12), 1169–1175.

American Psychological Association. (1978). Task force on sex bias and sex-role stereotyping in psychotherapeutic practice. Guidelines for therapy with women. *American Psychologist, 33*(12), 1122–1123.

Association for Counselor Education and Supervision. (1973). "Standards for the preparation of counselors and other personnel services specialists." Washington, DC: Author (mimeograph).

Association for Counselor Education and Supervision. (1978). Position paper on counselor preparation for career development/career education. *Counselor Education and Supervision, 17*(3), 178–179.

Arrendondo-Dowd, P. M., & Gonsalves, J. (1980). Preparing culturally effective counselors. *Personnel and Guidance Journal, 58*(10), 657–661.

Astin, H. S. (1984). The meaning of work in women's lives. *The Counseling Psychologist, 12*(4), 117–126.

Atkinson, D. R., Morten, G., & Sue, D. W. (1979). *Counseling American minorities: A cultural perspective.* Dubuque, IA: Wm. C. Brown.

Beane, J. (1981). "I'd rather be dead than gay": Counseling gay men who are coming out. *Personnel and Guidance Journal, 60*(4), 222–226.

Belkin, G. S. (1984). *Introduction to counseling.* Dubuque, IA: Wm. C. Brown.

Bell, A. P., & Weinberg, M. S. (1978). *Homosexualities.* New York: Simon and Schuster.

Brodsky, A. M., & Hare-Mustin, R. T. (1980). *Women and psychotherapy: An assessment of research and practice.* New York: Guilford.

Broverman, D. M., Broverman, I., Clarkson, F. E., Rosenkrantz, P. S., & Vogel, S. (1970). Sex-role stereotypes and clinical judgments of mental health. *Journal of Clinical and Consulting Psychology, 34*(1) 1–7.

Copeland, E. J. (1982). Minority populations and traditional counseling programs: Some alternatives. *Counselor Education and Supervision, 21*(3), 187–193.

Copeland, E. J. (1983). Cross-cultural counseling and psychotherapy: A historical perspective. *Personnel and Guidance Journal, 62*(1), 10–15.

Dohrenwend, B. P., & Dohrenwend, B. S. (1974). Social and cultural influences on psychopathology. *Annual Review of Psychology, 25,* 417–452.

Edwards, M., & Hoover, E. (1974). *The challenge of being single.* Los Angeles: J. P. Tarcher.

Fitzgerald, L. F., & Betz, N. E. (1984). Astin's model in theory and practice: A technical and philosophical critique. *The Counseling Psychologist, 12*(4), 135–138.

Fitzgerald, L. F. & Crites, J. O. (1980). Toward a career psychology of women: What do we know? What do we need to know? *Journal of Counseling Psychology, 27*(1), 44–62.

Garfield, S. L. (1978). Research on client variables in psychotherapy. In S. L. Garfield and A. E. Bergin (Ed.), *Handbook of psychotherapy and behavior change* (pp. 271–278). New York: John Wiley and Sons.

Glass, J. C., & Grant, K. A. (1983). Counseling in the later years: A growing need. *Personnel and Guidance Journal, 62*(4), 210–213.

Gray, J. D. (1980). Counseling women who want both a profession and a family. *Personnel and Guidance Journal, 59(1),* 43–45.

Groves, P. A., & Ventura, L. A. (1983). The lesbian coming out process: Therapeutic considerations. *Personnel and Guidance Journal, 62*(3), 146–149.

Hall, G. C. N., & Maloney, H. N. (1983). Cultural control in psychotherapy with minority clients. *Psychotherapy: Theory, Research, and Practice, 20*(1), 131–142.

Hare-Mustin, R. T. (1983). An appraisal of the relationship between women and psychotherapy: 80 years after the case of Dora. *American Psychologist, 38*(5), 593–601.

Herskovits, M. (1955). *Cultural anthropology.* New York: A. A. Knopf.

Hosie, T. W. (1979). Preparing counselors to meet the needs of the handicapped. *Personnel and Guidance Journal, 58*(4), 271–275.

Ibrahim, F. A. (1985). Effective cross-cultural counseling and psychotherapy: A framework. *The Counseling Psychologist, 13*(4), 625–638.

Irelan, L. M., Motley, D. K., Schwab, K., Sherman, S. R., & Murray, J. (1976). *Almost 65: Baseline data from the retirement history study.* U.S. Dept. of Health, Education and Welfare Research Report No. 49/HEW Publication No. (SSA) 76–11806.

Johnson, M. (1979). A knowledge base for counselors of women. *The Counseling Psychologist, 8*(1), 14–16.

Johnston, M. V. & Eklund, S. J. (1984). Life-adjustment of the never-married: A review with implications for counseling. *Journal of Counseling and Development, 63* (4) 230–236.

Knott, B. (1982). *Truly tasteless jokes.* New York: Ballantine Books.

Korchin, S. J. (1976). *Modern clinical psychology.* New York: Basic Books.

Korchin, S. J. (1980). Clinical psychology and minority concerns. *American Psychologist, 35*(3), 262–269.

Kroeber, A. L., & Kluckhohn, C. (1952). *Culture: A critical review of concepts and definitions.* New York: Vintage Books.

Larson, P. G. (1982). Counseling special populations. *Professional Psychology: Research and Practice, 13*(3), 843–857.

Locke, D. C. (1986). Cross-cultural counseling issues. In A. J. Palmo & W. J. Weikel (Eds.), *Foundations of mental health counseling* (pp. 119–137). Springfield, IL: Charles C Thomas Publisher.

Marsella, A. J., & Pedersen, P. B. (1981). Cross-cultural counseling and psychotherapy. New York: Pergamon Press.

Moore, H., & Strickler, C. (1980). The counseling profession's response to sex-biased counseling: An update. *Personnel and Guidance Journal, 59*(1), 84–87.

Nathanson, R. (1979). Counseling persons with disabilities: Are the feelings, thoughts, and behaviors of helping professionals helpful? *Personnel and Guidance Journal, 58*(4), 233–237.

O'Malley, K. M., & Richardson, S. (1985). Sex bias in counseling: Have things changed? *Journal of Counseling and Development, 63*(5), 294–299.

Paradis, F. E. (1981). Themes in the training of culturally effective psychotherapists. *Counselor Education and Supervision, 21*(2), 136–151.

Pedersen, P. B., & Marsella, A. J. (1982). The ethical crisis for cross-cultural counseling and therapy. *Professional Psychology, 13* (4), 492–500.

Raynes, A., & Warren, G. (1969). Some distinguishing features of patients failing to attend a psychiatric clinic after referred. *American Journal of Orthopsychiatry, 41*(4), 581–588.

Smith, M. L. (1980). Sex bias in counseling and psychotherapy. *Psychological Bulletin, 87*(3), 492–507.

Sophie, J. (1982). Counseling lesbians. *The Personnel and Guidance Journal, 60* (6), 341–345.

Subcommittee on Human Services of the Select Committee on Aging, U.S. House of Representatives, 96th Congress (1980). *Future directions for aging policy: A human services model.* Washington, DC: U.S. Government Printing Office.

Sue, D. W. (1978). Counseling across cultures. *Personnel and Guidance Journal, 56*(8), 451.

Sue, D. W. (1981). *Counseling the culturally different: Theory and practice.* New York: John Wiley and Sons.

Sue, D. W., & Sue, S. (1977). Barriers to effective cross-cultural counseling. *Journal of Counseling Psychology, 24*(5), 420–429.

Sue, S. (1977). Community mental health services to minority groups. *American Psychologist, 32,* 616–624.

Sue, S. (1983). Ethnic minority issues in psychology. *American Psychologist, 38*(5), 583–592.

Sundberg, N. D. (1981). Cross-cultural counseling: A research overview. In A. J. Marsella, and P. B. Pedersen (Eds.), *Cross-cultural counseling and psychotherapy.* New York: Pergamon Press.

Whitley, B. E. (1979). Sex roles and psychotherapy: A current appraisal. *Psychological Bulletin, 86*(4), 1309–1321.

Winkelpleck, J. M., & Westfeld, J. S. (1982). Counseling considerations with gay couples. *Personnel and Guidance Journal, 60*(7), 294–296.

Weinberg, G. (1973). *Society and the healthy homosexual.* Garden City, NY: Doubleday/Anchor.

Worell, J. (1980). New directions in counseling women. *Personnel and Guidance Journal, 58*(7), 477–484.

8

Consultation

GOALS OF THE CHAPTER

The primary aims of this chapter are to introduce the major models of consultation and to illustrate how these might be employed.

CHAPTER PREVIEW

1. Three major models of consultation will be presented: mental health, behavioral, and organizational.
2. The stages of consultation will be reviewed along with salient research findings.
3. Consultation will be contrasted with other interventions employed by counselors in terms of its efficiency, effectiveness, and acceptability.

INTRODUCTION

When used colloquially, "consultation" is often seen as synonymous with "advice giving." People regularly consult with their banker, stock broker, physician, and so forth. The type of process envisioned in these consultations, which involves relying on an expert, is an accepted model of consultation among human services workers. However, consultation has taken on a much broader meaning for most. Perhaps the best way to proceed with defining consultation is not to describe what it is, but rather to tell what it is not.

First, consultation and supervision are not the same (Brown, Pryzwansky, & Schulte, 1987; Caplan, 1970). Supervision is a process that involves a superordinate-subordinate relationship in which one party, the supervisor, has an evaluative role. Consultants, however, usually attempt to develop collegial relationships and have no evaluative role (Brown et al., 1987; Caplan 1970). Consultation and supervision do generally converge on one point: the recipients of the processes, the consultee and the supervisee, are expected to gain knowledge and skills as a result of their interaction with the consultant and supervisor, respectively.

One process that is often confused with consulting is training. It is not uncommon to hear counselors indicate that they have entered into a consulting relationship when in fact the service they are going to deliver involves a seminar or workshop. Training is a direct service and "is a process of imparting, in a planned, systematic way, a specified body of information" (Conoley & Conoley, 1982, p. 4). Consultation diverges from training in that it is an indirect service since the focus of the consultation (the client) is not present when the consultant and consultee meet. In addition, trainers often rely on one-way communication, are generally in positions of authority, and have set agendas. None of these conditions apply to consultation. It should be noted that while consultation and training are not analogous, it is not uncommon for consultants to employ training as an adjunct to consultation (Brown et al., 1987).

Consultation and organizational development (OD) are also frequently confused. "Organizational development" is a term used to depict a variety of services aimed at improving the functioning of organizations, including training (teaching), applied research and evaluation, and consultation (Lippitt & Lippitt, 1978). Organizational development is an umbrella under which a variety of developmental processes may be placed and in which counselors will be involved.

Perhaps the helping process that diverges most sharply from consultation is counseling. Consultation is an indirect service in that its aim is to help the consultee develop the skills needed to assist a client. Counseling is a direct service to clients. The aim of counseling is to assist clients with psychological difficulties that have already manifested themselves to some degree. Consultants refrain from dealing with the psychological difficulties of consultees, although they may have as one of their objectives helping consultees develop strategies to assist clients with psychological problems. When counseling and consultation are aimed at ameliorating an existing psychological difficulty, they are secondary or tertiary mental health prevention approaches. Secondary prevention efforts are aimed at eliminating problems before they have serious consequences, and tertiary prevention efforts have as their objectives the reduction of debilitating psychological problems, such as alcoholism, to reduce their overall impact. While consultation can be used as a secondary or tertiary mental health intervention, it can also be used as primary prevention strategy, that is, one aimed at preventing the onset of mental health problems (Brown et al., 1987).

CONSULTATION DEFINED

What then is consultation? It is first and foremost a problem-solving process with a twofold aim: (1) to assist consultees acquire the knowledge and skills needed to solve a problem of concern to them, and (2) to help consultees implement what they have learned to assist a third party, the client. The client may be an individual (a child), a group, a family, an organization, a business, or an entire community (Lippitt & Lippitt, 1978).

The consulting relationship, which is often preferred to as "triadic" because of the focus of the consultant and consultee upon the client, is an egalitarian one, and as a result consultation must be viewed as a totally voluntary process (Dinkmeyer & Carlson, 1973; Gallessich, 1982; Reynolds, Gutkin, Elliot, & Witt, 1984). In addition, effective consulting relationships are characterized by a collaborative spirit in which the consultant and consultee often share the responsibility for identifying the problem at hand, generating solutions to the problem, and implementing those solutions (Brown et al., 1987; Pryzwansky, 1974; Randolph, 1985). It should be pointed out that some consultants, most notably Caplan (1970), disagree with the idea that the consultant should be involved in implementing the intervention strategy. However, the rationale for this position is that the limited empirical data available on this issue suggest that consultees prefer this approach (Babcock & Pryzwansky, 1983).

Caplan's (1970) definition of consultation indicates that it occurs between two professionals (e.g., a counselor and a social worker), as opposed to between a professional and a lay person (e.g., a counselor and a parent). A number of authorities (Bergan, 1977; Lippitt & Lippitt, 1978; Meyers, Parsons, & Martin, 1979; Randolph, 1985) have taken issue with this assertion and have posited that consultation can occur between a consultant and either a professional or a lay person. Whether consultation occurs between a professional or a lay person, its purpose is to solve a "work problem" being experienced by the consultee. A teacher might be concerned about a misbehaving child, or a plant manager might focus on the productivity of his or her operation. Parents might seek consultation regarding an adolescent who is a drug abuser, and the head of a neighborhood action group might ask a consultant to assist the group to become more influential in the city's problem-solving strategies (Heller, 1985; Snapp & Davidson, 1982).

Consultants can operate effectively from either outside (external) or inside (internal) the agency or organization employing the consultee (Lippitt & Lippitt, 1978). Tradition has held that effective consultants can only operate from an external frame of reference (Caplan, 1970; Gallessich, 1982). However, during the past 10 years this position has given way to one that recognizes that the locus of the consultant, while influencing such factors as consultant status, knowledge of the consulting setting, ability to relate to individuals in authority positions, and a number of others, may not be the major factor in consultants' ability to function (Brown et al., 1987).

Finally, consultation moves through a number of rather well-defined stages, although not necessarily in lock step order. These stages are relationship, problem identification, goal setting, strategy development and implementation, and evaluation.

STUDENT LEARNING EXERCISE

Read the following descriptions of incidences and indicate whether what the counselor is doing is actually consultation or not. Circle Y for yes or N for no.

1. A mental health counselor is asked by a halfway house for alcoholics to assist in its staff development program by providing assertation training for all house parents.   Y   N
2. A school counselor assists a teacher to develop an achievement motivation program for underachieving mathematics students.   Y   N
3. A college counselor works with a group of residence assistants to assist them to develop a study skills program for the students in their respective residences.   Y   N
4. A mental health counselor routinely assists the mental health workers in his agency to assess the severity of eating disorders and to design appropriate treatment or referral programs.   Y   N

THE CONSULTING PROCESS—GENERAL CONSIDERATIONS

In the preceding section, an overview of consultation was presented along with a discussion of three major models of consultation. In the models sections, some insight was provided regarding the consulting process, which was defined at the outset as being roughly analogous to problem solving. In this section, more attention will be accorded the process. The intent here is to provide a generic overview of the steps in consultation and some of the significant empirical findings regarding them.

The Consulting Relationship.   The nature and quality of the consultation relationship are as important in consultation as they are in counseling and, not surprisingly, the development of this relationship requires many of the same types of skills needed in other helping relationships. Schowengerdt, Fine, and Poggio (1976) found that the presence of facilitative conditions such as empathy and warmth accounted for a large proportion of the variance (44%) in consultee satisfaction. The communication skills learned in basic counseling courses appear to generalize quite nicely to consultation.

Similarly, structuring the consulting relationship is viewed as essential to effective consultation (Brown et al., 1987). This involves establishing role relationships, agreeing that problem solving is important, making a commitment to spend the time needed to pursuing problem resolution, and planning for termination. Of these aspects of structuring, two probably require further elaboration: role relationships and planning for termination.

In the definition set forth in the early stages for this chapter, the consulting relationship was characterized as collaborative, which in this context is translated literally as assuming a joint responsibility for each phase of the consultation. Research has supported this idea (Babcock & Pryzwansky, 1983). One barrier to this is that consultees often ascribe expertise to the consultant, thus tilting the power relationship to the consultant. Caplan (1970) and Meyers, Parsons, and Martin (1979) warn against allowing this situation to occur, since the consultee may be reluctant to take an active part because he or she is intimidated by the consultant's knowledge or may feel coerced into accepting the consultant's suggestions because of the so-called expertise of the consultant. This can lead to lack of participation on the part of the consultee, and thus lack of ownership of the process by the consultee. Not only must consultants "structure in" egalitarianism, they must practice it as the relationship evolves (Brown et al., 1987).

It is also important that, at the outset, the consultant and consultee plan for termination. The goal of consultation is to produce a consultee who can function independently of the consultant. Establishing the expectation that termination will occur at the point the presenting problem has been resolved can assist in the attainment of this goal.

Problem Identification.   Problem identification depends on the ability of the consultant and consultee to generate sufficient information about the client, the consultee's interaction with the client, and the consultee to provide an adequate data base for assessment. A facilitative relationship will enhance this process. So will the ability of the consultant to introduce consulting leads that will elicit the needed information. Bergan (1977) suggests that these leads or elicitors as he terms them must be focused on seven categories. These are defined as follows:

1. *Background-environment:* historical variables that might influence the current situation.
2. *Behavior-setting:* the immediate environment in which the problematic behavior occurs.
3. *Behavior:* precise description of the client's problematic behavior.

4. *Observational data:* reports of systematic observation of the client.
5. *Client characteristics:* personality variables, intelligence, physical impairments, and so on.
6. *Plans:* reports of what the consultee has tried.
7. *Other:* material not falling into the foregoing categories.

Not surprisingly, Bergan and Tombari (1976) report that consultants who were either inefficient or ineffective in identifying the client's problem were unable to make much progress in consultation. Bergan, Byrnes, and Kratochwill (1979) and Bergan and Tombari (1976) have also found that the consultant's verbalizations can influence the manner in which consultees conceptualize problems and whether they expect to solve them. It appears that Bergan's beliefs about the importance of eliciting information from the consultee have some validity.

Goal Setting.   Once the problem has been defined, the goals of consultation must be established. Unlike the counseling process, where the only concern is the client's objectives, in consultation goals need to be established for both the consultee and the client. Client goals are similar to those established for counseling clients; that is, they involve facilitating the development of coping cognitions and behaviors that will reduce stress and enhance overall adjustment. Consultee goals are analogous in many ways to those established by teachers since they involve the acquisition of skills and attitudes that will enable the consultee to deal with similar problems without the consultant in the future.
The precision of the goals of consultation is to a large extent dependent on the consultant and consultee. However, most consultants opt for specific objectives since this eases the evaluation process.

Strategy Selection/Implementation.   Once goals are established, the consultant and consultee must select a strategy to achieve these goals. Strategies used depend on a number of factors, including the biases of the consultant and consultee, the setting in which the consultation is occurring, and the wishes of the client (Bergan, 1977; Brown et al., 1987). This last variable in strategy selection, the wishes of the client, may come as a bit of a surprise since consultation has been characterized as an indirect process. It should be noted, however, that it is indirect only insofar as the consultant is concerned. Consultees, whether they be parents, teacher, psychologists, or managers, must ultimately become directly involved with the client or client groups. Therefore, since good "therapeutic" practice requires involving clients in designing their own treatment, this rule applies in consultation as well.
As was shown earlier, Caplan (1970) recommended that consultants not become involved in the implementation process. Certainly there are times when, even in a collaborative approach, involvement in strategy implementation will not be necessary. However, the educational goals, that is, the goals for the con-

sultee, can probably be better attained through collaborative efforts, although there is limited empirical support for this.

The techniques utilized to attain consultee goals are fairly standard, regardless of the approach to consultation utilized. Modeling, role playing, bibliotherapy, and feedback seem to be effective. Techniques to be avoided as much as possible are those that will foster a dependency relationship, such as too much advice giving or assuming the consultee's responsibility for action when she is prepared to take action herself.

Evaluation. The consultant is a counselor/scientist at work. Specific problems are identified and solutions are advanced. Good science requires that the outcomes be systematically evaluated. Brown and co-workers (1987) suggests that a number of evaluation designs can be employed in the evaluation of consultation. Some of these will be discussed later in this book.

Termination. Termination occurs under a variety of circumstances, the most obvious of which is when goals have been attained. However, termination may also occur when it is obvious that the consultee does not have the necessary commitment, when the consultant or consultee cannot agree on goals for the client, and when the consultee wants assistance with an unethical/illegal act (e.g., establishing personnel procedures that will discriminate against a particular group).

The consulting process can be laid out in a series of neat steps, but in reality it rarely follows them precisely. It is certainly possible that a consultant and consultee could be assessing one problem while intervening on another. It is also likely that, once having moved into assessment, goal setting, or strategy implementation, factors such as resistance or interpersonal conflict may crystallize a need to return to relationship building.

MODELS OF CONSULTATION

Earlier in this book an overview of a number of major counseling theories was presented. This section is analogous to that presentation. Because the theoretical formulations regarding consultation are in a relatively early stage, the term "model" has been selected to describe the formulations that guide consultants rather than the term "theory" because of the connotations of the terms. One author, Gallessich (1985), has decried the current state of theory building in consultation and asserted that the lack of adequate models may lead to poor consultation practice. While it must be admitted that Gallessich's point about consultation models has some validity, particularly as it relates to the availability of a single model that can be generalized to all situations and to the clarity of the formulations, existing models, if used judiciously, can provide adequate guidelines for practice.

Overviews of the three major models of consultation—mental health, behavioral, and organizational development consultation—will be presented in this section. Of these, mental health consultation (Caplan, 1970) has probably had the greatest impact on the consultation of human services professionals.

Mental Health Consultation

Following World War II, Gerald Caplan worked in a child guidance center that had responsibility for providing mental health services to 16,000 children that had fled to Israel in the aftermath of the Holocaust. To complicate matters, the children were housed in a number of facilities covering a wide geographic area. Once a referral was made, members of the team of psychiatrists, social workers, and psychologists would travel to one of these cities to deliver the service. It soon became obvious that traditional diagnostic and therapeutic services were impossible, and thus the mental health workers began to "counsel" the professionals such as social workers about ways to manage the referrals rather than provide direct services themselves. Mental health consultation was born.

As indicated earlier in this chapter, Caplan (1970) defined consultation as an interaction between two professionals for the purpose of solving a work problem being encountered by the consultee. Caplan maintained that the relationship between the consultee and consultant must be coordinate (egalitarian) in nature, but structured so that the consultant would not get involved in implementing the solution to the problem derived in consultation. Finally, Caplan asserted that, in order to be effective, consultants should come from outside the employing agency of the consultee.

Caplan's (1970) general model actually includes four types of consultation. The type selected depends on whether consultees have concern with a particular problem, are experiencing administrative difficulty, need information in their area of specialization, or need to improve their problem-solving skills. These four approaches are discussed further below.

Client-Centered Case Consultation.   The primary objective of this form of consultation is to develop a plan to deal with a particular client or group of clients. In this mode, the consultants are very much in the expert role. They diagnose the nature of the client's problem and prescribe a treatment. In some instances, the treatment is to be carried out by the consultee, in others a referral will be made for the treatment. While Caplan generally views consultee skill development as an important aspect of consultation, consultee skill development is of secondary nature in client-centered case consultation. A part of the consultation process will necessarily focus on the skills of the consultee, since consultants must devise a treatment plan, and it is likely that the consultee will carry out the plan. But since much of the consultant's time is spent with the client performing diagnostic duties, consultees may benefit little from the process.

The typical tools used in the assessment of the client's problems are clinical interviews with the client, psychological and educational tests, and verbal reports from the consultee. The consultant also seeks to understand the work setting of the consultee in order to discern whether it is supportive of the work that needs to be conducted on the client. Once the diagnosis is completed and recommendations arrived at, this information is provided to the consultee, often in written form. Consultants may conduct information-giving sessions with consultees to make certain that they completely understand the recommendations that have been made (Caplan, 1970).

Consultee-Centered Case Consultation. Unlike client-centered case consultation, the primary goal of this form of consultation is the amelioration of the weaknesses of the consultees that contribute to their inability to deal with particular cases (Caplan, 1970). Caplan provides four diagnostic categories:

(1) Lack of knowledge of psychological or social factors that are contributing to the problem or information that might contribute to the resolution of the concern.
(2) Lack of skill. In this situation, the consultee seems to understand the psychological or social factors contributing to the problem, but does not possess the skill to implement a solution.
(3) Lack of confidence. In this case the consultee does not feel she can adequately deal with a problem even though she has the knowledge base and skills to do so.
(4) Lack of objectivity. Here the consultee's perceptions do not correspond with objective indicators regarding the client's problem.

Assessment in consultee-centered case consultation requires that the consultant ask the consultee to furnish descriptions of the difficulty that he or she is experiencing. When lack of objectivity appears to be the consultee's problem, the consultant may ask for repeated descriptions in order to make sure that the individual does in fact lack objectivity.

Lack of knowledge and skills deficits may be handled rather straightforwardly by supplying the knowledge needed or by developing the skills required to deal with the client. However, Caplan (1970) believes that when a number of knowledge and/or skills deficits are encountered within an organization a better approach to dealing with them is program-centered consultation. A school counselor who encounters a number of teachers with classroom management deficits might want to become involved in program-centered consultation with the school's principal in order to begin an in-service offering that would resolve the difficulties rather than deal with each teacher individually.

Caplan (1970) does not believe that consultants should become overly involved in providing support to the consultee who lacks self-confidence. Rather he suggests that the consultant attempt to identify sources of support within the organization and link the consultee to them. For example, a mental health counselor might be linked to a marriage and family therapist who would assume responsibility for helping the counselor gain confidence in the area of family therapy.

Caplan (1970) believes that there are five underlying causes of lack of objectivity: (1) personal involvement, (2) identification, (3) transference, (4) characterological distortion, and (5) theme interference. A counselor who, out of concern for a child, takes that child into his or her home has become personally involved. Caplan suggests that the consultant's role in dealing with this concern is to encourage the individual who has become personally involved to resume her or his professional role. This can be done by simply reviewing the importance of maintaining one's personal role or by providing a model of how a professional person would react in this situation.

Identification with the client may occur when the consultee has had a similar life experience to that of the client. For example, a manager who is unable to reprimand an alcoholic employee because he himself once had a drinking problem has an identification problem. Caplan (1970) again recommends that the consultant model appropriate objective behavior for the consultee.

Transference results from unresolved personality conflicts and usually is characterized by inaccurate perceptions of the client. A consultee who has an unresolved conflict with her mother may become hostile toward a secretary in her office who is having a similar problem even though that secretary is functioning effectively. Consultants should ask consultees to observe the secretary more closely, perhaps even suggesting that the consultee collect objective data about the secretary's performance. The consultant may also offer objective observations of the secretary's performance.

Characterological disorders are rather severe personality disturbances. While it is outside the consultant's role to deal with the disorder itself, Caplan (1970) believes that consultants can offer assistance by providing a model of objectivity. A mental health counselor, consulting with the supervisor of a group care home for emotionally disturbed adolescents, might discover that the consultee lacks the ability to establish meaningful relationships. The consultant in this case might assist the consultee in dealing with his or her anxiety in this area and provide a model of effective means of relating to the adolescents.

Theme interference is one of the most frequently occurring contributors to lack of objectivity, and Caplan (1970) believes it is fairly normal. Theme interference, like some of the other concerns mentioned, stems from an unresolved personality conflict and manifests itself in the form of a syllogism characterized by a faulty premise and an illogical conclusion. For example, a teacher might believe that all persons who make low grades will end up as failures in life. Thus, poor grades (A) always lead to failure in life (B). This syllogism is impenetrable by logic since some unresolved conflict provides the "logic" for it. Persons who experience theme interference may try a number of ill-conceived solutions to the problem they perceive and may report these "extensive" efforts to the consultant.

Two solutions to theme interference are possible: unlinking the faulty premise from the conclusion and theme interference reduction. Unlinking occurs when the consultant persuades the client that A and B are not necessarily related in the particular case (i.e., poor grades do not dictate failure in life). Caplan believes that unlinking is a gross error because it leaves the theme intact. He suggests that the consultant reduce the theme as follows.

The first technique for reducing theme interference is to examine case details in detail and consider all the possible outcomes and causes of the problem as presented. Thus, a consultant could help a teacher understand that a variety of correctable factors may be the cause of the problem as well as the possibility that outcomes other than failure are possible. Consultants may also tell parables based on their own experiences that contradict the inevitable outcome seen by the teacher. For example, to reduce theme interference in our hypothetical teacher, the consultant might tell of a situation in which a teacher predicted a gloomy outcome for a poor student in class. Later the student became motivated, did well, and was successful.

The consultant may also communicate to the consultee that his or her expectations regarding the client are unrealistic. Caplan (1970) cautions that this should not be done in a confrontive manner. Finally, Caplan notes that consultee's themes may manifest themselves in the consulting relationship. A police officer consultee—one who is absolutely certain that all juvenile delinquents will end up as convicted criminals—may have difficulty with authority. (A = People who defy authority by breaking the law; B = criminals incarcerated for their crimes.) The consultee might manifest this theme by taking issue with suggestions made by the consultant. The consultant should not engage in disputes with the consultee, that is, should not disprove the "logic" and utilize the interpersonal relationship as a means of theme reduction.

Program-Centered Administrative Consultation.   This form of consultation is most analogous to client-centered case consultation in that the consultant's role is to assess a current situation, diagnose the problem, and make recommendations regarding either the remediation of an existing problem or the initiation of a new one. It is characterized as program-centered administrative consultation because the "client" is a mental health program and the consultee is an administrator of that program.

During the problem assessment phase of program-centered administrative consultation, the consultant must be able to examine the characteristics of an organization (such as the counseling center of a community agency in which the program functions or is to function); make judgments about the human, fiscal, and physical resources available to support the program, and assess the managerial ability of the person or persons responsible for the program under consideration. As Caplan (1970) notes, this form of consultation requires far more than the usual clinical skills possessed by most mental health professionals. Caplan also notes that a number of specific factors must be examined during the assessment stage. Among these are the history of the organization, its goals, the support of the top administrator for the change being considered, as well as the aforementioned resources and managerial expertise.

Once initial judgments are made, it is recommended that the consultant seek staff input regarding them because successful outcomes are not likely to result unless individuals in the organization have some personal investment in the program. These judgments are then used to modify the tentative plan and a report is filed. As is customary in Caplan's model, the consultant does not participate in the implementation of the program.

Consultee-Centered Administrative Consultation.

Like its counterpart, consultee-centered case consultation, the goal of this approach to consultation is to improve the functioning of a member or members of the administrative team. Consultee-centered administrative consultation may develop as a result of other types of consultation. However, as Caplan (1970) specifies, it differs in many ways from any of the foregoing models.

During the initial or entry phase of consultee-centered administrative consultation, the consultant needs to seek sanctions from the chief administrator and then work to understand the function of the organization and the consultee(s). Ultimately, consultations may occur with one or more members of the administrative team, but it must be made clear that consultation is a voluntary process. Thus, the consultant works to uncover difficulties that are precluding the organization from delivering mental health services, brings these to the attention of the administrators, and hopes that they will volunteer for consultation. This process is necessarily a long-term one.

During the assessment phase, the consultant examines the personalities of the key administrators, the manner in which subgroups within the organization function internally, and how they relate to other groups within the organization. In addition, the consultant looks at vital organizational processes such as communication, leadership, decision-making, role assignments, and organizational patterns in order to identify problems in organizational functioning.

In keeping with the overall model of mental health consultation, the consultant intervenes with individuals either to increase their effectiveness or to develop an awareness of organizational difficulties in vital areas of functioning. The consultant does not design organizational interventions and does not participate in the implementation of interventions designed by the consultee.

STUDENT LEARNING EXERCISE

The following is a brief description of a mental health agency that is functioning below its potential. On the basis of the description, decide which of the mental health consultation approaches would be most acceptable to Caplan himself.

1. An external consultant has been called in because case loads are so heavy the staff cannot provide individual therapy. As a result, the waiting list is very long,

and many people in the community are questioning the management of the agency. The director has proposed alternative approaches to counseling (e.g., group counseling) a number of times without result. Preliminary interviews with the staff reveal that the director is viewed as a "political hack." Which approach should be used in light of the fact that the director has three years left on his contract?

2. Several counselors have had difficulties with cases involving PCP abuse. They have treated the cases in the same manner as other substance abuse cases, but without result. Which of Caplan's approaches fits the situation best?

3. It is clear that a teacher who is constantly referring poor children to the school counselor for help has a real "hangup" when it comes to children who are not middle class.

4. A wave of referrals dealing with step families engulfs a family counseling agency. Results of the contacts meet with mixed results at best.

BEHAVIORAL CONSULTATION

Three behaviorally oriented models of consultation have surfaced to date. Bergan (1977) has articulated a model that relies primarily on operant learning theory, Keller (1981) has set forth a behavioral-eclectic model that draws on a number of learning theories for its conceptualization, and Brown and others (1987) have set forth a cognitive-behavioral model. While these models differ significantly in a variety of ways, they share the behavioral tradition of emphasis on empirical support for their propositions and allegiance to a strict problem-solving model based on the scientific method.

Background

Behavioral consultation is a relatively new phenomenon that grew out of the behavior modification movement of the 1960s and early 1970s. However, a growing realization that personal variables such as cognitive and environmental factors beyond those related to immediate rewards and punishers caused most behaviorists to rethink their formulations. Bergan (1977) can justifiably be viewed as one of the genuine innovators in this area, in that he focused on the importance of the consultant-consultee relationship as a key variable in the consultation process. His view, which is somewhat controversial (Gallessich, 1982), is that the consultant essentially controls the consulting process through verbal processes such as eliciting key information through careful consulting leads and thoughtful input regarding psychological processes. Bergan does maintain that consultants should apprise the consultee of their intentions and that consultation must be a purely voluntary process.

More recently, Brown and others (1987) have set forth a social learning model (SLM) of consultation based on the thinking of Albert Bandura (1977, 1978). Bandura's social learning theory emphasizes that the environment, cognitions, and behaviors are all key variables in the functioning of human beings and has increasingly emphasized the importance of self-efficacy, or the confidence that one can perform in a specific situation (e.g., working calculus problems).

Relationship. Brown and others (1987) depart from the behavioral tradition, particularly that of Bergan (1977), in one significant way: the nature of the consulting relationship. They assert that the bases for the consulting relationship are the traditional facilitatie conditions of empathy, warmth, and genuineness. Their point of view is simply that the presence of these conditions facilitates the free flow of ideas in consultation in much the same way that they do in counseling or therapy.

Assessment. Assessment is a twofold process in the SLM. One aspect focuses on assessing client variables, including behavioral deficits, cognitions that relate to the problem, and environmental factors that may facilitate or impede the functioning of the client. When consulting with the parents of an alcohol abusing adolescent, the consultant might wish to know the rate, incidence, and circumstances under which alcohol is consumed (when, where, with whom, and how much), the adolescent's thoughts regarding the importance of drinking and confidence that he or she can stop (self-efficacy), and the environmental variables that may contribute to or act to maintain the drinking (e.g., alcoholic intake of parents, peers, etc.). The SLM consultant would also want to examine other personal variables such as health and alcohol dependency.

Similarly, the second aspect of the assessment focuses on the behavior, environmental variables, and cognitions of the consultee. What behaviors are now employed to deal with the problematic adolescent? How confident are the parents that they can cope with the problem? What environmental variables impinge upon them that will influence their own functioning? Are there physiological variables (e.g., alcohol dependency) that preclude altering certain home conditions.

Goal Setting. Goal setting may focus on one or more of the variables identified as contributing to the problem. The goal for the client is, of course, to reduce the problematic behavior by intervening in what appears to be the dominant factor in the problem. Similarly, the goal for the consultee is to develop the behavioral and cognitive behaviors needed to cope with the problem being presented by the client.

Strategy Selection and Implementation. In the SLM, the client is constantly apprised of the consultation conversation by the consultee. Thus, when the problem has been identified and strategies for correcting the client's problem are being selected, input is solicited from the client. In the final analysis, the selection and implementation of the intervention is a collaborative effort. However, the SLM consultant insists that the consultee handle as much of the intervention as his or her cognitive and behavioral repertoire permit, since successful performances are the key to building self-efficacy or the confidence that one can function in a specific area (Bandura, 1977).

Generally speaking, interventions are selected from among the following techniques (Brown et al., 1987):

1. Participant modeling	Guided practice includes coaching, rehearsal, and feedback.
2. Symbolic modeling	Desired behavior presented via audiovisual devices or through bibliotherapy.
3. Covert modeling	Involves imagining desired behaviors.
4. Cognitive modeling	Talking through desired cognitions by the consultant.
5. Cognitive restructuring	Involves identifying thought patterns surrounding problematic behaviors, including antecedents, performance related thoughts, and those that follow problem behavior, and then teaching new thoughts, often using cognitive modeling procedures.
6. Self-monitoring	Having an individual monitor one problematic behavior in order either to identify its dimensions *or* to determine progress toward goals.
7. Desensitization	Involves a family of procedures designed to eliminate phobic behavior, including approaches using imagery and *in vivo* (in the real situation) techniques.

STUDENT LEARNING EXERCISE

Complete the following quiz relating to Bergan's behavioral model and the SLM model outlined above. Circle T for true and F for false.

1. Bergan emphasizes a traditional or egalitarian consulting relationship in his model while the SLM approach does not.   T   F
2. Objective data are important in both behavioral models outlined, but Bergan emphasizes observational data more.   T   F

3. The client is involved in the intervention effort in both models (Bergan and SLM).　　　　T　F
4. Cognition is a more important variable in the SLM model than in Bergan's behavioral model.　　　　T　F
5. Neither approach emphasizes affect in the counseling relationship.　T　F

ORGANIZATIONAL CONSULTATION

Organizational consultation models are those most analogous to Caplan's consultee-centered administrative consultation, discussed earlier. However, as we shall see, organizational consultation grew out of a different background and is conceptually different from mental health consultation approaches to organizational change. The organizational development consultation model discussed here is based partly on the work of Huse (1980), Beer (1980), Lippitt (1982), and Morasky (1982).

Background

Organizational development consultation has a number of historical antecedents, including scientific management, the field theory of Kurt Lewin, and the humanism of Carl Rogers (Stryker, 1982). However, there can be little doubt that systems theory is having great impact on current thinking in this area. Systems theory holds that organizations are open systems that receive products from the environment (inputs), transform them as a result of technology and human processes (throughput), and export them back to the environment (output) (Katz & Kahn, 1978). Organizational development consultants hold that the human processes are most vital to the efficiency and effectiveness of the organization.

Certain key principles must be considered when examining organizations (open systems). These include the following:

1. There is a tendency for organizations to differentiate functions, thus creating specialization in roles.
2. All parts of the organization are interdependent. A problem in one part (subsystem) will inevitably be experienced in another. Because of the interdependence of the parts, solutions to problems in one subsystem may cause negative consequences in another. (See Figure 8.1.)
3. There is no single best solution to a problem (the principle of equifinality).

4. Effective organizations are adaptable. Adaptability requires that the organization respond to shifting external and internal conditions and change to meet the resulting demands.

5. Organizations have a tendency toward entropy or loss of energy. Adaptable organizations avoid entropy through change (Katz & Kahn, 1978).

An Overview

Organizational development consultants may be employed to function as a part of the sensing mechanisms needed to identify internal and external changes that may negatively influence the welfare of the organization. Often consultants

Figure 8.1 A systems view of organizational functioning. From *Psychological Consultation: Introduction to Theory and Practice* (p. 101) by D. Brown, W. B. Pryzwansky, and A. C. Schulte (1987). Newton, MA: Allyn & Bacon. Reprinted by permission.

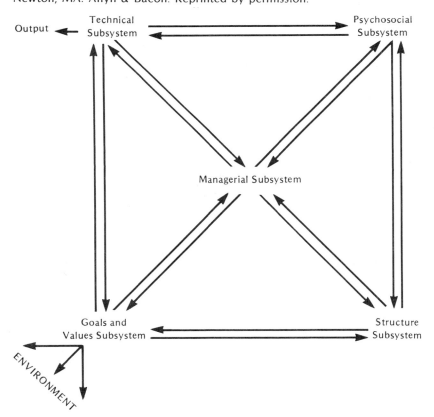

who serve to identify shifts in demands are internal consultants employed by the organization on a full-time basis. In other situations, consultants may be external, in that they are not employed by the organization as regular employees. These consultants may also act in a preventive way (i.e., may be employed to monitor organizational health), but they are more likely to be employed to assist with organizational problems *once they have developed.* There is nothing that precludes internal consultants from dealing with problematic situations, however, and in fact that is often the case. Regardless of the locus of the consultant (internal or external), certain steps must be followed. A description of these follows.

Entry.   Entry in the organizational consultation process can be broken down into a number of substages. A consultant, whether internal or external to the organization, may be contacted by an employee, usually a manager, because of a concern, either because a problem has arisen or because the manager wants to prevent difficulties. The manager may have identified a specific problem and may have made his or her own diagnosis of the basis for the problem. Most consultants resist accepting this diagnosis, insisting that they be allowed to work collaboratively with the organization to arrive at a mutual assessment of the concern. Some technical consultants (e.g., systems analysts) may assume full responsibility for this assessment. However, for the most part, consultants go through a process of reconnoitering prior to agreeing to becoming involved in a particular process. The objective of this reconnoitering process is to determine whether or not sufficient commitment and resources are available to deal with the problem at hand. If, in fact, motivation to solve the problem exists and human and fiscal resources are available to focus on the problem, the consultant contracts with the organization to assist with its problems (Beer, 1980; Lippitt, 1982).

Assessment.   Morasky (1982) suggests that the beginning point in assessing organizational problems is to identify the goals of the organization in order to determine whether they are clearly stated and are being followed. In some instances goals have been distorted. In others, they are not clearly stated and thus are misunderstood.

The second step in assessment, according to Morasky, is to examine the input/output boundaries. Inputs come into the organization in the form of (1) technology/information, (2) human resources, and (3) raw materials. If an organization has not kept abreast of the latest technology, cannot attract the needed labor supply, or has either inadequate supplies or inferior raw materials, it is unlikely to function effectively.

The examination of output boundaries is in reality looking at the marketing function. Is the product produced by the organization being "purchased" by the market? This may be easily discerned in the case of profit-making organizations. Nonprofit organizations such as community mental health centers and school counseling programs also have a marketing function (i.e., they need to sell their programs to different audiences). Needless to say, it is more difficult to determine whether the products of these organizations are being accepted in the "marketplace." Consultants may assist organizations to identify groups to which their products are to be marketed and identify marketing devices (Brown et al., 1987).

Third, organizational consultants need to examine the production processes. In community mental health centers, the focus of this investigation would be on the therapy, outreach, and consulting services. In goods-producing organizations, the consultant might look at the technology employed and how this interacts with the human side of the production.

Fourth, the consultant should look at the basic organizational processes (e.g., communications, decision-making, incentives system, etc.). Poor vertical communication plagues many bureaucratic organizations. Noninvolvement in the decision-making process can lower morale and generalize to the quality of the product produced. Disparate pay systems can have the same result.

Fifth, and finally, the consultant needs to examine the overall constraints on the system. Geography can serve as a barrier to the recruitment of personnel or to securing raw materials. Public agencies are often underfunded. Air pollution standards can result in the need to modernize. Zoning laws can preclude needed expansion. For example, a counselor who provided organization consultation to a small electric utility in a mideastern state identified the inability to recruit qualified technical staff as a major impediment to the functioning of the organization.

Problem Identification and Goal Setting.   Once the foregoing steps have been completed, the consultant and members of the organization must evaluate a mass of data. Lewin's (1951) force field analysis can be used for this purpose (Table 8.1). Driving forces are those identified that exert pressure to solve a problem. Staff morale, low profit, poor corporate image, and so forth are driving forces. Restraining forces are barriers to problem solving such as unavailability of sufficiently trained personnel, outdated equipment, space, and other similar factors. The result of the force-field analysis is to identify specific driving forces that can be accelerated and/or restraining forces that need to be reduced that will lead to problem solving. The goals of consultation then become to increase or decrease certain forces that exist within the organization.

Problem Solving.   Once driving and restraining forces are identified, specific strategies for dealing with the problem are generated by the consultant and members of the organization. Blake and Mouton (1976), Lippitt (1982), and Kurpius (1985) have classified these interventions according to their focus. Interventions such as skills development or attitudinal change are aimed at individuals who may be impairing the organization's functioning. Group interventions such as team building and collaborative problem solving focus on enhancing the effectiveness of problems with work groups. Mediation and conflict resolu-

Table 8.1   Example of Force-Field Analysis Technique

Step 1: Identify problem and set goals
Current Situation: Low worker morale, resulting in higher turnover and low productivity
Preferred Situation: High worker morale, low turnover, high productivity

Step 2: List forces that will influence problem resolution

Driving Forces	Restraining Forces
1. Low profit	1. Competition that requires low pay
2. High cost of recruiting and training new workers	2. Outdated company policies regarding work schedule
3. Desire to meet workers' needs, i.e., produce a desirable work environment	3. Available expertise
	4. Current management system

Step 3: Identify strategies to alter forces
(For example, explain technology that will increase productivity, redo company personnel policies, etc.)

tion are interventions aimed at improving intergroup relations. Finally, survey information feedback, culture building, and installing new communications systems attempt to positively influence the total organization.

MODELS OF CONSULTATION: POSTSCRIPT

The major models of consultation have been touched on rather lightly in this section. Space would not permit consideration of Schein's (1969) process model of consultation, which can be characterized as a client-centered approach. Neither could the eclectic model of organizational consultation developed by Blake and Mouton (1976) be covered in sufficient detail to do it justice. These models, and a fuller knowledge of the ones discussed, will have to be postponed for later coursework or reading.

STUDENT LEARNING EXERCISE
Complete the following quiz pertaining to systems theory and organizational consultation. Circle T for true and F for false.

1. The principle of equifinality suggests that the stages through which organizational consultation passes follow a linear model.   T   F

2. Most organizations have a tendency to lose energy. This is referred to as movement toward entropy.   T   F

3. Organizational consultants, after entry has been completed, may begin their work at a variety of places. Morasky suggests that they begin by identifying organizational boundaries.   T   F

4. Throughput and production are analogous terms.   T   F

5. The principles of product marketing are similar for goods and services producing as well as profit and nonprofit organizations.   T   F

6. A positive intervention is one subsystem that may have a negative impact on another.   T   F

THE EFFICACY OF CONSULTATION

Three questions should be asked in the evaluation of any intervention used by counselors. First, is it effective in achieving the changes sought? Second, compared to other approaches, is it more or less efficient? Does it take more or less time, energy, resources, etc.? Third, is it acceptable to the potential client group involved? In other words, will clients or consultees participate? None of these questions can be answered definitively for consultation.

There is evidence that consultation is as effective as, or possibly more effective than, counseling (Lauver, 1974; Palmo & Kuzniar, 1972; Randolf & Hardage, 1973), although the available data need additional support. Most of these studies were conducted in a school setting and generalization beyond that setting is limited. However, reviews of the consultation literature have generally supported the effectiveness of consultation (Bundy & Poppen, 1986; Fullan, Miles, & Taylor, 1980; Mannino & Shore, 1975; Medway, 1979) in a variety of settings, although all reviewers have pointed to methodological problems in the research.

The efficiency issue has not been addressed systematically, but research such as the Palmo and Kuzniar (1972) study that compared teacher/parent consultation efforts with group counseling indicates that consultation procedures were superior. One could speculate that this and other studies contrasting counseling and consultation (e.g., Lauver, 1974; Randolf & Hardage, 1973) that showed that consultation was more effective showed that it was more efficient as well.

Finally, Reynolds, Gutkin, Elliot, and Witt (1984) reviewed the literature regarding the acceptability of consultation in schools and concluded that few conclusions can be drawn at this time. Little research has actually been conducted that compares the acceptability of consultation with that of other interventions used by counselors.

SUMMARY

Three approaches to consultation have been discussed in this chapter along with a general discussion of the process of consultation and an examination of its efficacy. What should be obvious is that consultation is a relatively new intervention and, as such, is in a state of flux with regard to both conceptualization and practice. What should be just as clear is that consultation offers the counselor another approach to dealing with complex mental health concerns.

REVIEW QUESTIONS

1. Contrast the definition of consultation presented in this chapter with that advanced by Caplan. Speculate on why Caplan has taken the position he holds.
2. Outline the principles of systems theory. Tell how these might be applied to the assessment of an organizational problem.
3. Compare the diagnostic categories set forth by Caplan in his consultee-centered consultation model to the "diagnostic categories" that might be used in the social learning theory of consultation. Which provides the best background for designing an intervention? Why?
4. Caplan recommends that consultee-centered administrative consultation will necessarily be long-term in nature. Speculate on the reasons for this recommendation.
5. Outline the steps in consultation. Identify the prerequisite conditions that must be met at each step before one can move to the next step (except for termination, of course).
6. Caplan identifies five reasons why he believes consultees lack objectivity. Identify these and tell how a mental health consultation would deal with each.
7. Discuss the problem-assessment process in the social learning model of consultation.
8. In organizational consultation, the consultant examines each of the subsystems along with the entire structure of the organization. Why examine the entire system as opposed to concentrating on a single problematic subsystem such as production?

REFERENCES

Babcock, N., & Pryzwansky, W. B. (1983). Models of consultation: Preference of educational professionals at five stages of service. *Journal of School Psychology, 12,* 359–366.

Bandura, A. (1977). *Social learning theory.* Englewood Cliffs, NJ: Prentice-Hall.

Bandura, A. (1978). The self system in reciprocal determinism. *American Psychologist,* *23,* 344–358.

Beer, M. (1980). *Organizational change and development: A systems view.* Santa Monica, CA: Goodyear.

Bergan, J. R. (1977). *Behavioral consultation.* Columbus, OH: Charles E. Merrill.

Bergan, J. R., Byrnes, I. M., & Kratochwill, T. R. (1979). Effects of behavioral and medical models of consultation on teacher expectancies and instruction of a hypothetical child. *Journal of School Psychology, 17,* 307–310.

Bergan, J. R., & Tombari, M. L. (1976). The analysis of verbal interactions occurring during consultation. *Journal of School Psychology, 13,* 209–226.

Blake, R. R., & Mouton, J. S. (1976). *Consultation.* Reading, MA: Addison-Wesley.

Brown, D., Pryzwansky, W. B., & Schulte, A. C. (1987). *Psychological consultation: Introduction to theory and practice.* Newton, MA: Allyn & Bacon.

Brown, D., Wyne, M. D., Blackburn, J. E., & Powell, W. C. (1979). *Consultation: Strategy for improving education.* Boston: Allyn & Bacon.

Bundy, M. L., & Poppen, W. A. (1986). School counselors' effectiveness as consultants: A research review. *Elementary School Guidance and Counseling, 20*(3), 215–222.

Caplan, G. (1970). *The theory and practice of mental health consultation.* New York: Basic Books.

Conoley, J. C., & Conoley, C. W. (1982). *School consultation: A guide to practice and training.* New York: Pergammon Press.

Dinkmeyer, D., & Carlson, J. (1973). *Consulting: Facilitating human potential and change processes.* Columbus, OH: Charles E. Merrill.

Fullan, M., Miles, M. D., & Taylor, G. (1980). Organizational development in the schools: The state of the art. *Review of Educational Research, 50,* 121–183.

Gallessich, J. (1982). *The profession and practice of consultation: A handbook for consultants, trainers of consultants, and consumers of consultation services.* San Francisco: Jossey-Bass.

Gallessich, J. (1985). Toward a meta-theory of consultation. *The Counseling Psychologist, 13,* 336–354.

Heller, K. (1985). Issues in consultation to community groups: Some use distinctions between social regulations and indigenous citizens groups. *The Counseling Psychologist, 15,* 403–409.

Huse, E. F. (1980). *Organizational development and change* (2nd ed.). St. Paul, MN: West Publishing Company.

Katz, D., & Kahn, R. L. (1978). *The social psychology of organizations.* New York: John Wiley and Sons.

Keller, H. R. (1981). Behavioral consultation. In J. C. Conoley (Ed.), *Consultation in the schools: Theory, research and practice* (pp. 59-99). New York: Academic Press.

Kurpius, D. J. (1985). Consultation interventions: Successes, failures, and proposals. *The Counseling Psychologist, 13,* 368–384.

Lauver, P. J. (1974). Consulting with teachers: A systematic approach. *Personnel and Guidance Journal, 52,* 535–540.

Lewin, K. (1951). *Field theory in social sciences.* New York: Harper and Row.

Lippitt, G. L. (1982). *Organizational renewal* (2nd ed.). Englewood Cliffs, NJ: Prentice-Hall.

Lippitt, G., & Lippitt, H. R. (1978). *The consulting process in action.* San Diego, CA: University Associates.

Mannino, F. V., & Shore, M. (1975). The effects of consultation: A review of empirical studies. *American Journal of Community Psychology, 3,* 1–21.

Medway, F. J. (1979). How effective is school consultation? A review of recent research. *Journal of School Psychology, 17,* 275–282.

Meyers, J., Parson, R. D., & Martin, R. (1979). *Mental health consultation in the schools.* San Francisco: Jossey-Bass.

Morasky, R. L. (1982). *Behavioral systems.* New York: Praeger.

Palmo, A. J., & Kuzniar, J. (1972). Modification of behavior through group counseling and consultation. *Elementary School Guidance and Counseling, 6*(4), 258–262.

Pryzwansky, W. B. (1974). A reconsideration of the consultation model for delivery of school based psychological services. *American Journal of Orthopsychiatry, 44,* 579–583.

Randolph, D. L. (1985). *Micro-consulting: Basic psychological consultation skills for helping professionals.* Johnson City, TN: Institute of Social Sciences and Arts.

Randolph, D. L., & Hardage, N. C. (1973). A comparison of behavioral consultation and consultation with model-reinforcement group counseling for children who are consistently off task. *Journal of Educational Research, 67,* 103–107.

Reynolds, C. R., Gutkin, T. B., Elliot, S. N., & Witt, J. C. (1984). *School psychology: Essentials of theory and practice.* New York: John Wiley and Sons.

Schein, E. (1969). *Process consultation: Its role in organizational development.* Reading, MA: Addison-Wesley.

Schowengerdt, R. V., Fine, M. J., & Poggio, J. P. (1976). An examination of some bases of teacher satisfaction with school psychological services. *Psychology in the Schools, 13,* 269–275.

Snapp, M., & Davidson, S. L. (1982). Systems interventions for school psychologists: A case study approach. In C. R. Reynolds & T. B. Gutkin (Eds.), *The handbook of school psychology* (pp. 858–961). New York: John Wiley and Sons.

Stryker, S. C. (1982). *Principles and practices of professional consulting.* Glenelg, MD: Bermont Books.

9

Ethical Underpinnings of the Counseling Profession

GOAL OF THE CHAPTER

The purpose of this chapter is to identify the major principles that guide counseling professionals.

CHAPTER PREVIEW

1. The major purposes of codes of ethics will be discussed with an emphasis on the benefit of a code of ethics to a professional and the potential benefits to client groups served by the profession.
2. Eight principles of ethical conduct will be discussed and illustrated. Two codes of ethics will be drawn upon to illustrate these principles; these are *Ethical Standards of the American Association for Counseling and Development* (AACD, 1981), and *Ethical Principles of Psychologists* (APA, 1981).
3. A number of problems with the AACD *Ethical Standards* will be identified.
4. Initiating and adjudicating ethical complaints will be discussed.

INTRODUCTION

Ethics is the branch of philosophy devoted to the study of moral decision-making (Golightly, 1971). Philosophers concerned with ethics dedicate themselves to the understanding of the rise and implementation of moral standards among various societies and subgroups within those societies, including professions. Perhaps it goes without saying that cultures, subcultures, and occupational groups generate different sets of moral imperatives. However, professional groups (e.g., law, medicine, and psychology) within the United States have generated surprisingly similar ethical codes. These codes are the embodiment of the moral standards of these groups. While the general aim of a code is to provide practitioners with a guide to making ethical decisions, a code of ethics serves several other purposes (Van Hoose & Kottler, 1977).

PURPOSES OF ETHICAL CODES

The first purpose of a code of ethics is to provide a basis for regulating the behavior of the members of the professional group. Codes of ethics provide standards of practice regarding activities ranging from fee setting to deciding on which clients to serve. They also provide guidelines for action when certain types of difficult decisions arise (e.g., what to do with a suicidal client). These codes also tend to clarify the responsibilities of professionals to clients, to their employers, to society at large, and to their professional group.

But, as noted earlier, the purposes of codes of ethics are not restricted to providing guidelines for ethical decision-making and to regulating the behavior of members of the profession. As Van Hoose and Kottler (1977) point out, a code of ethics also protects the profession that promulgates it. All professional groups strive for autonomy from external regulation, particularly regulation by governmental agencies. In order to maintain their independence from regulatory bodies, a professional group must demonstrate not only a willingness to police itself, but also a method for self-regulation. The adoption and enforcement of a code of ethics is a clear signal to the public in general, and governmental regulatory agencies in particular, that this method is in place.

A code of ethics also enhances internal professional harmony because it establishes guidelines for professional practices and regulates intermember interactions such as referral of clients, consultation, and recruiting of new clients (Van Hoose & Kottler, 1977). Ethical guidelines for practice also protect the profession by establishing standards of practice that are often used in the adjudication of liability suits. For example, in the case of *Roy v. Hartogs* (1976) the judge ruled in favor of the client because her therapist had violated the professional standards of his field regarding sexual contact with a client. Conversely, counselors, psychologists, and other mental health professionals have routinely been absolved from guilt in liability suits when they have been found to be functioning ethically.

To summarize, a code of ethics is a set of moral guidelines designed to protect the professional, the profession, and the public served by the group. In 1981 the American Personnel and Guidance Association (now the American Association for Counseling and Development) adopted a revised set of *Ethical Standards* (see Appendix A) that at once reflects the values of the counseling profession and fulfills the functions of a code of ethics. The code is divided into nine sections: (1) preamble, (2) general concerns, (3) counseling relationship, (4) measurement and evaluation, (5) research and publication, (6) consulting, (7) private practice, (8) personnel administration, and (9) preparation standards. At this writing sections dealing with technology and advertising are being added. The existing sections and those being developed are thematic in that they address specific activities engaged in by counselors. However, the principles that guide the functioning of professional counselors cut across these sections.

In contrast to the AACD statement, the APA-sponsored *Ethical Principles of Psychologists* (1981) (see Appendix B) is organized around 10 principles that are designed to direct the professional psychologist. This approach has the advantage of clarity, and a "principles of ethical functioning" approach will be followed in the remainder of the chapter. The major focus of this discussion will be on the *Ethical Standards* of professional counselors, however. Statements from the APA (1981) document will be used for clarification or for illustrative purposes.

PRINCIPLES OF ETHICAL CONDUCT

Principle One: *Responsibility*

Professional counselors have various responsibilities, including those to clients, to the public at large, to other counselors, to the institutions that employ them, and to themselves. These responsibilities are enunciated generally in the preamble of the code in the following statement: The American Association for Counseling and Development "is an educational, scientific, and professional organization whose members are dedicated to the enhancement of the worth, dignity, potential, and uniqueness of each individual and thus to the service of society." The APA statement has a similar general statement in its preamble, but under principle one, responsibility, a number of specific obligations are detailed, including the responsibility to plan research carefully, clarifying in advance what will be done with research data; the responsibility of individuals who teach psychology to maintain high levels of scholarship; and the responsibility of practitioners not to misuse their influence.

While the APA statement emphasizes research, the AACD statement of *Ethical Standards* emphasizes the responsibility of counselors to their clients. The statement, "The member's *primary* obligation is to respect the integrity and promote the welfare of the client(s). . ." (Section B1) certainly makes this clear. This does not suggest that psychologists are less concerned with their clients, for this is not the case. However it does suggest a difference in emphasis on research between the two groups. When ethical decisions are to be made by either professional counselors or psychologists, the client's welfare and well-being should take precedence in the decision-making process. For example, a school counselor may find that one of his or her clients has been stealing from the school. Since that counselor also has responsibility to the school, an ethical dilemma presents itself. In resolving the dilemma, the client's well-being should be held in utmost importance if the foregoing statement taken from the code is interpreted literally. As we shall see, when the issue of institutional responsibility is discussed, the AACD *Ethical Standards* equivocates a bit.

One area of responsibility to individual clients that is particularly highlighted in the *Ethical Standards* pertains to recognizing individual differences, particularly as they relate to racial and sexual stereotyping. In the introduction to the code the counselor is told that an awareness of the negative impact of stereotyping helps guard "the individual rights and personal dignity of the client" (Section A8). Later, in the section on measurement and evaluation, counselors are warned to use the tests cautiously with minorities or others who are underrepresented in norm groups. These and other statements in the *Ethical Standards* caution counselors against stereotyping individuals while advocating deep respect for the uniqueness of the individual.

Several counselors have asserted that current ethical standards regarding culturally different groups do not go far enough and that changes need to be made to clarify the ethical issues in this area. Cayleff (1986) believes that counselors need an appreciation for the belief systems of culturally different clients and suggests that ethical guidelines should caution against imposing dominant cultural beliefs on culturally different clients. Casas, Ponterotto, and Gutierrez (1986) also believe that a change in the current ACCD *Ethical Standards* is necessary. They think that the *Standards* need to be more specific with regard to research with culturally different clients and preparation for working with cross-cultural clients, a position echoed by Ibrahim and Arrendo (1986).

One somewhat unusual aspect of the AACD code of ethics has to do with counselors' responsibilities regarding referral should a satisfactory arrangement not be possible because of finances. With regard to the latter, the statement of *Ethical Standards* specifies that, in the event that a fee, suitable to the client, cannot be established, assistance must be provided in finding comparable services at acceptable costs.

Principle 6d of the *Ethical Principles of Psychologists* is probably a more workable statement. It reads, "Psychologists make advance financial arrangements that safeguard the best interests of and are clearly understood by their clients" (p. 636). It is likely that a statement of this type will be adopted by the AACD as more counselors enter private practice. The AACD code is not nearly so rigid when referral becomes necessary in the counseling relationship. It does indiciate that it is an ethical duty of the counselor to be knowledgeable about referral resources. It goes on to suggest that, in the event referral becomes necessary, the counselor should identify referral resources. However, if the client rejects the referral, the counselor need not continue the relationship. In other words, a counselor's responsibilities are fulfilled once an appropriate referral resource has been identified and made known to the client.

Counselor's responsibilities to institutions or agencies are also addressed in the preamble to the *Ethical Standards* and elsewhere. In general, counselors are advised that acceptance of employment is essentially an agreement with the principles and policies of the institution. They are also admonished that if there is a conflict between the institution's practices and those standards established by the code, resignation from employment should be strongly considered.

Professionals who accept administrative jobs are also advised to foster accountability by making the organization's goals and policies explicit. Counselors who function as personnel administrators also have many other responsibilities, including developing an in-service training program for themselves and others, making the goals of their program known to the staff, and designing programs that guarantee the rights of the client group served. These responsibilities would, in all likelihood, be rather easy to meet. However, one ethical guideline that may be problematic for professional counselors can be found in Section G3. It states, "Members *must* alert their employers to conditions that may be potentially disruptive or damaging" (italics added). Would a school counselor inform the administration that a student was going to phone in a bomb threat or pull the fire alarm? Would a counselor working in a prison inform the administration that a sit-down strike was about to occur in protest of the overcrowded conditions? And how are these types of situations balanced against the directive regarding counselors' primary responsibility to clients? These questions cannot be answered without more information. Are people likely to be harmed if a fire alarm is sounded or a sit-down strike begins? With this and other information a plan of action can be developed. In many instances ethical principles provide guidelines for decision-making; they do not provide answers.

Counselors also have the responsibility to inform their employers of conditions that may impair their functioning as employees. This guideline is generally interpreted to mean that counselors who develop emotional problems, alcoholism, drug addiction, or related problems should report these difficulties because they may hamper their work. Counselors are naturally reluctant to place this type of information in the hands of employers since it may result in dismissal.

The *Ethical Standards* places a great deal of emphasis on responsibilities to institutions, primarily because many counselors are employed in institutional settings. As Patterson (1971) has indicated, AACD may have gone too far in its accommodation of employers. At the conclusion of the section on the counseling relationship, it is indicated that if the work setting calls for a variation in the guidelines established in the section, consultation with other professionals should be initiated *"whenever possible"* (italics added) to consider justifiable alternatives. Patterson believes that there are no justifiable alternatives to the good ethical practices that protect our clients. This section of *Ethical Standards* (Section B14) weakens it and should probably be struck.

As would be expected, *Ethical Standards* deals extensively with counselors' responsibility to the counseling profession. Two general areas of concern are raised in this regard. First, counselors are expected to influence the profession by exerting efforts that will improve professional practices. In particular, counselors are expected to involve themselves in continuous evaluation of their effectiveness and to engage in other activities that will enhance their functioning. Presumably these directives were included so that the counseling profession can assert with some certainty that it is comprised of a group of competent practitioners.

Counselors have a second area of responsibility to the profession: enforcing ethical behavior. Counselors are admonished that, when they possess evidence of unethical conduct on the part of another member, they should act first through local ethics committees and then through committees at state, regional, or national levels to correct the situation. In the section that follows the discussion of ethical principles, enforcement will be discussed in more detail. In the APA (1981) ethical statements, these and other matters dealing with professional relations are covered in a separate principle. However, both ethical statements try to clarify responsibility to clients, employers, and other professionals.

STUDENT LEARNING EXERCISE

Principle One
Indicate whether the following actions are ethical (E) or unethical (U).

1. A counselor fails to regularly upgrade his training.   E   U
2. A counselor utilizes an aptitude test for a multicultural group that has no Hispanics in the norm group.   E   U
3. A counselor ignores continued violations of a client's confidences by another counselor.   E   U
4. A white counselor, trained in cross-cultural counseling, takes a job in an all black institution.   E   U
5. A student personnel administrator decides that staff inservice is each person's responsibility and eliminates staff development from her budget.   E   U
6. A counselor who is an alcoholic continues to work.   E   U

Principle Two: *Competence*

In the foregoing section it was mentioned that counselors have a responsibility to the profession to develop and maintain their own competencies. A professional group cannot exist if there are substantial concerns in society about the competence of its members. The APA statement is very clear on this matter. It states, "The maintencance of high standards of competence is a responsibility shared by all psychologists in the interest of the public and the profession as a whole" (p. 634). Accordingly, most professional codes of ethics make numerous references to the importance of developing and maintaining the skills needed to function effectively. The AACD code of ethics is no different. Counselor educators are told that it is important that programs, insofar as possible, be competency based. In this way the profession attempts to ensure that counselors possess the needed competencies when they enter the field. In Section A1 of the code, counselors are advised that professional growth is expected throughout their careers, presumably as a means of maintaining competence. Competence is alluded to again in that same section, but in the context of representing one's own skills accurately. This theme is echoed again in the sections on private practice and personnel administration. The section on measurement and evaluation addresses the area of competence even more directly. It states (in regard to test usage), "Members must recognize the limits of their competence and perform only those functions for which they are prepared" (Section C4).

In sum, the AACD ethical guidelines indicate that ethical behavior requires that competency be developed in the training programs, that counselors have a responsibility to maintain their competency through continuous professional growth, and that their competency level should be represented accurately to clients, employers, and the general public.

STUDENT LEARNING EXERCISE
Principle Two
Indicate whether the following actions are ethical (E) or unethical (U).

1. A counselor gives an individual intelligence test for which she has little preparation.   E   U

2. After attending a workshop on hypnosis, a counselor engages in the activity under the supervision of the workshop leader.   E   U

3. An elementary school counselor attends an hour and a half session on music therapy. She then tries out what she has learned on her students.   E   U

4. A white counselor who has no cross-cultural counseling training is asked to counsel a "difficult" black client. He agrees to do this.   E   U

5. A counselor who has no training in counseling homosexual clients continues to counsel a gay client but consults an expert after every session.   E   U

Principle Three: *Confidentiality*

A hallmark of a professional group is when clients can discuss personal issues and have those disclosures kept in confidence. It should be noted that while a professional group can assert that it is necessary to safeguard clients by keeping personal disclosures in confidence, only a legislative body can grant the right to make disclosures privileged information (Bangs, 1971). This point will be discussed in detail in the next chapter, but the reader should be aware that unless privileged communication has been granted by legislative decree in a particular jurisdiction (normally a state), counselors may find themselves in conflict with the legal system since the ethical expectation of keeping confidences is not supported legally.

As would be expected, the *Ethical Standards* addresses confidentiality in numerous ways. However, and not unexpectedly, the strongest language is found in the section dealing with the counseling relationship. It indicates that information disclosed by the client must be kept in confidence *unless* "there is clear and imminent danger to the client or others" (Section B4). Counselors are told to take reasonable action whenever danger arises, presumably to prevent clients from harming themselves or others. Counseling records, data collected in the counseling relationship, and specific subject data collected in the course of research project are also viewed as confidential information and, therefore, should be protected against inadvertent disclosure.

The section of the code dealing with confidentiality does make one caveat with regard to confidentiality, that being with regard to group counseling. It states, "In a group setting, the member is also responsible for taking *reasonable* precautions to protect individuals from physical and/or psychological trauma resulting from interaction within the group" (Section B1) (italics added). This seemingly tentative statement is simply a recognition that maintaining confidentiality in groups is difficult since group members may disclose material outside the group. The guidelines provided indicate that the group leader should establish a norm of confidentiality in groups. But Davis (1980) reports that breaches of confidentiality are still problematic. While Davis' study is fraught with methodological problems, 57 participants in the groups studied leaked something that was said in the group to persons outside the group. The developers of the current AACD ethical statement were aware of this problem and worded the section on confidentiality in group counseling accordingly. The major implication of the section on confidentiality in groups is that the counselor needs to take reasonable steps to ensure confidentiality but that breaches are to be expected and anticipated.

One apparent oversight in the current ethical statement is the failure to address confidentiality in the consulting relationship (Robinson & Gross, 1983). While it would generally be assumed that information resulting from a consultation relationship with an individual would be accorded the same status as that disclosed during counseling, no guidelines are provided in this area.

Similarly, the organizational consultant, who should focus on the organization not the individuals, is left with no guidelines regarding confidentiality. This oversight must be corrected in future drafts of the AACD code of ethics. The statement contained in principle 5a (confidentiality) of the APA code of ethics would suffice. It states, "Information obtained in clinical or consulting relationships, or evaluative data concerning children, students, employees, or others, is discussed only for professional purposes and only with persons clearly concerned with the case" (p. 636).

STUDENT LEARNING EXERCISE
Principle Three
Indicate whether the following actions are ethical (E) or unethical (U).

1. An organizational consultant informs the plant manager that a number of the supervisors believe the manager is incompetent but does not reveal which ones hold that belief.   E   U

2. A school counselor fails to contact authorities after she learns that students intend to construct a barricade made of straw on a nearby interstate highway.   E   U

3. A school counselor informs the playground supervisor that John and Jim intend to throw rocks at three of the fourth-grade girls.   E   U

4. A counselor consults with the school social worker regarding one of his clients and gives detailed case information.   E   U

5. A counselor reveals interest test scores of one of his clients to an army recruiter.   E   U

Principle Four: *Public Statements*

Historically, ethical codes have been quite definitive about the types of public statements that could be made. Until recently, physicians, dentists, lawyers, and other professionals were precluded from advertising and were permitted only to make announcements regarding the opening of their practices. However, court cases and governmental rulings have changed this situation. All professional groups are entitled to advertise, and ethical codes have been revised to provide guidelines for these advertisements and other public announcements.

Like its APA counterpart, the AACD code of ethics emphasizes accuracy as the most important ingredient in advertising. In part, it states that "the member must advertise the services in such a manner so as to accurately inform the public as to services, expertise, profession, and techniques" (Section F2). Claiming credentials as a mental health counselor when one has been prepared as a school counselor would be unethical, as would offering services for which one has no expertise. More obviously, claiming degrees, preparation in areas outside of counseling (e.g., psychology), or other qualifications that are unearned would be unethical.

Figure 9.1 shows an advertisement used by a counselor in private practice to announce the opening of her practice. This advertisement follows ethical guidelines.

Advertisements are not the only form of public statements made by counselors. School counselors and others often make public statements about test scores and other data regarding the students they serve. In these instances counselors should give complete information and provide data that will allow the public to draw accurate conclusions. The AACD code of ethics makes particular mention of the need to avoid possible misinterpretation of information such as I.Q. test scores. Providing accurate and unbiased data to the general public, regardless of the nature of the information, is also stressed.

An example of an unethical statement by a counselor was published recently in a southern newspaper. The counselor, who works for a private academy, proudly announced that 12 of the school's students had qualified as National Merit Semifinalists on the basis of the Preliminary Scholastic Aptitude Test (PSAT) scores. The counselor went on to suggest that the high proportion of National Merit Semifinalists was the outcome of the academy's superior curriculum and outstanding instruction. Since the academy only accepts very bright students who normally come from middle-class and upper-middle-class homes, there is some likelihood that a number of them would have had outstanding PSAT scores regardless of where they went to school. Thus the conclusion that the scores were the result of the student's experiences at the academy was unsubstantiated and it was unethical to state this publicly.

STUDENT LEARNING EXERCISE
Principle Four
Indicate whether the following actions are ethical (E) or unethical (U).

1. A counselor in private practice indicates that the course he offers will raise college entrance examination scores "significantly" for those who complete it.   E   U

2. A MA level mental health counselor indicates that his training is equivalent to that of a clinical psychologist.   E   U

3. An AACD member, trained as a school counselor, hangs out a shingle as a career counselor/consultant.   E   U

Sondra Van Sant, M. Ed.
announces the opening of a practice in

Career Counseling
for adolescents and adults

- Career Direction
- Educational Planning

- Job-Finding Skills
- Vocational Testing

106 Sandy Creek Trail
Chapel Hill

**CAREER SUCCESS
WORKSHOP**

Strategies to:
    *Identify your strengths and market them successfully
    *Find unadvertised jobs
    *Improve your resume
    *Map your career path

conducted by
SONDRA VAN SANT
National Certified Counselor

6 Thursday Evening Sessions Sept. 29 to Nov. 3

7:30–9:30   **Call 967-3605**   Fee: $75
For Information and Reservations

**CAREER PLANNING
AND JOB FINDING**

Workshop Series
directed by
**Sondra Van Sant, M. Ed.,
Career Counselor**
Nine Thursday Evening Sessions
Sept. 23-Nov. 18.
7:30 p.m.
Fee: $75
Free Information Session
Thurs., Sept. 16
Carolina Inn
or call 967-3605
Registration Limited

Figure 9.1 Announcements of the Opening of a Private Practice. Reprinted by permission.

4. A person who is untrained as a counselor but is a member of AACD uses the following statement when opening a private job placement bureau: "Staffed by a member of the American Association for Counseling and Development. Skilled counseling and placement services offered to the job hunter."   E   U

5. An agency director, advertising drug rehabilitation services staffed by "experienced, qualified counselors," fails to mention that the staff is made up of paraprofessionals who were once themselves substance abusers.   E   U

Principle Five: *Relationships to Client Groups*

One of the important aspects of client-counselor relationship, confidentiality, was discussed above. However, other guidelines are provided for dealing with clients. For example, clients are to be advised of the nature of techniques to be used *prior* to initiating the counseling relationship. In addition, a counselor who determines that the counseling relationship cannot be helpful to the client is obligated to terminate the relationship. And in those counseling relationships that involve a fee, counselors are advised that the financial position of the client is to be considered in the fee-setting process. Counselors are also told to avoid relationships in which they might not be totally objective. These would most typically involve what are classified as "dual relationships," which are counseling relationships with friends, relatives, and business associates. Finally, counselors are admonished that sexual intimacies with clients are to avoided.

Counselors are involved with client groups other than those being seen in counseling relationships. Subjects in research projects must be conscientiously safeguarded so that no possible psychological or physical damage will result from the research procedures. For those counselors consulting with organizations, a clear understanding of "problem definition, change goals, and predicted consequences" (Section E2) must be developed. The AACD code of ethics, unlike most other ethical statements, deals with training. It also specifies that in preparation programs, students should receive an integrated academic and supervised practice, exposure to varied theoretical orientations, training in the ethical standards of their profession, and instruction from skilled teachers and practitioners.

Many of these guidelines obviously provide counselors with some difficult decisions to make. For example, when does one know that a particular counseling relationship will fail to be productive? It is not unusual for some psychoanalytically oriented therapists to see their clients several times a week for years. Therefore, the counselor's theoretical orientation comes into play in the decision-making process, along with that person's judgment about expected outcomes.

Protecting the welfare of clients involves taking a number of other steps, including explaining counseling techniques that might prove harmful or embarrassing. In general, the explanation should provide enough information so that the client can make an informed decision. For example, if a client will receive negative feedback in a group counseling environment, this should be explained and illustrated if necessary so the client can anticipate the situation and decide whether he wants to participate. Protecting clients also means not using them to meet one's own needs, such as sexual needs. One research study indicated that nearly 5% of the 507 male psychologists responding to a survey regarding sexual intimacies with clients indicated that they had been so involved. A significantly lower percentage (0.08%) of the female psychologists indicated that they had been involved sexually with their clients (Bouhoutos, Holyroyd, Lerman, Forer, & Greenberg 1983). But as Coleman and Schaeffer (1986) point out, sexual contact is not the only way that clients can be abused by counselors. Hugs, fondling, seductive behavior, and professional voyeurism (unnecessarily exploring intimate areas) may all lead to client confusion and disrupt the therapeutic relationship. As these authors point out, the counselor can avoid overt sexual abuse and psychological harm to clients by establishing clear boundaries between the counseling and the personal relationship. If this cannot be accomplished, the relationship should be terminated.

STUDENT LEARNING EXERCISE
Principle Five
Indicate whether the following actions are ethical (E) or unethical (U).

1. A counselor conducts several sessions with a client and then discovers that she is seeing a psychologist for the same problem. The counselor decides to continue counseling.   E   U

2. A school counselor accepts as a client the daughter of his best friend even though he has given his friend "advice" about the problem with the daughter for a number of months.   E   U

3. A school counselor accepts as a client the son of one of his best friends when he learns that the young man has a serious drinking problem that has been undetected by his parents.   E   U

4. A counselor becomes involved with one of his clients, stroking and embracing her, because he believes this will help her overcome her shyness with other males.   E   U

5. A counselor who leads growth groups based on encounter procedures does not inform a client that some sessions may involve intense negative feedback.   E   U

Principle Six: *Relationships to Colleagues and Other Professions*

The success of a professional group depends to a large degree on the extent to which there is harmony within the profession and with other similar groups. In two obvious attempts to maintain inter- and intraprofessional harmony, the AACD code of ethics specifies that (1) the member may not knowingly enter into a counseling relationship with a client who is being seen by another professional, and (2) if a counselor discovers that a client is being seen by another professional after the counseling relationship has been initiated, the relationship must be terminiated (if permission to continue cannot be gained from the second professional or unless the second relationship is terminated by the client).

The difference between the APA and AACD statements on this point is interesting: On this matter the former states,

> If a person is receiving similar services from another professional, psychologists do not offer their own services directly to such a person. If a psychologist is contacted by a person who is already receiving similar services from another professional, the psychologist carefully considers that professional relationship and proceeds with caution and sensitivity to the therapeutic issues as well as the client's welfare. The psychologist discusses these issues with the client so as to minimize the risk of confusion and conflict (76).

It may well be that the interest and involvement of more psychologists in private practice has led to this particular statement, which allows more freedom with regard to becoming involved with prospective clients. The guidelines do specify that a counselor may consult with another professional about a particular client if the need arises. This consultation is not restricted to counselors. However, the general position regarding consultation is that it should be restricted to those professionals who operate under ethical guidelines similar to those observed by counselors.

The AACD ethical statement also comments on the relationships among professionals in the area of research and publication. Counselors engaged in research have the responsibility to accord appropriate credit for research projects including joint authorship if the results are published. They must also communicate the full results of research to other counselors, even if that research reflects negatively on particular practices employed, services offered, and on the institutions generally.

When engaging in private practice involving other professionals, counselors must make clear the responsibilities of each, both among themselves and to the clients they serve. In the supervision of others, counselors are advised to "establish interpersonal relations and working agreements with supervisors and subordinates (Section G2). In this context "supervisors" refers to secondary or field supervisors. These types of relationships are deemed necessary so that ethical behavior can be maintained and so that competencies can be developed. Other intraprofessional relationships are covered by the code, including a section on the relationship between counselor educators and *students*. This section specifies that students should be the recipients of a well-designed and well-taught program. These statements and the ones alluded to earlier in this section should make it apparent that it is the intent of the code to regulate certain aspects of counselors' behavior as they deal with other counselors, counselor trainees, and professionals. Of particular concern is functioning in those areas that might result in ethical breaches or failure to fulfill responsibilities to client groups.

STUDENT LEARNING EXERCISE
Principle Six

Indicate whether the following actions are ethical (E) or unethical (U).

1. A mental health counselor tells a group of people at a cocktail party that social workers are not really prepared to perform psychotherapy.   E   U

2. Even though a student counselor has done a majority of the work on the research, a professor insists that he be senior author on the manuscript that has resulted from their collaboration. The student capitulates.   E   U

3. A professor in a theory of counseling class proclaims that there is only one theory that has been empirically validated and that is the one the class will study.   E   U

Principle Seven: *Relationships of Ethics and the Law*

Most codes of ethics, including the AACD code, either tacitly or directly recognize the relationship between the law and the profession. For example, the provision in Section B (Counseling Relationship) indicating that the counselor has a duty to warn others in the case of imminent danger to a client or others comes about as a result of a famous court case *(Tarasoff v. Regents of the University of California)* that will be discussed in detail in Chapter 10. A second provision of *Ethical Standards* deals with "the appropriation, reproduction, or modifications of published tests or parts thereof without acknowledgment and permission from the previous publisher" (Section C11). This is of course a recognition of copyright laws. References are also made to local statutes in the section dealing with private practice. Counselors are urged to be in compliance with local regulations in the establishment of corporations and to adhere to local regulations in the pursuit of their private practice. All of these admonishments came about partially to regulate member behavior, but also as means to make counselors aware of certain legal regulations which, if violated, would endanger the individual and demean the profession.

Future versions of the AACD code of ethics, and other such codes, will undoubtedly be shaped by legislature and governmental regulations just as the current version has been. In this way the profession can demonstrate to regulatory agencies not only an awareness of existing laws and governmental policies but also an intent to enforce them without assistance.

Principle Eight: *Research*

Section D of *Ethical Standards* deals with research and publication. In general, this section holds that counselors are to adhere to sound scientific principles when designing and conducting research, are to report their results fully, including results that are contrary to expectation, and are to assist other researchers who want to replicate or extend the research by providing original data and other types of assistance. Researchers are also advised to report results clearly so no misinterpretation is possible.

Another area of concern that is alluded to has to do with subjects in research studies. As was noted in the section on confidentiality, the anonymity of subjects is to be protected in the release or publication of all data. However, the guidelines address a broader set of issues than confidentiality. Researchers are also responsible for protecting the welfare of clients, which means that research subjects are not to be exposed to conditions that would result in psychological or physical harm. One means of assuring that subjects are protected is to fully inform them of the purpose of the research and to gain informed consent to participate. Informed consent is generally interpreted to mean that a prospective subject fully understands the nature and consequences of participation.

There is one equivocation about informed consent, however. The statement found in Section D5 indicates that subjects may be misinformed or not fully informed if such action is necessary to achieve the purposes of the investigation. This statement in no way lessens the investigator's responsibility to protect the welfare of the client. It does allow the continuation of research in which subjects are "blind" to the purposes of the investigation. Subjects in this type of research must be debriefed immediately upon completion of the research project. This debriefing process typically involves providing a full explanation of the purposes of the research and offering assistance if any psychological distress has occurred as a result of participation. Guidelines specify that both full explanation and assistance be provided.

STUDENT LEARNING EXERCISE
Principles Seven and Eight
Indicate whether the following actions are ethical (E) or unethical (U).

1. A research team decides not to report the outcomes of two analyses that, while they do not contradict the overall results of the resarch, do alter the conclusions that can be drawn. E U

2. A researcher does not write up a research study in which she obtained no significant results. E U

3. Aware that a few high school students have become mildly depressed after a study on the etiology of suicide, as a precaution researchers offer counseling services to students who participated in the study. E U

4. A school counselor promises that all information will be held in confidence even though the legislature has not granted privileged communication to school counselors. E U

SOME PROBLEMS WITH THE CODE

In the foregoing discussion several references were made to problems and deficiencies within the AACD (1981) *Ethical Standards*. As Mabe and Rollin (1986) note, not all situations can be covered by an ethical statement, but an attempt will be made to clarify what are veiwed as potential areas of difficulty in functioning as an ethical counselor. It is also the position taken here that the current code of ethics, as it now stands, provides some problems for counselors as they present themselves to governmental agencies, health insurance carriers, and others, and as they claim parity with other mental health service providers who have clearer statements of ethical guidelines. Only by clarifying and/or eliminating certain sections can these problems be eliminated.

Conflict between Client and Institution

Guidelines within the code of ethics indicate that the client is the primary concern of counselors (Section B1). However, if a counselor is obligated to report a potential disturbance to his employer (Section G3), there will probably be times when there will be conflicts of interest between the client and the institution. Counselors need to clarify this apparent contradiction. The statement contained in Section B14 that indicates that there may be justifiable alternatives to the ethical guidelines laid down in the section on counseling relationships, depending on the demands of the institution, should also be clarified. How can there be alternatives to confidentiality and protecting the welfare of the client? These equivocations may be misinterpreted by the public or the counseling profession. They also provide problems for counselors who rely on the code as a decision-making tool. It is suggested here that counselors follow the lead of the American Psychological Association (1981) guidelines and make it clear that the client comes first and institutional concerns are secondary. A statement such as the following could be included in the preamble: The essence of the counseling profession lies in assisting the clients that it serves; therefore in all matters the first responsibility of the professional counselor is to the client.

Other Apparent Contradictions

Section B11 indicates that a counselor who has an evaluative relationship with an individual should not serve as that individual's counselor. Then the *Ethical Standards* indicates that if no viable referral resource can be identified, the counselor may enter into or maintain a counseling relationship. One of these statements in Section B11 should be altered to indicate either that entering into a counseling relationship should always be avoided or that it should usually be avoided. The guidelines are currently confusing with regard to this issue. A statement such as the following would suffice: Dual relationships are generally to be avoided. However, in those situations in which there are no alternative sources of assistance, counselors may proceed if they are certain that objectivity can be maintained.

Omissions and Oversights

As Robinson and Gross (1983) have accurately noted, the section on consulting (Section E) is problematic. One problem is that there are no guidelines regarding confidentiality in consultation. Another area that presents problems is the definition of consultation. The authors of the code indicate that they took their definition of consultation from Kurpius (1978). However, the definition that appears in the code is rather limited in that it focuses on organizational consultation only. Inserting a broader definition of consultation would be a good beginning to revising this section of the code. More importantly, Section E needs to be revised to include statements on the consultation relationship, confidentiality, competency, responsibility, and termination of the consulting relationship.

A statement regarding confidentiality in consultation would necessarily begin by recognizing and defining the consultee and his or her rights. Since consultation often involves third parties (usually called "clients"), these parties would need to be defined as well. A statement regarding the confidentiality of information gained from consultees and clients should be incorporated into the current statement. It is suggested here that all information gained in consultation should be held in confidence, regardless of its source. The counselor functioning in the consultation role could use the data generated to draw conclusions and generate suggestions so long as the sources of the data were not identified.

A relationship is as important to consultation as it is to counseling (Brown, Wyne, Blackburn, & Powell, 1979). Of particular importance in the consulting relationship are the difficulties that can arise when the consultant and consultee are from different cultural backgrounds (Gibbs, 1985). A statement asserting the need to be aware of conflicts of values, linguistic styles, power-authority issues, and other concerns, particularly in cross-cultural consultation, should be incorporated into the current guidelines.

The AACD code of ethics now indicates that when making public statements about one's availability as a consultant, ethical guidelines should be followed. Apparently, misrepresentation of credentials among consultants is a fairly widespread problem (Robinson & Gross, 1985), but no hard data have surfaced to support this supposition. However, the current statement could be strengthened by including an admonishment against engaging in consultation without the proper skills.

Two additional statements regarding consultation should probably be added, one on responsibility and one on termination. The primary responsibility of the consultant is to the consultee, that is, the person who is receiving the consultation, unless that person (or persons) is involved in unethical or illegal conduct. When the consultee is engaged in illegal acts, consultation should be terminated. Termination should also be automatic when (1) the consultant has exhausted his or her expertise, and (2) there is a conflict between the consultant and consultee over values, issues, goals, or other factors that would cause dissonance in the consulting relationship.

All in all, the AACD code of ethics is similar in most respects to those of other mental health services providers. However, some clarifications and additions would enhance it and make it a more useful tool. These changes would also provide assistance in the enforcement of the code.

ENFORCING THE CODE OF ETHICS

The first question to be answered in enforcement is, "Who is covered by the AACD *Ethical Standards*?" The apparent answer is: anyone who calls himself or herself a counselor—but this is incorrect. Persons covered by the *Ethical Standards* include members of the American Association for Counseling and Development, counselors who are licensed or certified by state licensing/certification boards that have adopted this code of ethics, and counselors who have been certified by national agencies that have adopted the AACD code of ethics. Other counselors have an obligation to observe the code, but are unregulated.

The first line of enforcement of any code of ethics rests with the moral and ethical values of the individual counselor. As Gallessich (1982) aptly notes, self-discipline is the primary means by which any code of ethics is enforced. It is the basic responsibility of a training program not only to teach the principles of ethical conduct, but also to socialize neophyte counselors in a manner that will result in the internalization of the moral and ethical principles of the code of ethics (Tennyson & Strom, 1986). While there are no clear-cut guidelines for this socialization process, it seems that trainers (1) stimulate ethical sensitivity by emphasizing ethical dilemmas in all classes, (2) involve students in ethical decision-making processes, and (3) develop a tolerance for the ambiguities involved in ethical decision-making by modeling these difficulties (Kitchner, 1986).

But what if breaches in ethical standards do occur in practice? Just as counselors' self-discipline and personal ethical standards are the primary basis of ethical functioning, their vigilance against unethical practice among their colleagues is the basic safeguard against widespread unethical practice. Counselors must be alert to and act when unethical practice occurs. Since many ethical errors are simply oversights on the part of counselors, a reminder of the provisions of the code will suffice as an enforcement strategy in many instances. However, in the case of flagrant violations of various aspects of the guidelines, or when unethical behavior continues after it has been brought to the attention of the counselor, stronger steps must be taken to correct the behavior. This means reporting the behavior to the state division of the AACD Ethics Committee or, if the state does not have a committee formed, to the AACD Ethics Committee.

The AACD Ethics Committee has established guidelines for adjudicating complaints regarding ethical misconduct, and these guidelines have been adopted by approximately 24 states at this writing. It is anticipated that all states and territories affiliated with AACD will have ethics committees in place within the near future.

The first step in the adjudication process is the filing of a written statement with the state division ethics committee charging a member with unethical behavior. This complaint may be filed by either an AACD member or a nonmember. At this time there is no statute of limitations on filing these complaints. Therefore, a counselor who acts unethically is at risk for an indefinite period of time. Complaints should provide a detailed description of the unethical behavior and, when possible, indicate the section of *Ethical Standards* that has been violated. One warning is appropriate at this juncture. Counselors should *not* file complaints of ethical misconduct without carefully verifying through first-hand information that a violation of the *Ethical Standards* has occurred. To do otherwise is to run the risk of incurring a defamation suit.

Once the complaint is received, it is the ethics committee's responsibility to contact the accused member, inform him or her of the complaint, and ask him or her for information regarding the allegations. The committee may also collect data from other sources such as clients, other counselors, noncounselors, employers, etc. Once all data are collected, the committee considers the facts and reaches a decision.

If a counselor is found guilty of an ethical breach, a number of consequences may result. The mildest of these is a letter reprimanding the counselor, explaining the code of ethics, and warning the counselor to refrain from unethical conduct in the future. However, the ethics committee may also recommend delicensure or decertification, removal from registries, and suspension or expulsion from AACD. The groups to whom the recommendations are made would then have to take up the matter and render a decision. At this point in time we have insufficient data to indicate what these boards and organizations would do. However, in a sister discipline, psychology, the recommendation of the ethics committee is often followed and appropriate disciplinary action taken.

As was indicated in the foregoing paragraphs, dealing with ethical conduct is a rather new phenomenon for the counseling profession. Indeed, while the first ethics committee was established in 1953 (Allen, 1986), it has only recently become active in the enforcement area. However, the enforcement of the code of ethics is one of the most important activities for counselors since it is one of the factors that can be used to establish the status of counseling as a profession. A record of enforcing the code is also important as counselors seek parity in treatment from insurance companies, legislatures, and other governmental agencies.

SUMMARY

This chapter began with a review of the purposes of ethical codes, which were stated generally to be the protection of the public and the profession. This discussion was followed by the presentation of eight general principles of ethical functioning, including professional responsibility, maintaining competence, confidentiality, public statements, relationships to client groups, relationships to colleagues, ethics and the law, and ethical practice in research. The final two sections of the chapter dealt with some problems with the AACD ethical code and the enforcement issues.

REVIEW QUESTIONS

1. What are the goals that professional groups have in mind when they adopt a code of ethics? To what degree have these been achieved by the counseling profession?
2. Most professional groups now require continuing education for maintenance of licensure or certification. Which ethical principles can be cited as support for these requirements?
3. Outline the steps in the adjudicating of ethical complaints.
4. Why is the individual practitioner the most important ingredient in maintaining the ethical posture of a group?
5. Discuss the interface between the law and codes of ethics.

6. What are the differences and similarities between the AACD and APA codes of ethics?

REFERENCES

Allen, V. C. (1986). A historical perspective of the AACD ethics committee. *Journal of Counseling and Development, 64,* 293.

American Association for Counseling and Development. (1981). *Ethical standards.* Alexandria, VA: Author.

American Psychological Association. (1981). *Ethical principles of psychologists. American Psychologist, 36,* 633–638.

Bangs, A. J. (1971). Privilege and the counseling profession. *Personnel and Guidance Journal, 50*(4), 270–275.

Bouhoutos, J., Holyroyd, J., Lerman, H., Forer, B. E., & Greenberg, M. (1983). Sexual intimacy between psychotherapist and patient. *Professional Psychology: Research and Practice, 14*(2), 185–196.

Brown, D., Wyne, M. D., Blackburn, J. E., & Powell, W. C. (1979). *Consultation: Strategy for improving education.* Boston: Allyn & Bacon.

Casas, M. J., Ponterotto, J. G., & Gutierrez, J. M. (1986). An ethical indictment of counseling research and training: The cross-cultural perspective. *Journal of Counseling and Development, 64*(5), 347–349.

Cayleff, S. E. (1986). Ethical issues in counseling gender, race, and culturally distinct groups. *Journal of Counseling and Development, 64*(5), 345–347.

Coleman, E., & Schaeffer, S. (1986). Boundaries of sex and intimacy between client and counselor. *Journal of Counseling and Development, 64*(5), 341–344.

Davis, K. L. (1980). Is confidentiality in groups realistic? *Personnel and Guidance Journal, 59*(4), 197–201.

Gallessich, J. (1982). *The profession and practice of consultation.* San Francisco: Jossey-Bass.

Gibbs, J. T. (1985). The training and supervision of consultants: Must we continue to be class bound and color blind. *The Counseling Psychologist.*

Golightly, C. L. (1971). A philosopher's view of values and ethics. *Personnel and Guidance Journal, 50*(4), 289–294.

Ibrahim, F. A., & Arrendo, P. M. (1986). Ethical standards for cross-cultural counseling: Counselor preparation, practice, assessment, and research. *Journal of Counseling and Development, 64*(5), 349–352.

Kitchner, K. S. (1986). Teaching applied ethics in counselor education: An integration of psychological processes and philosophical analyses. *Journal of Counseling and Development, 64*(5), 30–310.

Kurpius, D. (1978) Consultation theory and process: An integrated model. *Personnel and Guidance Journal, 56*(6), 335–338.

Mabe, A. R., & Rollin, S. A. (1986). The role of a code of ethical standards in counseling. *Journal of Counseling and Development, 64*(5), 294–297.

Patterson, C. H. (1971). Are ethics different in different settings? *Personnel and Guidance Journal, 50*(4), 260–261.

Robinson, S. E., & Gross, D. R. (1983, March). *Ethics: The forgotten issue in consultation.* Paper presented at the APGA annual meeting, Washington, DC.

Robinson, S., & Gross, D. (1985). Ethics in consultation: The Canterville ghost revisited. *The Counseling Psychologist.*

Roy v. Hartogs, 381 N.Y. S. 2d 590 (1976).

Tarasoff v. Regents of the University of California, S.F. No. 23042, Superior Court No. 405694, 441 P. 2d. 345 (1976).

Tennyson, W. W., & Strom, S. M. (1986). Beyond professional standards: Developing responsibleness. *Journal of Counseling and Development, 64*(5), 298–302.

Van Hoose, W. V., & Kottler, J. A. (1977). *Ethical and legal issues in counseling and psychotherapy.* San Francisco: Jossey-Bass.

10

Legal Issues in the Counseling Profession

GOAL OF THE CHAPTER

The goal of this chapter is to present an overview of the major legal issues confronting professional counselors.

CHAPTER PREVIEW

1. The terms "privileged communication" and "confidentiality" will be discussed and the legal issues surrounding privileged communication presented.
2. Malpractice liability will be discussed in terms of the conditions under which it may occur and methods for avoiding legal liability outlined.
3. Defamation will be defined as a special case of potential legal liability and circumstances that might lead to slander and libel discussed.
4. Legal issues that confront school counselors will be presented, particularly those that may arise as a result of labeling, failure to provide due process, freedom of speech, right to services, records, dress codes, and abortion counseling.
5. Issues that should be of concern to private practitioners will be outlined, including honesty in labeling and breach of contract.
6. The final section of the chapter will deal with ethics and the law.

INTRODUCTION

Twenty-five years ago this chapter would have been unnecessary. Today legal concerns stand as one of the most serious issues confronting counselors. The dramatic rise in the importance attached to legal concerns can be attributed to two factors: the status of the counseling profession and the "legalizing" of American society. Even the most casual observer of current news events is aware that civil liability is of great concern to professionals, corporations, municipalities, and private citizens. This is primarily because juries have awarded increasingly large sums of money to plaintiffs when physicians, psychologists, or others have been found liable for damages in malpractice cases. But liability suits are not the only types of legal problems that make newspaper headlines. An associate superintendent of schools is prosecuted for not reporting a case of child abuse and subsequently is convicted. A state psychological licensing board is sued for defamation of character by a psychologist accused of unethical behavior. Parents file suit against two researchers because they allegedly have invaded the privacy of their child. The list of legal actions taken against all types of professionals is seemingly endless.

The "legalizing" of society is not the only reason that counselors need to be concerned about legal issues, since many legal developments have been quite positive. The last quarter-century has brought about substantial change to the point that Hopkins and Anderson (1985) observe that the emerging counseling profession of the 1960s and 1970s is the recognized profession of today. Many of the indicators of this recognition are legally based. Licensure laws are one example; privileged communication laws are another. But this recognition has also brought increased expectations with regard to the level of practice since counselors have argued convincingly that high levels of performance are the hallmark of their functioning. When high standards of practice are not adhered to, successful litigation can result.

As a result of increased recognition and increasingly aggressive lawyers, professional counselors need to be aware of laws that pertain to them, sources of civil liability, and the interaction of legal and ethical guidelines. The first section of this chapter will deal with laws that direct and/or restrict counselor practice, primarily in the areas of privileged communication and civil malpractice. The sections that follow will deal with legal issues for two groups of counselors in specialized settings: school counselors and counselors in private practice. Finally, a brief discussion of the interaction of ethics and law will be presented.

LEGAL RESTRICTIONS/DIRECTIONS

Privileged Communication

As we saw in Chapter 9, confidentiality is an important consideration in the ethical practice of counselors. Counselors are admonished to keep information gained in counseling relationships in confidence. "Confidentiality," then, is an ethical term having its origins in the codes of ethics of professional groups, including physicians, lawyers, counselors, and others. "Privileged communication," on the other hand, is a legal term, and was first granted to lawyers by the New York legislature in 1828 (Hopkins & Anderson, 1985). "Privileged communication" is a narrower term than "confidentiality" and refers to a privilege granted to a client to have information divulged in a professional relationship withheld from the courts. Normally, courts have a right to all evidence related to a particular litigation, and privileged communications statutes run contrary to this tradition (Hopkins & Anderson, 1985; Knapp & VandeCreek, 1983).

The rationale for awarding privileged communication to any group, including counselors, is that the communication must originate with the expectation that it will be kept in confidence, that confidentiality is essential to the maintenance of the relationship in which the communication occurs, that there is a belief in the community (legal jurisdiction) that the client-professional relationship ought to be fostered, and that the injury to the relationship resulting from the disclosure of the information gained would be greater than the benefit that would be derived from the impact of the disclosure on the litigation to which it pertains. Simply, a court or a legislature confronted with granting privileged communication must consider the nature of the relationship, the value placed on it by the community, the positive consequences involved in helping a relationship, and the negative consequences to litigation if privilege is awarded (Hopkins & Anderson, 1985; Knapp & VandeCreek, 1983).

Since 1828 most state jurisdictions have awarded privileged communication to the clients of physicians, lawyers, clergy, and psychologists. Many states have also extended privileged communication to counselors; for example, all licensure and registry laws for counselors contain provisions extending privileged communication to clients of the licensees. However, some states without licensing laws have privileged communication acts.

Privileged communication laws, whether they be freestanding or a part of another law, are of two general types: those granting absolute privilege and those granting some form of partial or limited privilege. Absolute privileged communication is rare, but is most often extended to the lawyer-client relationship or to those individuals who seek help or solace from the clergy. When absolute privileged communication is extended, presiding judges may not compel disclosure of the information, and even statutes such as those that dictate reporting child abuse often do not pertain to relationships so protected.

Most privileged communication statutes pertaining to mental health practitioners, including counselors, can be characterized as limited or qualified in nature. As Knapp and VandeCreek (1983) point out, the limitations applied to privileged communication are so diverse, the only way to ascertain those pertaining to the individual counselor is to consult those statutes that pertain to his or her jurisdiction (state) and situation. However, one of the major legal qualifications imposed on privileged communications where counselors are involved has to do with the right of a presiding judge to order disclosure of information gained in the confidential relationship, either in pretrial investigations or during the trial itself. Disclosure in this case pertains both to the verbal communication (counseling) and to the records kept regarding counseling. In these cases, the judge decides whether disclosure of information in the possession of the counselor is "in the best interest of justice" and makes a ruling regarding disclosure.

In addition to limitations placed directly on the privilege enjoyed by counselors and their clients within the privileged communication legislation itself, other legislation and case law also limit the degree of privilege extended. For example, all 50 states now have child abuse laws that require individuals who work with children (e.g., counselors, teachers, social workers, physicians) to divulge knowledge or suspicion of child abuse. It is also necessary to report criminal activity in some states (Hopkins & Anderson, 1985). These legal mandates override privileged communication statutes for counselors and their clients in many instances.

Case law, in particular *Tarasoff v. Regents of the University of California*, also has influenced the actual practice followed regarding privileged communication. In the Tarasoff case, a mental health worker was seeing a foreign student in an out-patient setting operated by the University of California at Berkeley. The student disclosed that he intended to kill a former girlfriend who, although not identified by name, could easily be identified by the therapist as Ms. Tarasoff. Subsequently, the therapist asked the campus police to detain Mr. Poddar, the client, which they did for a brief period of time. Mr. Poddar was released on order of the head of the psychiatric unit of the facility where he was confined, and he proceeded to kill Ms. Tarasoff. Her parents subsequently filed suit claiming that the therapist had a duty to warn both the parents and the intended victim.

The California Supreme Court upheld the suit, noting that when a special relationship exists between two persons, and the conduct of one of the persons needs to be controlled, a duty to warn is established. The therapeutic relationship was viewed as a special relationship. Mr. Poddar's explicit threats to kill and the identification of a specific, foreseeable victim established a duty to warn in the eyes of the court (Gehring, 1982).

The result of the Tarasoff case has been widely interpreted to imply that mental health workers have the duty to take appropriate steps to protect either the victims of a client or the clients themselves in the case of potential suicides (Denkowski & Denkowski, 1982). Hopkins and Anderson (1985) report that the result of the Tarasoff case has been tempered somewhat by a 1983 Colorado decision (*Brady v. Hopper*), which found that liability was dependent upon identification of "a specific threat to a specific person" (p. 15).

The counselor's duty to break confidentiality in cases in which clients may commit suicide has been established in a number of court cases. Earlier in a Wisconsin case (*Bogust v. Iverson*, 1960), a counselor was absolved from liability because the court held that he was not a psychiatrist and thus not qualified to make a diagnosis of potential suicide. However, this ruling probably has little relevance today because of the increase of recognition of the counseling profession. Liability can be avoided if the suicide is unforeseeable (e.g., no threats have been made), reasonable professional steps are taken to stop the suicide (e.g., a no-suicide contract is developed), and the counselor uses reasonable judgment in determining that the client can be depended upon to follow the contract (Gable, 1983). If a client threatens to commit suicide, and there is likelihood that the threat will be carried out regardless of the steps taken in counseling, the counselor should take appropriate steps to stop the suicide, including informing parents or guardians and/or seeing that the client is detained.

The implications of privileged communication are apparent in some instances and subtle in others. Obviously, ethical guidelines must be tempered by legal constraints. Under most statutes counselors have no discretion when they encounter child abuse. The information must be transmitted immediately to an agency designated in the statute, usually the Department of Social Services. Similarly, depending on local statutes, withholding information when disclosure has been ordered by a presiding judge places the counselor in violation of the law and subject to a fine and imprisonment.

Since privileged communication is granted to the client, not the counselor, a counselor may be freed from that restriction if permission of the client is obtained. Normally, this permission is breach the privilege would be obtained in writing and involves little difficulty if the client is an adult. But a client who has not reached the age of majority (18 in most instances) may not be able to provide permission to divulge privileged information. It is probable that only a parent or legal guardian will be able to give this permission.

Finally, counselors who carelessly divulge privileged information are guilty of a crime and, in addition to receiving professional sanctions, may find themselves accused of crimes or the subject of civil legal action because of malpractice.

Malpractice Liability

Malpractice liability grows out of four interrelated conditions. These are:

1. A counselor has a duty to a client to offer services that meet a standard of skill or care.
2. There has been a dereliction or breach of the duty.
3. Harm or injury results to the client or a member of society as a result of the breach of duty.
4. A causal link between the injury or harm and the breach of duty can be established. (Gable, 1983)

Although in the Tarasoff case cited in the preceding section, the mental health worker charged with malpractice was a psychologist, this case is illustrative of the relationship of a counselor's duty, a breach of duty, and a causal relationship between the breach and harm. As Gable (1983) notes, malpractice involves negligence, a failure to act according to accepted professional standards. Gable also points out that it is generally expected that professionals will have the skills necessary to provide reasonable care. In the Tarasoff case, possessing the skills to provide reasonable care involved being able to predict homicidal behavior and following acceptable professional standards to prevent the murder. The duty, then, was to diagnose and prevent homicidal behavior. The duty was breached, harm occurred, and a causal link was established between the dereliction of duty and Ms. Tarasoff's murder. As a result the courts ruled in favor of the plaintiffs, Ms. Tarasoff's parents.

Malpractice liability can result from a number of situations, including suicide (Berman & Cohen-Sandler, 1983), sexual intimacy with clients (Bouhoutsos, Holroyd, Lerman, Forer, & Greenberg, 1983), faulty supervision (Cohen, 1979; Cormier & Bernard, 1982), failure to get informed consent from children in a research project, improper diagnosis or evaluation of physical injury (Gable, 1983), providing abortion and birth control information, defamation, invasion of privacy, or breach of contract (Hopkins & Anderson, 1985; Slimak & Berkowitz, 1983). This list is lengthy, but it is not exhaustive. In the section on some special legal considerations for school counselors, other sources of malpractice liability will be discussed.

Just as certain conditions must be met before malpractice liability can be established, so are there major areas from which malpractice suits against counselors might result: (1) not following standard practice, (2) using procedures or techniques for which one is untrained, (3) failure to select the best procedure, (4) failure to explain the consequences of treatment, (5) defamation, (6) invasion of privacy, and (7) dereliction of duty. An eighth category, breach of contract, will be discussed in a later section.

Following Standard Practice.   A standard practice is a recognized approach to treating a particular concern. As Hopkins and Anderson (1985) note, determining a standard of care in a malpractice suit against a counselor is difficult. Most persons familiar with the counseling profession are aware that there are competing ideas about the most appropriate way to conduct individual and group counseling, consultation, and testing, although the standard practice regarding testing is probably less debatable.

However, while there is no standard way to conduct counseling, ethical guidelines establish some standards of care that must be followed. For example, sexual intimacies with the clients are prohibited in Section B11 of the AACD (1981) code of ethics. As Gable (1983) notes, sexual intimacy with clients, even in the guise of treatment, has consistently resulted in successful liabilty suits against mental health workers. In addition, in a number of cases in which therapists have engaged in sexual intimacies in the name of treatment, criminal suits have resulted.

Gable (1983) also indicates that innovative therapy involving physical contact with clients can be the basis for malpractice suits, particularly when the contact is extreme (e.g., hitting, choking).

While deviation from standard practice by hitting a client or becoming involved sexually is extreme, it seems likely that such practices occur, based on the data regarding other professions (Bouhoutos et al., 1983; Gable, 1983). However, failure to properly administer and interpret tests and inventories, and failure to warn to take appropriate steps in the face of homicide and suicide threats, appear to be areas in which counselors are more likely to fall short of recognized standards of care.

Training and the Use of Technique. During the past 20 years, a number of new counseling, consultation, and testing techniques have been developed and popularized, including most of the behavioral techniques, many group counseling techniques, some of the currently used interest inventories, and almost all of the computer assisted techniques (e.g., test administration). As a result many counselors either were not exposed fully to some of these techniques during their training or have little preparation in their use. These people are vulnerable to malpractice suits if damage results from the use of the procedures. A historical case in point the encounter groups of the 1960s and 1970s that were often led by counselors without proper training. A current-day example is the number of counselors using desensitization procedures to deal with phobic clients, again, in some cases, without proper training.

The question is, how does one attain a skill and demonstrate that he or she has applied it in a reasonable fashion? It seems that the courts have varying opinions about this matter, depending on one's profession, one's geographic location, whether one belongs to a professional organization (e.g., Association of Specialists in Group Work), and whether one claims to be a specialist (e.g., career counselor). The AACD (1981) code of ethics specifies in Section A4 that the members shall not claim or imply qualifications that exceed those possessed. The courts would carry this one step further. Counselors shall not engage in practices that require skills beyond those possessed. Those who do run the risk of professional malpractice if damage results from that practice.

Failure to Select Best Procedure. Counselors are confronted each day with decisions regarding the best approach to use with their clients. Since there is little evidence to support, say, group counseling over individual counseling, or counseling over consultation, there is little likelihood that malpractice suits will result from these types of decisions. However, a report in a major eastern newspaper gives an example of a decision made by a therapist that might lead to a malpractice suit. In this situation, a psychoanalytically oriented psychotherapist used traditional psychoanalytic procedures to treat a middle-aged woman with agoraphobia (fear of open places) for a number of years and at great expense. The woman did not improve and subsequently discontinued her psychotherapy, engaged a behavior therapist, and was cured in 18 months. The pain and expenses endured by the woman as the result of inappropriate treatment certainly are the basis for a malpractice suit. Counselors who continue to see clients when others might provide better assistance run the risk of malpractice suits, as does the person who selects the least potent treatment approach.

Failure to Explain the Consequences of Treatment. Few of the treatment strategies employed by counselors will cause the dangerous side effects of medical treatments, where this category of malpractice liability is of greatest concern. However, there are documented cases in which counselors have utilized techniques—such as nudity in groups, self-awareness techniques, touch exercises—that have caused psychological distress that might be interpreted by the courts as harm growing out of a breach of duty. Counselors need to recognize that when they are planning counseling activities, clients need to be fully aware of the nature and potential consequences (e.g., personal embarrassment) of the approach.

Defamation. Defamation of character involves slander, defaming someone orally, or libel defamation using the written word (Gable, 1983). Defamation occurs when information provided to a third party exposes the client to hatred, contempt, or pecuniary loss as a result of the communication. The defamed person must be alive and must suffer a loss, although the loss may be real or psychological (e.g., loss of job or reputation). As Hopkins and Anderson (1985) indicate, some states carry the definition of defamation a bit further, in that counselors and others can be found guilty of defamation if they give false information that (1) a client has committed a serious crime, (2) a client has a venereal disease, (3) negatively affects a person's business or profession, or (4) indicates that a female is promiscuous.

Hopkins and Anderson (1985) go on to indicate that there are two areas in which counselors may become involved in defamation: exposure of records and inadvertent disclosure of information received in counseling. To these should be added the area of recommendations, since many counselors are asked to attest to the character, work habits, academic ability, and other factors relating to clients' worth as students or employees.

Undoubtedly, the best defense against defamation is truth. However, the matter of truth and damage can be interpreted by the courts. In addition, the intent of the communication is of major concern in defamation cases. Successful defamation suits usually result from malicious statements, that is, those that are intended to harm one's client. However, false statements, regardless of content, that impune the reputation of one's clients (particularly those that relate to a woman's reputation or a client's ability to function on the job) may result in successful suits. Truthfulness and honoring the privilege accorded the communications of one's clients are always in order.

Invasion of Privacy. In 1970, the Russell Sage Foundation published a set of guidelines for collecting, filing, and maintaining student data because, as they noted, their current data-collection and record-keeping procedures constituted a serious threat to the privacy of individuals. In 1974 the Protection of the Rights of Privacy of Parents and Students Amendment to Education was passed with the intention of protecting students and parents from invasion of privacy. Invasion of privacy occurs when information about a client is gained without the client's full knowledge and consent or when the client is a minor or is impaired and is unable to give consent and the consent of parents or guardians is not obtained (Van Hoose & Kottler, 1977). Invasion of privacy can also occur when derogatory information gained with the consent of the client is knowingly *or* accidentally provided to another person (Hopkins & Anderson, 1985). In such cases, should either psychological or real damage result, the counselor may be held liable, even though the information disclosed is true.

Counselors are routinely involved in situations in which invasion of privacy might occur. The most obvious of these is the counseling situation, particularly if the counselor's duty to maintain confidence is breached. Tests may also constitute an invasion of privacy because, as Van Hoose and Kottler (1977) state, "Testing is by its very nature intended to discern subtle and disguised information that could not be obtained through verbal interviews" (p. 169). Allowing unauthorized individuals to access client records is another instance in which privacy of an individual might be abridged, as are certain research procedures that ask information about family relationships, sexuality, attitudes, values, and personality variables.

The most obvious defenses against malpractice liability action for invasion of privacy are keeping confidences and making certain that informed consent is received prior to collecting information. Informed consent depends on competency, knowledge, and voluntariness (Van Hoose & Kottler, 1977). Competency is affected by two factors—age and ability—with the latter being related to intellect and state of psychological functioning. In general if a student has not reached 18 years of age, parents or legal guardians must give consent for data collection or transmittal. Intellectual and psychological competence must also be established before informed consent can be established. Intellectual competence relates to individuals' ability to comprehend the purpose and nature of the data to be collected about them and its use. Mental illness may also impair a client's ability to comprehend the nature of a data-collection strategy.

Knowledge is also a prerequisite for informed consent and relates to the nature of the disclosure to a client about a data-collection procedure in a research project. Clients or research subjects must have enough knowledge about what is to be done to understand the personal ramifications of the procedure. For example, inmates in a minimum security prison who are to be given a personality inventory have a right to know the nature of the inventory (types of questions that are to be asked), what is to be done with the data once it is collected, and how the inventory profiles will be stored. In reality, full knowledge is often not provided to students, inmates, or other subjects in research experiments.

Voluntariness is the final condition that must be met in order to ensure informed consent. Voluntariness means that implicit and explicit coercion are not used to force compliance with a data-collection approach or participation in a research experience. It was not uncommon in the 1950s and 1960s for professors of psychology and counselor educators to require students to participate in three or four experiments as part of a course. (This is still a practice in some universities.) It would be hard to claim that consent in these cases meets the criterion of voluntariness, just as it might be difficult to convince a jury that many of our clients and subjects participate totally on a voluntary basis if teachers or guards suggest that involvement is a "good idea."

Failure to Provide Services. An area that has received little attention is the potential liability growing out of failure to provide the necessary services to students, particularly in the presence of state statutes or school board policies that indicate that certain types of counseling services should be made available to students or others. One set of parents brought a suit, which was dropped prior to litigation, against a counselor for not providing "adequate vocational guidance." Some schools are now initiating programs aimed at providing human sexuality and birth control information, suicide prevention programs, and a vast array of other services designed to combat drug and alcohol abuse, dropping out of school, etc. So long as these programs meet reasonable professional standards and are delivered in good faith, it seems doubtful that the circumstances needed for malpractice liability will be met. But, should programs not be properly and judiciously delivered, or not delivered at all in the face of policies to do so, the counselor and others could be found liable.

STUDENT LEARNING EXERCISE
Indicate that a statement is true by circling T or false by circling F.

1. The type of privileged communication afforded clients of most counselors is limited.   T   F

2. When a counselor-client relationship has been accorded limited privilege, the counselor must refuse to testify in a court of law unless a release is secured from the client.   T   F

3. If a counselor fails to provide some form of desensitization for phobic clients, which is documentably the best approach, legal liability may result, even if the client is helped by the alternative treatment.   T   F

4. Defamation may be either written or spoken.   T   F

5. A true report by a counselor indicating that a student has a venereal disease may be the basis for a defamation suit if the report harms the student.   T   F

6. Since counselors have very few standards of care to follow, they are, relatively speaking, free from successful malpractice suits.   T   F

7. A counselor may be found guilty of defamation if he writes a report indicating that a student performed poorly in a certain area when, in fact, he excelled in that area.   T   F

8. Current case law indicates that counselors must only inform the intended victim of a crime if their client is homicidal.   T   F

9. A researcher who works with children need only get permission from school officials to conduct research.   T   F

LEGAL ISSUES AND SCHOOL COUNSELORS

In a provocative article, Talbutt (1983) raised a number of special legal issues confronting school counselors, including those relating to search and seizure, labeling students, corporal punishment, dress, rights to due process, and a number of other areas. These will be discussed in this section.

Search and Seizure

As Hopkins and Anderson (1985) note, concerns about search and seizure grow out of the Fourth Amendment to the U.S. Constitution, which prohibits unreasonable search and seizure. As these authors and Talbutt (1983) also point out, the U.S. Supreme Court has consistently held that minors have the same protection growing out of the Fourth Amendment as adults. For example, the Supreme Court has ruled that the use of dogs trained to sniff out various drugs does not constitute a violation of Fourth Amendment rights, but that strip searches of those individuals identified by the dogs in the absence of a prior history of drug abuse, is an infringement of those rights. The key phrase in the foregoing has to do with the history of drug abuse because this relates to probable cause. Probable cause is evidence or likelihood that a crime has been committed and must be established before searches can occur (Kaplin, 1985). Thus random searches of school lockers for contraband such as weapons and drugs would probably constitute illegal search, but spot checking lockers of individuals who have histories of consistent drug abuse would in all likelihood not be illegal (Talbutt, 1983).

Labeling

An often debated issue in public schools today is the labeling of students. Generally the courts have supported the labeling of students for academic purposes (e.g., educably mentally retarded) because some reasonable basis exists for the process. However, the U.S. Supreme Court (*Merrihen v. Cressman*, 1973) has ruled that it is an invasion of privacy to label a student as a potential drug user on the basis of a test that has "error" in it because misclassification may result.

Due Process and Punishment

Both the Supreme Court and lower courts have consistently ruled that schools have the right to administer corporal punishment. The courts have also ruled that paddlings may be administered in the absence of due process, that is, without the student's facing his accuser and having the opportunity to rebut the charges brought against him (Talbutt, 1983).

The U.S. Supreme Court has also ruled (*Goss v. Lopez*, 1975) that students who are to be suspended from school have a right to know the charges against them, a chance to answer the charges, including reviewing the evidence against them, and an opportunity to present evidence on their own behalf (Talbutt, 1983). It should also be noted that while courts have consistently upheld the right of students to due process in matters of suspension, they have accepted situations in which students have been given very little notice of the intent to suspend in some cases.

Freedom of Speech

The U.S. Supreme Court has guaranteed students' First Amendment rights to freedom of speech in a number of cases, the most famous of which was *Tinker v. Des Moines Independent Community School District* (1969). In this landmark case the Tinker children wore black arm bands to school to protest the Vietnam war and were subsequently suspended. The U.S. Supreme Court held that the suspension was a violation of their constitutional right to free speech. However, freedom of speech is not a license to disrupt the activities of the school. The courts have consistently held that the school has the right to take appropriate action to maintain order (Kaplin, 1985).

Right to Services

In 1977 P.L. 94-142, Education of the Handicapped, became effective. The thrust of the law is to guarantee that handicapped students receive free and appropriate education. The law also has a built-in assurance that the rights of handicapped students will be protected because parents are given far-reaching powers to participate in the design of the education of their children. Specifically the law requires that parents be included in the development of an individualized education program (IEP) and the right to appeal to a state agency if they are not satisfied with the quality of the education being provided to their children.

Counselors have become involved with P.L. 94-142 in numerous ways. In some instances counselors are charged with the responsibility of overseeing the development of IEPs and thus must be familiar with the content of the law. IEPs require careful and systematic drafting of an educational plan for the handicapped child, according to Sproles, Panther, and Lanier (1978). These authors go on to indicate that the IEP must contain the following 10 components:

1. A statement of the child's current levels of academic performance (including academic achievement, social adaptation, prevocational skills, psychomotor skills, and self-help skills).
2. A statement of annual goals describing year-end educational objectives.
3. Statements of short-term instructional objectives to be met before annual goals.
4. Statements of the specific educational services needed by the child (determined without regard to the availability of those services).
5. Any special instructional media and materials needed.
6. The date and length of time the services will be given.
7. A description of the extent to which the child will participate in regular educational programs.
8. A justification of the record of educational placement the child will have.
9. A list of the individuals who are responsible for the implementation of the IEP.
10. Objective criteria, evaluation procedures, and schedules for determining (on at least an annual basis) whether the short-term instructional objectives are being achieved (Sproles, et al., 1978).

Not only does the IEP have to contain the aforementioned components, it must also be developed in a manner that will guarantee due process of laws to parents and children. Sproles et al. (1978) also identify 10 steps that must be followed to ensure that this provision of the law is met. These steps include (1) an annual review of the IEP, (2) scheduling a meeting to initiate the process of developing an IEP within 30 days after identification as a handicapped student, (3) involvement of all relevant individuals, including the parents, in the development of an IEP, and (4) complete disclosure of information to the parents in their native language. Other provisions regarding the IEP meeting itself are (5) gaining informed consent from parents, (6) involving surrogate parents (e.g., foster parents) if the biological parents are unable to act in an advocacy role for the student, and (7) scheduling meetings at places that are reasonably accessible to all parties. Finally, in order to ensure due process parents need to know that (8) they have a right to challenge both the evaluation of their child and the IEP, (9) they may access and review records regarding their children, and (10) all educational procedures initiated on behalf of their children will be fully documented and easily accessible to them.

Records

In 1974, another law with far-reaching implications for counselors, P.L. 93-380, Family Educational Rights and Privacy Act, was passed. This act applies to all public and private institutions that receive federal funds and has become the major legal consideration where student records are concerned (Kaplin, 1985). The major provisions of P.L. 93-380 are as follows:

1. Parents have the right to access the records of their children until the student reaches the age of majority (18), at which time that right to access passes to the student. This right to access contains five exceptions: personnel and private records of institution employees, some law enforcement records, some student employment records, alumni records, and some records regarding health care (Kaplin, 1985).

2. Parents of students have the right to challenge the content of their children's records.

3. Disclosure of personally identifiable information to persons outside the school is forbidden unless permission is given by the student or, if the student is under 18, the parent.

4. School personnel have restricted right of access. Right of access should be determined on a "need to know" basis, that is, those personnel who are directly involved with the student are typically those who need information about the student.

5. Schools have an obligation under the provisions of P.L. 93-380 to make parents and students aware of their rights regarding student records.

6. Students and/or parents have legal recourse if the provisions of the law are violated by filing a complaint to the Department of Education.

Dress Codes

Dress codes have been a part of most school policies for decades. These have included such odd requirements as requiring boys to wear socks and the exclusion of shorts and hats for both boys and girls. As a protest against what appeared to be discriminatory rules forbidding boys to wear shorts to school, a group of young men in Pennsylvania appeared in school in miniskirts, clothing that had been ruled as acceptable for girls. The boys were immediately suspended. Other protests against dress codes have found their way into the courts.

Courts have generally upheld school dress codes that are promulgated to protect the health and safety of the students, such as special clothing in physical education, where strenuous physical activity is required, or in shops and laboratory areas, where danger may be present (Talbutt, 1983). In some cases courts have gone beyond the health and safety guidelines to decide in favor of school rules that relate to maintaining decorum. In the case of *Fowler v. Williamson* 1979) the court held that a student could be barred from graduation for failure to follow dress-code requirements.

Abortion Counseling

Hopkins and Anderson (1985) believe that providing counseling to minors who are interested in having an abortion may have a number of legal implications, primarily because laws and court rulings regarding those laws vary from state to state. One particular concern raised by these authors is that a counselor might negligently interfere with parental rights to advise their children, either by giving inappropriate advice, overly influencing a student in favor of an abortion, or dissuading a student from having an abortion. In these cases the counselor may be held liable in a civil malpractice suit.

In the situation involving inappropriate advice, liability may result if the counselor fails to establish conditions in which the abortion decision could be fully considered. Options in these cases involve abortion, having the child and keeping it, or bearing the child and putting it up for adoption. A counselor who wrongfully uses his or her influence to persuade a client to have an abortion would be guilty of malpractice. Finally, a counselor who dissuades a student from having either the child or an abortion, particularly if the arguments involve any false information, is in legal peril.

Perhaps the best advice that can be offered with regard to dealing with clients who are considering abortions is to be fully familiar with local statutes and court decisions regarding them before proceeding. Also, as is the case in all matters, ethical guidelines should be carefully followed. Finally, personal values and opinions of the counselor should not interfere with professional duty in dealing with clients considering abortion (Hopkins & Anderson, 1985).

STUDENT LEARNING EXERCISE
Indicate that a statement is true by circling T or false by circling F.

1. P.L. 93-380 stipulates that parents have access to their children's records so long as they are in school.   T   F

2. P.L. 93-380 stipulates that all persons working in a school may have access to the records.   T   F

3. If a student in your school has applied for a scholarship from University X, a representative of that school automatically has access to the student's records.   T   F

4. Probable cause relates to the likelihood that a crime has been committed.   T   F

5. Students who are not yet age 18 have approximately the same constitutional rights as those over age 18.   T   F

6. A principal who suspends a student for wearing clothes that distract others is probably on safe legal grounds.   T   F

7. A student who asks to face his or her accuser prior to being suspended probably is on solid legal ground.   T   F

8. Freedom of speech is a right of students, so long as they do not up-
set other students or the staff.   T   F
9. Generally speaking, the courts have held that spankings are cruel and
unusual punishment.   T   F

PRIVATE PRACTICE

Increasingly counselors are entering private practice. Two major legal concerns
relating to this area of practice will be discussed in this section: honesty in labeling and breach of contract.

Honesty in Labeling

Winborn (1977), Trembly (1977), and Eberlem (1977) were among the first to
comment on legal and ethical concerns regarding consumers' rights, although
Witmer (1978) and Gill (1982) among others have commented on this issue since.
As Winborn states, "Consumers must have accurate information if they are to
make informed choices about goods and services" (p. 206). This need extends
to counseling and other services provided by counselors. Gill, drawing upon the
work of Witmer and others, has drafted a suggested list of factors that might
be included in a professional disclosure statement. These include (1) a statement of the purpose of counseling, (2) what the expected outcomes of counseling are, (3) the counselor's and the client's responsibilities during counseling,
(4) a description of the counselor's methods and techniques, (5) the types of
clients with whom the counselor is most effective, (6) when referrals are to be
made (e.g., need for medical treatment), and (7) the limits of confidentiality.

To date, no cases in which counselors have been sued for not making
the type of disclosure described above have surfaced, although they may have
occurred. One way of avoiding the possibility of being sued is for counselors to
draft disclosure statements and establish formal contracts with their clients.

Breach of Contract

A breach of contract occurs when either party fails to meet either their implicit
or their explicit obligations. For their part counselors are expected to deliver
the services contracted for and to do so using reasonable standards of care. To
do otherwise is to court breach of contract suits.

Legally speaking, contracts may be of two types, expressed or implied.
The result is that a counselor may be sued for breach of contract, even though

no formal contract exists. Counselors and other helping professionals enter into implied contracts with their clients regarding the benefits that the client will receive from counseling and in a number of other areas including confidentiality, quality of care to be provided, and techniques to be employed. As can be readily seen, the recommendations made in the preceding section that relate to professional disclosure statements have direct implications for the types of contracts that counselors need to establish with their clients.

Contracts protect clients by delineating the nature of the service to be provided. They also protect the counselor by setting forth length of treatment and terms of payment, although clients' liability with regard to the length of treatment is limited since they terminate treatment at will without incurring liability. However, a contract does legally obligate the client to pay for services received.

Gable (1983) warns against entering into implicit special agreements with clients such as reassurance that the treatment will be effective or that "everything will be fine." The courts have held that these types of reassurances constitute warranties when given by other professionals such as psychiatrists. Thus a counselor who provides reassurances may be in breach of contract should the treatment not be effective. Gable suggests that some assurances can be given to clients that counseling is effective, but that these should not overshadow the fact that counseling can fail. The counselor should also inform the client of the risks involved in the treatment if they exist.

ETHICS VERSUS THE LAW

Mappes, Robb, and Engels (1985) contend that there are apparently a number of conflicts that exist between the ethical and legal expectations of counselors. In fact, a relationship exists between statutory and case law and ethics, and this is that the former restricts or shapes the latter. Court cases such as *Tarasoff v. Regents of the University of California* have resulted in the reshaping of ethical statements regarding confidentiality to conform to apparent legal expectations. Child abuse reporting laws simply supercede codes of ethics and thus restrict the extent of a client's privilege. Similarly, P.L. 93-380 gives the parents of minor children and adults the right to access their records, which again shapes counselors' ethical behavior with regard to records. Finally, legislative bodies are continuously reviewing the privileged communication laws and reshaping them based on their view of the best interest of justice and clients. For example, the privileged communication law for school counselors in North Carolina was recently amended to make it possible for judges to order disclosure of information in pretrial investigations. Previously, disclosure could only be ordered at the trial stage.

Legal action by the Antitrust Division of the U.S. Department of Justice has also restructured ethical codes and thus ethical behavior in the area of advertising (Mappes et al., 1985). It can be expected that this type of incursion into the ethical conduct of counselor behavior, and those already mentioned, will continue. While some may see these incursions as negative, the result in some cases has been better services, more disclosure of information, and greater protection of the client.

SUMMARY

During the past two decades, juries have awarded huge sums of money to successful plaintiffs in malpractice suits. As a result, mental health practitioners have become increasingly aware of their legal obligations to their clients. Avoiding liability suits involves practicing ethically and following standards of care where they exist. It also involves offering only those services that one is qualified to deliver.

Counselors in schools and in private practice have some particular concerns. School counselors need to be aware of the constitutional and statutory rights of their clients with regard to search and seizure, freedom of speech, protection from invasion of privacy, and rights to services, to name a few of the more important areas. Private practitioners have many of the same legal concerns that other counselors have, but need to be particularly concerned about breach of contract and honesty in advertising.

Finally, the relationship between ethics and law is a dynamic one. Both statutory law and case law will continue to shape the code of ethics and thus the definition of ethical behavior of counselors.

REVIEW QUESTIONS

1. Contrast confidentiality and privileged communication.
2. Outline the conditions that must be present before legal liability can be proven and the steps that should be taken to avoid malpractice suits.
3. What are the conditions to the steps outlined in number 2?
4. Distinguish between slander and libel.
5. Define due process and tell the conditions that must be met in a school setting to ensure that students are guaranteed their constitutional rights in this area.
6. Identify the major areas in which statutes and case laws have changed the ways that counselors function.

REFERENCES

American Association for Counseling and Development. (1981). *Ethical Standards,* Alexandria, VA: Author.
Berman, A. L., & Cohen-Sandler, R. (1983). Suicide malpractice: Expert testimony and standard of care. *Professional Psychology: Research and Practice, 14,* 6–19.

Bogust v. Iverson, 102 N.W. 2d, 228 (1960).

Bouhoutsos, J., Holroyd, J., Lerman, H., Forer, B. R., & Greenberg, M. (1983). Sexual intimacy between psychotherapists and patients. *Professional Psychology Research and Practice, 14*, 185–196.

Brady v. Hopper, 83-JM 451 (D. Colo) Sept 14, 1983.

Cohen, R. J. (1979). *Malpractice: A guide for mental health professionals.* New York: Free Press.

Cormier, L. S., & Bernard, J. (1982). Ethical and legal responsibilities of clinical supervisors. *Personnel and Guidance Journal, 60*, 486–491.

Denkowski, K. M., & Denkowski, G. C. (1982). Client-counselor confidentiality: An update of rationale, legal status, and implications. *Personnel and Guidance Journal, 60*, 371–375.

Eberlem, L. (1977). Counselors beware! Clients have rights! *Personnel and Guidance Journal, 56*(7), 219, 223.

Fowler v. Williamson, 251 S.E. 2d, 889 (1979).

Gable, R. K., (1983). Malpractice liability of psychologists. In B. D. Sales (Ed.), *The Psychologists' Handbook* (pp. 460–491). New York: Plenum.

Gehring, D. D. (1982). The counselor's "duty to warn." *Journal of Counseling and Development, 61*, 208–212.

Gill, S. J. (1982). Professional disclosure and consumer protection in counseling. *Personnel and Guidance Journal, 60*, 443–446.

Goss v. Lopez, 419 U.S. 565 (1975).

Hopkins, B. H., & Anderson, B. S. (1985). *The counselor and the law.* Alexandria, VA: AACD Press.

Kaplin, W. A. (1985). *The law of higher education* (2nd ed.). San Francisco: Jossey-Bass.

Knapp, S., & VandeCreek, L. (1983). Privileged communications and the counselor. *Personnel and Guidance Journal, 62*, 83–85.

Mappes, D. C., Robb, G. P., & Engels, D. W. (1985). Conflicts between ethics and law in counseling and psychotherapy. *Journal of Counseling and Development, 64*, 246–258.

Merrihen v. Cressman, 364 F. Supp. 913, (E.D. P.A. 1973).

Russell Sage Foundation (1970). Proposed principles for the management of school records. Excerpt. *Personnel and Guidance Journal, 49*, 21–24.

Slimak, R. E., & Berkowitz, S. R. (1983). The university and college counseling center and malpractice suits. *Personnel and Guidance Journal, 61*, 291–294.

Sproles, H. A., Panther, E. E., & Lanier, J. E. (1978). PL 94-142 and its impact on the counselor's role. *Personnel and Guidance Journal, 57*, 210–213.

Talbutt, L. C. (1983). Recent court decisions: A quiz for APGA members. *Personnel and Guidance Journal, 62*, 355–357.

Tarasoff v. Regents of the University of California, 551, p. 2d 334 (Cal. Sup. Ct., 1976).

Tinker v. Des Moines Independent Community School District, 393 U.S. 503, 506, 89S. Ct. 733, 21 L.Ed.2d 731 1969.

Trembly, E. (1977). Three steps toward consumer advocacy. *Personnel and Guidance Journal, 56*, 214–218.

Van Hoose, W. H., & Kottler, J. A. (1977). *Ethical and legal issues in counseling and psychotherapy.* San Francisco: Jossey-Bass.

Winborn, B. B. (1977). Honest labeling and other procedures for the protection of consumers of counseling. *Personnel and Guidance Journal, 56*, 210–213.

Witmer, J. M. (1978). Professional disclosure in licensing. *Counselor Education and Supervision, 18*, 71–73.

11

Credentialing of Counselors and Programs

GOALS OF THE CHAPTER

The purposes of this chapter are to present an overview of individual credentialing and program accreditation in the counseling profession and to discuss the implications of credentialing for the profession.

CHAPTER PREVIEW

1. A brief history of credentialing in the counseling profession will be presented. The intention of this presentation is to illustrate both the recency of the movement and the rapidity with which credentialing is being adopted by the profession.
2. The terminology of individual credentialing (e.g., licensure, certification, etc.) will be defined and illustrated.
3. Program accreditation will be discussed, including its purpose and the processes involved.
4. Implications of credentialing for the counseling profession will be examined.

INTRODUCTION

We live in a credential-conscious society. Physicians display their certificates and licenses on office walls. Termite exterminators paint local permit numbers and state certification numbers on their vehicles. Barbers, beauticians, real estate sales people, and nurse practitioners all are credentialed by regulatory bodies in the states in which they practice. The result is that credentials have taken on a variety of meanings. The most important one is that these certificates are now viewed, by both the public and the occupational groups involved, as indicators that those who hold them are legitimate practitioners.

Credentialing began to protect the public at large, and this continues to be its main purpose. Unscrupulous individuals have performed surgery, accepted construction jobs for which they had no expertise, sold worthless property to unsuspecting clients, and practiced psychotherapy. Professional groups and legislators alike view credentialing as a means of identifying those individuals who possess the needed skills and expertise to perform certain services, such as the general practice of medicine.

Credentialing serves other purposes as well. It is a means by which professional groups act to communicate which of its members meet certain speciality standards (e.g., plastic surgery, career counseling). It is also used by professional groups to restrict entry into certain job markets by unqualified individuals. Finally, credentialing provides state legislators with a means by which they can control the entry into, and practice of, various professional groups.

As is perhaps obvious from the foregoing discussion, the impetus for credentialing can come from two sources: professional groups and governmental agencies. Often these two groups work in concert. For example, in one state the attorney general's office received more than 400 complaints within a relatively short period of time regarding the nature of career counseling and placement by private employment agencies. Lawyers in the attorney general's office contacted members of the professional association in the state, and legislation to regulate career counselors via licensing was drafted. However, in another state that was experiencing the same problem, the attorney general's office successfully promulgated legislation that was totally unsatisfactory to the professional counselors. As early as 1976, MacKin warned counselors to monitor themselves or run the risk of governmental intervention. Certainly his warning seems appropriate given the turn of events described above.

Credentialing involves more than issuing licenses or certificates to individuals, however. Training programs have also come under scrutiny by professional groups, and the counseling profession is no exception. In addition to the credentialing of individuals, the accreditation of counseling preparation programs will also be discussed in this chapter.

A BRIEF HISTORY OF CREDENTIALING:
COUNSELORS AND PROGRAMS

The movement to credentialing in the counseling profession has been dramatic. While some of the background of the credentialing effort was presented in Chapter 1, a brief history of this effect should graphically portray the priority placed on credentialing within the profession. Material in this section was abstracted in part from publications by Warner, Brooks, and Thompson (1980), and McFadden and Brooks (1983).

- 1972—*Welden v. Virginia Board of Psychological Examiners*. John I. Weldon was enjoined from practicing as a counselor by a Virginia court because counseling used the tools of psychology but was unregulated by statute.
- 1973—The Commission on Rehabilitation Counselor Certification met for the first time in Chicago. Four years later credentialing of rehabilitation counselors (Certified Rehabilitation Counselors) began.
- 1973—The Southern Association of Counselor Education and Supervision adopted a position supporting licensure efforts.
- 1974—A special issue of the *Personnel and Guidance Journal*, "Licensure and the Helping Professions," was published under the editorship of Sweeney and Sturdevant.
- 1974—The American Personnel and Guidance Association, APGA (now the American Association for Counseling and Development, AACD) called for licensure legislation efforts in all 50 states.
- 1975—The APGA (AACD) Senate established a licensure commission with Thomas J. Sweeney of Ohio University as its chair.
- 1975—*State of Ohio v. Culbreth B. Cook*. Mr. Cook was charged with practicing psychology without a license by the Ohio State Board of Psychology, arrested, and tried. Mr. Cook did not represent himself to be a psychologist but was engaged in private practice as a counselor specializing in assessing children in academic difficulty. The court found Mr. Cook not guilty.
- 1976—Virginia passed the first counselor licensure law.
- 1977—Licensure and certification issues were addressed in a special issue of *Personnel and Guidance Journal* edited by Gerald R. Forster.
- 1977—Bruce Shertzer of Purdue University was appointed to head a special committee to study credentialing. Later that year the committee recommended continued efforts in support of licensure, accreditation of counselor education programs, and the development of a national registry for professional counselors.
- 1977—Association for Counselor Education and Supervision (ACES) adopted *Guidelines for Doctoral Preparation in Counselor Education*.

These along with the *Standards for the Preparation of Counselors* and *Other Personnel Services Specialists*, adopted in 1973, would underpin program credentialing efforts.

- 1978—*Personnel and Guidance Journal* published a third special issue on licensure and credentialing.

- 1978—Acting upon the recommendation made by the committee chaired by Bruce Shertzer, the APGA Board of Directors approved committees for Counselor Preparation and Standards, Licensure, and Registry. ACES was directed to proceed with the accreditation of preparation programs.

- 1979—Idaho State, Ball State, University of Washington, and University of Virginia began the first ACES accredited counselor education programs.

- 1979—The National Academy of Certified Mental Health Counselors administered its first examination.

- 1979—Arkansas passed a second licensure law in March. In July, Alabama became the third state to achieve licensure.

- 1981—Twenty-one states announced their intention to introduce counselor licensure laws at the APGA convention.

- 1981—In June Texas became the fourth state to pass a licensure bill. In July Florida became the fifth.

- 1981—CACREP held its first meeting. It became the official accreditation arm of AACD.

- 1981—National Vocational Guidance Association (NVGA) intiated NCCC, the Nationally Certified Career Counselor program.

- 1982—Idaho became the sixth state to pass a licensure law.

- 1982—The National Board of Certified Counselors (NBCC) held its first meeting. More than 3,000 counselors submitted applications for certification that year.

- 1983—North Carolina passed the first counselor registry law.

- 1984–85—Nine additional states pass licensure laws: Ohio, Tennessee, Georgia, Mississippi, Montana, Oklahoma, South Carolina, Missouri, and Oregon.

- 1985—The National Career Counselors certification program merged with the National Board of Certified Counselors. After July 1 eligibility for certification was dependent upon prior certification by NBCC.

- 1985—The NBCC newsletter *NBCC News Notes* reported that more than 1,400 counselors had qualified for certification.

- 1986—Nebraska and West Virginia became the 17th and 18th states to pass counselor licensure or registration laws.

- 1987—Forty-eight counselor education programs had been accredited by CACREP. Washington, Wyoming, Kansas, Delaware, and Rhode Island have passed credentialing laws.

In approximately 15 years, the counseling profession has advanced from a position of no credentialing of programs or individuals to a fully developed preparation program accreditation effort with a number of state and national credentialing efforts as well. In the section that follows additional details will be provided regarding credentialing and its meaning to professional counselors.

STATE-LEVEL CREDENTIALING FOR INDIVIDUALS

The credentialing movement has resulted in a plethora of titles that are at times confusing to both professionals and lay people alike. In this section the various titles connected with the state-level credentialing of counselors will be identified, defined, and, where possible, illustrated.

Licensure: Title and Title/Practice Laws

A license is a credential authorized by a state legislature that regulates either the title, practice, or both of an occupational group. As a result, there are title acts and title/practice acts. Acts that license counselors, psychologists, social workers, and marriage and family therapists are typically title acts since they usually do not set forth areas of practice, but they do reserve the use of the title to the professional groups. Licensure laws for dentists are title/practice acts since they restrict the use of the title "dentist" to qualified individuals *and* set forth the parameters of dental practice. For example, in many states, dentists are entitled to prescribe certain types of medicines. On the other hand, the practice of counseling may be defined in legislation, but usually no attempt is made either to restrict counseling to counselors or to set forth the conditions under which it may be practiced. The Ohio law varies from this format, however. Two provisions of that law follow.

Section 4757.01 (A) H.B.205 of the Counselor and Social Work law states,

> "Practice of professional counseling" means rendering or offering to render to individuals, groups, organizations or the general public a counseling service involving the application of clinical counseling principles to assist individuals in achieving more effective personal, social, educational, or career development and adjustment. "Practice of professional counseling" does not include the diagnosis and treatment of mental and emotional disorders unless a professional counselor has received from the counselor or social worker board created in section 4757.03 of the revised code the endorsement provided for under division B of section 4757.07 of the revised code, or unless a professional counselor is supervised by another professional counselor who has that endorsement, a licensed psychologist, or a psychiatrist.

Another section of the Ohio statute deals with the title. Section 4757.02 (A) of H.B. 205 states,

Except as provided in section 4757.16 of the revised code, no person shall engage in or hold himself out as engaging in the practice of professional counseling under the title of "professional counselor" or "counselor assistant" or any other title or description incorporating the word "counselor" for a fee, salary or other consideration unless he is currently licensed as a professional counselor or registered as a counselor assistant under this chapter and rules adopted under it.

The above section of the Ohio statute restricts the use of the title to licensed professionals, although a number of exemptions, such as school counselors, are provided for in the act. Section A of the statute also defines counseling practice and provides that only licensed counselors may engage in that practice unless they are exempted by the law. By setting forth these standards the Ohio statute becomes a title/practice licensing act.

Virginia, Texas, Florida, and a number of other states have adopted title licensure laws. Section 490.12 of Florida's bill to license mental health professionals (S.B.82) illustrates the language used in these acts to preclude the use of the title by unlicensed persons. It states,

No person shall hold himself out by any title or description incorporating the words, or permutations of them, . . . "mental counseling," "marriage therapist," "marriage counselor," "marriage consultant," "family therapist," "family counselor," "family consultant," "mental health counselor," "sex therapist," or "sex counselor," unless such a person is licensed under this chapter or is exempt from the provisions of this chapter.

The last sentence in the passage of the Florida mental health licensing law should be noted since it indicates that exemptions from the law are possible. This is a typical statement. To date, counselor licensure laws have been aimed primarily at regulating private practice only; that is, counselors in public agencies do not have to be licensed in most states where licensure laws exist.

As Forster (1977) points out, licensing legislation, in addition to restricting the use of title and/or practice, establishes a licensing board that is a quasi-legislative body empowered to establish rules that govern the licensing and delicensing process. This board is typically appointed by the governor of the state, is comprised largely of members of the professional group being regulated by the licensing legislation, and may have a representative of the public at large as a member. Including lay people on licensing boards is increasingly popular because the basic purpose of licensure boards is to protect the welfare of the public in a particular state, and some legislators feel that licensing boards have become too concerned with the welfare of their own occupational group. The Texas licensure law (SB606) is illustrative. SB606, Section 4 Nature and Composition of Board states,

(a) The board is composed of nine members appointed by the governor with the advice and consent of the senate; (b) Not later than the 30th day after the effective date of this Act, the executive committee of the Texas Association for

Counseling and Development shall submit to the governor a list of qualified candidates for the board, including the names of four qualified counselor educators and 12 qualified practicing counselors. Not later than the 60th day after the date the list is received, the governor shall select from the list the membership of the board consisting of one counselor educator and four counselors to provide practice. The governor shall appoint four citizens from the general public who have no direct or indirect affiliation with the practice of counseling or delivery of mental health services.

Section 6 of SB606 delineates the responsibilities of the board: These are to (1) hold at least two regular board meetings per year, (2) keep an information file about each complaint filed, (3) "determine the qualifications and fitness for licenses, renewal of licenses, and reciprocal licenses," (4) develop rules that enable the board to carry out the intent of the Act, (5) "examine for, deny, approve, issue, revoke, suspend, and renew licenses," and (6) make consumers of counseling services aware of the purposes of the board and means by which they may register complaints.

Certification: State Level

Of all terms dealing with credentialing, none is more confusing than certification. Because certification has been used historically in connection with the process of becoming qualified to practice in public schools, this is the usual connotation of the term. However, certification laws can also be passed that have essentially the same impact as licensure laws, although they do not generally provide the status associated with licensure (Forster, 1977). It is therefore necessary to distinguish between these two types of certification.

Certification for Schools. The U.S. Constitution empowers states to regulate education within their jurisdiction. Typically, legislators have delegated this authority to state boards of education who, in turn, establish certification standards for counselors, teachers, administrators, and others. Representatives from state departments of education are then charged with enforcing the rules that have been established by the state board of education. This is accomplished in two ways. The most popular is the approved program approach in which a team from the state department of education peruses the course offerings, field experiences, laboratory facilities and experiences, and other factors related to the quality of preparing educators and approves a certification program in a particular area such as school counseling. A recommendation from that program results in certification.

A second approach is for a Division of Teacher Training and Certification or a similar named office within the state department of education to review credentials of prospective educators and render decisions regarding whether they are qualified to perform in the public schools.

Two things need to be emphasized about the foregoing presentation. First, the constitutional authority of the state and its designee(s) to regulate entry into the public schools is absolute if it chooses to maintain that authority. Licensing laws passed to regulate the use and/or practice of psychology or counseling cannot generally supercede this authority. Therefore, many licensing laws make note of this authority or contain some form of caveat regarding holding the title of counselor or psychologist in the school. Second, state boards of education have little control over private schools, particularly those that are church-related, and thus these schools are usually able to set training standards for their counselors and other personnel independently.

Certification for Title Restrictions.   Some occupational groups have petitioned legislatures for permission to designate individuals that have met higher standards. Often these standards are higher than those for other members of that occupational group and involve passing a competency examination, completing a distinct number of years of practice, and holding a graduate degree. Probably the best known occupational group that has pursued this route are the accountants, with only those accountants who have met the higher standards allowed to use the title "certified public accountant." Some states have a similar provision for marriage and family counselors. Any mental health professional may advertise that he or she performs work in those areas, but only those practitioners who have met the standards established by the certification board may advertise themselves as certified marriage and family counselors. In other states, marriage and family counselors are licensed, so the procedure for designating professional groups is not the same from state to state.

Registry for Title Restriction.   Another way of allowing an occupational group to designate individuals who have met a set of specified standards is for a state legislature to pass a registry law. A register is a document that lists by name and other pertinent information those individuals who have been certified by a professional certification board (AACD, 1985–86, p. 9). Nursing has traditionally used this means to identify those individuals who meet high standards (registered nurses). At least one state, North Carolina, has a registry law that empowers a registry board to set standards and establish and publish a listing (register) of registered practicing counselors. Some key excerpts from the North Carolina Registration Law (E.B.553) follow:

> 90.325 Definitions
> (1) A "counselor" is a person engaged in the practice of counseling who is not a "Registered Practicing Counselor" as defined in this article.
> (2) A "Registered Practicing Counselor" is a person engaged in the practice of counseling who holds a certificate as a Registered Practicing Counselor issued to him under provisions of this article.
>
> and
>
> 90.326 Unlawful Use of Title
> It should be unlawful for any person who has not received a certificate of qualification as a Registered Practicing Counselor to assume or use such a title, or to use any words or other means of identification indicating that the person

has been certified as a Registered Practicing Counselor but such a person may use the term "counselor" in connection with his name relating to his services as a counselor.

When this wording is compared with that cited earlier from the Florida law, it should become clear that title licensure laws are much more restrictive than registry laws, with licensure laws forbidding even the use of permutations of the word "counselor." However, wording in the Idaho Licensure Law (HB492) illustrates how title licensure acts and registry acts converge, since the Idaho law is considerably less restrictive in its intent than the Florida law. It states,

> Chapter 34—section 54-3402
> It shall be unlawful for any person to represent himself/herself to be a licensed professional counselor or licensed counselor unless he/she shall first obtain a license pursuant to this chapter. Nothing in this chapter, however, shall be construed to limit or prevent the practice of an individual's profession or to restrict a person from doing counseling provided that the person or individual does not hold himself/herself out to the title or description as being a licensed counselor or a licensed professional counselor.

Implications: State Level Credentialing. It is obvious that licensure laws that restrict the title, certification, and registry laws perform very much the same function: They identify those professionals who can utilize certain titles (e.g., professional counselors). One important difference among them that has already been noted is that licensure has more status. This is probably because medicine, law, and dentistry have been granted licensure privileges, and licensure laws are typically more preclusive in that they often totally restrict the use of the title "counselor" *or* its derivatives, as is obvious in the Ohio and Florida counselor licensure laws cited earlier. Certification and registry laws only restrict the use of the title certified public accountant or registered practicing counselor, while permitting almost anyone to use the generic occupational title in context (e.g., sales counselor, credit counselor, etc.). Therefore, most occupational groups, and particularly counselors, are striving to secure licensing in all 50 states. Currently, nearly half of the states have licensing laws in place.

CREDENTIALING FOR INDIVIDUALS:
NATIONAL LEVEL

In many ways, state level laws that give counseling groups the right to set standards within that jurisdiction are the most important because of the legal penalties (typically a violation is a misdemeanor) that can be imposed by a licensing, certification, or registry board for individuals who violate the regulations governing the group. However, many occupational groups, including counselors,

have initiated additional credentialing efforts at the national level that promote excellence within the group by promoting standards of training, requiring that counselors demonstrate a knowledge base, and asking individuals to
maintain their qualifications through in-service training. Within the counseling profession these efforts are in the form of certification boards that offer
credentials to qualified individuals.

AACD (1985–86) defines certification as "a process by which the professional certifying board grants formal recognition to an individual who has
met certain predetermined professional standards as specified by that group"
(p. 9). Currently, there are four boards certifying counselors at the national level:
The Commission on Rehabilitation Counselor Certification, the National
Academy of Certified Clinical Mental Health Counselors, The National Council for Credentialing Career Counselors, and the National Board for Certified
Counselors (NBCC). Because the last of these, NBCC, is generic in nature, it
will be discussed first.

NBCC

NBCC was established in 1982. The purposes of the certification, according to
NBCC (1986), are to

- Promote professional accountability;
- Identify to the public and professional peers those counselors who have
  met specific professional standards;
- Advance cooperation among groups and agencies actively involved in
  professional credentialing activities;
- Encourage the continuing professional growth and development of National Certified Counselors.

Eligibility.   NBCC offers three routes to certification. The first of these is obtaining a graduate degree in a counseling or related field that has been accredited by CACREP. Applicants must submit an official transcript, have supervised counseling experience, document their training, and pass the NBCC
examination.

The second certification option is for those people who do not graduate
from CACREP accredited programs. These applicants must have earned a graduate degree in counseling or a related professional field, document that coursework has been completed in counseling theory and supervised practice as well
as six other areas, complete two years of at least half-time work, and pass the
NBCC exam. Historically, a third option was available to persons who had passed
licensure examinations and received licensure in states affording that option.
These people were exempt from the NBCC exam, but had to meet the coursework requirements listed under option two, and hold licensure as a profession-

al counselor in a state requiring a licensure examination. In 1986, NBCC decided to phase out this option, a decision that illustrates the pattern of most certification efforts: they become more restrictive.

Certificate. Counselors meeting eligibility requirements are credentialed as National Certified Counselors (NCC) for a period of five years. Renewal of the certificate requires completion of 100 clock hours of continuing education or reexamination and continuing ethical practice.

NCCC

In 1981, the National Vocational Guidance Association (now National Career Development Association) established the National Council for Credentialing Career Counselors (NCCC) as a means of improving career development practice. Originally, this council operated independently, but on July 1, 1985, it merged with NBCC. One of the results of this is that NCCC credentialing currently requires NBCC certification as a prerequisite to certification. Other eligibility requirements follow.

Eligibility. In addition to the NBCC certification requirements already listed, individuals seeking certification as a career counselor must demonstrate that they have compiled coursework in career development, assessment, and fieldwork that includes 25% time focused on career counseling or equivalent experience. Additional coursework in career counseling procedures, education and labor market structure and trends, consultation strategies and methods, and career development program management and implementation is also required. Applicants must also pass a career counseling specialty examination and document that they have at least three years of professional career counseling experience in at least a half-time position.

Certificate. Counselors who meet the requirements are designated as Nationally Certified Career Counselors (NCCC) for a period of five years. In addition to completing 100 clocks hours for NBCC recertification, career counselors must complete an additional 25 hours of continuing education. Fifty hours of the total (125) must focus on career development. In addition, NCCC recertification requires continuing ethical practice throughout the certification period.

NACCMHC

The National Academy of Certified Clinical Mental Health Counselor (NACCMHC) published its first registry in 1979. The objectives of this certification program, much like those already listed for NBCC, are to identify dedicated mental health counselors and establish a national network of mental health counselors who can provide services to the public at large.

Eligibility.   In order to be eligible for certification as a clinical mental health counselor, individuals must have graduated from a program accredited by CACREP or must have completed a two-year master's degree program resulting in a degree in an accepted mental health field. Applicants also must have successfully passed the NACCMHC examination, have two years of post-master's experience as a mental health counselor (a 1000-hour internship can substitute for one of these years), document that they have completed 3000 clock hours of supervised clinical work, and have received 100 hours of face-to-face supervision during this period (NACCMHC, 1986).

The specification that members of allied mental health professions such as psychiatry, psychology, psychiatric social work, and psychiatric nursing are eligible for certification is a unique feature of this particular counselor credential.

Certificate.   Successful applicants receive certification as Certified Clinical Mental Health Counselors (CCMHC). This certificate is valid for five years and may be renewed by completing 100 hours of competency-based continuing education and paying an annual recertification fee. NACCMHC stresses that continuing education should be related to maintaining and enhancing skills and not merely be academic in nature (NACCMHC, 1986).

CRCC

The Commission on Rehabilitation Counselor Certification (CRCC) was established in 1974 (CRCC, 1986), and thus is the oldest of the counselor credentialing agencies. The primary purpose of the program "is to provide assurance that professionals engaged in rehabilitation counseling will meet acceptable standards of quality in practice" (CRCC, 1986, p. 1). A second purpose is to provide agencies that employ rehabilitation counselors with a standard against which applicants can be compared.

Eligibility.   CRCC delineates eight routes to certification and specifies that an applicant must meet *all* requirements listed within one of the categories. All applicants must complete a certification examination. The first of the paths to certification is completion of a master's degree program in a rehabilitation counselor preparation program fully accredited by the National Council on Rehabilitation Education (CORE) and completion of an internship (480-hour quarter system, 600-hour semester system) supervised by a Certified Rehabilitation Counselor (CRC). No employment experience is required under this option. The second option for certification is similar except that provision is made for graduates from programs not accredited by CORE, in which case the applicant must have one year of experience under the supervision of a CRC. Option three, like option one and two, is designed for graduates of rehabilitation counseling programs. However, in the event that the program is not accredited by

CORE and the individual has no internship, two years of experience supervised by a CRC are required as a prerequisite to certification.

The fourth and fifth options, which will be phased out in 1992, establish procedures for individuals who have master's degrees unrelated to rehabilitation counseling and for individuals with bachelor's degrees. Those categories require five and seven years of supervision, respectively, but at this juncture are of little importance because they are soon to be terminated.

The sixth option for certification is for students and specifies that students must be enrolled in an accredited rehabilitation counseling program, have completed 75% of his or her coursework, have completed the internship under the supervision of a CRC, and provide a letter verifying that he or she is a student in good standing. While this is a special category for students seeking certification, examination results profiles and certificates are not released until students have completed the master's degree. Thus, the effect is to give students a head start on the certification process, not to actually certify them.

The final two categories of certification are for individuals who do not hold U.S. citizenship and for individuals who hold a doctorate in rehabilitation counseling. In both cases, the general requirements set forth for the other categories must be met.

Certificate.   Successful applicants are credentialed as Certified Rehabilitation Counselors and the certificate is valid for five years. In order to receive recertification without reexamination, applicants must complete 150 contact hours of approved continuing education credit.

AAMFT

Although marriage and family therapists are not usually included as members of the counseling profession per se, many practicing and potential counselors are interested in this area. The American Association for Marriage and Family Therapists (AAMFT) has promoted high standards of preparation for marriage counselors since 1942 (Kosinski, 1982). With the aim of promoting better practice in this area, in 1979 AAMFT established standards for what it terms "clinical membership."

Eligibility.   The academic requirements for clinical membership in AAMFT involve completing a master's program or other program in allied mental health, with courses in human development, marital and family studies, marital and family therapy, professional studies (e.g., ethics), supervised clinical work, and research methodology. Additional eligibility requirements specify the completion of 200 clock hours in the practice of marital and family therapy, of which only a total of 100 may be completed during the master's training program. Also, 1500 hours of face-to-face clinical practice are required. Prior to being granted clinical membership in AAMFT, an applicant must have treated at least 50 cases and must have completed two years of work under the direction of an AAMFT approved supervisor (Kosinski, 1982).

Clinical Membership. Clinical membership in AAMFT is the designation used for a member who meets the above standards. The member must continue to engage in a rigorous program of continuing education designed to improve his or her skills.

SUMMARY OF INDIVIDUAL CREDENTIALING

The numbers and forms of licenses and certification are considerable. What is obvious is that the counseling profession as a whole, and the subgroups within the profession, are enthusiastically pursuing various forms of credentialing. The rationale for this movement was set forth in the introduction: legitimizing the profession and its specialties to the public at large. Other implications of the credentialing movement will be discussed in the final section of this chapter.

STUDENT LEARNING EXERCISE

Match the answers in the right-hand column with the credentials listed in the left hand column.

_____ 1. Title licensure act

_____ 2. Title/practice licensure act

_____ 3. Registry/certification laws

_____ 4. Certification for school counseling

_____ 5. NCC

_____ 6. NCCC

_____ 7. CCMHC

_____ 8. CRC

a. voluntary rehabilitation counselor certification program

b. aimed at improving vocational counseling

c. precludes the use of the term counselor by unqualified individuals

d. generic national certificate

e. state level voluntary credentialing effort

f. preclusive acts that specify areas of practice as well as title usage

g. credential sought by counselors who work in community agencies

h. usually given by approved counselor preparation programs

TRAINING PROGRAM ACCREDITATION

In 1977, Forster defined program accreditation as follows: "This is a process whereby an association or agency grants public recognition to a school, institute, college, university, or specialized program of study that has met certain established qualifications or standards as determined through initial and periodic evaluations. Program approval is another name for accreditation" (p. 373).

Forster went on to establish the link between program accreditation and credentialing by indicating that in some professions graduates of accredited or approved programs are considered to be credentialed. In others, such as counseling, the link is not so direct. However, as was noted in the foregoing discussion, graduation from an accredited program allows individuals preferential treatment in the certification processes described. What is not so obvious from the previous section is that this relationship generally holds in the acquisition of other credentials, such as licenses, as well.

The roots of accreditation of counselor education programs can be traced in part to the 1964 adoption of "Standards for Counselor Education in the Preparation of Secondary School Counselors" by the Association of Counselor Education and Supervision (ACES) and the American Personnel and Guidance Association (now AACD) (Stripling, 1978). Today, two accrediting bodies are involved in approving counselor preparation programs. CORE accredits rehabilitation counselor preparation programs and CACREP accredits school, mental health, and related counselor preparation programs. Standards used in the latter process were first adopted in 1973 (ACES, 1977).

The Accreditation Process

Wittmer and Loesch (1986) identify six features of the accreditation process. The first of these is that accreditation is voluntary. In some of the older, more established professions, training programs must be accredited before graduates can practice. However, this is not the case in the counseling profession. The result is that fewer than 15% of counselor preparation programs are accredited at this juncture, although this number is expected to rise dramatically in the next decade.

The second and most obvious of the points made by Wittmer and Loesch (1986) is that accreditation is based on standards. CACREP, for example, relies upon two sets of standards: *Standards for Preparation of Counselors and Other Personnel-Services Specialists* and *Standards for Advanced Preparation (Doctoral) in Counselor Education* (CACREP, 1985). These standards address a number of features of the training program, ranging from the care with which program objectives are spelled out to the quality of the faculty. Consideration is also given to the quality of students enrolled in the program, the curriculum offered, the nature of the field experiences, the facilities available to students and faculty, administrative support for the program, and a variety of other factors. To some degree, the standards are aimed at quantitative factors (e.g., number of hours spent in field experience), but for the most part the concern is on qualitative factors (e.g., are students adequately prepared to perform as counselors?).

If a program faculty determines that they wish to become accredited, they conduct an intensive self-study using the aforementioned standards as a guide. This self-study is presented to, and reviewed by, CACREP. CACREP has three courses of action at this point in the process. One of these is to accept the application and send an accreditation team to the university or college housing the applicant program. This team's responsibility is to verify that the information contained in the self-study is accurate. CACREP may also reject the application on the grounds that the program clearly does not meet standards *or* the council may request more information (CACREP, 1985).

If an accreditation team is sent to a program, it interviews faculty, students, administrators, and field supervisors, and conducts a review of appropriate records to determine whether CACREP standards have been met. The team files a report with CACREP that is considered along with the original application. Here again, the council has three options: denial, provisional accreditation, or full accreditation. Full accreditation indicates the program under consideration has fully met accreditation standards. Provisional accreditation is awarded when a training program has met all but a few of the accreditation standards and shows clear promise of remedying its deficiencies within the two-year period for which accreditation is given (CACREP, 1985). Programs that are denied accreditation are provided precise feedback about their deficiencies and encouraged to reapply once problems have been addressed.

The third feature of the accreditation process is that it costs money (Wittmer & Loesch, 1986). One of these costs is the application fee. If the program is approved, a continuing fee must also be paid each year. However, these are not the major costs of accreditation. High-quality counselor education programs cost considerable amounts of money to staff and support because of faculty teaching student loads, the employment of higher-quality faculty, increased expenditures for facilities, and so on. It is the increased cost that precludes some counselor education programs from pursuing the process.

As we have seen, accreditation requires self-study. This is the fourth feature of the process delineated by Wittmer and Loesch (1986). However, the self-study does not end with accreditation. In fact, the self-study at the outset is barely the beginning of this process. Each year, the faculty, field supervisors, and students of a CACREP approved program review the status of each program to make certain that they are still in compliance with the standards.

Wittmer and Loesch (1986) point out a fifth aspect of the accreditation process: It has a geographic limit. However, unlike the Department of Education program approval process described earlier in this chapter, accreditation has a national geographic limit.

Sixth, accreditation is not reciprocal (Wittmer & Loesch, 1986). The American Psychological Association or the American Association of Marriage and Family Therapists will not recognize the accreditation given by CACREP and, of course, CACREP does not recognize APA's or AAMFT's accreditation processes either. Perhaps this can best be understood when one considers that the various accrediting agencies represent different professional groups, and thus reciprocity would, to a very large degree, be inappropriate.

A seventh and final feature of the accreditation process is that it is curriculum specific. Many counselor education programs offer specialties in school counseling, mental health counseling, rehabilitation counseling, student personnel services, etc. Accreditation is awarded not to an entire department, but to the specialty curriculum (CACREP, 1985). Thus it is entirely possible that one program within a counselor education program unit could be accredited and another not.

There are a number of results of the adoption and implementation of accreditation standards for the preparation of counselors. First, the profession has an adopted set of criteria for judging preparation programs that may be utilized by prospective students, employees, and clients, and by insurance carriers and others to evaluate the quality of preparation of counselors. The criteria also provide a set of standards by which counselors and others may compare their preparation to that of other mental health professionals. Finally, and as already noted, these standards allow credentialing bodies to make judgments about the preparation of persons who apply for certification and licensure. The result is typically preferential treatment for graduates of these programs.

STUDENT LEARNING EXERCISE

Read each statement and place a T in the blank if it is true, and an F if it is false.

_____ 1. Program accreditation and individual credentialing are often linked in some manner.

_____ 2. Program accreditation is primarily a quantitative effort, that is, aimed at auditing credit hours, examining the credentials of instructors, and examining facilities.

_____ 3. Evidence has been advanced that students completing accredited programs are better prepared than those completing nonaccredited programs.

_____ 4. AAMFT will accept graduates of CACREP-approved programs for credentialing.

_____ 5. At this point, program accreditation by CACREP is a voluntary process.

_____ 6. One of the primary reasons for advancing program accreditation is to increase the credibility of counselors.

IMPLICATIONS OF CREDENTIALING

Any discussion of the implications of credentialing must be divided into two sections: those for the individual and those for the profession. Students and others often ask, "If I am licensed or certified, what does it mean for me?" In a number of instances, particularly with regard to certification, the answer is that in tangible terms it means nothing. In professional or personal terms, the benefit to the individual may be substantial. Let us look at the tangible rewards for the individual first.

Licensing for counselors in states like Virginia and Florida may mean that the individuals can receive payment for the provision of mental health services specified in the health insurance coverage of a client. Since fees for counseling vary widely, from as little as $15 per hour to as much as $100 per hour, it is difficult to estimate what the actual tangible return might be.

The intangibles of meeting the highest standards of one's professional group are the reward sought by most counselors. Licensure in many states and certification by NBCC, NCCC, CCRC, or NACCMHC carry no automatic reward, yet thousands of counselors have pursued these credentials to illustrate their commitment to professionalism.

The implications of credentialing for the counseling profession are profound. One of these that is relatively certain is that both program accreditation standards and certification requirements will continue to escalate. This will place increasing pressure on counselor education programs because higher standards translate also quite directly into increased costs in many instances. Since accreditation, licensure, and certification are linked, preparation programs unable to meet accreditation standards may be less able to compete for prospective students. These are points of conjecture, to be sure, since there is no evidence that program accreditation improves the quality of the graduates.

It is also quite likely that licensure and certification will become hiring requirements for some types of counseling jobs in the future. For example, the American Rehabilitation Counselor's Association has lobbied unsuccessfully to require that all counselors hired under the auspices of the Rehabilitation Act of 1973 be Certified Rehabilitation Counselors (Guidepost, 1986). There are also movements afoot in some states to require that mental health counselors working in state agencies be certified or licensed. These initiatives will continue to intensify and be successful in some instances.

It can also be expected that the counseling profession will gain in stature with the public at large, among mental health professional groups, and among legislators as a result of credentialing. The result will be an extension of professional self-control and rewards such as third-party payments from health insurance carriers. This is not to suggest that these things will occur just because of credentialing. However, credentialing efforts will provide counselors interested in advancing the profession with the rationale and support needed to convince legislators that the profession meets the criteria necessary for further recognition.

SUMMARY

The history of individual and program credentialing in the counseling profession is a brief one when compared to many professional groups. However, given its brief history, credentialing is also a highly successful movement, and one with so much momentum that it is likely to accelerate in the future.

Credentialing varies from state to state, with a large number of states having no licensing or regulatory statutes for counselors in place at this time. However, in almost all states that have no licensing laws in place, movements are underway to correct this situation.

Program accreditation began officially in 1979, although concern about formal training standards in the profession can be traced to the early 1960s. Program accreditation, like licensure and certification processes, is a quality control measure.

REVIEW QUESTIONS

1. Compare and contrast title/practice and title licensing laws.
2. How do certification and licensing laws differ? How are they similar?
3. Discuss the pros and cons of credentials such as NCC, given that there are few tangible benefits associated with holding these certificates.
4. What are the advantages that accrue to the accredited counselor education program? What are the disadvantages? What are the advantages and disadvantages to the student, given the fact that there is no assurance that he or she will actually be better prepared to function as counselors?
5. If all states adopted licensure laws such as the one in Ohio that precludes certain counselors from diagnosing mental health problems, what would be the impact on the counseling profession?
6. Given the definitions set forth, is the Idaho law a licensure law or a registry/certification act, even though it is called a licensure law?

REFERENCES

Accredition of Counseling and Related Educational Programs. (1985). *Accreditation Procedures Manual and Application for Counseling and Related Educational Programs.* Alexandria, VA: Author.

American Association for Counseling and Development. (1985–86). *American Association for Counseling and Development*, 1985–86. Alexandria, VA: Author.

Association for Counselor Educational Supervision (1977). Standards for the preparation of counselors and other personnel services specialists. *Personnel and Guidance Journal, 55*(10), 596–601.

Commission on Rehabilitation Counselor Certification (1986). *Guide to rehabilitation counselor certification.* Arlington Heights, IL: Author.

Council for the Accredition of Counselors and Related Educational Programs (1985). *Standards for Preparation of Counselors and Other Personnel-Services Specialists* and *Standards for Advanced Preparation (Doctoral) in Counselor Education.* Alexandria, FA: Author.

Forster, J. R. (1977). What shall we do about credentialing? *Personnel and Guidance Journal, 55*(10), 573–580.

Guidepost. (1986). ARCA pursues rehabilitation bill. *Guidepost, 28,* 1986, p. 2.

Kosinski, Jr., F. A. (1982). Standards, accreditation, and licensure in marital and family therapy. *Personnel and Guidance Journal, 60*(6), 350–352.

MacKin, P. K. (1976). Occupational licensing: A warning. *Personnel and Guidance Journal, 54*(10), 507–511.

McFadden, J., & Brooks, Jr., D. K. (Eds.). (1983). *Counselor licensure action packet.* Falls Church, VA: AACD.

National Academy of Certified Clinical Mental Health Counselors. (1986). *Application instruction and information.* Alexandria, VA: Author.

National Board of Certified Counselors. (1986). *Certification information and application.* Alexandria, VA: Author.

National Council for Credentialing Career Counselors. (1986). *Certification information and application.* Alexandria, VA: National Board of Certified Counselors.

Stripling, R. O. (1979). Standards and accreditation in counselor education: A proposal. *Personnel and Guidance Journal, 56*(10), 608–611.

Warner, Jr., R. W., Brooks, Jr., D. K., & Thompson, Jean A. (Eds.). (1980). *Counselor licensure: Perspectives and issues.* Falls Church, VA: AACD Press.

Wittmer, J. P., & Loesch, L. C. (1986). Professional orientation. In M. D. Lewis, R. L., Hayes, & J. R. Lewis (Eds.). *An Introduction to the Counselors Profession* (pp. 301–330). Itasca, IL: F. E. Peacock Publishers.

12

Counselors in Educational Settings

GOAL OF THE CHAPTER

The goal of this chapter is to describe the functioning of counselors in various educational settings.

CHAPTER PREVIEW

1. The controversy regarding the roles of counselors in educational settings will be presented.
2. Counselor functions in elementary, junior high, high school, and post-secondary educational institutions will be discussed.
3. The diverse factors that influence counselor functioning will be discussed.

INTRODUCTION

The *Occupational Outlook Handbook* (Bureau of Labor Statistics [BLS], 1985–86) reports that of the 148,000 counselors working in the United States in 1982, nearly two-thirds were working in educational programs, primarily in elementary and secondary schools, colleges, and universities. It is undoubtedly true that the number of counselors working in educational institutions exceeds 100,000 at this point. It is a major objective of this chapter to examine the diverse functions these counselors perform and to give the reader a sense of both the commonalities and differences that exist, not only across educational levels, but within the levels as well. It is not the intention of this presentation to infer that there are prototypical ways of functioning, or that one function (e.g., counseling) is superior to another (e.g., consultation), although there are those within the profession who would do so, and with good reason.

COUNSELORS' ROLES AND FUNCTIONS: AN OVERVIEW

The matter of counselors' roles has not been overlooked by professional organizations, particularly the American School Counselor Association (ASCA), which has continuously provided leadership in the area of clarifying the role of counselors in educational institutions. This association began with two publications, "The Unique Role of the Elementary School Counselor" (Lamb & Deschenses, 1974) and "The Role and Function of Postsecondary Counseling" (ASCA, 1974). It continued with a revision of the elementary school role statement in 1978 (ASCA, 1978) and publication of "The Role of Secondary School Counselors" (ASCA, 1977). Another document, "The Role of the Middle/Junior High School Counselor," was also developed, but never published, in the 1970s. The most recent statement, "The Practice of Guidance and Counseling by School Counselors" (ASCA, 1981), consolidates all previous role statements into a single document. Before discussing the specific roles of the elementary school, middle/junior high school, high school, and college counselors, some of the generic aspects of counselor functioning set forth in this latest document will be discussed.

Perhaps the most striking feature of the latest (ASCA, 1981) role statement for school counselors is its emphasis on the developmental/preventive orientation of counselors, as opposed to a focus on remediation. Statements such as the following highlight this emphasis.

> Counselors as developmental facilitators function as school-based members of student support teams. (p. 8)
> Counseling and guidance is an integral function in the school that is maximized when counselors provide consultation and in-service programs for staff regarding the incorporation of developmental psychology into the curriculum. (p. 8)
> The clinical skills and knowledge base of the counselor is most effectively used if effort is directed in an organized way toward making the school, the teachers and the curriculum sensitive to those aspects of personal development most associated with life success. (p. 8)

This positive, developmental philosophy embodied in the ASCA (1981) statement is aimed at directing counselors to adopt a set of generic interventions that would be tempered to fit the developmental stages of the client group served. This set of intervention strategies would include structured developmental experiences such as classroom units designed to promote human growth in areas such as career and moral development. Consultation is also viewed as an important intervention, particularly consultation with teachers and parents aimed at assisting these two groups in providing better learning environments for students.

It is a curious aspect of the ASCA (1981) statement that the counseling function receives relatively little attention. Counseling is viewed as a technique that can be useful in facilitating the development of students. The role statement states that "individual and small group counseling is provided when the needs [of students] deserve more attention or privacy" (p. 9).

This apparent deemphasis on counseling in the 1981 role statement is certainly at odds with the recommendations found in many current articles. For example, recent articles have recommended counseling functions with families and stepfamilies (Lutz, Jacobs, & Masson, 1981; Wilcoxen, 1986), emotionally disturbed students (Levinson, 1985), special education students generally (Skinner, 1985), potential dropouts (Gadwa & Griggs, 1985), students suffering from eating disorders such as anorexia nervosa (Hendrick, 1984) and bulimia (Hendrick, 1985), and students who are potentially suicidal (Delisle, 1986; Wellman, 1984). While no one questions the importance of counseling students suffering from a vast array of psychological difficulties, the intent of the latest role statement for counselors (ASCA, 1981) is to emphasize the prevention of psychological problems by engaging in activities that will impact students' psychological development.

Finally, the 1981 ASCA statement indicates that there should be variation in functioning of counselors working in educational institutions because of the differences in psychological development evidenced by students in elementary school, middle/junior high school, high school, and postsecondary institutions.

PREOCCUPATION WITH ROLE

The relative importance of the counseling function is but one of the variables that has received attention in the counseling literature. In fact, there seems to be a preoccupation with the roles of counselors in educational institutions. More than two dozen articles have appeared in the *School Counselor* and *Elementary School Guidance and Counseling* since 1976 that dealt with the roles of school counselors, and a number of others have appeared in other journals. A dozen and a half articles have also appeared in publications such as the *Journal of College Student Personnel*, the *Journal of Counseling Psychology*, and the *Journal of Counseling and Development* that address this same area for college counselors. And this current preoccupation is not new. In fact, the roles that counselors in educational settings should fill have been the subject of debate since counselors began to deliver mental health services in addition to career and educationally oriented assistance. But why the concern? There are a number of interrelated answers to this question.

Counseling is relatively new and, as such, is an evolving profession. Counseling services were first offered extensively on college campuses in the late 1940s, although there were a number of campuses with counseling centers prior to 1945 (Heppner & Neal, 1983). As was pointed out in Chapter 1, counseling in public schools has been available since the turn of the century, but it was not until the late 1950s and 1960s that counseling services were widely offered in high schools and junior high schools. Although there has been a rapid growth in the number of counselors in elementary schools, many schools are still without the services of counselors (Gibson & Mitchell, 1986). The newness of counseling services in our educational institutions almost mandates that there be an ongoing search for more effective means of delivering services to client groups.

The nature of the clients served has changed over time, and this has also changed perspectives on counselor functioning. Veterans returning to college campuses with their spouses after World War II increased concerns about marriage and family counseling services in institutions of higher education. This concern has been so greatly amplified today that it is not uncommon for job announcements for college counselors to specify that applicants have skills in marriage and family counseling. Similarly, elementary school counselors find that a variety of society trends, including increased divorce rates and both parents working, have increased their need to offer services to parents in the form of parent education, parent consultation, and, in some instances, family counseling. Skyrocketing increases in teenage pregnancy have forced high school counselors to alter their activities to include support groups for pregnant teenagers and to become involved in human sexuality programs. As these changes have occurred and will continue to occur, counselors may have to continue to shift the focus of their activities.

Another factor that contributes to the concern about roles is a sense of vulnerability among counselors in educational institutions. This perception was heightened in the late 1970s and early 1980s when economic recession brought cutbacks in public school and university counseling staffs in states such as Michigan and Pennsylvania, and property tax reduction referendums in California and Massachusetts lowered public school revenue, resulting in a reduction in counselor positions. Gladding and Hageman (1984) characterized the situation as "a professional season of fading. It is a crisis" (p. 166). Crabbs (1984) blamed not only the economic cycle, but increasing social and political conservatism for the current situation, and offered an accountability model for counselors that would enable them to justify their positions and stem the outward tide of reduction in force.

While there is no question that counseling services are to some extent vulnerable since they do not represent instruction—the major function of educational institutions—there is a countertrend, a growing awareness of the need for counseling services. As Herr (1986) observes, the doomsayers are not accurate forecasters of the demise of counseling in educational institutions. In fact, as Herr also notes, there are many current indicators that counseling services are valued. He cites as one source of support the prestigious Carnegie Foundation document *High School, A Report on Secondary Education in America* (Boyer, 1983), which recommends that high school counseling loads be reduced to one counselor for each hundred students. This ratio probably approaches 1:500 in most situations currently. Of note also are a modest expansion of college counseling centers in many institutions and the passage of legislation in some states. Virginia, Tennessee, and South Carolina recently have required the addition of school counselors to educational staffs.

To be sure, the picture for counselors is not uniformly bright. As Gladding and Hageman (1984) observed, there are states in which counseling services may have difficulty recovering. In others, cutbacks in counseling staffs may still result, or, at the very least, no gains in numbers of counselors or services offered are likely.

Still another factor that continues to fuel counselors' concerns about their roles is a certain amount of discrepancy between what the public perceives them to do and what professionals themselves believe they are about. Recently, Bishop (1986) found that 85% of the faculty on the University of Delaware campus were aware of the services offered by the counseling center. Most (81%) also knew that personal counseling was offered to students, and 62% knew that educational counseling was offered to the same group. However, only 30% recognized that consultation services were available to them, and 17% believed that they could receive personal counseling, a service not offered by the center. Bishop concluded that faculty members were not aware of the career development services offered by the counseling center since only 52% knew that career counseling for students was available.

Ibrahim, Helms, and Thompson (1983) studied the role perceptions of high school counselors held by students, administrators, members of the business community, and counselors themselves and, like Bishop (1986), found some discrepancies. For example, counselors saw research and consulting with the staff as less important than administrators. It should be pointed out, however, that these two groups agreed on a majority of the functions of the high school counselor.

In the aforementioned study, counselors and administrators had significantly different perceptions from parents or members of the business community with regard to providing help to parents, public relations, educational and occupational planning, and referral of problems to outside agencies. Counselors and administrators attached more importance to public relations and helping parents, and parents and members of the business community placed greater emphasis on career and educational planning and referral (Ibrahim et al., 1983).

A Kansas study (Bonebrake & Borgers, 1984) in many ways paralleled the one conducted by Ibrahim et al. (1983), with two important exceptions. These variations were that only principals and counselors were included in the study and the focus of the study was on junior high/middle school counseling. The results of the study are reported in Table 12.1. As can be seen, principals and counselors disagreed only to a slight degree in their rankings of the functions of counselors. Bonebrake and Borgers concluded that the slight discrepancies they observed in perceptions of the counselors' role and functioning were not as great as those observed in earlier studies.

School Counselors and Mental Health

A recent College Board report (College Entrance Examination Board [CEEB], 1986) argued that counselors working in K–12 settings have as their primary responsibility fostering the educational development of students, including facilitating course selection and transition to postsecondary educational institutions. This same report recommends that counselors focus less on the personal problems of their clients. This is not a new argument, but it is advanced with the same naiveté as previous arguments of this kind.

Students experiencing stress arising out of family disputes, or those with emotional problems of their own, are unlikely to be concerned about school subjects or the transition to postsecondary institutions. In fact, they are often unable

Table 12.1   Task Rankings

Rank	Group	
	Counselor items	*Principal items*
1	Individual counseling	Individual counseling
2	Teacher consultant	Student assessment
3	Student assessment	Teacher consultant
4	Parent consultant	Evaluation of guidance
5	Evaluation of guidance	Parent consultant
6	Referral services	Career education
7	Group counseling	Classroom guidance
8	Career education	Group counseling
9	Classroom guidance	Referral services
10	Scheduling	Scheduling
11	Research	Research
12	Functioning as principal	Supervision of lunchroom
13	Supervision of lunchroom	Functioning as principal
14	Discipline	Discipline
15	Teach nonguidance classes	Teach nonguidance classes

Note. From "Counselor Role as Perceived by Counselors and Principals" (p. 196) by C. R. Bonebrake and S. B. Borgers, 1984, *Elementary School Guidance and Counseling, 18.* Copyright, 1984 AACD. Reprinted by permission. No further reproduction is authorized without further permission of AACD.

to take advantage of their current educational opportunities. Students do not function in separate spheres, with their personal lives being detached from their educational functioning. Counselors who expect to be helpful in the educational arena will have to address personal problems either directly or by referral of those students experiencing difficulty to outside agencies.

The fact is that school counselors are in an ideal situation to provide personal counseling, although circumstances such as pupil load, facilities, and noncounseling duties may prevent them from functioning in this area. Mental health counselors working in community agencies have little contact with their clients other than a weekly appointment that may or may not be kept. School counselors interact routinely with teachers and thus have an opportunity to get first-hand feedback on a client's progress and even to exert influence on environmental factors that may facilitate desirable change. They can also follow up easily whenever a student misses an appointment. Support groups such as peers and families are also easily accessible to school counselors in many instances.

The extent to which school counselors will become involved in personal counseling will depend on a variety of factors. However, to argue that this is not a role of this group seems inappropriate.

COUNSELORS IN ELEMENTARY SCHOOLS

As Tolbert (1982) pointed out, and as was noted in Chapter 1, elementary school counselors are the newest addition to the cadre of counselors working in school settings. As was also noted earlier in this chapter, elementary school counselors represent the fastest growing group of counselors at this juncture, partially because there is increasing recognition of the impact of certain societal problems such as family breakup on children and, to some degree, because there is an expectation that elementary school counselors will prevent serious educational and psychological problems from arising. While there are numerous expectations of how elementary school counselors should function, the fact is that they operate quite differently.

Marsha is the only counselor in an elementary school with an enrollment of 650 pupils. Her district requires that every counselor deliver classroom guidance activities to every classroom each week. The result is that the majority of Marsha's time is spent preparing for or delivering units on topics dealing with friendship, values clarification, understanding and appreciating people who are different (e.g., from different ethnic groups, with handicaps), self-concept development, and an array of others to the 30 classrooms in her building. In her remaining time, she runs small groups dealing with classroom achievement, consults with parents and teachers, serves on the committee to accept and process referrals for students who may need placement in special education classes, and does a limited amount of individual counseling, primarily with students who are having educational adjustment problems. Students with moderate or severe psychological problems are referred to private practitioners or to the local community mental health center.

Sarah's school, like Marsha's, enrolls more than 600 students. However, Sarah has more freedom to design her own program and has elected to work collaboratively with teachers to incorporate units into the regular curricular activities. As a result, all teachers include units on career-related activities such as parent's careers (kindergarten), community helpers (first grade), and workers in our state (fifth grade). Teachers have also incorporated into the curriculum units on study skills and how to take tests. Sarah also coordinates the sex education program for fifth and sixth graders. In all of these activities, Sarah acts as a resource person in that she helps teachers locate appropriate materials and she often acts as an active participant in that she is a co-presenter. These coordination/consultant activities take up well over 50% of Sarah's time. The remainder is spent in individual and group counseling, conducting parenting skills classes, designing and delivering in-service training for teachers on topics such as creative discipline, conferencing with parents, and developing communications skills.

Tom serves a school of 350 students, and his role is probably more in keeping with the stereotypical role of the elementary school counselor. Classroom guidance takes only about 25% of his time, while small groups based on the needs of students occupy another 30%. Tom also sees three to four individuals per day for 30 to 45 minutes, consults with teachers and parents, and serves on the special education screening team.

Sarah's activities most closely approximate the recommended role and function statement set forth in the most recent ASCA (1981) role statement. The recommendations in that document are for elementary school counselors to consult with and deliver in-service training to teachers so that they can deliver services to children directly, develop parenting skills, work in the identification and remediation of students with developmental deficiencies or handicaps, and assist with curriculum development that will facilitate an understanding of the relationship between school and work.

It is interesting to note that none of the counselors described above emphasizes individual counseling. A 1977 study conducted by the North Central Association of Schools and Colleges found that elementary school educators such as teachers, administrators, and counselors ranked individual counseling as the most important activity performed by elementary school counselors. Consultation with teachers and group counseling ranked second in importance, consultation with parents third, behavior modification fourth, parent counseling fifth, values clarification activities sixth, assessment activities seventh, career guidance eighth, and so forth (Gibson & Mitchell, 1986). There is no current study that provides a perspective on the importance attached to the individual counseling area, although one would expect that individual and group counseling would be rated as important activities by counselors and noncounselors alike. However, from the 1981 role statement, from sources such as Gibson and

Mitchell (1986) and Tolbert (1982), and from observation, a picture can be developed of the roles filled by elementary school counselors.

- *Individual Counseling*—These sessions, lasting from 30 to 45 minutes, depending on the age of the child, range in focus from support for the child who has experienced a loss such as a death in the family, to skills building for the child who has difficulty making friends. The duration of counseling may be from one to several weeks.
- *Group Counseling*—These sessions typically involve six to eight children and revolve around a central theme such as school achievement, friendship, coping with stepfamilies, etc. Usually, they are scheduled once a week for six to eight weeks, but may last longer.
- *Consultation with Teachers*—These sessions may be initiated by either counselor or teacher and focus on a concern that will assist the teacher to be more effective with students. Counselors act collaboratively, in that they become actively involved in all phases of the process.
- *Consultation with Parents*—This activity may also be initiated by either a counselor or a parent. Consultation is typically short term and focuses on a specific process in the family that is leading to difficulty for the child. An example might be that a child who is undisciplined at home exhibits unruly behavior at school.
- *Classroom Guidance*—These sessions, which typically last from 30 to 45 minutes, focus on developmental issues confronted by most youngsters such as communication, decision-making, getting along with others, etc.
- *Coordination*—This involves the identification and facilitation of activities that will promote the child's development. Elementary school counselors may coordinate the testing program, career development activities, and referral to community agencies.
- *Orientation*—Students new to the school are presented information about their new environment in small groups and by other means. They are also given an opportunity to explore their feelings about their new experiences. Students leaving the school are familiarized with the middle/junior high school, generally in cooperation with counselors from that level.
- *Educational Activities*—In-service training activities are conducted with teachers in order to increase their skills and enable them to be more effective with students. Similarly, parent education activities are held to develop parenting skills.
- *Other*—Elementary school counselors fill a number of other roles such as serving on committees charged with screening students referred for special services, serving as advisors to student councils, and acting as the school's liaison with community agencies such as the Department of Social Services.

COUNSELORS IN MIDDLE/JUNIOR HIGH SCHOOL

It is true that middle school (typically grades 5 through 8) and junior high school (7 through 9) counseling have received short shrift in terms of attention and concern. It seems to be the case that most authors believe that material from both senior high school and elementary school will generalize to these grade levels. However, students at this educational level are undergoing some dramatic physical and psychological changes that place unique demands on counseling staffs. This uniqueness is recognized in the latest role statement (ASCA, 1981), in that it is recommended that counselors facilitate students' adjustment to the less confining atmosphere of the upper grade levels, emphasize career guidance, and work with teachers to assist them to incorporate into the curriculum developmental units.

The Bonebrake and Borgers (1984) study reported earlier is a bit more specific regarding the roles a middle school/junior high school counselor should fill, with individual counseling, teacher consultation, student assessment, and parental consultation being listed as the top four functions by counselors. Interestingly, career education was ranked as the eighth most important function by counselors in the study of counselors in Kansas. To some degree, however, the functioning of a middle school counselor and two junior high school counselors is more illustrative of the impact of the setting and the students on counselor functioning.

Doug is responsible for 350 junior high school students and spends more than 50% of his time counseling individual students in the junior high school where he works because "it is virtually impossible to get groups of students together." He does run two support groups per week, one for new students and another for minority students. He is involved in teacher consultation and has been instrumental in getting drug and alcohol abuse units strengthened in health and biology classes. He also has been successful in getting English and social studies teachers to develop units on careers that extend over a nine-week grading period. Doug coordinates the achievement and aptitude testing program, as well as the administration of interest inventories to all first-semester ninth graders. The remainder of his time is spent in scheduling, working with community agencies, "administrivia" (filling out forms), and general school responsibilities.

Julia, formerly an elementary school counselor, now works in a new middle school that enrolls more than 900 students. She has been assigned half of these students. She has found that students have less free time to see the counselors than those in the elementary school where she had worked. She has designed classroom guidance units for students, and each year, each class will receive a nine-week unit based on the developmental needs of the students. Units include human sexuality (conducted with the health educator), school and you, boy-girl relations, getting along with parents, and career exploration. Individual counseling, some group counseling, teacher consultation, parent education, serving on the special education referral committee, scheduling, and referral make up the bulk of the remainder of Julia's schedule.

Sharon works in a rural area where she has responsibility for more than 700 junior high students. She has convinced the administration to make students available for group work and spends more than 35% of her time in group counseling. Fifty percent of her time is spent in individual counseling, with the rest spent on parent and teacher consultation, scheduling, and referral of students to community agencies. She spends no time in the classroom, but she believes this is a weakness in her program because she feels she is not reaching all the students.

In summary, the functions that comprise the middle school/junior high school counselor's role are as follows.

- *Individual Counseling*—Sessions are geared to school periods or parts of school periods (30 to 55 minutes) and, for the most part, are spread over a few weeks. Problems discussed typically focus on peers, boy-girl relationships, family concerns, and adjustment in school.
- *Group Counseling*—Group counseling sessions, like individual counseling sessions, have to be tailored to the school day. Problems discussed in groups are similar to those addressed in individual counseling.
- *Teacher Consultation*—Generally, consultation sessions are short term in nature and focus on educational concerns such as discipline, parent relationships, and curricular concerns such as integrating career development concepts into the curriculum, strengthening drug abuse programs, and developing programs such as those involving study skills.
- *Classroom Guidance*—This is not a major role for many junior high school counselors, although many middle school counselors are extensively involved in delivering classroom units. Topics parallel those offered in elementary schools, with more emphasis on career development, life planning, human sexuality, drug abuse prevention, and dealing with parents.
- *Parental Consultation*—Topics involved range from motivating students to do school work to dealing with rebellious adolescents. Generally, consultation is relatively short term, and some of the sessions may be followed up with telephone calls to offer support or assistance.
- *Referral*—A number of serious problems arise among young adolescents, including bulimia, anorexia nervosa, and suicidal ideation. Depending on the severity of the problem, counselors may refer these types of problems to outside agencies because of time constraints.
- *Coordination*—Many counselors working at this level are charged with extensive scheduling responsibilities or, at the very least, coordinating the scheduling process. Counselors also coordinate testing and career development programs in many instances.
- *Orientation*—A part of orientation may come in the form of support groups for new students. However, middle and junior high school counselors, in collaboration with elementary and high school counselors, are

often involved in orientation of new students or preparing students for the next level.

- *Research and Evaluation*—These activities are not emphasized in many school districts but occupy a portion of most counselors' time.

HIGH SCHOOL COUNSELORS

Counseling services have been offered in some high schools for more than 85 years and, in some ways, if one considers the ASCA 1981 role statement as a guide, roles have changed greatly. Career choice and planning, and assessment of personal characteristics so that adequate life decisions can be made are emphasized in that document. However, in a departure from the earlier secondary school counseling programs and from recommendations for the other levels, the role statement (ASCA, 1981) suggests that high school counselors provide "remedial interventions" for individuals who are having difficulty with career planning, school adjustment, or personal development.

Ibrahim et al. (1983) presented a relatively recent study that asked parents, counselors, administrators, and members of the business community to rate the roles and functions of counselors. Some of the results of this study were alluded to earlier in this chapter, but a more detailed analysis of that study will be presented here. In this study, counselors rated individual counseling for personal and educational problems as their most important function, followed closely by providing information to students about course content and helping students make personal plans. Providing individual counseling for students with career choice problems, providing students with information about careers, disseminating information about postsecondary educational opportunities, referring students with special needs, consulting with the school psychologists, conducting orientation programs, public relations activities, consulting with teachers, counseling parents, and administering tests and interpreting the results also were deemed important by the high school counselors in the study. The counselors surveyed were much less positive in their rating of job placement activities, conducting classroom guidance activities with teachers, research, and publishing a guidance newsletter. It is interesting to note that those activities favored by counselors in this study parallel the recommendations of the ASCA (1981).

Sandra is a high school counselor who rotates with her class each year, following sophomores until they are seniors and then picking up another group of sophomores. Because of this rotation, her role varies considerably from year to year. One constant is her involvement in scheduling and general educational planning, which culminates with assisting seniors and those who leave school prior to graduation with selection of postsecondary educational opportunities. Another constant is a steady stream of personal counseling clients who are seen, for the most part, individually. Group counseling focuses on career planning, race relations, and, from time to time, problem pregnancies. Referral of students involved with drugs and alcohol abuse and those who have relatively severe personal problems, such as suicide threats, bulimia, and anorexia nervosa, also occupy a fair amount of each day. Finally, because so many of her students go on to college, writing recommendations, seeing that transcripts are mailed, and helping students with financial aid applications also take much of her time.

Jerry is a vocational counselor in a large high school and works only with vocational students. Although he helps students with personal, educational, and vocational problems, a great deal of his time is spent on career planning, job placement, testing, and the development of employable skills. He also has developed and maintains an extensive career information library. Because Jerry's program is partially supported by federal funds, he spends a small amount of time completing forms such as activity reports.

Marian's principal sees her as an extension of the administration in her school and, as a result, she spends nearly half of her time in scheduling, drop-add, telephoning students who are absent, record keeping, and computing grade point averages. The remainder of her time is spent in individual, educational, and career planning, disseminating postsecondary educational and career information, coordinating the program, serving as a member of the curriculum reform committee, and meeting with parents, usually about students with academic problems or for college planning. She admits to being frustrated by her inability to meet the vast number of personal-social needs among the study body.

The functions filled by secondary school counselors can be summarized as follows.

- *Individual Counseling*—These sessions, usually spanning a few weeks, deal with a wide range of developmental and moderately severe personal problems. Sessions are geared to school schedules and typically last from 30 to 55 minutes. Typical problems addressed include making educational choices, career planning, family concerns, drug and alcohol abuse, and peer relationships.
- *Group Counseling*—Like individual counseling, group counseling addresses a wide range of developmental and personal problems. Group counseling typically lasts from 8 to 10 weeks but may be somewhat shorter or longer depending on the school situation.
- *Teacher Consultation*—Consultation with teachers focuses on such topics as the infusion of activities such as study skills programs into the curriculum and, to a smaller degree, classroom management and the motivation of students.
- *Parent Consultation*—This function typically occupies less of the counselor's time than at other levels. The focus ranges from assisting parents to deal with alcohol and drug abuse to educational planning.
- *Orientation*—Orientation of new students to the high school is a continuing problem for counselors in this setting because of the frequent arrival of new students. Counselors at this level are also often involved

in orienting students to postsecondary educational institutions and the world of work. To cope with the latter, counselors arrange seminars in which graduates of the school discuss work situations with current students; they also plan field trips, internships, career days, and other relevant activities.

- *Educational Planning and Advising*—These activities range from assisting in course selection and registration on a semester-by-semester basis to activities focusing on long-range planning such as planning a high school course of study and selecting a postsecondary educational program. In some instances, this planning is coordinated with career planning, particularly as students near graduation. Some of these activities result in considerable clerical work such as duplicating and mailing transcripts to colleges and universities.

- *Coordination*—Counselors may coordinate such activities as the testing program, career development activities, substance abuse programs, and other similar programs.

- *Job Placement and the Development of Employable Skills*—Some high school counselors are charged with identifying job opportunities in the community, placing students in jobs in the community, and preparing students to secure jobs and be successful in them.

- *Referral*—Students with serious psychological problems such as severe depression, anorexia nervosa, or bulimia are typically referred to outside agencies. Secondary school counselors often are continuously involved with identifying and making referrals to appropriate external agencies and with follow-ups to those referrals.

COUNSELORS IN POSTSECONDARY SCHOOL SETTINGS

Counselors are widely found in vocational-technical schools, community colleges, four-year colleges, and universities. ASCA's (1981) role statement for this group emphasizes the development of programs that will assist high school students make the transition to adulthood. These programs would involve personal, educational, and career counseling, developing the skills to function independently, assisting with job placement, and assisting in areas such as moral development.

Research regarding counselors in postsecondary institutions has focused for the most part on college counselors. Some of this research has focused not on the role of the college counselor but on certain aspects of the agency itself. For example, Brown and Chambers (1986) found that students indicated that they would be more willing to go to a counseling center called a Personal and Career Counseling Service than they would a service named Psychological and Career Counseling Service; Counseling, Career, and Consultation Service; or Psychological and Career Exploration Service. The authors concluded that their research supported earlier findings that the name of a counseling center influences how it is perceived by students and faculty.

In a more relevant study, Troy and Magoon (1979) researched the actual use of time by the counselor staff at the University of Maryland. They also asked members of the staff to indicate how they preferred to use their time in order to see whether preference is related to actual function. In Table 12.2 it can be seen that counselors preferred remedial and rehabilitation counseling, administration, maintenance and development, and instruction, and that this is where they spent their time. On the other hand, improvement of campus ecology, developmental counseling, developing new personal sources, and working on accountability were the least preferred activities and the activities in which counselors spent the least amount of time.

It is obvious that Troy and Magoon (1979) found a high correlation between preferred ways of spending time and how time was actually spent. What is unfortunate in this study is that the researchers did not examine personal and career counseling in terms of preferences for actual time spent. After an extensive review of the research literature by Heppner and Neal (1983), the authors concluded that there is a general trend with regard to the changing role of counseling centers. This change is marked by an increased emphasis on personal-adjustment counseling and, of course, a corresponding decrease on other types of services, particularly career counseling. A fairly recent study (Pinkney & Jacobs, 1985) revealed that new counselors studied ranked titles that involved

Table 12.2 Ranking of Hours Spent Per Week and Preferences for Various Activities in One Counseling Center

	Activity	Hours spent	Preferred number of hours spent
1.	Remedial and rehabilitative counseling services	240	244
2.	Administrative, maintenance, and development	192	144
3.	Instruction, training, and supervision	127	122
4.	Off-campus professional services	59	42
5.	Research	53	87
6.	Alternative treatment models	52	57
7.	Miscellaneous activities	28	29
8.	Campus consultation	26	50
9.	Accountability procedures	15	5
10.	Developmental counseling	2	5
11.	Development of new personal services	1	1
12.	Improving campus ecology	0	3

Note. Data from "Activity Analysis in a University Counseling Center: Daily Time Recordings or Time Estimates?" by W. G. Troy and T. M. Magoon, 1979, *Journal of Counseling Psychology,* 18.

career counselors (e.g., job placement counselor) lower than those relating to personal counseling (e.g., psychological counselor). This same group was also less likely to be interested in narrative descriptions of cases involving career-related problems. Relating these preferences and interests to the Troy and Magoon study suggests that career counseling is suffering an image crisis and may not receive the attention it deserves in some counseling centers. Some counseling centers have compensated with differentiated staffing patterns.

Gary is a career counselor in a relatively large counseling center. More than 50% of his time is actually spent in career counseling, with the remainder being spent in leading career exploration groups, teaching a career exploration class for undergraduates, and working collaboratively with the Career Planning and Placement Service to develop employable skills such as resume preparation and interviewing behaviors in students.

Lorraine works in the same center and spends three-quarters of her time seeing individual clients with personal adjustment problems. Problems that require long-range treatment (more than 12 weeks) are referred to the local mental health center because of time constraints. Personal development groups, such as those dealing with sex role identity and becoming more assertive, occupy her remaining available hours.

John works in a small community college and wears a "number of hats," including recruiter, job placement officer, and, of course, counselor. Much of his time is spent with orientation and registration activities as well as with those already mentioned. He estimates that he spends less than one-quarter of his time counseling and this is mostly focused on educational and career planning.

The major functions of counselors in postsecondary institutions can be summarized as follows.

- *Individual Counseling*—These activities typically are longer term in nature than individual counseling in other educational institutions and embrace a wider variety of problems. Personal adjustment counseling makes up the bulk of the counseling activity in many agencies, but career counseling is still a very important activity.
- *Group Counseling*—Group counseling may span an entire semester or more. Topics addressed include career exploration, assertiveness, bulimia, anorexia nervosa, developing a sex role identity, and a host of other problems growing out of educational and personal experiences and problems of students.
- *Consultation and Outreach*—Counselors consult with faculty, residence hall personnel, and others involved with students. They also develop educational programs such as those designed to make residence hall advisors better able to identify and refer students who are manifesting psychological problems.
- *Training and Supervision*—Some, but not all, college counselors have adjunct appointments in training programs and are actively involved

with teaching courses and the supervision of the field experiences of counselors in training.

- *Research and Evaluation*—A substantial number of college counselors have ongoing research programs and contribute regularly to the professional literature. Some of these and others also are involved in periodic or continuing efforts to evaluate the impact of their agency on the setting where it is located.

- *Testing*—Larger counseling services often employ psychometrists to administer tests. However, in small centers counselors administer tests to their own clients. In community colleges, it is not uncommon for counselors to be charged with the administration of the screening tests used to place students in mathematics and English classes.

- *Referral*—Because of the availability of staff, most counseling centers find it necessary to refer certain types of clients to external agencies. On large college campuses, the counseling center may be one of several agencies delivering services to students, with each agency specializing in a particular function such as career counseling or dealing with pregnant students. In these situations, in-house referral systems are developed and utilized to make appropriate referrals.

FACTORS THAT INFLUENCE ROLE AND FUNCTION

In the preceding sections of this chapter, concerns about the role and function of counselors in educational institutions were discussed first. This was followed by a look at the role and function of counselors at various levels of the educational enterprise. Three different types of information were included in each of the discussions of counselors' roles at the various levels: professional recommendations, roles suggested by research, and brief narrative descriptions of the function of counselors at each of the levels. What should have been obvious is that there may not be much correlation between the actual functioning of counselors, the suggestions growing out of professional associations, and the empirical literature.

It is the position here, and one held over a long period of time by the authors (Brown & Srebalus, 1973), that counselors are professionals and thus must be involved in shaping their own role to suit their personal characteristics and those of the institution in which they are employed. This process is ultimately a reciprocal process, with the professional counselor exerting influence based on a variety of factors and the institutions placing demands on the individual that must be met. It should also be noted that the reciprocal process is a dynamic one and thus the role of a counselor is likely to shift over time as the individual and the institution change. At this point, some of the factors that influence this dynamic process will be examined.

The needs of the client groups to be served are among the most influential of the factors shaping the counselor's role in a given institution. On an informal basis, needs may be perceived quite differently by counselors, administrators, parents, and the community. Increasingly, counselors are involved in needs assessment programs that involve approaches such as surveying students, parents, teachers and administrators to ascertain perceptions of student, parent, and teacher needs, examining school records to identify needs (e.g., look at the dropout rate), and perusing test information to identify academic deficiencies. Once needs are developed, mutually agreed on strategies can be developed to meet the needs.

While it would seem logical that the needs of the clients to be served would dictate counselor functioning, this may not be the case. As we saw in the Troy and Magoon (1979) study, counselors' preferences for various functions seemed to have a considerable impact on how they spent their time. Perhaps in that situation, preferences were based on perceptions of needs, but in many instances, preferences for various functions are based on the skills of the counselor and probably on the personality of the counselor as well.

Not only do the preferences of counselors influence their roles, but so do the expectations of administrators and other role senders. It may be recalled that Marian, a high school counselor, found herself extensively involved in administrative duties because her principal viewed her as an extension of his office. Other counselors have found themselves in similar circumstances.

Tradition is also a powerful force in determining how the counselor will actually function. All too often, counselors hear, "We've always done it this way." Assertive professionals are able to break with tradition and function in different ways over time if they can convince the persons around them that a new method is more effective.

The resources of the institution also are tremendously important determiners of the counselor's roles. Underfunded community colleges press counselors into roles in financial aid, recruitment, registration, etc. Elementary school counselors find themselves checking on truants and giving psychological tests because of the unavailability of attendance officers and school psychologists. High school counselors confronted with massive numbers and no secretarial help may be reduced to functioning as registrars and college placement officers because of the demands placed on them.

Professional organizations such as the American School Counselor Association influence roles by the development of role statements such as the one cited frequently in this chapter (ASCA, 1981). These statements provide baselines by which professional counselors may judge their own functioning against that established by their peers.

Finally, training programs exert considerable influence on the function of counselors by the selection of areas to be emphasized in the training programs. School counselors (Sheeley & Jenkins, 1986) have been critical of training programs for being too theoretical and not providing enough techniques that have practical application. However, it is probably not accidental that in the surveys cited earlier in this chapter individual counseling was viewed as the most important activity in which counselors engage and emphasis is placed upon this activity in training programs.

SUMMARY

School counselors represent a significant portion of the counseling profession. Because they are employed largely in public institutions, their functioning is influenced by the same societal forces that have an impact on schools. Cutbacks in funding for schools have resulted in reduction in force among counselors in some places, but in many states the number of school counselors is advancing steadily.

The functioning of counselors in educational settings varies tremendously, depending on such factors as student needs, administration expectations, counselor preferences, and the availability of other resources. It seems likely that a number of current issues such as the "back to basics" movement will continue to influence how counselors in educational settings function.

STUDENT LEARNING EXERCISE

After you have read this chapter, the following activities may help you understand more completely the functioning of counselors in educational settings.

1. Interview practicing counselors from various levels that interest you. Ask them the following questions:
   a. How much time do you spend on various counseling related activities? Non-counseling related activities?
   b. Which of your activities is the most rewarding?
   c. If you could change your role, what would you do?
   d. What impact does your supervisor have on your role? Your setting? The age of the client group?
   e. What changes have you seen in your role since you became a counselor?
2. Interview a school psychologist or a mental health counselor and contrast their roles to those of school counselors.

REVIEW QUESTIONS

1. Identify the major roles of counselors in educational institutions. Then discuss how each role might be used to meet student needs. Finally, rank those roles you personally would like to offer to students and tell why.

2. Discuss counseling and consultation as possible intervention strategies. Tell how the educational level would have an impact on your use of these two interventions.

3. Outline the pros and cons of school counselors' providing therapeutic services to bulimics, potential suicides, and others who would require large amounts of the counselors' time.

4. Which counselors working in educational settings are in the best position to have an impact on the mental health of their clients? Why?

5. Some have argued that counselors working in K–12 settings do not need to be as rigorously trained as counselors working in mental health settings. Do you agree? Why or why not?

6. Counselors working in some educational settings are saddled with many noncounseling duties. How would you avoid having that happen to you?

REFERENCES

American School Counselor Association. (1974). The role and function of postsecondary counseling. *The School Counselor, 21,* 330–334.

American School Counselor Association. (1977). Role statement: The role of the secondary school counselor. *The School Counselor, 24,* 228–233.

American School Counselor Association. (1978). The role of the elementary school counselor. *Elementary School Guidance and Counseling, 13,* 91–96.

American School Counselor Association. (1981). Role statement: The practice of guidance and counseling by school counselors. *The School Counselor, 29,* 7–12.

Bishop, J. B. (1986). A faculty review of a university counseling center: Knowledge, perceptions and recommendations. *Journal of College Student Personnel, 27,* 413–417.

Bureau of Labor Statistics. (1985–86). *Occupational outlook handbook.* Washington, DC: Author.

Bonebrake, C. R., & Borgers, S. B. (1984). Counselor role as perceived by counselors and principals. *Elementary School Guidance and Counseling, 18,* 194–199.

Boyer, E. L. (1983). *High school, a report on secondary education in America.* New York: Harper and Row.

Brown, D., & Srebalus, D. J. (1973). *Contemporary guidance concepts and practices: An introduction.* Dubuque, IA: William C. Brown.

Brown, M. T., & Chambers, M. (1986). Student and faculty perceptions of counseling centers: What's in a name? *Journal of Counseling Psychology, 33,* 155–158.

College Entrance Examination Board. (1986). *Keeping the options open: Recommendations—Final report of the commission on precollege guidance and counseling.* New York: Author.

Crabbs, M. A. (1984). Reduction in force and accountability: Stemming the tide. *Elementary School Guidance and Counseling, 18,* 167–175.

Delisle, J. R. (1986). Death with honors: Suicide among gifted adolescents. *Journal of Counseling and Development, 64,* 588–560.

Gadwa, K., & Griggs, S. A. (1985). The school dropout: Implications for counselors. *The School Counselor, 33,* 9–17.

Gibson, R. L., & Mitchell, M. H. (1986). *Introduction to counseling and guidance* (2nd ed.). New York: Macmillan.

Gladding, S. T., & Hageman, M. B. (1984). Reduction in force: Proactive suggestions and creative plodding. *Elementary School Guidance and Counseling, 18*, 163–166.

Hendrick, S. S. (1984). The school counselor and anorexia nervosa. *The School Counselor, 31,* 428–432.

Hendrick, S. S. (1985). The school counselor and bulimia. *The School Counselor, 32,* 275–280.

Heppner, P. P., & Neal, G. W. (1983). Holding up the mirror: Research on the roles and functions of counseling centers in higher education. *The Counseling Psychologist, 11,* 81–98.

Herr, E. L. (1986). The relevant counselor. *The School Counselor, 34,* 7–13.

Ibrahim, F. A., Helms, B. A., & Thompson, D. L. (1983). Counselor role and function: An appraisal by consumers and counselors. *Personnel and Guidance Journal, 61,* 597–601.

Lamb, J., & Deschenes, R. (1974). The unique role of the elementary school counselor. *Elementary School Guidance and Counseling, 8,* 219–223.

Levinson, E. M. (1985). Vocational and career-oriented secondary school programs for the emotionally disturbed. *The School Counselor, 33,* 100–106.

Lutz, E. P., Jacobs, E. E., & Masson, R. L. (1981). Stepfamily counseling: Issues and guidelines. *The School Counselor, 28,* 189–194.

Pinkney, J. W., & Jacobs, D. (1985). New counselors and personal interest in the task of career counseling. *Journal of Counseling Psychology, 32,* 307–332.

Sheeley, V. L. , & Jenkins, D. E. (1980). Tomorrow's school counselors: Directions revealed for their education. *The ASCA Counselor, 2315,* 15.

Skinner, M. E. (1985). Counseling and special education: An essential relationship. *The School Counselor, 33,* 131–135.

Tolbert, E. L. (1982). *An introduction to guidance: The professional counselor.* Boston: Little, Brown and Company.

Troy, W. G., & Magoon, T. M. (1979). Activity analysis in a university counseling center: Daily time recordings or time estimates? *Journal of Counseling Psychology, 26,* 58–63.

Wellman, M. M. (1984). The school counselor's role in the communication of suicidal ideation by adolescents. *The School Counselor, 32,* 106–109.

Wilcoxen, S. A. (1986). Family counseling practices: Suggested reading guide for school counselors. *The School Counselor, 33,* 272–278.

Wilson, N. J., & Rotter, J. C. (1982). School counseling: A look into the future. *Personnel and Guidance Journal, 60,* 353–357.

13

Mental Health Counselors

GOAL OF THE CHAPTER

The purpose of this chapter is to portray mental health counseling as a career option.

CHAPTER PREVIEW

1. Typical duties of mental health counselors will be depicted.
2. The history and funding of community mental health will be surveyed.
3. The early history of the American Mental Health Counselors' Association will be sketched.
4. Treatment strategies in community mental health will be described.
5. Special attention will be directed toward the outpatient and emergency services in mental health.

INTRODUCTION

The purpose of this chapter is to provide an overview of community mental health settings as employment options for counselors. At the outset an illustration will be provided of mental health counseling, with issues that confront counselors being highlighted. Historical influences, such as federal funding, will be reviewed, including how such influences helped structure the philosophy and services offered by mental health centers. Particular attention will be paid to the counselor's role in outpatient and emergency services, since by training and orientation these are likely to be areas of specialization. The chapter will close with commentary on the specialized training required of the mental health practitioner.

Working in Mental Health: An Illustration

Brad has worked for three years in western Maryland as a mental health counselor. Prior to that he spent three years working at an inner city crisis center. Street tough since a child, Brad has rarely been surprised by the sometimes zany and difficult challenges he has faced over the past six years. While Brad may have been more adventurous than some, his caseload represents the typical responsibilities of a mental health counselor treating outpatients. Brad works with children, adolescents, and adults in a moderate-sized facility. In a larger center with a larger, more diversified staff, Brad might have had a more specialized set of duties.

Today is going to be a long one. Brad will fill in this evening for a colleague at the first meeting of a new DWI (Driving While Intoxicated) Group. While he need only have the group complete forms for the court and self-assessment inventories, show a film on how alcoholism progresses, and lead a brief discussion, he realizes that resistances among the members may be high. Information from the court shows that many of them have a long-term, chronic problem with alcohol abuse.

Brad is able to substitute in the DWI Group because he was originally hired at the center as a substance abuse counselor but applied for a vacant mental health position immediately upon completion of his probationary period. In his center, general outpatient mental health and substance abuse treatments are administered separately. The more diverse nature of the outpatient service attracted him.

On his way to check his mailbox, Brad notices and greets Brenda, a protective custody worker from Social Services. She is waiting by the elevator while one of her child cases has an appointment. Brenda looks tired. Brad remembers their most recent collaboration: Cindy, sexually abused for years by her uncle, was showing real improvement, but not quite enough to keep her out of trouble in school. When she was finally expelled from school for a lengthy string of minor offenses, she lost her foster care placement and was relocated in a group home 70 miles away. It was a frustrating case; both Brad and Brenda thought they had turned the corner with Cindy, but ended up without enough time to solidify some of the gains that had been made through counseling. She had been able to walk away from fights, get three passing grades last term, and iron out problems with her foster mother's daughter. It wasn't enough. Both Brad and Brenda felt a sense of loss.

Brad's mailbox is full. Nancy, the secretary, has pulled the records he has requested. Behind in his paperwork, Brad needs to complete more than a dozen records by next week when the team from Baltimore arrives for the annual site review. Under the records is a returned MIS Form (Management Information System); Brad forgot to write the correct disposition code when he discharged Henry yesterday. The computer needs to know whether his client was discharged because he died, simply quit coming, was arrested, achieved the goals sought in counseling, or any of a number of coded categories. He laughs thinking the computer may have gotten heartburn if it had to decipher that code.

The form reminds him again of Hank; he was one of Brad's first clients at the center. Violent in his struggles with his stepparents, underachieving in school, and without friends, Hank is a child case Brad could discharge, having achieved all stated treatment goals related to the problems listed above. While some of his youthful clients have relatively uncomplicated problems, more have pervasive developmental delays related in part to questionable family circumstances. Even successful counseling does not eliminate all their problems.

On his way to his office Brad passes the waiting room. It is packed. Today one of the part-time psychiatrists will conduct medication checks. The case aides have brought in the partial care (day hospital) clients for this reason. They do not need full hospitalization, but can remain in the community by coming three or so days a week for recreational and supportive therapy. Most of them and their families are well known by the staff after the many years of treating their chronic and severe conditions.

As Brad enters his office the phone rings. James, attending treatment as part of his parole plan, tells Brad he will miss his appointment due to car trouble. In the past James has had difficulty with drug abuse and depression while in prison. It seems that three out of the last five weeks he has had some similar excuse. Brad resolves to discuss the case with the clinical director. Brad's report to the parole officer regarding James' attendance is not due for another two months, but a decision of the value of seeing him must be made before then. The client waiting list is too long in his opinion. Why not make room for some new clients by discharging some who seem uncommitted to treatment?

The phone rings again; the receptionist indicates that Jason has arrived. Brad originally saw Jason's wife. She wanted to discuss her marital dissatisfaction and growing determination to leave Jason. Both of them were seen conjointly by Brad, but now only Jason remains to work through the emotional aftermath of his wife's departure. He has been doing better the past few weeks.

Before Brad goes to get Jason he looks over the day's schedule. Since James cancelled for 10:00 A.M., he might try to get a few signatures on some reports from his supervisor, Dr. Johnson, a paid consultant. Dr. Johnson is in private practice in an adjoining county and is at the center two days each week.

An 11:00 meeting has been scheduled for the Staffing and Assignment Team. He learned yesterday that the team must assign 12 new clients who received intakes the previous week. They also plan to review new grievance procedures for clients, proposed by the state. Barbara comes at 1:00; she has just been released from the general hospital after a four-day stay related to her cyclical depression. At 2:00 Brad sees Martha. He has increased the frequency of her sessions to twice a week, and it seems to be working. His supervisor has helped him understand her borderline condition; a disorder he had not studied when in graduate school. At first Brad viewed Martha superficially as just a burdensome individual. She was very demanding, challenging what he said more often than most clients. Through supervision he learned that her frequent phone calls, demands for immediate and special treatment, suspiciousness, and continual reports of conflict with family and neighbors were manifestations of the disorder Brad was supposed to treat. He's become more patient and comfortable with Martha, but has been reminded by Dr. Johnson not to take anything for granted in his relationship with her.

Getting away from Martha is often difficult because of her last-minute requests and questions, and at 3:15 Brad must be at the high school to co-lead a group with the school counselor. The executive director at the center has emphasized the importance of making sure the service contract with the schools is renewed. Several salaries would be at stake if it were not. The group is not going well. Most of the members have been in conflict with teachers, administrators, and other students. They probably would have been expelled if it were not for this cooperative program with the mental health center to keep them in regular classrooms. They are not well prepared for group experiences. The pressure is on to get it going.

Brad's involvements for this day illustrate some of the diverse responsibilities a counselor working in community mental health may encounter. Brad's caseload includes a high percentage of youth with frequent school contacts, but other counselors at the center have a heavier involvement with other client populations. Brad, however, is similar to many mental health counselors; they all get called upon to fill many different roles, being more generalists than specialists. To meet such challenges one's professional preparation ought to provide a broad base of personal skills along with an awareness of even larger resources necessary to provide service to the varied clients seeking assistance at a mental health center.

COMMUNITY MENTAL HEALTH: ITS HISTORY AND FUNDING

Bloom (1984) provides a careful review of important events and practices behind the development of the mental health care system in the United States. During the late 18th and early 19th centuries this country made an effort to improve the treatment given to the chronic mentally ill through the construction of more than 300 state psychiatric hospitals. By the mid-20th century this system, built to remedy the inadequate care given to psychiatric patients, had deteriorated badly. The hospitals were in poor physical condition, were very overcrowded, and demonstrated increasingly lower patient recovery rates.

By the 1950s significant advances had taken place in the field of psychopharmacology. New drugs proved effective in controlling psychotic symptoms; antianxiety and antidepression medications were being developed also. Such medications began to speed the rate of recovery in state hospitals; they also enabled many patients, who would otherwise require the protected environment of the hospital, to function in the community. In both Europe and the United States community-based mental health programs were being developed and evaluated.

In 1946 Congress passed the National Mental Health Act (P.L. 79-487) that established the National Institute of Mental Health (NIMH). NIMH and other public and private organizations began to develop mental health care recommendations that drew the attention of John F. Kennedy and his administration. Kennedy spoke eloquently before the 88th Congress in favor of restructuring the mental health care system. One month before his death Kennedy signed the Community Mental Health Centers Act (P.L. 88-164), through which considerable funds were made available to build and staff centers.

Under the Johnson administration this legislation was amended and expanded several times. New responsibilities included treatment for substance abuse, expanded child services, rape prevention, and special programs for the elderly. In some respects this expansion taxed the capabilities of the mental health care system beyond the resources that would be available during the Nixon and Ford administrations.

The Carter administration once again energetically promoted mental health care, with particular attention to minority populations. One month before his defeat in the 1980 election, President Carter signed the Mental Health Systems Act (P.L. 96-398). It updated mental health legislation to meet a larger set of needs. However, following Reagan's election, budgetary authorizations for P.L. 96-398 were rescinded in favor of block grants to the states. Funds originally intended for mental health were spent by the states for other purposes.

The content of these federal laws structured much of what exists in community mental health today. Public Law 88-164 divided states into what are called catchment areas, each having a population limit, usually 200,000 residents. The act required each center to offer inpatient, outpatient, and partial care, crisis intervention, and consultation and education. Prevention was viewed as an important part of each center's program. Treatment of the chronic mentally ill, though, remained at the center of the legislation. While community mental health centers were not viewed in these laws as replacements for state mental hospitals, they were to work in tandem with the latter. Bloom (1984) believes that a dual system was actually developed—one being the existing state hospital system, and the other the mental health centers. All the goals of community mental health have not been accomplished, but there has been more mental health care within local communities, with greater attention being paid to short-term services and indirect services to other agencies.

During the last several decades important court decisions have supplemented the influence of mental health legislation. In particular, during the 1950s and 1960s the Warren Court heard cases previously rejected by the Supreme Court. Some of these cases centered on the rights of psychiatric patients. Through them occurred dramatic revisions in commitment procedures, with a dual emphasis on the rights of patients to treatment and to treatment via the least restrictive alternative. The latter led to the process called deinstitutionalization, i.e., releasing back to the community patients who had experienced long-term hospitalization. Also, conscious effort was made to avoid as much as possible long-term hospitalization as a treatment option. The impact of this was a need to find a cost-effective way to care for mentally ill persons who might otherwise overstress their families or be forced to live on the streets.

Patient advocacy groups ensured that legislative mandates and court decisions favoring the rights of mental health clients were implemented. Today all citizens are less likely to be restrained or secluded except for brief periods of emergency. Mental health clients are guaranteed much greater confidentiality of their records; also they are able to access the information in these records. Current procedures in mental health mandate periodic review of treatment plans along with the right of clients to refuse treatments that they believe to be unnecessary or overly burdensome. These policies represent a dramatic shift away from the historic position that the state automatically knows what is best for its troubled citizens.

The historic influences described have created a mental health care system that serves much of the United States. Knesper, Wheeler, and Pagnucco (1984) surveyed the country and found mental health professionals in public and private practice serving 1,393 counties. They also found that 1,682 counties were without mental health professionals. Underserved areas were more likely to be in the western half of the nation, especially the plains states. Rural sections of the South were also understaffed by such professionals. Such gaps in the system ensure that many troubled individuals do not receive mental health care. Kiesler (1982) notes that in recent years 60% of all mental health hospitalizations have occurred in general hospitals, with an average stay of 11.6 days. Only 25% of the mental health patient days have occurred in private or state/county psychiatric hospitals. For these patients the average stay is 189 days. Kiesler notes that as of 1978 one-quarter of all inpatient days in hospitals of all kinds were for mental health reasons.

One can still wonder whether our mental health care system can really serve all persons in need of treatment. For example, Knitzer (1984) reports that the President's Commission on Mental Health estimates that 5% to 15% of all children and adolescents (3–9 million children) require some type of mental health service. She notes that as of 1976 only 665,000 children received services from mental health agencies, and only 350,000 more were treated by the schools. Ware, Manning, Duan, Wells, and Newhouse (1984) note that, in spite of lip service to preventive care, the likelihood that mental health care will actually be given is related to the degree of psychological distress experienced by the person in need of service. It seems that at present both clients and the treatment system itself often respond only when mental health problems have become serious.

MENTAL HEALTH COUNSELING AS A PROFESSION

Since its inception in the 1940s NIMH has included within the category of mental health professions the following: psychiatry, psychology, social work, and nursing. It was only in 1986 that NIMH added mental health counselors as the fifth mental health profession.

The counseling profession, with its emphasis on serving a cross-section of the population, most of whom fall in the "normal" category, has had a different mission from mental health practice, which has tended to emphasize the chronic mentally ill. However, by the mid-1970s more and more counselors became employed in settings other than schools. In particular, there was a need to develop an identity for the master's level counselor working in a variety of agencies and community programs. Weikel (1985) notes that in 1976 formal efforts began to form an association to serve the interests of this group of practitioners. During that year the American Mental Health Counselors Association (AMHCA) was formed. In 1977 its members voted by a narrow margin to join American Personnel and Guidance Association (APGA). Its priorities became licensure, third-party payments, full parity with other mental health professionals, private practice, and the treatment of special populations in community and private settings. The growth of AMHCA has been rapid. In late 1985 AMHCA became the largest division of American Association for Counseling and Development (AACD) and currently retains that position. AMHCA's members come from such diverse backgrounds as psychiatry, nursing, psychology, social work, and the clergy. The record to date indicates that this active and energetic group will effectively influence the mental health care system in the future.

TREATMENT PHILOSOPHIES AND STRATEGIES IN MENTAL HEALTH

The allied helping professions have an enormous task serving a broad range of clients, whether they operate in a mental health center, another community agency, or a private practice. Serving diverse clients requires the development of many varied treatments. For example, some clients may be relatively normal persons experiencing mild crises, while others may be suffering from a combination of seriously disabling conditions. Frances, Clarkin, and Perry (1984) use the title "differential therapeutics" to describe an approach to treatment selection that has application to mental health clients. They base treatment selection on (1) the physical setting in which treatment takes place, (2) the format of the treatment, and (3) the theoretical orientation behind the intervention.

Setting

In mental health practice decisions about how to help a client must often be made quickly, especially for clients in crisis who are possibly dangerous to themselves or others. In some instances the safest treatment may be hospitalization, i.e., inpatient care; in other instances the client may be assisted by partial hospitalization or day hospital care; still other patients are not in immediate danger and have the resources to benefit from regular outpatient treatment. The decision to hospitalize is often made by a team of mental health professionals, and the actual prescreening for admission is most often done by a psychiatrist. The mental health counselor, however, may be the first contact for a client in need of hospitalization and must be alert to that ultimate setting-related decision.

In mental health practice the selection of setting coincides with the general goals of treatment, whether treatment is seen as a form of acute care, an effort at rehabilitation or prevention, or an attempt to maintain a person with a chronic, possibly deteriorating condition. For example, partial hospitalization is frequently the choice for individuals with chronic, deteriorating conditions.

Treatment Format

Frances, Clarkin, and Perry (1984) note that the next set of decisions after choice of setting has to do with the use of one or more of the following types of therapy: group, family, marital (couples), or individual. These authors conceptualize emotional problems as resulting from one of many different systems, from molecular/cellular systems, through family/community systems, to society in general. The location of the problems via this conceptual framework helps to dictate treatment format.

Decisions regarding format must also take into consideration those factors that enable a client to benefit from such treatments. If those enabling conditions are not present, an alternative treatment may need to be sought. For example, an adolescent client in trouble with the police may be part of a family that is experiencing considerable stress, handling their problems by projecting blame on one another. They may be unable to deal with this or other problems because communication among members is vague and misdirected. It would seem that the client and the entire family unit are good candidates for conjoint family therapy (see Chapter 4). However, within this family the mother manifests extreme agitation along with severe distrust. Because of her personal pathology, the usefulness of family therapy would be reduced. The adolescent might have to be treated individually even though many of the problems are family related.

Treatment Orientation

Various theoretical approaches have differential application across client groups. As indicated in Chapter 3, one client may be more likely to comply with one approach and not another. For example, some clients may find it untenable to reveal negative feelings as an avenue to greater psychological strength. They might find an expressive therapy, such as person-centered therapy, too uncomfortable to endure. Other clients may be poor candidates for the more "directive" therapies since they might have little inclination to take suggestions from others, complete homework assignments, or possibly expose themselves to uncomfortable situations in order to practice new behaviors. For these clients, such approaches as reality or behavior therapy may receive considerable resistance.

Other Considerations

Adopting a view of differential treatment that utilizes varying forms of interventions sometimes allows one to consider the combination of several treatments. For example, a client may be in a partial-care program but may also receive an antidepressant medication plus regular counseling. It can be argued that such combinations have additive effects: One ensures immediate safety for the client, another is quick-acting, and another is likely to produce long-lasting gains. The disadvantage of combined treatments are that some may negate others, side effects may develop, and, ultimately the treatment team may never learn what outcomes any individual treatment produced (Frances, et al, 1984). With multiple interventions available in mental health that can be used effectively or misused, the need to collaboratively plan treatment increases in importance. In a well-managed center multidisciplinary client staffing sessions can provide an important training benefit for the counselor-in-training as well as those employed in the setting.

THE OUTPATIENT SERVICE

Mental health counselors have been trained primarily to work in the outpatient service of a mental health or other community agency. Prior to assignment to a counselor, outpatient clients usually have completed intake interviews in which data have been gathered about their social history, current complaints, previous treatment history, and current resources. Many outpatient clients also will have seen a psychiatrist for a medical evaluation and the prescription of medication.

When treatment begins the outpatient worker has a written record of the intake, identifying data (including billing information) taken by an office worker, and notes regarding medications. The records of clients with chronic problems will often contain special psychological evaluations, reports sent by psychiatric hospitals, interview notes of previous therapy, and so forth. To this the counselor will need to add, usually within the first two to four interviews, a treatment plan. Such plans include a statement of the client's problems, a diagnosis (*DSM-IIIR*), a list of client strengths and weaknesses, short-term and long-term goals, the treatment modality to be used, a list of support services, a prognosis, criteria for discharge, and a plan for follow-up services (Brands, 1978). Notes or interview summaries to be included in the record at later dates should be referenced to this treatment plan, especially to the treatment goals.

A caseload of between 15 and 20 active clients appears to be manageable for counselors working primarily in outpatient service. The balance of these counselors' schedule will include meetings, time for the completion of paperwork, on-call duty (including walk-in standby), supervision, consultation and education, and special projects.

Over several years the outpatient counselor can expect to be assigned a wide variety of clients, ranging from persons confronting predictable developmental challenges to individuals with life-long histories of adjustment problems. Some clients assigned to outpatient treatment do not have the resources to benefit from such treatment; they are not well enough organized to manage transportation to the center, remember appointments, and other such things. However, their situation does not warrant assignment to another setting. Such clients will be in and out of the center. Other clients with chronic disorders (e.g., cyclical depression), will end treatment when their condition improves but will return at a later date. This cycle may be repeated many times. Thus the counselor is likely to find that an hour may be set aside each week to accommodate the likelihood that old clients will be returning in sufficient numbers.

Counselors may wish to control some of the client assignment process by specializing in serving particular populations (e.g., conduct disordered youth) or by offering special treatments. Specialization provides other advantages, such as (1) recognition to the agency for providing special service, (2) an opportunity for the counselor to devote time to areas of special interest, (3) greater job security by being needed to maintain a special set of services offered by the agency, and (4) clear indications of professional development. In the course of a career the counselor may respecialize several times, broadening expertise with each change.

When clients achieve treatment objectives or for some reason choose to discontinue treatment, the counselor usually documents the end of treatment through a written discharge summary that becomes part of the client's record. If clients remain in the mental health care system for long, clearly their records become rather large. The intent of the paperwork required of mental health professionals is to ensure regular review of client care. In many places state law will specify the types of records that must be kept both to protect client rights and to ensure quality service. Well-managed centers require that every outpatient worker be under supervision regardless of experience level or degree and that treatment plans and discharge summaries be signed by a supervisor.

Centers vary across the country with regard to how the outpatient service may be divided into special units. One center may divide its service between an adult and a children/adolescent unit. Another may separate substance abuse treatment from regular mental health outpatient service. In many cases the funding methods for supporting special treatments may require an administrative separation of different units. Administrators below the executive director of the center who are involved in the management of outpatient services usually include the medical director (chief psychiatrist), the clinical director (usually a licensed psychologist), and directors of special programs (e.g., children services or addictions). A counselor may coordinate yet another smaller unit, say, a school intervention program.

STUDENT LEARNING EXERCISE

Read the following descriptions of counselor activity and indicate whether they are appropriate for a mental health setting. Circle Y for yes or N for no.

1. The counselor has little background in psychopathology and its diagnosis.   Y   N
2. The counselor believes that all individuals can become fully functioning through group counseling.   Y   N
3. The counselor firmly believes that there is seldom, if ever, a valid reason to refer a client to a psychiatrist for medication.   Y   N
4. The counselor enjoys working in a multidisciplinary treatment setting with a wide variety of clients.   Y   N

THE EMERGENCY SERVICE

Closely connected with outpatient and other units is the emergency service. When mental health crises arise in the community, mental health professionals coordinate with medical and law enforcement agencies to assist those persons dangerous to themselves or others, or those threatened by a third party. A mental health center usually has at least one person and a backup on call at all times. During office hours that person is free of scheduled appointments; during nonoffice hours he or she is available through a telephone hotline, through both the center's regular telephone number and the 911 service. Many mental health counselors earn "comp time" (that is, time for which they are compensated with time off) for off-hour emergency duty. This service is very important to a community.

Managing the behavior of people in a state of active crisis mandates the involvement of mental health professionals. Such persons may manifest loss of control, disorganized thinking, acute anxiety, immobilizing fear or panic, escape through substance abuse, and other problematic responses (Everstine & Everstine, 1983). Crisis situations call for quick assessment and assistance. Assessment was treated in Chapter 5.

Treating Assault Victims

Many crisis situations involve victims. They may have been beaten, sexually assaulted, involved in a natural disaster (e.g., tornado or flood), or seriously threatened by some such situation. Prompt attention to these individuals can have the benefit of both relieving a portion of the current pain and also helping to prevent future complications. Many believe that an acute, crisis situation, if left unattended, can have lasting psychological damage.

Treatment begins with helping the victim express feelings associated with the situation, be they feelings of guilt, anger, grief, or fear. The counselor then helps the person identify resources within himself or herself along with support from other persons and organizations, including the police and medical professions. Underlying this effort is an emphasis on helping the victim anticipate what is needed and to plan for it. For the person in danger, providing refuge is an essential part of treatment. Although mental health centers are unlikely to operate their own shelters, staff members frequently work in cooperation with agencies that do. For example, a church in a small community may give a battered spouse money for a motel room and meals. In addition, the church will make the arrangements and provide transportation at the request of the mental health center. A larger community may have a "safe house" for the temporary protection of a battered spouse. Even the mental health center staff may not know the location of this house, but can refer clients to it through the agency that operates it. Often in the case of abuse and neglect of children, social service workers have already intervened, with custody of the child having been transferred to the state. In such cases the child will be presumed to be safe through placement in foster care.

Orzek (1983) discusses some of the complexities of assault cases for females in committed relationships: how the assault affects them, their male partner, and their relationship. Rape produces more than a need for immediate medical attention and support for the victim; after several days have passed the quality of psychological care that follows will influence the prognosis. Orzek warns counselors to pay attention to the client's reaction to the violence of the assault and not just its sexual nature. The woman's male partner at that time may feel very protective, expressing this with physical closeness, but his closeness may be timed too near to the assault. Orzek recommends that sexual activity between partners be curtailed, if for no other reason than to control the transmission of venereal disease. It is probably better to have the partners agree that sexual contact will be initiated by the female when she is ready. As time passes the female victim may appear outwardly to have healed from the rape, but usually much more psychological healing must follow. If the victim remains in counseling, working through her feelings and issues of trust and dependence are important.

Suicide

One of the most common situations affecting the emergency service worker is suicide. It is estimated that 1 million people report attempting to kill themselves each year, with 25,000 being successful (Perr, 1979). This makes suicide the 10th leading cause of death, responsible for 1% of all fatalities in the United States. The rates of suicide for portions of our population are much higher. For example, suicide is the second or third leading cause of death for people under the age of 30.

It is likely that the persons who make up these statistics will have contacted someone before committing suicide. While most persons committing suicide are depressed and very unhappy, most are not absolutely sure they want to die (Shneidman, Farberow, & Litman, 1976). Consequently, they almost always cry out to someone else for assistance before actually reaching the point of suicide. Fujimura, Weis, and Cochran (1985) note that this ambivalence provides a major opportunity for the counselor to intervene and help. Many individuals attempt suicide repeatedly and eventually succeed, but many others will abandon suicide as a solution to their problems. The response of the emergency service counselor can promote this change.

The first step for both an intake worker and the emergency service worker—the assessment of suicidal potential—was treated in Chapter 5. The next step is to decide how to treat the crisis if it is deemed real. Motto (1976) recommends hospitalization when the person (1) is unsure of being able to resist the suicidal impulse, (2) has just made a serious attempt, (3) lacks supportive family and friends, or (4) is under the influence of alcohol or some drug that loosens impulse control. Hospitalization may be avoided if there are suitable persons available to care for the suicidal individual, and intense outpatient contact can be provided to both the person contemplating suicide and her or his family.

Motto (1976) emphasizes the need for the emergency worker to recognize the client's feelings of alienation and abandonment—viewing the world as rejecting and contemptuous. The presence of these feelings mandates the communication of a desire to understand and accept the individual in an active manner in order to provide quick symptom relief so the life-threatening crisis might end. Such swift and energetic action can convince the suicidal person that something really will be done to improve her or his situation (Fujimura et al., 1985). At times the counselor may try with no avail to get the voluntary cooperation of the individual. In such cases the counselor, in cooperation with other staff members, may file a petition to have the person involuntarily hospitalized. However, if the person does not appear delirious, psychotic, or panic-stricken, and denies suicidal intent, she or he probably will be discharged from the hospital shortly after being transported there by law enforcement personnel.

If emergency service personnel can intervene to prevent a suicide attempt and if they remain in contact, follow-up treatment can be planned and delivered. A therapeutic team that includes the person's family, friends, minister, and physician can develop a more comprehensive approach to changing the situation. Treating the depression is central. Most references (e.g., Motto, 1976) warn the treatment team about the dangerousness of the point when the depression begins to lift; at that time the individual has the energy necessary to commit suicide and may do so if pessimism about the future has not changed. Also, medication, such as a tricyclic antidepressant, may have been prescribed for the individual. Careful monitoring of such medications is required when the client is referred to the outpatient service since these drugs are extremely toxic. Since feelings of alienation are so common among persons contemplating suicide, group therapy may provide another means of support. The group could be one more vehicle to help the individual develop a feeling of inclusion within a social system.

When an individual in crisis does commit suicide, friends and family may need assistance in coping with the complex feelings associated with such a loss. This may also apply to the community personnel who attempted to prevent its occurrence.

Dealing with a crisis can be unsettling to the beginning counselor. One consoling feature of such work is the careful effort made to provide back-up assistance to the on-call counselor. When in doubt, the beginning counselor should use this support. Kahn (1981) offers the following recommendations to a crisis worker:

1. Develop a working relationship with the client.
2. Get the right information from the client. Write it down. Get his or her name and address.
3. Consider both the precipitating factors and the client's personality in assessing the situation.
4. Try to share with the client a view of the situation that might produce more adaptive responses.
5. Explore actual ways the client might approach the problem right away.
6. Work at getting the client to agree upon goals that support a new approach to the situation.
7. Arrange for future contacts with the mental health center and other appropriate agencies.

PRIMARY PREVENTION IN COMMUNITY MENTAL HEALTH

Earlier in this chapter trying to prevent major mental health problems was described as one of the principal objectives of the community mental health movement. Unfortunately, because of funding cutbacks and the obligation to respond to the urgent needs of already troubled clientele, this objective has not been given adequate means (Goodyear & Shaw, 1984). Mental health counselors and community psychologists have the background and motivation to increase primary prevention efforts if resources become available. Bloom (1984) notes, however, that major resistance to the development of preventive interventions may always remain, since the power base in the culture may recognize that such efforts ultimately require major social system changes.

Primary prevention efforts can still occur within the current structure and with current funding in mental health. Citing the President's Commission on Mental Health (1978), Lewis and Lewis (1984) list three major thrusts for prevention in mental health: (1) interpersonal competency building, (2) programs for populations facing life crises, and (3) advocacy directed toward modifying and improving social environments.

Targeting special populations because of the long-term implications of the problems they present is an important way of utilizing the three prevention thrusts listed. People coping with powerful stressors such as poverty, divorce, other disturbed domestic relationships, educational and occupational failure, and loss of jobs and loved ones are good candidates for both crisis intervention and prevention work. If left unattended, present circumstances may lead to further potentially serious and chronic difficulties. Just as public health agencies have maternal and infant care as a priority because of their impact on the next generation, mental health prevention efforts are recommended for school-age clients, mothers on public assistance, and other stressed populations (Bloom, 1984). Because of this, Goodyear and Shaw (1984) see cooperative efforts between school and mental health systems as a necessary alliance for primary prevention.

THE FUTURE OF MENTAL HEALTH COUNSELING

At present there seems to be a major effort to contain health costs—an issue to receive further attention in Chapter 14. In many areas health maintenance organizations (HMOs) are restructuring health care service delivery so greater attention can be given to wellness. Cummings (1986) notes that his corporation, which manages numerous HMO operations, has a tendency to employ counselors instead of psychologists as their mental health service providers. With health costs amounting to 11% of the gross national product (Cummings, 1986), continued effort will be directed toward finding cost-effective ways to provide mental health services. As the newest of the mental health professions, counseling may become the most responsive to new trends.

PREPARING FOR A CAREER IN COMMUNITY MENTAL HEALTH

Graduates of counselor education programs have excellent backgrounds for careers in mental health. As described earlier in this book, their skills in interviewing, assessment, understanding special populations, and consultation fit directly into their job description.

But as in most community-based programs, the mental health counselor will work hand-in-hand with many other helping professionals and must learn to understand them and relate to their perspectives on client care. Practicum and internship in mental health settings provide an opportunity to gain experience with these different helping professionals. To prepare specifically for this phase of training, the counselor-in-training may be well-advised to:

1. Learn the specific procedures to follow in conducting an intake interview, and become familiar with its elements, such as the mental status examination. These were described briefly in Chapter 5.

2. Intensify your study of psychopathology. Develop an adequate understanding of the *DSM-IIIR* format for the diagnosis of mental disorders; this is the basic system used to classify clients undergoing treatment. It is also the way of reporting the types of clients treated.

3. Prepare yourself to relate to clients with fewer resources to solve problems than those commonly used by counselors working in educational settings.

4. Practice becoming proficient in writing reports, treatment plans, and progress notes. A great deal of paperwork is involved in mental health counseling. This paperwork is continually reviewed by funding agencies, and thus it is very important to administrators in mental health centers.

5. Recognize that there are many governmental laws and regulations affecting mental health care. Be prepared to learn about them when employed as a counselor.

SUMMARY

This chapter reviewed the historic influences affecting the mental health care system in the United States. It is a system developed by helping professions other than counseling, with counselors being the most recent service providers to join the system. Originally intended to correct some of the deficiencies in the treatment of persons with chronic mental illness, mental health centers have developed a wide variety of services for a diverse population of clients. While mental health counselors may develop unique and special job descriptions, they are primarily trained to work as outpatient therapists and to participate in the emergency service. Because of the seriousness of the problems of certain clients, the mental health counselor will often be part of a treatment team that may include a psychiatrist, a licensed psychologist, and a case worker; together these professionals will provide multiple interventions, including medications, counseling, and environmental control. Since important decisions are often made to protect people's lives, mental health counselors usually develop special skills in diagnosis and crisis intervention.

REVIEW QUESTIONS

1. Describe the kinds of clients served in community mental health centers.
2. How does the role of the mental health counselor compare to that of a school counselor?
3. What is the relationship between community mental health and historic efforts to care for the chronically mentally ill?
4. What might explain the rapid growth of the American Mental Health Counselors Association (AMHCA)?
5. Describe some of the issues related to outpatient counseling in a mental health center.
6. What are some of the important issues related to the emergency service in mental health?
7. What graduate courses might a counselor-in-training take to prepare for a career in mental health?

REFERENCES

Bloom, B. L. (1984). *Community mental health: A general introduction* (2nd ed.). Monterey, CA: Brooks/Cole.

Brands, A. B. (1978). *Individualized treatment planning for psychiatric patients.* Washington, DC: U.S. Department of Health, Education, and Welfare.

Cummings, N. A. (1986). The dismantling of our health system: Strategies for the survival of psychological practice. *American Psychologist, 41*(4), 426–431.

Everstine, D. S., & Everstine, L. (1983). *People in crisis: Strategic therapeutic interventions.* New York: Brunner/Mazel.

Frances, A., Clarkin, J., & Perry, S. (1984). *Differential therapeutics in psychiatry: The art and science of treatment selection.* New York: Brunner/Mazel.

Fujimura, L. E., Weis, D. M., & Cochran, J. R. (1985). Suicide: Dynamics and implications for counseling. *Journal of Counseling and Development, 63*(10), 612–615.

Goodyear, R. K., & Shaw, M. C. (1984). Introduction to the second special issue on primary prevention. *The Personnel and Guidance Journal, 62*(9), 507–508.

Kahn, M. W. (1981). *Basic methods for mental health practitioners.* Cambridge, MA: Winthrop Publishers.

Kiesler, C. A. (1982). Public and professional myths about mental hospitalization: An empirical reassessment of policy-related beliefs. *American Psychologist, 37*(12), 1323–1339.

Knesper, D. J., Wheeler, J. R., & Pagnucco, D. J. (1984). Mental health services providers' distribution across counties in the United States. *American Psychologist, 39*(12), 1424–1434.

Knitzer, J. (1984). Mental health services to children and adolescents: A national view of public policies. *American Psychologist, 39*(8), 905–911.

Lewis, J. A., & Lewis, M. D. (1984). Preventive programs in action. *The Personnel and Guidance Journal, 62*(9), 550–553.

Motto, J. (1976). The recognition and management of the suicidal patient. In F. Flack & S. Draghi (Eds.), *The nature and treatment of depression.* New York: John Wiley and Sons.

Orzek, A. M. (1983). Sexual assault: The female victim, her male partner, and their relationship. *The Personnel and Guidance Journal, 62*(3), 143–146.

Perr, I. N. (1979). Legal aspects of suicide. In L. D. Hankoff & B. Einsidler (Eds.), *Suicide: Theory and clinical aspects.* Littleton, MA: PSG Publishing Company.

President's Commission on Mental Health. (1978). *Report of the Task Panel on Prevention.* Washington, DC: U.S. Government Printing Office.

Shneidman, E., Faberow, N., & Litman, R. (1976). *The psychology of suicide* (2nd. ed.). New York: Jason Aronson.

Ware, J. E., Manning, W. G., Duan, N., Wells, K. B., & Newhouse, J. P. (1984). Health status and the use of outpatient mental health services. *American Psychologist, 39*(10), 1090–1100.

Weikel, W. J. (1985). The American Mental Health Counselors Association. *Journal of Counseling and Development, 63*(7), 457–460.

14

Counseling in Corporate and Other Settings

GOAL OF THE CHAPTER

The purpose of this chapter is to describe corporate and community settings other than mental health centers as career options for counselors.

CHAPTER PREVIEW

1. Examples of how counselors can help meet the needs of business and industry will be given.
2. Workers' problems that counselors can help resolve will be surveyed.
3. Employee Assistance Programs (EAPs) will be described.
4. General personnel management as an option for counseling graduates will be discussed.
5. Training and career development activities in business will be described.
6. Career opportunities for counselors in vocational rehabilitation, criminal justice, medical settings, and private practice will be described.

INTRODUCTION

The purpose of this chapter is to provide an overview of employment opportunities for counselors in nontraditional settings. Employment in business and industry will receive the most emphasis, since it offers a diverse set of opportunities for people trained in counseling, though often in roles somewhat different from those in public agencies. Other employment settings in organizations, such as vocational rehabilitation, criminal justice, medical facilities, and private practice, will also be reviewed. A secondary focus of this chapter will be to illustrate how counseling skills generalize from setting to setting so that counselors are prepared to face challenges in many different organizations.

Public and private educational systems have been the primary employers of counseling professionals (Papalia & Kaminski, 1981). In particular, counseling and counseling psychology have been dedicated to helping young people identify and utilize personal resources in education and work (Osipow, 1982). This thrust in the profession was described in greater detail in Chapter 12. In Chapter 13 the development and expansion of the mental health care system was described, along with how counselors and other social service professionals fit into that system. The fields of education and mental health offer the most significant employment opportunities for counselors.

In recent years corporations have been identified as potential employers of graduates from counselor education programs (Christiani & Christiani, 1979). These authors argued that counselors have skills useful in meeting corporate goals. In the past decade American business seems to have needed help, especially with increased competition worldwide and America's shrinking share of world markets. To increase productivity of workers, the counseling profession may be able to do for business what it achieved for education during the era of the National Defense Education Act (NDEA). (Papalia & Kaminski, 1981).

THE NEEDS OF BUSINESS AND INDUSTRY

Most people recognize that the principal purpose of a business is to make a profit. For example, a steel corporation is dedicated not to making steel but to turning a profit. If a steel company can make more money investing in the stock of other corporations than it can in making steel, the "steel" company will become an investment company rather than one that manufactures steel products. The company will close steel mills and will invest its resources in more profitable ventures.

Companies do business by amassing capital and then investing that capital in the means necessary to develop, manufacture, and market their products. Capital in general takes on two forms, according to Leonards (1981); one is technical capital, including machines and material goods, and the other is human capital, representing the workers who manipulate these machines and goods.

To be competitive, a company strives continually to improve productivity, i.e., the output of products per worker hour. If the machines or equipment used or the workers develop problems (e.g., need repair, become obsolete, etc.), productivity will begin to decline. With declining productivity, especially in comparison with companies with increasing productivity, the company will produce less at a greater cost. Its products will need to be sold for more money though they will not be of higher quality. Such products are unlikely to sell well; markets will decline, and the company will face the prospect of bankruptcy. To prevent this, companies attempt to cut losses by lowering costs by reducing their workforce, closing unprofitable plants, and so forth.

Huddleston and Fenwick (1983) note that, following World War II, productivity increased in this country around 2.4% annually. In 1966 productivity growth began to stall, with a drop to 0.8% between 1973 and 1978, while the productivity of other industrial nations continued to improve. Since 1978 productivity has continued to decline in America. The American economy has been in need of revitalization. This can be achieved in part through new machines and new technology; another part of this applies to people and what they can provide. Just as machines become worn out and obsolete, so do people "break down" and require "retooling." Both people and modern machinery cost huge sums of money to develop, maintain, and replace.

Worker Problems

Business and industry, by virtue of their enormous investment in human resources, experience many productivity problems as a result of a troubled and dissatisfied workforce. Placement of employees in jobs for which they are unsuited can start a history of low productivity. Reassignment of workers after initial placement is costly, especially when the workers have few generalizable skills.

Workers can also bring to their jobs personal problems that hinder their work performance. Poor mental health among even a small percentage of employees can drastically reduce profits. Acute stress, brought on by domestic or other conflict, can distract and de-energize, further reducing performance.

Alcoholism and the Workplace

Probably the best examples of worker mental health affecting productivity are alcohol and drug abuse. Quayle (1983) estimates that there is a $30.1 billion loss annually in productivity resulting from employee substance abuse. Between 5% and 10% of the workforce use illicit drugs or abuse alcohol daily. These workers are 16 times more likely to be absent from work, have 4 times the accident rate, and have 5 times the number of compensation claims as nonabusers. Alcohol- or drug-abusing workers have a 40% higher fatality rate on the job and 47% more industrial injuries. One can see that early identification and treatment of such problems is not only humane but also potentially cost-effective for a company.

At first glance it may seem easy enough to deal with such problem workers by simply terminating their employment. However, dismissal of employees is very expensive when one adds up the costs of severance benefits and the recruiting and training of new employees.

Managing an Evolving Workforce

Related to some of the personnel management problems faced by companies is the fact that lowered productivity and major changes in the type of work expected of employees occurred roughly at the same time. Schuster (1978) notes that, as productivity began to decline in the early 1970s, for the first time manual laborers became outnumbered by workers who depend on mental rather than physical skills in their jobs. With this change arose a need to revise systems of managing people in work environments. Schuster proposed that this shift has mandated the use of Douglas McGregor's "Y" theory of management.

McGregor's theory is now a classic in the management literature. McGregor (1960) proposed what he called a conventional view of management (Theory X) and a more recent view (Theory Y) that takes into consideration Maslow's Need Hierarchy to better describe the motivations of contemporary workers. Theory X fits well with the view that workers are used best when they are used as if they were machines. Management must be responsible for the economic enterprise since people must be directed, motivated, controlled, and changed in order to fit the needs of an organization. This is difficult because the average person is by nature indolent, working as little as possible. He or she lacks ambition, dislikes responsibility, and prefers to be led. These workers are inherently self-centered, resistant to change, and indifferent to organizational needs. However, they are not very bright and can be coaxed into making an effort by a more shrewd individual.

In contrast, Theory Y proposes a more optimistic view of workers. People are not by nature passive or resistant to organizational needs; they only become that way as a result of their negative experiences within organizations. The capacity to assume responsibility and direct behavior toward organizational goals is potentially available if recognized by management and cultivated.

Thus, Theory Y attempts to approach the "new" workers with heavy emphasis on self-direction and self-control, while Theory X relies almost exclusively on external control. The experience of the 1970s with declining productivity has pointed to managing personnel more in accord with "Y" principles in an attempt to reverse that downward trend. Peters and Waterman (1982), in their very popular review of how some of America's most successful companies are run, document the value of having employees think independently, challenge one another, and personally view their efforts as essential to both their success and that of the company.

These successful companies (e.g., IBM), stick by their employees, encouraging their self-development. The employees return to the company imagination and energy that drive the organization toward decisive action in pursuit of excellence.

The Partnership Between Management and Counselors. The directions taken in personnel management over the past decade, as described above, have provided an invitation to individuals trained in the social and behavioral sciences to continue those trends. With Theory Y and other similar systems has come the need in work environments to decentralize and delegate, improve performance appraisal, and refine new participative approaches to running a company. This has given rise to a wide variety of psychological approaches to productivity improvement. Katzell and Guzzo (1983) demonstrate the success of efforts that utilized such approaches in pursuit of (1) training and instruction, (2) appraisal of worker performance, (3) goal setting in relation to productivity objectives, (4) work redesign to humanize the workplace, (5) supervisory methods based on psychological factors, (6) organizational structure, (7) decision-making techniques, (8) work schedules, and so forth.

Within climates that value expertise in developing human resources, a counselor-trained manager can arrive, who may or may not have the title "counselor" in the organization. Nevertheless, a market exists for the skills that these workers bring to the organization. The next section reviews some of the ways counselors can be of use.

STUDENT LEARNING EXERCISE

Read the following needs of corporations and determine whether each is an area in which counselors can contribute. Circle Y for yes and N for no.

1. To evaluate equipment needs.   Y   N
2. To save on personnel recruitment costs by maintaining the effectiveness of existing workers.   Y   N
3. To help identify, treat, and refer substance abuse problems.   Y   N
4. To help corporations revise management approaches to incorporate more employee participation.   Y   N

CORPORATE EFFORTS INVOLVING COUNSELORS

Employee Assistance Programs

Employee Assistance Programs (EAPs) represent one of the company-based efforts to which counselor training generalizes most directly. Over the last 10 years the growth of such programs has been remarkable. Quoting from several sources, Forrest (1983) estimates that the number of EAPs has risen from about 50 in

1950 to more than 5,000 in 1981. Certainly, that number has increased since 1981 to the point that most major corporations are offering some form of mental health/career development assistance to their employees.

The beginning of systematic efforts to assist employees with debilitating personal problems began in the 1940s with occupational alcoholism programs by such companies as Dupont, Kemper Insurance, and Eastman Kodak (Presnall, 1981). For much of its history employee assistance has been concerned primarily with alcohol and drug abuse. From its start, the growth of employee assistance programs was slow until 1970, when P.L. 91-616 was passed, establishing the National Institute on Alcohol Abuse and Alcoholism. Called the Hughes Act because of its sponsorship by Senator Harold Hughes, himself a recovering alcoholic, this legislation mandated the development and maintenance of alcohol programs for federal employees and funded demonstration programs for other employees and occupational program consultants for each state.

In the 1970s, the decade of declining productivity, research was discovering that properly managed alcohol programs in industry could avoid lawsuits from employees terminated because of alcohol abuse and could produce significant savings to the company. A review of follow-up evaluations of EAPs by Masi and Teems (1982) reports returns ranging from $5 to $17 for every dollar invested. The savings result from decreased personal damage or injury (indemnity) costs, decreased hospital/medical/surgical costs, lower employee insurance premiums, less absenteeism, less sick leave, lower employee turnover costs, and improved production rates.

In part EAPs have proven to be so effective in the treatment of alcohol and drug abuse because of the contractual relationship between the employer and the employee. This relationship permits the employer to intervene if a worker's productivity seriously declines. With the threat of termination, the employer can help the worker penetrate the denial so common with alcohol and drug abuse problems. Family and friends often have more difficulty confronting the problem, are damaged themselves by the chemical dependency problems, and are not as well trained in identifying the warning signs of substance abuse.

With the success noted, the operational aspects of EAPs have broadened in the 1970s and 1980s. More effort now is directed toward other mental health problems. Helping employees cope with domestic problems (marriage and child-rearing), clinically significant depression, and other problems now receive attention. Occupational stress management is another significant component of many EAPs. Further treatment of this topic is given in Chapter 16 when counselor burnout is discussed.

Successful companies believe strongly that trained employees are extremely valuable assets; it is more cost effective to rehabilitate and keep healthy a competent employee than to hire and train a new one (Witte & Cannon, 1979). As top management has recognized this, and as labor has increasingly held employers liable for emotional problems related to working conditions, support continues to increase for broader views of employee assistance (Roman, 1981).

How EAPs Work.   In most cases an EAP does not represent a mental health clinic on corporate property. Rather, problem identification, referral, and supervisory/employee education predominate over the provision of on-site therapy.

The first stages of program development involve getting a strong endorsement from top management and assessing needs and available resources. Development of a written policy that ensures complete understanding is essential. This includes statements regarding program authority to treat and refer, eligibility for services, descriptions of personnel involved and staff membership criteria, procedures for program use, and the confidentiality of the records kept in the program (Forrest, 1983).

Staffing the program requires someone with administrative expertise, plus counselors with a broad repertoire of skills who can work in an industrial setting as generalists. These skills include:

1. Special knowledge in the identification and treatment of substance abuse.
2. Thorough knowledge of treatment resources within the community and the ability to develop a referral network that fully utilizes those resources.
3. An interest in training and consultation with managerial and union personnel.
4. A willingness to refer long-term cases, with emphasis on treating more acute, short-term ones.
5. Research skills to evaluate program dollar cost savings to the company.

Since alcohol abuse is a disorder that usually develops over a 7 to 10 year period, early identification of the problem produces long-term savings. Training supervisory personnel to identify symptoms of poor mental health becomes central to an EAP. In addition, the program provides very practical health education that attempts to reach employees and their families through brochures, posters, home mailings, etc. Self-referrals are likely to increase if the EAP counselor is a good writer/media specialist who can produce materials that clearly portray the seriousness of problems and the means available to treat them.

Personnel Management

An employment option for graduates from counseling programs in business is to assume the role of personnel or human resource manager. In doing so they must prove to the company that their training provides benefits beyond that of a graduate from a business school in personnel management or industrial relations.

According to Dessler (1981), the basic responsibilities of personnel managers include (1) recruitment and placement of employees, (2) determining effective compensation and other motivators for enhancing performance, (3) appraising performance, (4) training and developing employees within the organization, (5) assisting with labor relations and associated grievances, and (6) attending to employee health and safety and the governmental regulations associated with them.

Most likely counseling graduates will be less well trained than their business counterparts in such areas as determining compensation (salary), managing payroll, writing job descriptions, and knowing governmental regulations regarding health and safety. However, their intensive training in the behavioral sciences and their human relations skills may more than compensate for these deficiencies, particularly in areas of employee training and development, performance appraisal and feedback, and employee discipline and outplacement. Special training in career counseling and career planning may even give the counseling graduate an edge in intensive employee development projects.

When assessing the contribution of counselor training to careers in personnel or human resources management, it is important to recognize that the principal purpose of such managers is to assist a company's primary decision-makers by assuring an adequate supply of manpower for current and future needs. This includes assessing labor supply and demand within the organization. It basically results in managing two forms of career development: one for individual employees and one for the organization itself. These forms of career development are fundamentally different, but they can complement one another, as will be described later. Connected to both forms of development is training. Thus, in training and career development rests a strong foundation for corporate employability of individuals trained in counseling.

Employee Training and Development

Development may be viewed as promoting the growth of something, while training has to do with directing or disciplining that growth. In a sense a human resource trainer/developer is much like a gardener, only he or she is working with people instead of plants. It would seem difficult to separate training from development in either situation.

With the current emphasis on improving productivity through the use of new technologies and new management styles, there exists an enormous need for training and retraining in American business and industry. Huddleston and Fenwick (1983) estimate that as much as 80 percent of the workers currently employed will need to be retrained.

While it is true that much of this instruction is related to employee utilization of new technology (e.g., computers), much of the training relates directly to what counselors learn during their own training. For example, Smith and Walz (1984) list the following as popular industry-based training programs:

stress management, how managers can "counsel" a troubled employee, how to refer, how to conduct small groups, how to facilitate meetings, how to motivate employees, and how to discipline.

What's attractive about the training ventures mentioned by Smith and Walz (1984) is the ways in which such training can generalize. Increased effectiveness in human relations equips employees to deal with problems within many settings. Such skills are less likely to become obsolete than those related to operating equipment.

PROMOTING CAREER DEVELOPMENT
IN A CORPORATE SETTING

Programming for employee career development is more complicated than similar efforts directed toward students in educational settings. In the latter there exists an unambiguous concern for the individual student's welfare. Career counselors in educational settings can proceed directly with the goal of helping clients gain control of their future through planning and action.

In the workplace human resource development specialists see career development as career counseling that is person-centered in its approach, with little concern for the organization's needs. However, few companies believe that what is good for the person is automatically good for the company (Becker, 1976). Career development in the workplace must take on different meanings. The purpose of a career development program must be to match an employee's career aspirations with the opportunities and challenges available within the company (Aplin & Gerster, 1978). Thus, promoting career development within corporate settings must reflect a dual obligation; it must attempt to serve the individual employee, and it must satisfy organizational needs. When combined, the right of the company to assign jobs to employees works with the employee's desire to assume responsibility for greater career advancement and satisfaction.

With the need to work for the welfare of both the employee and the company, the career counselor in a corporation can offer many of the same services available at other settings. Lipsett (1980) describes his experiences in a multinational, high tech corporation in which he was able to offer career planning services without much structure from the company's management. Of the employees who sought him out for counseling and consultation, most were interested in planning moves within the company that could lead either to career advancement (promotion) or at least to a less routine, more satisfying job. A lesser number simply wanted assistance with the problems they were having adjusting to the workplace.

Thus, many of these self-referred, adult workers wanted assistance in planning the future through the examination of possible choices that would influence their employment, much like vocational clients in educational settings. However, much of this planning was in the context of planning moves within the company. This type of planning, called career pathing, represents a fusion of individual and organizational needs. Both can get together early in the career of the individual to plan a trajectory upon which job changes can be made in anticipation of the employee's growth and the company's needs. Such career coaching is usually done by a supervisor (Walz, 1982), but he or she can be better equipped to perform such tasks through training and consultation with the counseling-trained human resource manager.

Managers trained in this fashion not only understand how to promote career decisions but have also learned how to visualize career success and advancement. Often this occurs within the realistic appraisal of opportunities within the company, rather than through simple occupational daydreams. Also, corporate-based career development specialists need to satisfy the employee's need for self-appraisal as part personal planning, while overseeing performance appraisal for the sake of managing overall organizational manpower.

The Status of Career Planning in the Workplace.   From her intensive review of career planning activities in actual work settings, Brooks (1984) concluded that much interest exists for encouraging career development among employees. However, there appears to be little agreement regarding what kind of activities are included under the label "career development." In addition, little systematic research has been undertaken to assess employer-sponsored career planning assistance programs.

Career planning services in the workplace are delivered to employees in one of three ways: through one-to-one counseling, through workshops or special groups, or through self-directed materials (Brooks, 1984). As mentioned earlier, one-to-one career counseling has traditionally occurred between workers and their supervisors, with increasing emphasis on the use of career specialists. Recommended workships often take the form of a one-day program that allows for self-assessment, information sharing, goal setting, and planning (Morgan, Hall, & Martier, 1979). Parker (1982) describes how "take home" packets are especially cost effective for career planning programs in small companies.

Because employees may be at varying points in their career or adult life stage, programs must be adapted to take this factor into account. Hill and Miller (1982) underscore the relevance of using developmental theories, such as Levinson's (see Chapter 2), in anticipating the issues relevant to employees at different stages. For example, workers in their mid-20s might benefit from exploring varied job activities, with the idea of facilitating continued goal selection. On the other hand, mid-career employees may need technical updating if advances in their area have outstripped earlier training.

While many people associate career development in the workplace with earning promotions, many other forms of movement are possible. Kaye (1980) identifies the following forms of career mobility: vertical, lateral, realignment, exploratory search, job enrichment, and relocation. With this range of possibilities in mind, it becomes strikingly clear how intimate the tie can be between career planning programs and the various transitions adults make in their lives. This planning helps buffer adults from the predictable crises that occur during these passages. It can help to make work-related changes fit better into a broader scheme to satisfy multiple needs.

Outplacement Counseling. One form of career assistance that deserves special mention is outplacement counseling. This means professional assistance to terminated workers seeking other employment. Graduates from counseling programs are well prepared to do outplacement work, yet the counseling profession has attended little to this effort in comparison to personnel management (Davenport, 1984).

Many companies offer outplacement assistance to their executives as part of their severance benefits. Procedures currently used are well known to counselors; they include (1) recognition but minimization of the grieving associated with job loss, and (2) the maximizing of task-oriented behavior in such areas as resume writing, sharpening of interviewing skills, and the making of contacts with employers (Davenport, 1984). A terminated employee's rapid involvement in job-seeking saves the company money and also lessens the stress experienced by the terminated worker.

Preparing for a Corporate Career

Smith, Piercy, and Lutz (1982) have described a training program for counselors interested in human resource development that has been developed at East Texas State University. In addition to taking typical counseling and psychology courses, doctoral students at East Texas State also take coursework in business, such as Personnel Methods, Organizational Behavior, Executive Development, Small Business Consultation, Supervisory Management, and Administrative Behavior and Organizational Theory.

At West Virginia University counseling students interested in human resource development (HRD) are encouraged to consider as electives, in addition to those cited above, the following:

Department	*Course Title*
Health Education	Community Health: Drug Education
Industrial Relations	Industrial Relations Psychology
	Work Group Dynamics
	Equal Employment Opportunities
	Quality of Work Life
	Collective Bargaining
Public Administration	Public Employees Labor Relations
Safety Studies	Controlling Environments and
	Personnel Hazards
Speech	Theory and Research in
Communications	Organizational Communications

Besides planning graduate coursework, a person may need to rethink other life experiences in terms familiar to the corporate world. This is illustrated in Exhibit 14.1. While the American Association for Counseling and Development (AACD) remains an organization of relevance for graduates of counseling programs anticipating a corporate career, affiliation also is worthwhile with the American Society for Training and Development (ASTD) and the American Society of Personnel Administration (ASPA). Regular contact with members of these organizations can provide opportunities for learning the vocabulary and perspectives of the business world.

Exhibit 14.1   The Case of Jan and Her Search for a Corporate Career

Jan had been a high school English teacher for five years before becoming a school counselor. After three more years as a counselor, Jan decided that she wanted to relocate from her small town in Pennsylvania to a large city on the east coast. In addition, she wanted to leave public education and work in business and industry. A management position in human resource development appeared attractive but out of reach. How could a former school teacher and counselor compete for a position in corporate management?

Jan discussed her occupational daydream with several of her friends, who put her in contact with a former educator-turned-corporate manager. He impressed upon Jan the importance of reframing her experiences as an educator and counselor in terms that people of the business world would understand and appreciate. So Jan took stock of her experiences in education with the help of her consultant. She prepared for her job search by converting her work-related experience into language the corporate world could understand. Here are some of her conversions:

Educational Experiences	*Converted to*
Classroom teaching	Managing learning environments
	Managing people in groups
Instructional plans	Plans for long-term and short-term programs
	Establish performance objectives
Testing students	Evaluating human performance
Summer graduate courses	Continual self-development
Structured group counseling	Human relations training

Teacher support groups	Occupational stress management
Job placement—students	Employment evaluation

In addition, Jan was prepared to sell herself as a person with the unusual experience of being able to evaluate her efforts by observing her clients in a variety of climates (school, work, at home) and by working with the same individuals under both structured (curricular) and unstructured (extracurricular) situations. Also, her access to her clients over their educational career gave an unusual opportunity to evaluate her efforts through extended follow-up. Public education provides workers the opportunity to work under a multitude of rules and regulations. It also operates loosely structured programs that demand creativity and imagination. Together these experiences prepare a person for a career in human resource management.

STUDENT LEARNING EXERCISE

Read the following competencies. Indicate whether or not it is important for a counselor to have each competency when employed in a corporate setting. Circle Y for yes or N for no.

1. Resolve conflict, bargain, and negotiate.   Y   N
2. Review governmental safety regulations.   Y   N
3. Write pamphlets and brochures.   Y   N
4. Conduct needs assessments.   Y   N
5. Understand how to promote success motivation.   Y   N
6. Confront and discipline employees.   Y   N

COUNSELING IN REHABILITATION SETTINGS

Since early in the 19th century when special schools and training programs were begun for deaf, blind, mentally retarded, and physically disabled children, rehabilitation services have emerged with an extensive set of medical, social, and psychological services. From World War I to the present numerous pieces of federal legislation have been passed to help fund these services. In 1973 it was estimated that 31 million persons in the United States were disabled in some way (Disability and Health Economics Research Section, 1975). The economic impact of this situation has helped mobilize resources toward broad-based rehabilitative treatments.

Rehabilitation counselors play a central role in managing the rehabilitation process. They assess clients for eligibility and study and report their condition to community agencies, making referrals when needed. Counselors provide clients with personal and vocational counseling and assist with job placement. Counselors work with clients in groups and with their families.

Most rehabilitation counselors work for governmental agencies, primarily state divisions of vocational rehabilitation. Marinelli (1982) notes that large numbers of rehabilitation counselors also work for the Veterans Administration, state employment services, hospitals and medical centers, correctional facilities, welfare agencies, the Social Security Administration, and workmen's compensation insurance firms. There are also sheltered workshops, independent living centers, colleges and schools, and nonprofit organizations that employ rehabilitation counselors. Recently, private-for-profit agencies have increased in number, employing many recent graduates of rehabilitation counseling programs, largely through support of these agencies by the insurance industry.

The preparation of rehabilitation counselors has become well defined through the accreditation of training programs by the Council on Rehabilitation Education (Berven & Wright, 1978) and the certification of individual counselors by the Commission on Rehabilitation Counselor Certification. Because of this, persons interested in working primarily with physically and mentally disabled populations are wise to explore training programs holding accreditation and providing eligibility for certification.

A traditional view in rehabilitation has been that employment is therapeutic for most individuals. Job placement and work adjustment become important themes in the rehabilitation process. Counselors typically develop refined skills in vocational evaluation of individuals and in job survey and analysis.

COUNSELING IN CORRECTIONAL SETTINGS

The American justice system is a massive, complex system involving many different professions with many useful roles for counselors. At each step in the system, from apprehension of suspects to final release of prisoners, counselors can participate with other law enforcement and corrections officials in attempting to ensure the safety of citizens and the rehabilitation of law offenders.

Pretrial Intervention

The prosecution, conviction, and subsequent confinement of law offenders has become such a burdensome and costly process that alternatives have been sought. Diversion programs represent one such alternative; they suspend the criminal justice process in favor of providing counseling and other services for individuals likely to benefit from them. Common offenses treated in such a manner include shoplifting, passing bad checks, property destruction, and battery and disorderly conduct resulting from a temper outburst, often triggered by alcohol (Gotteil & Ghosh, 1983). In such a program a prosecutor may choose to have a suspect assessed by a screening panel, mandatory counseling, and some effort at restitution for the damage done.

While this alternative opens opportunities for counselor involvement in treating offenders, Gotteil and Ghosh (1983) note that client resistance to mandatory counseling often exists. In work with juvenile offenders, a court counselor often is responsible for extensive intake work resulting in a written report to the juvenile court judge that strongly influences the final action taken by the court. In such pretrial work the justice system often views the counselor as already beginning the treatment to reduce recidivism by exploring the probable consequences of the current offense and of future ones.

Trial-Related Counselor Involvements

Expert testimony during criminal trials usually falls in the domain of the psychiatrist or licensed psychologist. Doctoral-level counseling psychologists can contribute to this process. The master's level counselor is more likely to function as a social caseworker employed by the court, working much like the mental health counselor when visiting a jail. For juveniles especially, court counselors are likely to maintain contact with the offenders following an initial hearing with the judge for the purpose of making presentencing recommendations. Many states have diagnostic centers where juvenile offenders may be placed for a period of time, usually 20 to 60 days, and where they are tested, interviewed, and generally observed by counselors and other correctional staff. Following this placement, juveniles may be put on probation or placed in a group home, a psychiatric facility, or another correctional center.

Correctional Counseling in Prisons and Other Facilities

Prisons and other correctional facilities regularly employ psychiatrists, psychologists, and counselors. These staff members have responsibilities for (1) assessment, (2) treatment, (3) training, (4) consultation, and (5) research (Whiteley & Hosford, 1983). In addition to performing these usual duties, the correctional counselor is viewed as a member of the institution's staff and is responsible for protecting that institution and ensuring security throughout. In most prisons there is a clear division between inmates and officers, with fierce loyalty on both sides (Toch, 1978). While at times counselors might be portrayed as intermediaries between inmates and the institution, both sides clearly want counselors identified with the correctional staff. At one time prisons were justified as rehabilitation centers for law offenders; today imprisonment is seen as a punishment for social injury (Geis, 1983). This view of imprisonment maintains the division between inmates and staff.

Problems of prison costs and overcrowding have accelerated the search for alternative forms of incarceration, especially for the nonviolent offender. Community programs such as half-way houses and other supervised living environments often emphasize vocational and interpersonal skill acquisition. Counselors fit well into such programs; however, in recent years there has been a tendency to move away from these types of treatment (Whiteley & Hosford, 1983).

With the demise of the alternatives to incarceration in large prisons, counselors in prisons are usually left with large caseloads. Because of this, group counseling has become a favorite intervention; it fits well with the large caseloads. These groups often address problems of substance abuse, since this problem is widespread among inmate populations (National Institute of Drug Abuse, 1981).

Probation and Parole

Law offenders put on probation or released from prisons on parole often receive counseling from mental health counselors or counselors employed by the courts. Counselor training among parole officers varies from none to advanced degrees. While the mental health counselor is free to give full attention to the person on probation and follow a traditional therapist role, the court counselor has a dual role of both counselor and enforcer of the limits and structure set by the probation/parole plan (Lee & Klopfer, 1978). The latter may call for such non-counseling methods as lecturing, persuading, threatening, and punishing. In addition, since the court counselor must report the activities and progress of his or her caseload back to the court, confidentiality is more limited, and consequently so is the degree of trust between counselor and client. The same is true for correctional counselors working in prisons.

Preparing for a Career in Corrections

The brief overview given of counselor involvement in the criminal justice system identifies some of the problems and challenges one must face when working in such settings. Yet law offenders often have emotional problems that have contributed to their status, and they can benefit from contact with counselors. Besides the differences noted in treating law offenders, similarities between them and other clients also exist.

Page and Shearer (1980) provide a number of recommendations for the training of correctional and court counselors. Learning how to build trust with mistrustful clients, deal with authority games, and generally surviving a harsh physical working environment head their recommendations. In addition, counselors need to understand how the criminal justice system works, the types of lifestyles led by offenders, and how to use special confrontational skills. Such work, while potentially rewarding, is not for the faint-hearted.

PASTORAL COUNSELING

There is quite a bit of literature, both pro and con, on the relationship between counseling/psychotherapy and religion. The professional debate notwithstanding, people turn to clergy more often for help with emotional problems than they do to any other group of professionals (Clemens, Corradi, & Wasman, 1978). This is not surprising since more than 90% of our population hold some form of religious beliefs (Benson, 1981). These believers turn to their clergy for help with both religious and other problems.

In studying attitudes toward religious and secular counseling, Quackenbos, Privette, and Klentz (1985) showed that lay people do see religious and secular counseling as different. Thirty-five percent surveyed preferred some form of religious counseling, 79% thought religious values were an important topic to be discussed in therapy, and 53% stated they would seek counseling at a pastoral center if it were available. The authors conclude that many people want religion to be included in counseling and psychotherapy.

Counselors, however, are often hesitant to discuss spiritual issues with their clients (Loeninger, 1979). Some of the reasons for this suggested by Russo (1984) include:

1. Fear of imposing personal values on clients.
2. Negative attitudes toward organized religion.
3. Lack of a theoretical model that can aid in the exploration of religious and spiritual issues and values.

Russo (1984) believes that forms of transcendental logic are available that can confront spiritual issues. Apparently more and more counselors are becoming interested in such topics. The Association for Religious and Value Issues in Counseling (ARVIC) has been one of the fastest growing divisions of the American Association for Counseling and Development (AACD) with one of the highest percentages of student members (Bartlett, Lee, & Doyle, 1985).

CHRISTIAN COUNSELING

One example of pastoral counseling, relevant to a large number of individuals, is Christian counseling. Strong (1980) defines this as a synthesis of psychological procedures for achieving therapeutic change in an interview with the values and realities of faith in Jesus Christ.

Christian thinking holds both the responsibility of the person for self-development and the availability of divine assistance for that development. The secret for the Christian is to become open to the help of God, allowing it to break through the many barriers between God and people. Knowledge of divine assistance is available to the Christian via scripture, especially through the model of Jesus Christ. Prayer and meditation allow God to influence the person's actions that move him or her toward achieving desired changes and growth. By following the tenets of Christianity, the believer can achieve greater adaptation to life challenges and greater emotional health.

Theodore (1984) notes that strong religious convictions are often condemned as being dogmatic and inflexible. He suggests that empirical science can be used, as suggested earlier by Bergin (1980), to test the useful aspects of religion from a mental health viewpoint (see Table 14.1). These can be compared to the humanistic-atheistic tenets suggested by Ellis (1980).

Christian Counseling can be offered at pastoral care centers staffed by clergy and lay persons of interdenominational faiths. Since clergy represent a significant portion of many counselor education programs, many lay therapists and clergy at pastoral care centers receive similar training.

COUNSELING IN MEDICAL SETTINGS

Hospitals, health maintenance organizations (HMOs), private medical practices, and hospice care facilities are medical settings that counseling graduates might consider for employment. Unfortunately, to date such settings have not accounted for a large percentage of job placements for counselors. These and other facilities and services account for the massive health care system in this country that consumes 11% of the gross national product (Cummings, 1986). More efforts seem to be underway to reduce the size of this system than to expand it. This will have a negative effect on the future employment of counselors.

Public and private hospitals are dominated by the allied health professions (medicine, nursing, pharmacy, physical and occupational therapy, etc.); even psychologists represent a small percentage of the personnel working at such facilities. It is estimated that only 10% of the membership of the American Psychological Association work in hospitals (DeLeon, Pallak, & Hefferman, 1982). And it has been only recently that guidelines have been relaxed by the Joint Commission on Accreditation of Hospitals to allow psychologists hospital privileges (Manning, Wells, Duan, Newhouse, & Ware, 1984).

More promising has been the trend toward HMOs, which have recently showed an interest in hiring mental health counselors (Cummings, 1986). These are large corporations that offer prepaid health plans. It is estimated that by 1993 more than 50 million persons will be served by these plans, which began in the 1900s. After 1993 a 10% annual growth rate is estimated (DeLeon, Uyeda, & Welch, 1985). Since the 1970s and the passage of P.L. 93-222, HMOs have been seen as a major factor in reshaping the American health care system. The

Table 14.1   Testable Hypotheses From a Theistic and a Humanistic-Atheistic Frame of Reference

Theistic hypothesis (Bergin, 1980, pp. 102–103)	Humanistic-atheistic hypothesis (Ellis, 1980, p. 638)
Religious communities that provide the combination of a viable belief structure and a network of loving, emotional support should manifest lower rates of emotional and social pathology and physical disease.	Atheistic communities that provide a balanced, undogmatic belief structure and a cooperative, forgiving community without any absolutistic commandments will manifest lower rates of emotional, social pathology, and physical disease.
Those who endorse high standards of impulse control (or strict moral standards) have lower than average rates of alcoholism, addiction, divorce, emotional instability, and associated interpersonal difficulties.	Unequivocal and eternal fidelity or loyalty to any interpersonal commitment, especially marriage, leads to harmful consequences—both interpersonally and intraphysically.
Disturbances in clinical cases will diminish as these individuals are encouraged to adopt forgiving attitudes toward parents and others who may have had a part in the development of their symptoms.	Teaching clients forgiveness and selective love, commitment, service, and sacrifice for others will help heal interpersonal difficulties and reduce intrapsychic distress. Teaching them unselective, universal, and unequivocal love, commitment, service, and sacrifice for others will help sabotage interpersonal relations and increase intrapsychic distress.
Infidelity or disloyalty to any interpersonal commitment, especially marriage, leads to harmful consequences—both interpersonally and intrapsychically.	
Teaching clients love, commitment, service, and sacrifice for others will help heal interpersonal difficulties and reduce intrapsychic distress.	Personal suffering consisting of appropriate feelings like sorrow, regret, frustration, and annoyance at one's own or another's undesirable behavior will often increase one's compassion and potential for helping others. Personal suffering consisting of inappropriate feelings like panic, horror, depression, and hostility will usually decrease one's compassion and potential for helping others.
Improving male commitment, caring, and responsibility in families will reduce marital and familial conflict and associated psychological disorders.	
A good marriage and family life constitute a psychologically and socially benevolent state. As the percentage of persons in a community who live in such circumstances increases, social pathologies will decrease and vice versa.	
Properly understood, personal suffering can increase one's compassion and potential for helping others.	
The kinds of values described herein have social consequences. There is a social ecology, and the viability of this social ecology varies as a function of personal conviction, morality, and the quality of the social support network in which we exist.	

Note. From "Utilizing of Spiritual Values in Counseling: An Ignored Dimension" (p. 164) by R. M. Theodore, 1984, *Counseling and Values,* 28. Copyright AACD. Reprinted by permisssion. No further reproduction authorized without written permission of AACD.

emphasis in HMOs is on health maintenance and the treatment of illness, rather than solely the latter. Since hospital costs are lower, HMOs seem to offer more cost-effective health care. HMOs can now offer short-term mental health services (up to 20 visits). Thus, enrollees can come to see counselors at their HMO for "free" (i.e., as part of their prepaid program) rather than pay a fee for services at a mental health center or to a private practitioner.

In addition to HMOs, more traditional health care settings have been recommended as employment settings for counselors. Shanks (1978) argued for the value of hiring counselors to assist physicians in their practices. Counselors could accompany and support the physician, attending directly to the psychosocial needs of the patient. Also, the counselor could help reinforce the physician's directives and help the patient work through decisions related to his or her health care. In many ways this would humanize the practice. In the future counselors may form an interest group within their professional organizations to pursue such employment possibilities.

In recent years hospice care for the terminally ill has become more available. As an alternative to hospitalization, hospice care in the home or in a center could take advantage of counselor expertise with respect to death and dying. However, Liss-Levinson (1982) provides a realistic perspective on hospice work—it is of value to patients and their families, but includes the often undignified nature of the dying process.

PRIVATE PRACTICE

Many counselors working for schools and agencies fantasize about private practice. Appealing is the idea of being one's own boss, having a nicely decorated office, a secretary, and so forth. The reality of private practice is more than designing an office and offering a counseling service—one operates a business. This venture includes becoming licensed in many states, paying higher liability insurance rates, providing various treatments, marketing them, and the management of all other services in support of the treatments. Many counselors are not prepared for all these facets of private practice. For this reason many find it wise to join an already established firm, at least in the beginning. In this way one can rely on others with more experience in the business side of private practice.

Staying in business as a private practitioner is not easy or automatic. Adding pressure to the practice is the fact that counselors and counseling psychologists are more likely to see clients with less debilitating problems than psychiatrists. This is because of preference, receipt of third-party payments, and access to hospital privileges (Norcross & Wogan, 1983). Less debilitated clients stay in treatment for fewer sessions (Taube, Burns, & Kessler, 1984). Thus, the private practice must attract a larger number of clients at more frequent intervals. This affects income security.

In spite of some of the problems, private practice can be lucrative. A

1984 survey of private practitioners (Psychotherapy Finances, 1984) showed the average hourly rates for therapy as follows: psychologists, $65; marriage counselors, $60; social workers, $50; pastoral counselors, $50. The average net income (after expenses) was $48,500 for psychologists and $34,400 for social workers. However, these figures do not include fringe benefits (e.g., paid vacation and holidays, health insurance, pension, workman's compensation). Only 34% of the private practitioners surveyed contributed in that year to a Keogh (retirement) Plan. Public employees may receive fringe benefits packages worth from 20% to 50% of their salary. If an employee's benefits package is worth 35%, a salary of $26,000 returns to the employee a combined salary/benefits package of $35,100. Fringe benefits are a definite consideration no matter where one is employed.

SUMMARY

This chapter has attempted to provide an overview of a variety of employment options for counselors. Many of them are less traditional than school or mental health counseling, but each represents a unique set of challenges with varying rewards. The options explored demonstrate the versatility of counselor preparation and the possibilities for work environment changes throughout one's career.

REVIEW QUESTIONS

1. How would a counselor working in a corporate setting argue for the cost effectiveness of an employee assistance program?
2. What are some of the differences in promoting career development between educational and corporate settings?
3. How can a counselor-in-training prepare for a career in business and industry?
4. What are some unique aspects of rehabilitation counseling?
5. Describe how counselors fit into the criminal justice system.
6. Define Christian counseling.
7. What are some of the issues related to working in medical settings? Private practice?

REFERENCES

Alpin, J. C., & Gerster, D. K. (1978). Career development: An integration of individual and organizational needs. *Personnel, 55*(2), 23–29.

Bartlett, W. W., Lee, J. L., & Doyle, R. E. (1985). Historical development of the Association of Religious Values and Issues in Counseling. *Journal of Counseling and Development, 63*(7), 448–451.

Becker, S. P. (1976). Look before you leap to take charge of career development. *Training, 13*(9), 50–52.

Benson, J. M. (1981). The polls: A rebirth of religion. *Public Opinion Quarterly, 45*, 576–585.

Bergin, A. E. (1980). Psychotherapy and religious values. *Journal of Consulting and Clinical Psychology, 48*(1), 95–104.

Berven, N. L., & Wright, G. N. (1978). An evaluation model for accreditation. *Counselor Education and Supervision, 17*(2), 188–194.

Brooks, L. (1984). Career planning programs in the workplace. In D. Brown, L. Brooks and Associates (Eds.), *Career choice and development* (pp. 388–405). San Francisco, CA: Jossey-Bass.

Christiani, T. S., & Christiani, M. F. (1979). The application of counseling skills in the business and industrial setting. *The Personnel and Guidance Journal, 58*(3), 166–169.

Clemens, N., Corradi, R., & Wasman, M. (1978). The parish clergy as a mental health resource. *Journal of Religion and Health, 17*, 227–232.

Cummings, N. A. (1986). The dismantling of our health system: Strategies for the survival of psychological practice. *American Psychologist, 41*(4), 426–431.

Davenport, D. W. (1984). Outplacement counseling: Whither the counselor? *The Vocational Guidance Quarterly, 32*(3), 185–191.

DeLeon, P. H., Pallak, M. S., & Hefferman, J. A. (1982). Hospital health care delivery. *American Psychologist, 37*(12), 1340–1341.

DeLeon, P. H., Uyeda, M. K., & Welch, B. L. (1985). Psychology and HMOs: New partnership or new adversary? *American Psychologist, 40*(10), 1122–1124.

Dressler, G. (1981). Personnel management (2nd ed.). Reston, VA: Reston.

Disability and Health Economics Research Section (1975). *An evaluation of the structure and function of disability programs: Year one summary report.* New Brunswick, NJ: Rutgers University.

Ellis, A. (1980). Psychotherapy and atheistic values. A response to A. E. Bergin's "Psychotherapy and religious values." *Journal of Consulting and Clinical Psychology, 48*, 635–639.

Forrest, D. V. (1983). Employee assistance programs in the 1980s: Expanding career options for counselors. *The Personnel and Guidance Journal, 62*(2), 105–107.

Geis, G. (1983). Criminal justice and adult offenders: An overview. *The Counseling Psychologist, 11*(2), 11–16.

Gotteil, D., & Ghosh, S. A. (1983). Pretrial intervention: Counseling in adult diversion programs. *The Counseling Psychologist, 11*(2), 17–25.

Hill, R. E., & Miller, E. L. (1982). Career changes: Implications and suggested response strategies for the individual and the organization. In G.R. Walz (Ed.), *Career development in organizations* (pp. 21–46). Ann Arbor, MI: ERIC/CAPS.

Huddleston, K. F., & Fenwick, D. (1983). The productivity challenge: Business/education partnerships. *Training and Development*, April, 96–100.

Katzell, R. A., & Guzzo, R. A. (1983). Psychological approaches to productivity improvement. *American Psychologist, 38*(4), 468–472.

Kaye, B. (1980). How you can help employees formulate career goals. *Personnel Journal, 59*(5), 368–372.

Lee, R. E., & Klopfer, C. (1978). Counselors and juvenile delinquents: Toward a comprehensive treatment approach. *The Personnel and Guidance Journal, 57*(4), 194–197.

Leonards, J. T. (1981). Corporate psychology: An answer to occupational mental health. *The Personnel and Guidance Journal, 60*(1), 47–51.

Lipsett, L. (1980). A career counselor in industry. *The Vocational Guidance Quarterly, 28*(3), 269–273.

Liss-Levinson, W. S. (1982). Reality perspectives for psychological services in a hospice program. *American Psychologist, 37*(11), 1266–1270.

Loeninger, R. J. (1979). Therapeutic strategies with "religious" resistances. *Psychotherapy: Theory Research, and Practice, 16*, 419–427.

Manning, W. G., Well, K. B., Duan, N., Newhouse, J. P., & Ware, J. E., Jr. (1984). Cost sharing and the use of ambulatory mental health services. *American Psychologist, 39*(10), 1077–1089.

Mardinelli, R. P. (1982). Rehabilitation services. In H. B. Mitzel (Ed.), *Encyclopedia of educational research* (pp. 1580–1587) (4th ed.), New York: Macmillan and Free Press.

Masi, D. A., & Teems, L. A. (1982,) March/April. The history, the philosophy and the essential components of employee assistance programs. Paper presented at the International Conference on Alcoholism, Christ Church College. Oxford University, Oxford, England.

McGregor, D. M. (1960). *The human side of enterprise.* New York: McGraw-Hill.

Morgan, M. A., Hall, D. T., & Martier, A. (1979). Career development strategies in industry—Where are we and where we should be? *Personnel, 56*(2), 13–30.

National Institute on Drug Abuse. (1981). *Drug abuse treatment in prisons.* Washington, DC: Department of Health and Human Services.

Norcross, J. C., & Wogan, M. (1983). American psychotherapists in independent practice: Some findings and issues. *Professional Psychology: Research and Practice, 14*(3), 529–539.

Osipow, S. H. (1982). Counseling psychology: Applications in the world of work. *The Counseling Psychologist, 10*(3), 19–25.

Page, R. C., & Shearer, R. A. (1980). Some curriculum ideas for training public offender counselors. *Counselor Education and Supervision, 19*(4), 293–300.

Papalia, A. S., & Kaminski, W. (1981). Counseling and counseling skills in the industrial environment. *The Vocational Guidance Quarterly, 30*(1), 37–42.

Parker, C. L. (1982). Facilitating career development in a small business. *The Vocational Guidance Quarterly, 31*(1), 86–89.

Peters, T. J., & Waterman, R. H., Jr. (1982). *In search of excellence: Lessons from America's best run companies.* New York: Warner Books.

Presnall, L. (1981). *Occupational counseling and referral system.* Salt Lake City: Alcoholism Foundation.

Psychotherapy Finances (1984). 1984 survey report. *Psychotherapy Finances, 11*(8), 1–8.

Quackenbos, S., Privette, G., & Klentz, B. (1985). Psychotherapy: Sacred or secular? *Journal of Counseling and Development, 63*(5), 290–293.

Quayle, D. (1983). American productivity: The devastating effect of alcoholism and drug abuse. *American Psychologist, 38*(4), 454–458.

Roman, P. (1981) From employee alcoholism to employee assistance. *Journal of Alcohol Studies, 47*(3), 165–173.

Russo, T. J. (1984). A model of addressing spiritual issues in counseling. *Counseling and values, 29*(1), 42–48.

Schuster, F. (1978, December) Human resources management: Key to the future. *The Personnel Administrator,* 33–36.

Shanks, J. (1978). A staff counselor in family practice. *Behavioral Medicine, 5*(6), 26–29.

Smith, R. L., Piercy, F. P., & Lutz, P. (1982). Training counselors for human resource positions in business and industry. *Counselor Education and Supervision, 22*(2), 107–112.

Smith, R. L., & Walz, G. R. (1984). *Counseling and human resource development.* Ann Arbor, MI: ERIC/CAPS.

Strong, S. R. (1982). Christian counseling: A synthesis of psychological and Christian concepts. *The Personnel and Guidance Journal, 58*(9), 589–592.

Taube, C. A., Burns, B. J., & Kessler, L. (1984). Patients of psychiatrists in office-based practice: 1980. *American Psychologist, 39*(12), 1435–1447.

Theodore, R. M. (1984). Utilization of spiritual values in counseling: An ignored dimension. *Counseling and Values, 28*(4), 162–168.

Toch, H. (1978). *Living in prison.* Glencoe, IL: Free Press.

Walz, G. R. (1982). The career development diamond: Touching all the bases. In G. R. Walz (Ed.), *Career development in organizations* (pp. 1–20). Ann Arbor: ERIC/CAPS.

Whiteley, S. M., & Hosford, R. E. (1983). Counseling in prisons. *The Counseling Psychologist, 11*(2), 27–34.

Witte, R., & Cannon, M. (1979, June). Employee assistance programs: Getting top management support. *The Personnel Administrator,* 23–25.

15

Research, Evaluation, and Accountability

GOALS OF THE CHAPTER

The purposes of this chapter are threefold. The first of these is to address a long-standing issue, the differences between research and evaluation. The second is to provide an overview of the major models of research and to outline some of the strengths and weaknesses of each. The third is to discuss the major approaches to evaluation and to tie these to accountability, an increasing concern of counselors.

CHAPTER PREVIEW

1. Research and evaluation will be distinguished. Some distinctions will also be made between applied and basic research.
2. The strengths and weaknesses of some basic research designs will be presented.
3. The implications of research for the counseling profession will be discussed, including issues in this area.
4. The purposes and processes of program evaluation will be overviewed.
5. Accountability as it relates to evaluation will be discussed.

INTRODUCTION

At the outset it should be made clear that research and evaluation are *not* two distinctly different processes; in fact they have more commonalities than differences. For many years these similarities tended to confound scholars and practitioners who attempted to differentiate between the two (Drew & Hardman, 1985). However, in the late 1960s and early 1970s, progress toward meaningful differentiation between these two processes was made. Today it is widely accepted that research and evaluation differ in three ways: the purpose for which they are conducted, concern about the generalizability of the findings (external validity), and their relationships to theory. A fourth distinction between research and evaluation that is sometimes made lies in the area of applicability of findings. Evaluation efforts are typically more concerned with generating data that are immediately applicable to the work of the counselor, with research being less concerned with this applicability of findings. However, this distinction does not apply in all cases, as we shall see.

The purpose of evaluation is to provide information that will allow those charged with program management to make decisions regarding the value of an entire program or part of that program (Burck, 1978; Drew & Hardman, 1985). Some have likened evaluation to the parliamentary move of calling for the question, a move that indicates that it is time to move from discussion of an issue to a vote aimed at determining whether the issue at hand passes or fails (Bardo, Cody, & Bryson, 1978). This analogy is an apt one, but evaluation does not focus just on the end product, that is, whether a program succeeds or fails. It is also aimed at determining what factors contributed to the outcome. Evaluation that focuses on outcome is called "summative" or "product evaluation." Summative evaluation tries to determine whether those individuals who received the program actually benefited in a meaningful way. Evaluation that focuses on the factors that contribute to outcomes is called "process" or "formative evaluation." Process evaluation tries to identify key variables that have contributed to or retarded the observed outcomes.

Much social science research is initiated to establish cause and effect relationships, although approaches to research do not allow the researcher to draw casual conclusions directly. Researchers are concerned with whether a particular counseling technique or program is effective, but they are more concerned with establishing a causal link between the intervention (A) and the observed outcome (B). Does A produce B? In order to answer this question, all extraneous variables that might produce B, and thus reduce the certainty that A and B are linked causally, must be controlled. Because of the desire to control extraneous variables, research is less likely to be conducted in field settings, such as college counseling centers, because variables that might influence the results cannot be adequately controlled. Evaluation, on the other hand, is always conducted in a field setting. Although evaluators also wish to control extraneous variables and establish causal relationships, projects to be evaluated are in the field.

Evaluation is conducted to fuel the decision-making process. Research is aimed at advancing our knowledge base by determining cause and effect. Researchers are concerned about the generalizability of their findings to other settings and groups. Evaluators are not as concerned about this issue. Generalizability or external validity refers to the extent to which an intervention such as a group counseling program will work in other settings. Will a group treatment program in prison A work in prison B? If the program was established only with the special characteristics of Central Prison in mind, it may not work in Southeastern Prison, but the question being asked in evaluation is, "Should we retain this program in Central Prison?" Researchers attempt to design programs that would be applicable in a number of settings (generalizability). Thus, the researcher attempts to utilize counselors who are typical of counselors in general (i.e., counselors in all prisons), to verify that the inmates being counseled are also representative of other inmates (i.e., in terms of age, race, type of crime committed, etc.), and to be sure that the treatments employed can be utilized in other settings.

As is probably obvious, questions of evaluation grow out of concern for the effectiveness of the technique or program being employed. In applied research, as opposed to basic research, questions may grow out of this same concern. However, in applied research, questions asked may also stem in part from theoretical considerations. This is partially because research, unlike evaluation, is aimed at advancing science, which in addition to explaining *what* works is aimed at explaining *why* things work. Thus a researcher may not simply be concerned with whether a particular technique can increase job interviewing effectiveness in high school students. That researcher may wish to know which techniques drawn from a theoretical perspective such as modeling theory (e.g., written directions, live models, live models plus practice, etc.) produce the most effective learning. While not all research is theory based, much of it is linked to theoretical as well as applied questions.

Some research has little immediate applicability and in fact is not pursued for practical reasons. This research is typically referred to as basic research. Counselors are little concerned about the research that examines the retention rate of nonsense syllables learned under conditions of stress. Nor are they usually interested in knowing about the maze-running habits of rats or the problem-solving skills of great apes. This research becomes relevant only when it is translated into practical application.

The commonalitites between research and evaluation outweigh the differences. There are differences between the two but, as Asher (1976) and Posavac and Carey (1985) indicate, evaluation is a process of generating information or facts using research methods. As has already been noted, both research and evaluation are concerned with internal validity—establishing that the program or technique under study produces the observed outcome. Those methods used to control extraneous variables from influencing the outcome are utilized in both processes. These methods involve using no-treatment (control) comparison groups, randomly assigning clients to treatment and control groups, and keeping those who deliver and receive treatments unaware of the research and evaluation design so that they will not inadvertently influence the outcomes of the study.

To illustrate these ideas, let us consider the counselor who is interested in determining whether or not a group counseling intervention enhances occupational choice-making skills. She would begin by identifying a group of students who have deficits in the occupational choice-making areas, perhaps as indicated by the inability to make an occupational choice when asked to do so. She would then design a treatment to remedy this deficiency. Students would then be randomly assigned to the treatment or control (no-treatment) group. Students and counselors leading the groups would be made aware of the general purpose of the groups but not the specific measures to be used in the study to avoid "teaching to the test." After the treatment, the treatment and control groups would be compared, usually by means of a statistical test. This process would be the same whether research or evaluation is involved. Thus while the purposes for which the study was initiated, the selection of counselors and clients to ensure generalizability of results, and the relationship of the research questions to theory may vary, the basic processes involved in research and evaluation are quite similar.

STUDENT LEARNING EXERCISE
Indicate whether the following statements are true or false.

1. Evaluation and research are more similar than they are different.   T   F
2. Evaluation is more concerned about threats to internal validity, that is, being able to specify that the results are caused by the treatment, than is research.   T   F
3. Generalizability is an issue related to external validity.   T   F
4. Evaluators are more concerned about generalizability than are researchers.   T   F
5. Evaluators use research designs.   T   F

RESEARCH

In the preceding section two types of research were described: applied and basic. This section will briefly describe the various types of applied research approaches, which include approaches in which variables are manipulated (experimental research), relationships explored (correlational research), the status quo described (descriptive research), or development monitored over time (longitudinal research).

Experimental Research

Extensive Designs.   Experimental research designs are of two types: extensive and intensive. Extensive design involves the study of groups; intensive design focuses on the individual. Extensive designs are those usually associated with experimental research and typically involve measuring the impact of an experimental manipulation by comparing an experimental group to a control group. A counselor who wishes to determine the impact of an intervention on snake phobics begins by identifying a group of snake phobics, randomly assigning the phobic subjects to two groups (experimental and control), administering the treatment, and then taking a follow-up measure of the phobic behavior and comparing the two groups, usually using some statistical procedure. This classic research design, if properly conducted, allows maximum control of competing hypotheses, and thus fulfills the most basic requirement of experimental research by increasing the researcher's ability to imply cause (treatment) and effect (reduction in snake phobia reactions).

It should be pointed out that there are many other legitimate experimental designs, most of which are described in a classic work by Campbell and Stanley (1963). However, there are also a number of pretenders, that is, research designs that do not allow any semblance of control, that are frequently employed by researchers, and that find their way into the counseling literature. One of these, the one-shot case study, is frequently used and involves only one group (experimental) and one measurement (posttest). This design, if applied to our snake phobia problem, would involve only the selection of the phobic subjects, the administration of the treatment, and a posttest. Since there is no comparison group (control) and no pretest, no real conclusions can be drawn regarding the effectiveness of the treatment.

The one-group, pretest-posttest group (Campbell & Stanley, 1963) design does improve on the one-shot case study approach, but only slightly. Research using this approach identifies subjects using a pretest, follows this by the administration of a treatment and then a posttest. Because a comparison can be made between the pretest and posttest, many naive individuals believe that control has been established. However, without a control group this is not the case. To illustrate, let us assume that during the course of the research on snake phobics, a local television station decided to air a series of spots on its local news regarding the value of snakes, and each night for a week the news team ran a 10-minute segment on snakes. Without a control group the researcher is unable to separate the impact of the television series from his or her treatment and is left to wonder whether extraneous variables or the treatment reduced the intensity of snake phobia.

Extensive designs have been criticized (Goldman, 1978, 1986) because what often occurs is that over the course of treatment some of the subjects get better and some get worse, with the result being that the control and experimental groups are not significantly different with regard to the criterion measure (e.g., intensity of snake phobia). As a result, intensive research designs are increasingly popular.

Intensive Designs.   Intensive designs, also called case study or $n = 1$ designs, were developed by behaviorally oriented psychologists and counselors (Tawney & Gast, 1984), but are now used by researchers with a variety of points of view (Anton, 1978). These designs have a number of advantages for counselors because they were developed for use in applied settings, focus on the individual, use the individual as his or her own control, and have a high level of control and thus allow inference of cause and effect. Their one weakness lies in the area of generalizability. Since only one subject is studied at a time it is difficult to argue that the "sample" of subjects adequately represents a broader population. However, even this deficiency can be overcome by repeating the design (replication) (Tawney & Gast, 1984).

Conducting intensive design research begins with making three basic decisions: (1) "What behavior is to be changed?" (2) "How will the target behavior be changed or what will our intervention be?" and (3) "What will be our goal in the behavior change process?" The behavior to be changed (e.g., the ounces of alcohol ingested) is referred to as the dependent variable, and the method for changing it (e.g., drug rehabilitation group) is the independent variable. The goal of the change is the criterion (Tawney & Gast, 1984).

Once the target behavior is identified, a method of measuring the behavior must be determined. As Anton (1978) states, the first principle of single subject research "requires the counselor/researcher to make a series of observations over some period of time" (p. 122). The method of measurement in intensive design research is, typically, systematic observation. However, in many school settings data regarding target behavior can often be determined through existing and ongoing records such as attendance and tardiness reports, grades, proportion of homework handed in, and percentage of work completed correctly.

The units of measurement of the target behavior must also be determined. Those typically used involve a simple count of the target behavior (how often did it occur during a time period), percentage (number of problems completed correctly), rate, number of times a behavior occurs during a time period (calories ingested per day), duration (how long a temper tantrum occurs), latency (how long it takes to respond), and trials to criterion (how many trials before a child learns to add two-digit numbers) (Tawney & Gast, 1984).

Once the units of measure are established, the target behavior must be operationally defined (what is a drunk?; what constitutes name calling?), observers trained, and an observational scheme devised. With regard to the latter, it is usually not possible to observe a subject continuously and thus some form of time sampling procedure is employed. For example, it may be that the subject is observed or only five minutes per hour, with the segments being selected randomly.

Data collection begins with the collection of baseline information regarding the target behavior, which is simply determining the occurrence of the behavior in the units selected under typical circumstances. Determining what is typical is done by simply observing the incidence of the behavior being observed. Once the occurrence stabilizes, the researcher can be relatively certain that a typical pattern for the behavior has been established. Not surprisingly, this is referred to as a "stable baseline." A stable baseline is illustrated in Figure 15.1, and is designated the A phase of data collection.

Note that the rate per half hour fluctuated between nine per period and eight per period during the four observations. A stable baseline cannot be determined with fewer than three observations, but typically more than three are required.

Once a stable baseline is established and the intervention is introduced, the B phase of the research begins. As can be seen in Figure 15.1, the intervention, which in this case was involving the student in individual counseling, produced significant changes in the student.

The design in Figure 15.1 is referred to as the AB design and is the most basic of the intensive research designs. While the AB design is useful for practitioners, it does not fulfill the qualification of greatest concern to researchers—the ability to say with some certainty that the observed change in the B phase is in fact due to the intervention. The teacher may have imposed stricter

Figure 15.1   Incidence of Out-of-Seat Behavior of Fourth-Grade Boy.

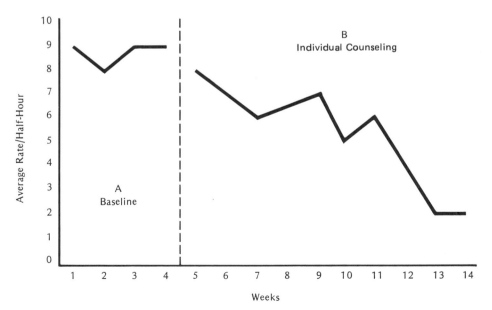

disciplinary standards, or parents, hearing of the child's problem, may have offered a reward for "good behavior." However, there are a number of intensive research designs that meet the criteria established by researchers.

Withdrawal/Reversal Designs.   A number of designs fall into this category, but because of space, only the most basic of these, the A-B-A-B and some closely related designs will be discussed. As the letters suggest, the A-B-A-B design begins with baseline (A), the baseline is followed by an intervention (B), the intervention is withdrawn and the baseline reestablished (A), and then the intervention (B) is reintroduced. The logic behind this design is quite simple. If the target behavior returns to baseline once the intervention is withdrawn and then responds to the intervention a second time, it can reasonably be assumed that the target behavior is under the influence of the intervention and thus a reasonable case for cause and effect can be established. Figure 15.2 shows an A-B-A-B design.

A researcher who attained the results observed in Figure 15.2 could be reasonably certain that homework completion was in fact influenced by behavioral contracts offering rewards for completing teacher assignments. This same researcher could establish that this intervention generalizes by replicating this same experiment with a number of deficient students who were failing to complete homework, and so in one sense the A-B-A-B design meets both the need to establish causal relationships and generalizability. The design is also

Figure 15.2   Percentage of Homework Completed by Eighth-Grade Boy Using Contingency Contracting.

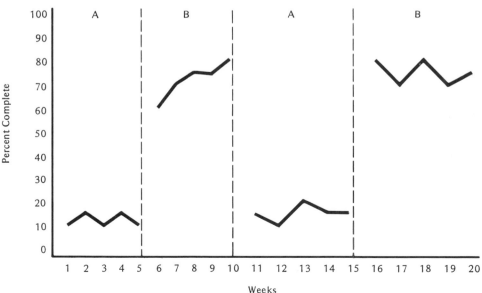

of some use to practitioners because it allows the substitution of other interventions when the first one fails *or* if the practitioner is simply interested in knowing if one approach to dealing with a problem is superior to another. Therefore, it is possible to have designs in which C represents a second intervention (A-B-A-B-C), where B and C are being compared for effectiveness.

From a scientific point of view the A-B-A-B design gets high marks. From practical and ethical points of view it does not. Practically speaking, behavior, once changed, rarely returns to a baseline condition. Another practical problem with the A-B-A-B design is an ethical one. How does one justify withdrawal of an intervention that is working? It seems, and is, unethical to withdraw an intervention that is helping a client or a subject. These practical problems make the reversal/withdrawal designs all but useless in the applied setting of the counselor. Fortunately, there are alternatives.

Multiple Baseline Design. These designs are conceptualized in much the same way as A-B designs except the design is being carried out simultaneously across three or more data sets. As Tawney and Gast (1984) indicate, a data set may involve three target behaviors under the same condition, the same behavior under three different conditions, or the same behavior for three different people.

Multiple baseline designs require, as do intensive designs, that the target behavior(s) and, if appropriate, target situations be identified and criterion levels (goals) be established. In multiple baseline design in which three different problem behaviors of one individual are to be targeted for one individual in one situation, *independent* behaviors such as spelling, incidence of hitting others, and keeping area around desk free from trash should be selected and base-rated. Then the intervention, perhaps teacher reinforcement, is introduced for behavior one (spelling achievement). Once the goal of the intervention has been attained, the intervention is introduced for behavior two, and so forth. If all three target behaviors respond in the same way, a researcher can say that the observed results can be attributed to the intervention. A similar pattern is followed if the same behavior (incidence of smoking) is to be modified across three situations, or if three individuals with the same problem (binge eating) are to be studied. A multiple baseline design is illustrated in Figure 15.3.

From a research point of view, the multiple baseline approach has few flaws, particularly if the researcher replicates the design with several individuals in a number of situations. One difficulty with the design is identifying three functionally independent behaviors in an individual. Functionally independent behaviors are those that are not a part of some habit pattern. For example, smoking and drinking are functionally linked for many individuals and would not make good target behaviors. However, since there are alternatives to selecting three or more behaviors in the same individual, this problem does not pose a serious limitation. A more serious concern for the practitioner, and perhaps the researcher, is the monitoring of three behaviors/individuals/situations at the same time (Tawney & Gast, 1984). Observational procedures are time consuming and monitoring three behaviors may be more than can be adequately

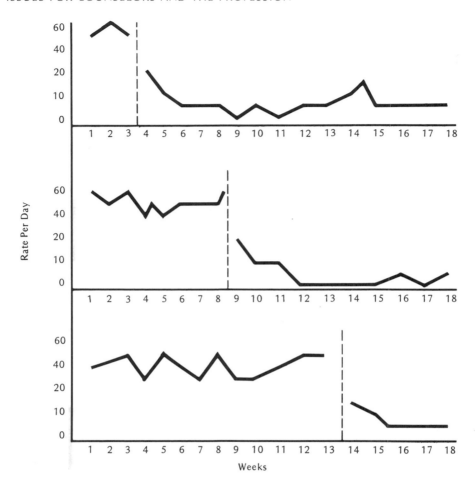

Figure 15.3 Cigarette Smoking in Three Clients Before and After Self-Monitoring/Reinforcement Intervention.

managed. Finally, just as there was an ethical problem with withdrawing a successful intervention in the withdrawal/reversal designs, a similar problem arises in the multiple baseline design when more than one individual is involved, since a successful treatment is being withheld from a client or subject. Each researcher will have to weigh the relative impact of withholding treatment and make a decision on a case-by-case basis.

Other Designs. There are a number of other intensive research designs that are essentially extensions of those already discussed. For example, a researcher might wish to determine the simultaneous impact of numerous interventions on a single target behavior. These designs are discussed in detail in Hersen and Barlow's (1976) *Single Case Experimental Designs: Strategies for Studying Behavior Change* and need a more detailed treatment than can be provided here.

Interpreting Intensive Research

The interpretation of the outcome of extensive research design relies primarily on the results of statistical tests. The interpretation of the outcomes of intensive designs is usually done through inspection of the data. This process begins by inspecting baseline data for stability and continues as the researcher collects data. One of the concerns, of course, lies with the extent to which the criterion has been attained. Normally, the expected outcome of this is established using a practical approach such as determining what is "normal" for the individuals being studied. For example, how many times is a typical third grader out of his seat? In other instances the goal may be cessation of smoking or drinking. These goals become important factors in determining whether or not an experiment is judged successful as does the stability of the data line. Just as a stable baseline is important as a prerequisite for determining when to introduce an intervention, a stable treatment data line is necessary before an experiment can be judged successful. If that treatment line is moving back toward the baseline, it may be that the treatment has had only a short-term impact.

Correlational Research

In correlational research we are usually interested not in manipulating variables but merely in establishing relationships between or among them (Cozby, 1981). For example, college admissions officers want to establish the relationship between high school grades and college achievement. Personnel officers are interested in knowing whether tests of clerical speed and accuracy really do relate to functioning as a secretary. These questions and others are answered using correlational research methods. Two of these methods will be discussed briefly here.

Relationships between two variables are examined using an entire family of correlational procedures, the most common of which is the Pearson Product Moment correlation. Like others, this yields a coefficient ranging from +1 to −1 that indicates the degree of relationship among the variables of interest. A coefficient of +1 is a perfect positive correlation and would indicate, as in the case of grades and college achievement, that there is a direct correspondence between high school grades and college achievement; that is, if one gets straight A's in high school, the same thing will occur in college. Negative correlations are just as revealing as positive correlations. The only difference in interpreting negative correlations is the direction of the relationship, since in negative relationships when one variable goes up, another goes down. If there were a −1 relationship between high school grades and college grades, the straight A high school student would be the straight F student in college.

Correlational research gets a bit more difficult to interpret, although the principles are the same, when we are interested in determining the relationship between two or more predictor variables (say high school grades and college entrance examination scores) and a dependent variable (college grades).

These relationships are determined using what are called multiple correlation procedures. These procedures are particularly useful in that they allow us to build predictor equations using multiple measures and thus increase our accuracy of predicting such variables as college and job success, likelihood of dropping out of school, and so on.

As indicated at the outset, multiple correlation coefficients are interpreted in the same manner as simple correlations, that is, a +1 correlation between high school grades, Scholastic Aptitude Test scores, family income, and college grade point average are still indicators of a perfect relationship, only this time three variables have to be used to account for college grades.

Perfect relationships are rarely, if ever, attained, and thus we are frequently interpreting correlation coefficients of considerably less than 1.0. There are some straightforward ways of making these interpretations, but generally correlations that exceed .70 are considered to be high, .30–.69 moderate, and less than .30 low. For example, typically, the correlation between Graduate Record Examination scores and success in graduate school falls well below .30, while the relationship between a variety of factors and success as an undergraduate is likely to be much higher. However, even a low correlation may be considered highly valuable in some situations (admission of graduate students) when no other variables are available to suggest who might be successful.

There are a number of limitations in correlational research, but the most important one is that cause-effect relationships cannot be inferred from the correlational data. We know, for example, that there is a high relationship between scores on intelligence tests and grades in school. Does that mean that intelligence causes higher grades, which is the commonly held view? Or is it possible that success in schools results in high intelligence test scores? It is also possible in this IQ-grades relationship that a third variable such as family socioeconomic status is influencing the observed correlation. Therefore, researchers using correlational methods should be cautious not to make causal inferences from their data (Cozby, 1981).

Survey Research

Survey research methods, like those of correlational designs, do not involve manipulating variables. They are utilized to answer two types of questions. The first of these is, "What are the characteristics of a given group, institution, or geographic region?" In answering this question, we may simply want to know the gender and racial and ethnic background of U.S. citizens. We may also want to know how many graduates of Philosophy University took jobs the first year out. At other times, we may wish to describe the attitudes and opinions of voters regarding an issue or issues.

More frequently, survey research in the social sciences is embarked upon, not only to describe a given situation, but to make comparisons among different situations. For example, we might wish to know how many juvenile delinquents were produced by towns or cities with various economic conditions.

Survey research studies are conducted using two basic approaches, printed surveys and interviews. As Drew and Hardman (1985) note, regardless of the approach, the most important aspect of survey research is to ask questions that can clearly be understood by the potential respondent. Lack of clarity in the questions, survey instruments that are too long, poor introduction to the research material, and the timing of the arrival of the interviewer or questionnaire are all important factors in determining not only the quality of the responses but also the quantity, that is, the number of actual responses received.

Survey researchers typically begin the process by carefully identifying the goals of the study, determining what types of data are needed to attain those goals, and then drafting questions that will elicit that data. Questionnaires or interview procedures are then field-tested and revised. Once data are received, depending on the purposes of the study, they may be subjected to sophisticated statistical analysis and interpreted much as one would interpret experimental research findings, or the data may be presented matter-of-factly, using percentages and means. In the latter situation, the interpretation is much the same as that resulting from intensive designs; that is, the researcher's judgment comes very much into play.

Longitudinal Research

As the name suggests, longitudinal research involves collecting data on a group of students over a long period of time, perhaps as long as 30 or 40 years. Sanborn (1978) believes that the term "longitudinal research" frightens some individuals because of the time involved. He believes that it is most useful to think about this form of research as a method for providing answers to immediate questions, such as how many graduates got jobs. He also suggests that the usual idea that longitudinal research requires expensive, laborious procedures need not be true. In agencies such as schools, colleges and universities, and prisons and rehabilitation agencies, some data are collected routinely over time. In many instances, additional data collection could occur within the usual data collection framework with little difficulty.

Sanborn (1978) indicates that planning longitudinal research studies begins with considering the agency's goals for its clientele. If these goals are not well defined, this would be the first step in the design of the study. Out of these goals, criteria to be assessed in the longitudinal study will emerge. Generally, these are of two types: attitudes, beliefs, or satisfaction, and behavioral or personality change. To illustrate, a longitudinal study might try to determine whether clients at a mental health center were satisfied with the services they received and the degree to which they believe those services have helped them with various adjustment problems. On the other hand, the researchers might look at their personal adjustment (jobs held, marital relationships, etc.). Sanborn suggests that a variety of data sources and types be used in longitudinal research. It is also suggested that using different types of criteria may be worth considering.

Once goals and criteria for judging outcomes are established, counselors should carefully document their activites that relate to the goals, identify sources of data that will relate to the client group, plan for repeated assessments, and analyze data as they are generated.

Longitudinal research studies offer school and college counselors, and others who have client groups, an excellent means of establishing that counseling services have a meaningful impact. One question that must be asked when planning longitudinal research is how long the data collection should continue. Sanborn (1978) suggests that one answer to this can be drawn from how long we expect to make an impact. It is unrealistic to expect a counseling intervention in the elementary school to have a life-long impact, and thus follow-up through high school may be a sufficient period for the study. However, there are also practical matters to consider when planning data collection. A concern about the reasonableness of the data collection period must be addressed.

STUDENT LEARNING EXERCISE

Indicate that a statement is true by circling T or false by circling F.

1. The one group, pretest-posttest design is a true experimental group.   T   F
2. Extensive research designs are easy to use in an applied setting.   T   F
3. A baseline in an $n = 1$ design must consist of two observations of the target behavior.   T   F
4. A is the baseline phase in the A-B design.   T   F
5. It is inappropriate to have more than one intervention in an intensive design study.   T   F
6. Multiple baseline designs are those that require that at least three baseline periods be established prior to intervention.   T   F
7. Correlational designs give indications of relationships, not cause and effect.   T   F
8. Longitudinal designs answer only long-term problems.   T   F
9. A recidivism study in a penal instituion would probably employ survey techniques.   T   F
10. Process evaluation focuses on variables that influence outcome.   T   F

RESEARCH RESULTS AND THE COUNSELING PROFESSION

Since the mid-1970s, there has been a great deal of controversy regarding the meaning of research to the counseling profession. In 1978, Goldman, writing in the introduction to his edited book on research for counselors, stated that "all authors in this book, to varying extents, agree with the position that much or most of the research published in the counseling field has made little contribution to practice in the field" (p. 3). Recently, Goldman (1986) restated this point and reiterated that the reason research has not made a great contribution to the counseling field is not because of research per se, but because of the type of research being done. Goldman (1978, 1986) has recommended that we deemphasize research that focuses on groups, relies on paper and pencil measures, puts too much emphasis on objectification of data, relies heavily on complex statistical methods, and relies too heavily on experimental designs.

The title to one of Krumboltz's (1986) recent articles clearly denotes that his point of view differs from that of Goldman. The title is "Research is a Very Good Thing." Krumboltz makes the point that literally dozens of techniques now employed by counselors grow out of the traditional scientific tradition. Krumboltz does make the point that research deserves to be criticized and that many research studies are trivial or seriously flawed. He even goes as far as to state, "Most research studies contribute nothing to the field and waste the time of readers, researchers, and editors" (p. 161). Krumboltz also agrees with Goldman that research needs to focus more on individuals, although he does not endorse deemphasizing extensive designs.

Krumboltz's position regarding research seems to be the more prudent one, since many counseling techniques, including the basic interviewing skills taught to most students, almost all of the so-called behavioral and cognitive behavioral techniques, many of the current ideas about groups, and so forth, have come forth from research efforts. The trick, it seems, is to be able to weed through the studies that are being produced and take from them those that produce worthwhile data, not to discard the proverbial baby with the bath water. Lichtenberg's (1986) comment about counselors and research seems relevant here. He wrote, "They [counselors] would be empirical in their practice and accountable for their interventions through awareness of counseling and behavior change procedures showing evidence of effectiveness or promise and of factor mediating or mitigating therapeutic change. Minimally, such practitioners would be good consumers of research" (p. 366).

EVALUATION

In the introduction to this chapter, it was suggested that from a technical point of view, evaluation utilizes the methodology of research. The differences between the two processes lie in the basic purposes for which they are conducted, their link to theory, and their concern with generalizability. To reiterate, evaluation originates to inform the decision-making process, is likely to be tied to practical concerns (as opposed to theoretical ones), and is not as concerned about generalization of findings to other settings as is research. In the evaluation process, investigators use extensive and intensive designs, correlational methodology, and survey techniques. This section will deal in more detail with the purposes of research, the models of evaluation that may be utilized to achieve these purposes, and the link between evaluation and accountability.

Purposes of Evaluation

Earlier in the chapter, it was noted that evaluation is conducted for the purpose of informing the decision-making process. Anderson and Ball (1978) have elaborated on this idea and generated six purposes. The first is to determine whether a program should be installed. In this type of evaluation, attempts are made to determine the need or demand for a particular service or program (Posavec & Carey, 1985). Gathering data about program continuation or expansion is the second type of evaluation. The essential question answered in this evaluation is, "Does the program work?" Third, and closely related to one and two, is to inform the decision-making process as a group modifies a program. The fourth and fifth purposes stated by Anderson and Ball could be called public relations purposes, since one involves rallying support for a program and the other rallying the opposition. The sixth purpose of evaluation is more in keeping with the purpose of research—to contribute to our understanding of sociological and psychological processes.

Program evaluators may pursue all or a few of these purposes simultaneously. They may ask four types of questions, two of which have already been alluded to in the preceding paragraph. One of these questions, "What is the need for this program?" is answered by examining the socioeconomic profile of a community, looking at the peculiar needs of a community with regard to the type of program being comtemplated, and trying to ascertain what type of program would be most attractive to potential consumers (Posavac & Carey, 1985).

The second type of question to be answered deals with the processes of the program: "Is the program, as designed and implemented, serving the target population?" To answer this question, a number of subquestions must also be answered, including, "Are sufficient numbers of clients from the target group being attracted to the program?" "How does the workload match that expected when the program was planned?" and "Are there differences among the staff in terms of time and energy spent on the program?" (Posavec & Carey, 1985). Note that the effectiveness of the program does not come up in process evaluation.

The third and fourth questions relate to effectiveness and efficiency. Summative, or outcome, evaluation relates to the gains to the client group in the program, and efficiency issues relate to the cost of the program, particularly the cost per unit of outcome. An individually oriented counseling program might be proven effective, but the costs relative to the gains might be high. A group counseling program might achieve the same ends at a lower cost.

Blocher (1987) has identified eight steps in the evaluation process. These are paraphrased below, and a ninth step has been added.

1. Identify the purpose of the evaluation, including the decisions that need to be made.
2. Determine who will make the decisions once the evaluation data are collected.
3. Determine what criteria will be used to make decisions. How will the decision makers decide whether a program is successful or unsuccessful?
4. Determine relevant sources of process and outcome data about the program being evaluated.
5. Design methods for collecting data, including data about comparison groups or programs.
6. Collect the needed data.
7. Analyze the data.
8. Interpret the data and present it to the appropriate individuals.
9. Make decisions about program continuation, revision, etc.

The actual process of evaluation should begin when a program is being planned. Specific goals and objectives make outcome evaluation easier. Job descriptions, role relations, documentation of decision-making processes, clear budget statements, etc., ease process evaluation as well. Clear timelines for goal attainment can also be instrumental in determining when evaluations should be scheduled. Finally, the purposes and questions to be answered will determine the model of evaluation to be employed.

Evaluation and Accountability

During the 1970s, it became clear that educational, mental health, and other social programs were not going to be funded in many places unless they could demonstrate their value. This age of accountability provided a tremendous impetus to the evaluation movement. In terms of counselors, referendums in California and Massachussetts, and recessions in many of our industrial states and more recently our agricultural states, resulted in reduction in force (RIF) in schools and other public institutions where counselors are employed. Public Law 94-63 requires that mental health centers funded by federal funds document many of their activities and spend no less than 2% of their funds on program evaluation (Peterson & Burck, 1982). As Posavac and Carey (1985) state, "No professional is above being held accountable. . . . Increasingly, respect and status have to be earned by performance, not by certification or status" (p. 19).

Peterson and Burck (1982) suggest that there are five basic elements in an accountability model for human services programs. These are:

- Diagnosis of needs
- Prescription of a plan of action
- Therapeutic, educational, and training processes in accord with plan of action
- Outputs in the form of new skills, knowledge, and attitudes gained by clients
- Outcomes that are the result of clients utilizing their newly acquired competencies

The evaluation models and approaches discussed in the preceding section would, of course, lend themselves to documenting the worth of a program. Given the current demand for accountability, counselors involved in program development would be well advised to plan for evaluation in the program planning process.

STUDENT LEARNING EXERCISE

Indicate that a statement is true by circling T or false by circling F.

1. Research results are embraced generally as a way of selecting the correct counseling technique to use.   T   F
2. Outcome evaluation is equivalent to summative evaluation.   T   F
3. Formative evaluation is equivalent to summative evaluation.   T   F
4. In the best approach to evaluation, outcomes as well as contributing forces would be examined.   T   F

SUMMARY

Research and evaluation have much in common, but can be distinguished on a number of grounds. Typically, evaluation occurs in the field, while research is likely to occur in a more controlled environment. Research is more concerned with generalizability of results than is evaluation, since the focus of most evaluation efforts is on the worthiness of local programs. However, both research and evaluation are wedded to the scientific tradition in that, if used properly, they can provide counselors with empirical support for their approaches.

The major research designs that counselors employ are extensive, intensive, correlational, longitudinal, and descriptive. Both extensive and intensive designs lend themselves to detecting cause-and-effect relationships if they are carried out properly; the other designs are less useful in this regard. All these designs can be used in evaluation efforts.

There is some debate about the utility of empirical data in the counseling field, with some contending that little of worth has emerged from our research and evaluation and others holding the opposite position. There is little debate, however, about the need to systematically document the value of our programs and to be accountable, however. Recent years have seen the elimination of counseling programs in which counselors have not been accountable.

REVIEW QUESTIONS

1. Compare and contrast research and evaluation, paying particular attention to their purposes.
2. Extensive and intensive designs both get high marks from a scientific point of view. Why?
3. Give several examples of the use of correlational research by a practitioner.
4. Give several examples of the use of survey research designs by practitioners.
5. Contrast A-B-A-B designs and multiple baseline intensive designs in terms of their strengths and limitations.
6. Tell how an intensive design could be used as an evaluational device by a counselor.
7. Contrast process and outcome evaluation approaches. What types of evaluation designs lend themselves to each?
8. How can the techniques/designs identified in this chapter be used as the basis for establishing counselor accountability?

REFERENCES

Anderson, S. B., & Ball, J. (1978). *The professional practice of program evaluation.* San Francisco: Jossey-Bass.

Anton, J. L. (1978). Studying individual change. In L. Goldman (Ed.), *Research methods for counselors: Practical approaches in field settings* (pp. 117–154). New York: John Wiley and Sons.

Asher, J. W. (1976). *Educational research and evaluation methods.* Toronto: Little, Brown and Company.

Bardo, H. R., Cody, J. J., & Bryson, S. L. (1978). Evaluation of guidance programs: Call the question. *Personnel and Guidance Journal, 57,* 204–209.

Blocher, D. H. (1987). *The professional counselor.* New York: Macmillan.

Burck, H. D. (1978). Evaluating programs: Models and strategies. In L. Goldman (Ed.), *Research methods for counselors: Practical approaches in field settings* (pp. 177–202). New York: John Wiley and Sons.

Campbell, D. T., & Stanley, J. G. (1963). *Experimental and quasi-experimental designs for research.* Chicago: Rand McNally.

Cozby, P. C. (1981). *Methods in behavioral research* (2nd ed.). Palo Alto, CA: Mayfield Publishing Company.

Drew, C. J., & Hardman, M. L. (1985). *Designing and conducting behavioral research.* New York: Pergamon.

Goldman, L. (1978). Introduction and point of view. In L. Goldman (Ed.), *Research methods for counselors: Practical approaches in field settings* (pp. 3–26). New York: John Wiley and Sons.

Goldman, L. (1986). Research and evaluation. In M. D. Lewis, R. L. Hayes, & J. A. Lewis (Eds.), *An introduction to the counseling profession* (pp. 278–300). Itasca, IL: F. E. Peacock.

Hersen, M., & Barlow, D. H. (1976). *Single case experimental designs: Strategies for studying behavior change.* New York: Pergamon.

Krumboltz, J. D. (1986). Research is a very good thing. *The Counseling Psychologist, 14,* 152–158.

Lichtenberg, J. W. (1986). Counseling research: Irrelevant or ignored? *Journal of Counseling and Development, 64,* 365–360.

Peterson, G. W., & Burck, H. D. (1982). A competency approach to accountability in human services programs. *Personnel and Guidance Journal, 60,* 491–495.

Popham, W. J. (1975). *Educational evaluation.* Englewood Cliffs, NJ: Prentice-Hall.

Posavac, E. J., & Carey, R. G. (1985). *Program evaluation: Methods and case studies.* Englewood Cliffs, NJ: Prentice-Hall.

Sanborn, M. P. (1978). Longitudinal research: Studies in a developmental framework. In L. Goldman (Ed.), *Research methods for counselors: Practical approaches in field settings* (pp. 203–232). New York: John Wiley and Sons.

Tawney, J. W., & Gast, D. L. (1984). *Single subject research in special education.* Columbus, OH: Charles E. Merrill.

16

Career Issues
for Counselors

GOAL OF THE CHAPTER

The purpose of this chapter is to look beyond entry into the counseling profession to the promises and pitfalls of a counseling career.

CHAPTER PREVIEW

1. Stages in a counseling career will be portrayed.
2. Strategies for growth as a counselor will be proposed.
3. Advancement in a counseling career will be outlined.
4. Occupational stress or burnout will be described along with other threats to counselors' physical and mental health.
5. Strategies for burnout prevention will be discussed.
6. Time management, networking, and mentoring will be discussed as specific career advancement strategies.

INTRODUCTION

Early in a counselor preparation program the emphasis is on introducing the profession to students with the hope of stimulating interest in its mission. A training program can be looked on as a socialization process in which professional norms are conveyed along with some of the ritual involved in being a member of the professional group.

With a commitment to join the profession follows the need to learn the theories and techniques used. Much information needs to be amassed and synthesized even prior to working with the first "real" client. As this process continues, personal enthusiasm for the work increases, followed by a commitment to continue growth after graduate school.

The first counseling job can be unsettling; most counselors do not feel fully prepared to do the work assigned. Entry-level preparation is useful, since it gets beginners started. However, the development of a competent counselor is an ongoing process. In most cases the full potential of a counselor will not be realized for many years.

Regrettably, all counselors do not meet their potential in the years following entry into the profession. With some the quality of service they offer to clients actually deteriorates. In part this may have been supported unknowingly by the reluctance of counselor educators to forewarn counselors-in-training of the frustrations and disappointments commonly experienced after entry into the profession (Freudenberger & Richelson, 1980).

Again, the reality of being a counselor makes one realize quickly that a caseload of real clients is much more of a challenge than a friend in a counseling class role-playing a client or the internship caseload, which is often carefully selected by a supervisor. Passages in an extended counseling career are not easy. This chapter will attempt to provide an overview of career issues following entry. The processes and pitfalls to being more fully formed as a help-giver will be portrayed.

PHASES IN A COUNSELING CAREER

Once graduates from an entry-level program become employed, they usually must complete an initial probationary period during which they are scrutinized by the employer and they in turn evaluate the appropriateness of the placement for themselves. The objective of this period is to test the counselor's work identity as she or he attempts to conform to the standards of the employer. Crites (1976) argues that most new employees, no matter how carefully they made their career plans and choices, find that a new job is not quite what they expected; they must make a series of adjustments in order to cope with its demands. All too often beginning employees are on their own as they struggle with the changes and surprises attached to a new job.

Levinson and his associates (1978) note that most younger employees are not immediately accepted as equals by veteran employees. Rather, they are often treated as apprentices, not as peers. It seems that it takes time to earn collegial respect. Thus, beginning a new job as a young adult can be stressful.

Entry-level performance is judged by self and others on a number of dimensions: (1) quality and quantity of work, (2) steadiness of effort, (3) ability to listen and follow instructions, and (4) ability to sustain effort or display stamina. While demonstrating these qualities, a new employee must also maintain interpersonal relationships with co-workers and supervisors (Oetting & Miller, 1977).

Both the formal and the informal parts of the probationary period end when a worker is judged to be capable of independent work. With this increased confidence in his or her ability from others, the new counselor is more easily able to assume responsibility for clients without close reliance on the support of supervisors. Still, approval from supervisors and peers must be earned.

When a counselor has been accepted as a peer and trusted by supervisors, he or she enters a period in which career advancement becomes an attainable goal. In order to move toward this goal, the individual must recognize advancement opportunities, their requirements, and how in the future one can obtain one of those positions. One can then begin to work to attain promotions and other changes connected to a career development plan.

Career paths of counselors are rarely steady and direct. Most go through a cycle of periods of energy/achievement, stagnation, and even decreased effectiveness. Super (1984) describes how a worker's emotional involvement in a job tends to increase or decrease at different stages of life. For example, between 40 and 45 (midlife transition) a male's job is of less importance to him emotionally than at earlier and possibly later times.

As one progresses through different adult stages entry-level training will become dated, possibly obsolete. Retooling and revitalization will remain constant needs.

While a small number of counselors may be dismissed early in their careers, more will self-select themselves out of the profession. Still others will wither in the profession, becoming "dead wood"; they emerge as problems to themselves and to the profession.

WHAT IT TAKES TO SURVIVE AND GROW AS A COUNSELOR

Assuming Responsibility for One's Own Career Development

Chapter 3 described a career as an individual's life-long involvement with work. A distinction can be made between "career-oriented" and "job-oriented" counselors. Career-oriented counselors develop a more comprehensive attitude toward their employment than their job-oriented counterparts. The latter are concerned primarily with what is expected of them from others in the present—what they must do to retain employment. They rarely think beyond present issues and problems. They rarely visualize different work roles for themselves. Career-oriented individuals take a broad view of themselves and work, synthesizing the social roles they play within many time dimensions.

Career-oriented counselors are interested in career pathing, that is, the process of planning routes along which their careers will follow; this includes the consideration of important occupational choices, work tasks selected while employed, and self-development activities (Gutteridge, 1976). Most professionals, and particularly counselors, rarely work for an organization that assumes responsibility for employee career pathing; professionals must do this for themselves.

In his discussion of adult development, Gould (1978) identifies the true beginning of adulthood as when one realizes that what a person becomes is entirely up to that individual. Prior to that time individuals believe that powerful parental-like figures know how one should perform; and if one does what he or she is supposed to do, rewards will follow. Thus, people waste much time attempting to conform to imaginary standards and pathways instead of getting down to business and taking control of their own lives.

If a counselor begins to assume responsibility for his or her career development, the chances for success in that career are greater (Scheele, 1979). This responsibility begins with planning. Time is set aside regularly to think about current affairs and the promises and risks for the future.

Planning to Be a Successful Counselor

At first glance occupational success seems to be tied to the process of career advancement. The more successful one becomes, the more one achieves promotions, titles, higher salary, and status. However, Howes' (1981) analysis of operational definitions for success in empirical research identifies job satisfaction as the most often-used index. This makes sense, since satisfaction is a subjective evaluation of experience, one intrinsically tied to a sense of well-being that ultimately becomes more important than impressing others and amassing material wealth.

Anticipating change in the profession and changes for oneself can add to an individual's chances for success, whether success is defined as promotions, wealth, or job satisfaction. Learning about options, present and future, makes sense. This becomes more than simply storing information; it becomes making a commitment to the learning of information-seeking skills that can be applied to one's own personal and professional development.

Developmental changes within an individual are also worth noting. At age 30 one's job will have a personal context entirely different from what it will have at age 45 or beyond. Anticipating personal passages, as described in Chapter 2, will soften the adjustments required. For example, at age 30 a person is often ready to settle into a permanent position for the first time; at age 45 a worker may be interested in developing new skills following an intense appraisal of his competitiveness with younger colleagues (Super & Thompson, 1981).

Selecting a Quality Employer

When faced with the anxiety of job-seeking, the counselor-in-training may find it difficult to envision being offered several positions at one time and needing to decide which job offer to accept. Nevertheless this does happen, and the job-seeker must develop a set of criteria to use in evaluating job possibilities (see Table 16.1). Amico (1981) notes that professional growth, not financial gain, is the prime reason for workers to seek job changes. Professional growth may also be an important criterion for one's first job. Starting salary is another important criterion. Most counselors work for public agencies, and these that often give annual raises in the form of a percentage of salary increase. Thus, the basis for salary increments over many years is the initial salary accepted.

Good employers do more for workers than offer salary and salary increases. It is wise to judge a prospective employer on his or her record for improving employee productivity and enhancing the quality of the workplace. Since professional competence is developed throughout life, the training and development opportunities offered by the organization are important. Through them personal needs can be satisfied as skills keep pace with changes at the workplace. The best chance of improved effectiveness for the counseling practitioner is achieved through continuous supervision and feedback on the job.

There will be times in the career of a counselor when evidence confirms

Table 16.1 What to Look For in a Job

Salary
Fringe benefits
Special fringes (e.g., supplemental retirement plan)
Opportunity for advancement
Formal supervision
Supervisory feedback past probation period
Availability of mentors
Adequate support staff (e.g., clerical)
Automated office (e.g., computers, word processors, etc.)
Peer review/feedback
Support for continuing education
Employer respect for personal/family commitments
Pleasant physical environment
Strong financial support of agency/organization
Promotion and retention based on merit
Staff and supervisors free of personal problems
Absence of worker factions/cliques
Conscientious reimbursement of employee business expenses
Access to professional and legal counsel
Job satisfaction of other employees.

the inability of one's current employer to contribute substantially to continued professional development. It is then time to move on; the factors described in this section re-emerge as criteria in the selection of the next employer.

Doing One's Job Well

Most will agree that the basis for career advancement rests on doing one's current job well. In appraising an employee's suitability for promotion, employers look for potential to fill the role defined in the next position; they rarely encourage or advance an already mediocre employee.

The following profile of the valued employee is based on a synthesis of the personnel management literature. Such an employee (1) is neither too political nor apolitical, (2) demonstrates energy and enthusiasm, (3) is a "team player," (4) is able to meet quotas and deadlines, (5) has no known bad habits that could embarrass the organization (e.g., alcohol abuse, promiscuity, etc.), (6) is even-tempered, (7) makes few mistakes and learns from mistakes made, (8) accepts constructive feedback, (9) can communicate both orally and through written documents, and (10) seems to share the same goals as the organization.

Doing one's job well may not seem very attractive at times; most job descriptions, especially those of employees with the least seniority, include some unpleasant tasks. Sometimes being an employee is like being drafted into the armed services or being "forced" to take a graduate course simply because it is "required." Reframing such experiences can open up new opportunities for learning that would otherwise have gone unnoticed (Sheele, 1979). It's like saying, "I don't like being here, but while I have to be, how can I make the most of it and get the most out of this time in my life?" The alternative to this is saying, "I don't want to be here, and I'll be darned if I'm going to give them the satisfaction of seeing me comply with something I've already decided I can't stand." As described in Chapter 3, one statement is a coping device, the other is self-defeating.

Preserving Mental Health and Job Effectiveness

Research on counselor/therapist mental health, while not extensive, provides a glimpse of the emotional problems faced by members of the allied helping professions. When a counselor seeks the assistance of another therapist, it is usually to (1) work on a relationship difficulty (e.g., poor marriage), or (2) deal with problem emotions (usually depression) or (3) cope with an alcohol or drug problem (Deutsch, 1985). While some of these problems may result from long-standing personal traits, it is believed that the work of counselors makes them susceptible to problems of this sort.

Watkins (1983) describes some of the intrapersonal and interpersonal hazards of being a counselor. The counselor's or therapist's role in the community isolates him or her emotionally therapist/counselor while paradoxically taking away personal privacy. This difficulty can be compounded by poor boundary management between one's private/personal life and one's professional life. For example, counselors are likely to maintain poor domestic relations (Watkins, 1983) by treating their spouses, friends, and children as they treat their clients. Most of us remember how our friends reacted when we first learned to reflect feelings in a counseling techniques class and tried it on them. In most cases our friends saw this behavior as unauthentic. Most family members and intimate friends do not respond well when the interpretations and procedures designed for clinical use are used on them; they feel manipulated and offended, and such practices are often perceived as an attempt to preserve a subordinate role for the loved one.

Gilbertson, Larson, and Powell (1978) explain such counselor behavior as a result of one's need to accept the identity of therapist. Switching identities back and forth from counselor to family member can be difficult. Just being a counselor requires great amounts of energy in empathizing with troubled persons and helping them solve their problems. These dificulties can lead to a form of work-related exhaustion called "burnout."

Coping with Counselor Burnout

Like most forms of occupational stress, burnout is an extremely serious health problem; next to infectious diseases and illness resulting from environmental pollution, work-related stress is viewed as the most serious health hazard facing society today (Kasl, 1978). In addition, since burnout is the single most discussed reason for the deterioration of service from experienced and once effective therapists and counselors, it is a major professional concern as well (Maslach, 1982; Perlman & Hartman, 1982).

Burnout is most often defined as a syndrome, prevalent in the human services professions, in which practitioners manifest a complex set of symptoms—some physiological, others attitudinal and behavioral in nature (Spicuzza & DeVoe, 1982). Freudenberger (1974) believes that burnout is best described as physical and emotional exhaustion. Faced with the demands of their work, human service professionals simply wear out over time, becoming less effective, even inoperative. This form of exhaustion is special in that ordinary rest periods do not relieve the fatigue. A counselor may retire for the day only to awaken the following morning still depleted of energy. The burned-out counselor is different from a lazy one; to "burn out," a person must have been "on fire." Burned-out counselors are often the ones who before burnout sought additional responsibilities and responded to requests for additional service (Freudenberger & Richelson, 1980). It is the deterioration in energy and enthusiasm for the job in the course of a career that marks the presence of burnout.

As this exhaustion progresses, other changes occur. Maslach (1976) reported that the social service workers she interviewed tried to deal with their occupational stress by distancing themselves from their clients. These help-givers became increasingly more negative and cynical in their attitudes, often dehumanizing their clients when discussing them. Maslach also found that burn-out was correlated with increased use of alcohol, emotional problems, and suicide. Freudenberger (1974) drew an analogy between these symptoms and what has come to be known as "battle fatigue." Again, the pressures and challenges of the helping professions place such demands on an individual that without some plan to buffer oneself from such pressures, and without a plan to renew and revitalize one's energy, more than likely a dedicated counselor (one who is "on fire") will evenutally burn out.

Stressors Affecting the Helping Professions.   Factors that produce stress in individuals are called stressors. Stressors that affect counselors and other human service workers include (1) overwork, (2) money issues, (3) job politics, (4) boredom, and (5) lack of control over client outcomes (Forney, Wallace-Schultzman, & Wiggers, 1982). Maher (1980) pinpoints lack of felt control over client outcome as the principal stressor for therapists. He also adds as stressors (1) long working hours, (2) a difficult caseload, (3) poor working relationships, (4) role ambiguity (no clear role description), and (5) role expansion (repeatedly assigned additional duties). Stressors on counselors are summarized in Table 16.2. In general, the longer the list of stressors, the more rapid and intense should be the burnout.

The Stress-Prone Counselor.   It can be assumed that all professional help-givers will be exposed to the stressors being discussed, but it is not clear whether

Table 16.2   Counselor Stressors

Work-related
   Intense interpersonal contacts
   Insensitive administration at work
   Not part of the policy-making process
   Peer isolation
   Results of work often unknown
   Inadequate feedback/supervision
   Low salary/economic hardships
   Role ambiguity
   Qualitative work overload

Personal
   Too idealistic
   Merge work/nonwork (poor boundaries)
   Poor marriages
   Life too public
   Cannot set boundaries
   High expectations

or not certain personality characteristics in the worker may make that person more susceptible to burnout. Melendez and DeGuzman (1983) believe that no one trait predisposes a person to rapid burnout. Freudenerger and Richelson (1980) state that naiveté and excessive idealism come closest to predicting burnout. Aloofness and distance from one's family may also be related to burnout (Small, Small, Assure, & Moore, 1969). Maslach (1982) believes that introverted, unassertive, impatient, intolerant, and conventional individuals as well as those lacking self-confidence are the most susceptible to burnout. In general, negative life events (e.g., divorce, problems with children, natural disasters) promote and aggravate burnout (Justice, Gold, & Klein, 1981).

Type A behavior often is associated with individuals most likely to become stressed (Keenan & McBain, 1979). Friedman and Rosenman (1974) characterize Type A behavior as manifesting the following: hard-driving effort, striving for achievement, competitiveness, aggressiveness, haste, impatience, restlessness, alertness, and hurried motor movements. Time consciousness best represents the Type A person. For example, the Type A person is always in a hurry, cannot wait in line, is impatient with the speed at which others respond, likes to work on several tasks at one time, and often interrupts others and finishes for them what they are trying to say.

Arguments have raged for years about the relationship between Type A behavior and coronary heart disease. Type A behavior is supposed to predict susceptibility to coronary heart disease, which in turn is viewed as a stress-related disease. Diamond's review of the literature (1982) suggests that hostility is a major component of Type A personalities. One might conclude that any or all these personality dimensions may make a counselor more stress-prone. Focusing only on the clearly observable, we can say that the stress-prone counselor will work long hours, take little time off, manage a difficult caseload, and maintain poor working relationships with peers (Maher, 1983). Thus, personality characteristics that explain such behavior enter into the effort to control this damaging situation.

Antidotes for Burnout.   Reducing burnout among counselors best proceeds with the recognition that this syndrome is a protective mechanism, an attempt to insulate oneself from the physical and emotional damage resulting from occupational stress. It seems wise to begin treating burnout by first reducing contact with the factors causing the stress. Where such stressors cannot be eliminated or reduced (e.g., a caseload of difficult clients), buffers need to be put in place to reduce the impact of those stressors (see Table 16.3).

The most discussed and promising buffer for occupational stress among helping professionals seems to be social support, given by primary partners at home and by colleagues at work (Cooper & Marshall, 1978; Levi, 1978; Kyriacou, 1981; Spicuzza & DeVoe, 1982). Social support means more than merely having someone to talk to; it works best when family and work colleagues recognize the potential for burnout and actively plan to maintain an emotional atmosphere that permits acceptance of work-related strain. Watkins (1983) thinks associa-

Table 16.3 Antidotes to Counselor Burnout

Time and boundary management
Detached concern for clients
Work sharing and job rotation
Supervision for professional development
More effective peer/supervisor feedback
See counseling as a job not a "calling"
Cultivate nonwork friendships
Realism about the power of counseling interventions
Written professional development plan
Join a social support/mutual aid group
Treat spouse and children as different from clients
Improve body image
See health as holistic
Preserve privacy better
Cultivate hobbies/take vacations
Reevaluate personal/professional ambitions

tion with "healthy souls" in particular helps ward off burnout, since interacting with well-adjusted individuals enhances the mental development and well-being of the professional help-giver.

Support at work might take the form of a mutual help group that has a formal structure, has clearly identified members, and meets regularly. Silverman (1980) describes such groups as providing assistance on a variety of fronts. First, these groups disseminate information that can be used in problem solving. For example, stressors in the workplace can be identified, as can escape routes from them. In addition, such groups might provide material assistance if needed; more often they will make earnest attempts to maintain an emotional climate in which members feel cared for and supported. It is also important for the group to recognize when a colleague is in crisis and to help mobilize aid rapidly to confront problems before they are compounded. For example, a colleague in the midst of a deteriorating marriage often is not asked to talk about his situation. Friends and colleagues are reluctant to interfere in personal business. The person in crisis may begin to drink excessively as his marriage continues to decline. If this negative behavior is not stopped, employment may be jeopardized. A support group hopefully would recognize and treat a problem before it progressed that far.

Just as a support group can prevent burnout, training programs might help reduce the risk of rapid burnout for new helping professionals by providing realistic rather than idealized views of their professions (Savicki & Cooley, 1982). The overall adjustment of most new employees seems best served by realistic job previews (Dugoni & Ilgen, 1981).

Since loss of energy is one of the major symptoms of burnout, the conservation of physical and psychological energy becomes an obvious antidote. Maher's review of important theoretical positions (1983) from Freud to Durkheim supports the notion that humans do not have unlimited energy and stamina. Counselors must make choices regarding situations they should avoid in order to conserve their energy. The conservation of energy includes taking time off from work—"mental health days" and vacations. In addition, social services workers, according to Maher, need to understand what factors in themselves and their lifestyles help create energy. One example might be an investment club in which colleagues pool money for purchasing securities. Seeing the value of investments rise and fall can be entertaining and exciting, that is, if they rise more than they fall.

Probably the most commonly recommended antidote to stress, and thus burnout, is the regular incorporation of relaxation into one's lifestyle. Benson (1975) has provided an extremely popular review of various techniques aimed at relieving stress and tension. He offers a simple meditative technique that engages the body's "relaxation response"; Benson says it is biologically opposite of the arousal response, called stress. It is Benson's thesis that contemporary society has erroneously devalued the "the relaxation response" and has failed to teach people strategies for relaxing, as earlier civilizations did. The helping professionals need to compensate for this attitude by offering systematic instruction or practice in such techniques as biofeedback, meditation, progressive relaxation, yoga, and so forth.

Keeping Counselors Healthy

It can be argued that reliance on any one strategy or set of techniques to cope with stress will inevitably be fruitless, since stress and subsequent burnout are related to a complex array of lifestyle factors. Ultimate success in coping with stress, especially for those already damaged by it, lies in making lifestyle changes that not only help avoid illness but also promote increased states of wellness.

It is important for counselors to recognize that stress is not simply a synonym for nervous tension; stress is a biological response, centering on the mobilization of the endocrine system, that is intended to help organisms cope with the challenges and demands of life. It is a form of arousal that can have devastating effects on personal health if not intelligently managed (Selye, 1976). The personal and social cost of allowing individuals to slowly undergo a process of biological destruction, as is the case in imprudent maintenance of stress states, is simply unacceptable.

In recent years periodicals have been filled with articles describing how companies have attempted to keep their employees healthy. The cost of developing managers and technical specialists (e.g., engineers and applied scientists) is simply too great to allow such resources to be squandered by ignoring unhealthy lifestyle habits among these workers. The same is true for people in the social service professions. Thus, stress management becomes equated with lifestyle management, where serious attention is given to habits and behaviors that affect illness, death, health, or wellness. In this regard, Romano (1984) identifies the following as behaviors in need of careful attention: diet, physical exercise, and cigarette smoking.

Succeeding in the Counseling Profession Through Proper Nutrition.
Vast amounts of material are published each year regarding diet. While many opinions exist to the contrary, there still seems to be an emerging consensus concerning what foods one should eat and what substances one should avoid consuming in order to be healthy (Lapple, 1975; Mahoney & Mahoney, 1976; Pritikin, 1980; Brody, 1983; Haas, 1983).

Basically, a healthy diet is one that:

1. Greatly minimizes the intake of all fat, in particular animal fat.
2. Relies on complex, "slow-burning" carbohydrates (starches) as the principal nutritional base; these include fruits, vegetables, and whole grains.
3. Greatly minimizes the intake of simple carbohydrates (sweets); these include processed foods, principally those that have a high percentage of refined sugar.
4. Restricts the intake of high protein foods below average levels for industrialized nations. This means lowered amounts of all meats and seafood, especially red meats.
5. Pays attention to the kinds of additives or manmade chemicals—in particular those that are known to cause cancer—found especially in processed foods.
6. Minimizes the consumption of alcohol and caffeine.
7. Reduces or eliminates smoking. Breaking the smoking habit can have significant health benefits even if one quits in his or her 50s or 60s (Cooper, 1985).
8. Includes the frequent intake of fluids, especially water.
9. Spreads the eating schedule across the entire day, with an emphasis on smaller, more frequent meals, especially early in the work day.

This view of nutrition can be understood by drawing a simple analogy between food and fuel (Haas, 1983). Some foods are clean-burning fuels; others are "dirty," with many toxic by-products that tax bodily mechanisms trying to remove such poisons. Complex carbohydrates (starches) are clean-burning; fats and proteins are not. Toxic substances within the body, even in minute doses, are irritants to tissue, thus increasing the risk of cancer and other diseases.

The benefits of proper nutrition go beyond the delay or avoidance of health problems; increased well-being, both physical and psychological, can result. Such benefits include:

1. Better weight control, which in turn can lead to a more positive body image and greater self-esteem.

2. Increased attractiveness to others, which can result in increased social effectiveness.

3. Greater energy through more efficient oxygen exchange in the cardio-vascular system.

4. Fewer digestion problems, which in turn lead to fewer sleep and rest problems.

5. Less risk of sudden death (heart attack) along with increased enjoyment of physical fitness activities.

Brody (1985) provides a vivid description of how employment demands interfere with sound nutrition. The time pressure associated with work encourage the skipping of especially important meals (breakfast and lunch) and overeating at other times. The lack of access in most workplaces to nutritious foods forces the overuse of high and nutritionally "empty" calories, often dispensed through machines. Such practices can rob counselors of health and energy, which in turn reduces their ability to help clients.

Succeeding in the Counseling Profession Through Increased Physical Fitness. In general, physical fitness is defined according to an individual's endurance (stamina), strength, and flexibility. Also relevant are balance, weight control, and muscular definition (Schwartz, 1982). Of these factors, the most important according to many different experts is cardiovascular endurance. The only real way one can become physically fit is through exercise.

Physically fit employees are more valuable. It is important to understand that physical fitness for workers is different from physical fitness for athletes.

McCullagh (1984) notes that part of the "fitness revolution" that began several decades ago is the emphasis on life-long pursuits that promote physical fitness. Called "lifesports," these include such activities as swimming, racketball, running, bicycling, and other sports that promote cardiovascular fitness while being enjoyable and habitual.

Cardiovascular fitness is developed through what is called aeorbic exercise (Cooper, 1970). Aerobic means "living in air." Aerobic exercise is any activity that exercises the heart (raises the heartbeat to 70% maximum rate) but is not so strenuous that it causes an oxygen deficit so the participant becomes out of breath. An aerobic exercise regimen is one that exercises the heart in such a way for a minimum of 20 minutes three or four times a week.

Such exercise, while beneficial, is not without risk (see Table 16.4). Every year hundreds of people experience sudden death (heart attack) while exercising; most of these are middle-aged individuals. However, in almost all cases (Cooper, 1985) autopsies confirm that coronary heart disease (usually hardening of the arteries) was present over a long period of time before death. For this reason Cooper (1985) recommends an ECG stress test, particularly for exercisers over age 40.

Table 16.4   Popular Forms of Aerobic Exercise

Type	Advantages	Disadvantages
Aerobic dance	Widely available Fun	Some instructors lack expertise Injuries increase when studio is crowded
Cross-country skiing	Achieves best conditioning Aesthetic and fun	Requires skill Snow and trails often not available Can get lost in woods and bad storms
Cycling	Enjoyable	Dangerous in traffic Equipment often expensive Dependent on dry weather
Indoor exercise (rowing/cycling)	Safe in bad weather Readily available	Boring Can become irregular
Racket/handball	Fun	Encourages Type A personalities Access limited Requires a partner Injuries common; protect eyes
Running/jogging	Very popular Strengthens bones Easy access	Injuries to joints On roads can be dangerous Easy to overdo
Swimming	Safe in a pool Few injuries possible Good while recovering from injuries	Requires skill Does not strengthen bones Infections (eyes/ears)
Walking	Safe Aesthetic/interesting Can provide social contact	Low aerobic effect/must walk fast or longer Requires considerable time

CAREER ADVANCEMENT FOR COUNSELORS

Research suggests that physical fitness training contributes significantly to one's improved mood, self-concept, and work behavior (Folkins & Sine, 1981). Improved work behavior includes less absenteeism, reduced errors, and improved output. It would seem that career advancement should follow from this state of wellness (see Table 16.5).

Earlier in this chapter career advancement was touched on when counselor career stages were briefly reviewed. To date there is little data on what happens to counselors after their entry-level training. Two studies (Walton, 1980; Birashk & Kaczhowski, 1984) provided 10- and 13-year follow-ups of

Table 16.5 A Holistic Health Plan

Description: This outline represents a summary of the key issues discussed with regard to burnout and healthy lifestyles. Use it in constructing your own health plan.

I. Review of current health habits and important stressors
   A. Habits that are problematic.
      1. Use of exercise; general level of activity.
      2. Nutritional habits.
      3. Smoking.
      4. Unhealthy beliefs or personality traits (e.g., Type A).
   B. Stressors in own environment
      1. Complaints I have regarding daily living conditions.
      2. Complaints I have regarding my job or schooling.
      3. Disappointments in my private life.
   C. Summary evaluation of personal health habits
II. My health plan
   A. Improving my physical health to better tolerate stress
      1. My physical fitness plan.
      2. How I plan to relax.
      3. Improved eating habits.
   B. Personality improvement ideas
      1. Restructuring unhealthy ideas and beliefs.
      2. Plan to seek counseling or not.
      3. A reading plan for personal growth.
   C. Controlling stress at work and at school
      1. How I'll avoid stressors listed above (I.B.2).
      2. How to improve relationships with colleagues/supervisors.
      3. Getting control of my ambitions.
      4. My new self-image as a worker or student.
   D. Keeping change rates within limits
      1. Staggering changes to avoid the stress of too much change
   E. Improving my support network at home and with friends
      1. How to become less of a complainer.
      2. People I will support more, who can return the support.
      3. How I can improve communication with loved ones.
   F. My revised philosophy of life
      How my new health can change the way I see meaning in life.

master's level counselors who had graduated from National Defense Education Act (NDEA) Training Institutes. While the majority of these graduates accepted school counseling positions on the completion of their degrees, fewer than half remained in counseling positions a decade or so later. A few of these graduates left the counseling profession completely, returning to the classroom or entering some other field with little direct relation to counseling. A number of graduates from both studies completed doctorates in counseling, with most of these accepting university positions as counselor educators. A fair number of these subjects entered administrative positions as guidance directors in school systems or as administrators of counseling-related programs in higher education.

From this data it seems that the career paths followed by counselors are broad in the sense that they "spread out" into related fields, with higher salaries and greater status tied to additonal education. This may be the case since career ladders specific to the direct practice of counseling and related interventions are not very long, at least in comparison to other occupations. A mental health center or other agency may have several grades of employment, such as Counselor I and Counselor II. Most practicing counselors who are interested in higher pay, greater status, and more leadership and responsibility, have to leave counseling for the most part and accept administrative positions. Some exceptions to this exist, but they are few in number.

Compare this situation to careers in business administration. Lipsett (1980) has developed career path charts demonstrating the many advancement levels possible for someone with a bachelor's degree in business or accounting. Some of these charts show as many as 10 labor grades one could advance through with that degree alone. Another shows six different levels one could be promoted through in just a purchasing department.

Some changes in career direction for counselors probably are a result of personal changes that affect occupational interests and motivation for continued skill development. Stress resulting from comparisons of salary, responsibilities, and skills with other professions may provide additional incentive to leave counseling (Spicuzza & DeVoe, 1982).

Important to remember, however, is the fact that follow-up studies of counselors (Walton, 1980; Birashk & Kaczhowski, 1984) show that graduates from counselor preparation programs are usually satisfied with their training and with the direction their careers take. The chance is good, based on this evidence, that 30% to 50% of a graduating class of master's level counselors will initially be employed as counselors and remain so for more than a decade. The majority of those who seek other positions will advance in terms of salary and status by accepting positions offered to those with further education and work experience. These positions are like entry-level positions; they reflect similar patterns of career interests and worker traits or abilities, as described by the U.S. Department of Labor. (See *The Dictionary of Occupational Titles* and *The Guide for Occupational Exploration* for descriptions of the systems of both interests and worker traits.)

Table 16.6 Occupations with Worker Trait Codes Similar to Counselors

Occupational Titles	Occupation	Worker Trait Code
Religious	Christian Science Practitioner	129.107–014
	Director of Religious Activities	129.107–018
	Clergy Member	120.007–010
Counseling and Social Work	Director of Counseling	045.107–018
	Psychologist, Clinical	045.107–022

THREE STRATEGIES FOR CONTINUED CAREER GROWTH

Whether one remains a counselor or moves to another position, three popular strategies can facilitate achieving desired ends. They are effective time management, the development of networks, and the use of mentoring.

Effective Time Management

The concept of time management has been popularized in recent years (e.g., Mackenzie, 1972; Lakein, 1973) as a label for a set of strategies that allow people to be more judicious in how they invest their time.

When people with many different responsibilities say they "never get anything done," what they usually mean is that they never get around to doing really important things. Most overworked people manage to complete many small tasks every day; their discontent often centers on their failure to achieve long-range goals. Part of the reason for this is that important, long-range goals constitute the basis for ultimate self-esteem. So much is at stake in meeting these goals that most become anxious when just thinking about them. To escape this anxiety, people avoid dealing with these big life goals, substituting instead work on immediate, less significant tasks. This process becomes one of the most common forms of procrastination.

Time management strategies help people overcome procrastination. The emphasis in most time management approaches (Mackenzie, 1972; Lakein, 1973) is on goal identification, prioritizing of goals, identification of activities that waste time, and planning work space and time. The emphasis is on not only what one should do, but also what one should avoid doing. When this process works, people find that more time becomes devoted to large, significant life goals. The goals, sometimes overwhelming by their dimension, become more attainable as people learn how to divide them into smaller, more easily achieved parts.

Not all people need to learn better time management methods; many have largely uninvolved lives in which boredom is more of a problem than is overwork. Time management is especially relevant for such workers as full-time homemakers, dual career couples, business managers, and others that have a tendency to take on too many responsibilities. Many excellent references on time management are available at most book stores.

The Development of Networks

Networking is merely a recent term used to describe the process of making connections with other people, especially those that can be useful in the future. Rawlins and Rawlins (1983) identify a number of benefits resulting from the development of helpful contacts. People who can help us procure needed resources, important information, job leads, opportunities, and feedback can be identified and filed for future reference. Actively networking with others builds participation and self-confidence. Here are some common networking suggestions for beginning counselors:

1. Have a plan on how to file names, addresses, and telephone numbers of people you meet. Select a system (e.g., rolodex or computer file) that can be updated and reorganized easily.

2. Make an effort to get others to know you and remember your name, address, and phone number. Purchase business cards if your employer does not supply them. Use them liberally.

3. Make a specific effort to get people to remember you. For example, some professional counselors are rarely without postcards or "speed memos" so they can easily send a note of appreciation or a request for additional information to someone of potential use in the future.

4. Volunteer to work on committees or groups that will enable you to meet influential people. For example, being a student representative on a college committee may give you access to a dean or vice president from whom most graduate students ordinarily would not get recognition. Scheele (1979) calls this "catapulting" in that one can be projected over barriers that ordinarily block access to important people.

5. Maintain your own identity but remember that psychologically healthy and adaptive people display a broad wardrobe of behaviors; they are not limited to being just a certain way, regardless of circumstances. Practice acquiring such a wardrobe by forcing yourself into a variety of social situations.

The Use of Mentoring

The recent labeling of an older person as a "mentor"—one who has an impact on the career and personal development of a younger person—seems to have begun with Levinson and his associates (1978). A mentor is not viewed either as a parental figure or as a peer; rather a mentor is seen as an individual roughly one-half generation older than another who teaches, advises, opens doors for, encourages, promotes, cuts red tape for, show the politics and subtleties of the job to, believes in, and thus helps a protegé succeed (Rawlins & Rawlins, 1983).

Having a mentor has been linked to faster promotions and higher pay for the protegé (Roche, 1979). The relationship, however, is mutually beneficial; mentors often get some of the same benefits as protegés. These may include (1) job advancement, (2) creation of a support system, (3) access to system resources, (4) more control over the work environment, (5) development of a reputation, and (6) personal satisfaction (Gerstein, 1985).

Alleman, Cochran, Doverspike, and Newman (1984) note from their review of mentoring literature that same-sex and opposite-sex mentor-protegé relationships are very similar. Mentors look for potential, not similarity with self, in the protegé. Protegés, though, perceive mentors as like themselves. These same authors note that mentoring in part can become a solution for workers who have reached a plateau (i.e., are not promotable); such employees can contribute much to the organization and to their own meaning by preparing another generation for the work to be done.

SUMMARY

In this chapter issues related to the career development of counselors were briefly reviewed in order to provide the counselor-in-training with a preview of some of the issues and potential problems that might arise. It is hoped that readers will be better prepared both to avoid the damaging aspects of counseling-related work and to capitalize on opportunities available for advancement. In particular, burnout was treated at length as one of the major threats to quality service in the profession. Strategies for avoiding burnout and other health-related problems were explored.

REVIEW QUESTIONS

1. Describe the typical stages in a counseling career.
2. What are some common views regarding success as a counselor?
3. What are some typical mental health problems of counselors?
4. What is burnout? How can it be treated? How can it be minimized?
5. What are the characteristics of the stress-prone counselor?
6. What are some ways to remain healthy as a counselor?
7. What are some advancement strategies for counselors?

REFERENCES

Alleman, E., Cochran, J., Doverspike, J., & Newman, I. (1984). Enriching mentoring relationships. *Personnel and Guidance Journal, 62*(6), 329–332.

Amico, A. M. (1981). Computerized career information. *Personnel Journal, 60*(8), 632–633.

Benson, H. (1975) *The relaxation response.* New York: Morrow.

Birashk, B., & Kaczhowski, H. (1984). Career patterns of NDEA elementary school counselors. *Vocational Guidance Quarterly, 32*(4), 263–270.

Brody, J. (1983) *Jane Brody's guide to personal health.* New York: Avon.

Brody, J. (1985) *Good food book: Living the high-carbohydrate way.* New York: W. W. Norton.

Cooper, K. H. (1970). *The new aerobics.* New York: Bantam Books.

Cooper, K. H. (1985). *Running without fear: How to reduce the risk of heart attack and sudden death during aerobic exercise.* New York: M. Evans and Company.

Cooper, C. L., & Marshall, J. (1978). Sources of managerial and white collar stress. In C. L. Cooper and R. Payne (Eds.), *Stress at work* (pp. 81–105). New York: John Wiley and Sons.

Crites, J. O. (1976). A comprehensive model of career development in early adulthood. *Journal of Vocational Behavior, 9(1),* 105–118.

Deutsch, C. (1985). A survey of therapists' personal problems and treatment. *Professional Psychology: Research and Practice, 16*(2), 305–315.

Diamond, E. L. (1982). The role of anger and hostility in essential hypertension and coronary heart disease. *Psychological Bulletin, 92*(2), 410–433.

Dugoni, B. L., & Ilgen, D. R. (1981). Realistic job previews and the adjustment of new employees. *Academy of Management Journal, 24*(3), 579–591.

Folkins, C. H., & Sime, W. E. (1981). Physical fitness training and mental health. *American Psychologist, 36*(4), 373–389.

Forney, D., Wallace-Schultzman, F., & Wiggers, T. T. (1982). Burnout among career development professionals: Preliminary findings and implications. *Personnel and Guidance Journal, 60*(7), 435–439.

Freudenberger, H. J. (1974). Staff burnout. *Journal of Social Issues, 30*(1), 159–165.

Freudenberger, H. J., & Richelson, G. (1980). *Burnout: The high cost of achievement.* Garden City, NY: Doubleday.

Friedman, M. & Rosenman, R. H. (1974). *Type A behavior and your heart.* Greenwich, CN: Fawcett Publications.

Gerstein, M. (1985). Mentoring: An age old practice in a knowledge-based society. *Journal of Counseling and Development, 64*(2), 156–157.

Gilbertson, D., Larson, C., & Powell, T. (1978). Therapist burnout: Perspectives on critical issues. *Social Casework, 59,* 563–565.

Gutteridge, T. G. (1976). *Organizational career development: State of the practice.* Buffalo, NY: SUNY-Buffalo Human Resources Institute.

Haas, R. (1983). *Eat to win.* New York: New American Library.

Howes, N. J. (1981). Characteristics of career success: An additional input to selecting candidates for professional programs. *Journal of Vocational Behavior, 18,* 277–288.

Justice, B., Gold, R. S., & Klein, J. P. (1981). Life events and burnout. *Journal of Psychology, 108,* 219–226.

Kasl, S. V. (1978). Epidemiological contributions to the study of work stress. In C. L. Cooper and R. Payne (Eds.), *Stress at work* (pp. 3–50). New York: John Wiley and Sons.

Keenan, A., & McBain, G. D. (1979). Effects of Type A behavior, intolerance of ambiguity, and locus of control on the relationship between role stress and work-related outcomes. *Journal of Occupational Psychology, 52,* 277–285.

Kyriacou, C. (1981). Social support and occupational stress among schoolteachers. *Educational Studies, 7.* 55–60.

Lakein, A. (1973). *How to get control of your time and your life.* New York: New American Library.

Lapplé, F. M. (1978). *Diet for a small planet.* New York: Ballantine Books.

Levi, L. (1978). *Quality of the working environment: Protection and promotion of occupational mental health.* (Reports from the Laboratory for Clinical Stress Research, No. 88, 25p).

Levinson, D. J. , Darrow, C. N., Klein, E. B., Levinson, M. H., McKee, B. (1978). *The seasons of a man's life.* New York: Ballantine Books.

Lipsett, L. (1980). Career path charts as counseling aids. *Vocational Guidance Quarterly, 28*(4), 360–368.

Mackenzie, R. A. (1972). *The time trap.* New York: McGraw-Hill.

Maher, E. L. (1983). Burnout and commitment: A theoretical alternative. *Personnel and Guidance Journal, 61*(7), 390–393.

Mahoney, K., & Mahoney, M. J. (1976). *Permanent weight control.* New York: W. W. Norton.

Maslach, C. (1976). Burnout. *Human Behavior, 5,* 16–22.

Maslach, C. (1982). *Burnout: The cost of caring.* Englewood Cliffs, NJ: Prentice-Hall.

McCullagh, J. C. (1984). *The complete bicycle fitness book.* New York: Warner Books.

Melendez, W. A., & DeGuzman, R. M. (1983). *Burnout: The new academic disease.* Washington, DC: Clearing House on Higher Education.

Morgan, M. A., Hall, D. T., & Martin, A. (1979). Career development strategies in industry: Where are we and where should we be? *Personnel, 56*(2), 13–30.

Oetting, E., & Miller, C. D. (1977). Work and the disadvantaged: The work adjustment hierarchy. *Personnel and Guidance Journal, 56*(1), 29–35.

Pearson, J. M. (1982). The transition into a new job: Tasks, problems, and outcomes. *Personnel Journal, 61,* 286–290.

Perlman, B., & Hartman, E. A. (1982). Burnout: Summary and future research. *Human Relations, 35,* 283–305.

Pritikin, N., & McGrady, P. M., Jr. (1979). *The Pritikin program for diet and exercise.* New York: Grosset and Dunlap.

Rawlins, M. E., & Rawlins, L. (1983). Mentoring and networking for helping professionals. *Personnel and Guidance Journal, 62*(2), 116–118.

Roche, G. R. (1979). Much ado about mentors. *Harvard Business Review, 57*(1), 14–16, 20, 24, 26–28.

Romano, J. L. (1984). Stress management and wellness: Reaching beyond the counselor's office. *Personnel and Guidance Journal, 62*(9), 533–537.

Savicki, V., & Cooley, E. J. (1982). Implications of burnout research and theory for counselor educators. *Personnel and Guidance Journal, 60*(7), 415–419.

Scheele, A. M. (1979). *Skills for success: A guide to the top.* New York: Morrow.

Schwartz, L. (1982). *Heavyhands: The ultimate exercise.* Boston: Little, Brown.

Selye, H. (1976). *The stress of life.* New York: McGraw-Hill.

Silverman, P. R. (1980). *Mutual help groups: Organization and development.* Beverly Hills, CA: Sage Publications.

Small, I., Small, J., Assure, C., & Moore, D. (1969). The fate of the mentally ill physician. *The American Journal of Psychiatry, 125*(10), 1333–1342.

Spicuzza, F. J., & DeVoe, M. W. (1982). Burnout in the helping professions: Mutual aid groups as self-help. *Personnel and Guidance Journal, 61*(2), 95–99.

Super, D. E. (1984). Career and life development. In D. Brown & L. Brooks (Eds.), *Career choice and development.* San Francisco: Jossey-Bass, 192–234.

Super, D. E., & Thompson, A. S. (1981). *Adult career concerns inventory.* New York: Teachers College, Columbia University.

Walton, J. M. (1980). NDEA participants prepared for inner-city counseling: A ten year follow-up. *Counselor Education and Supervision, 20*(1), 50–55.

Watkins, C. E., Jr. (1983). Burnout in counseling practice: Some potential professional and personal hazzards of becoming a counselor. *Personnel and Guidance Journal, 61*(5), 304–308.

17

Unresolved Issues in the Counseling Profession: Setting Future Directions

GOAL OF THE CHAPTER

The purpose of this chapter is to present major unresolved issues confronting the counseling profession, and to make recommendations for action.

CHAPTER PREVIEW

1. Ten major unresolved issues will be discussed and recommendations made for addressing them. The issues pertain to:
   a. The use of technology.
   b. The legal basis for the profession.
   c. Empiricism and counseling practice.
   d. The future of career counseling.
   e. Training requirements.
   f. Approaches to mental health problems.
   g. Acceptance of counselors as allied health professionals.
   h. Dealing with the "back to basics" movement.
   i. Impact of the moral majority in school counseling services.
   j. Counseling services in the corporate setting.

INTRODUCTION

What should be quite clear at this juncture is that the counseling profession is in a state of flux. Many important steps have been taken, but much remains to be done. In this chapter, the unresolved issues will be discussed briefly and recommendations will be made as to how the counseling profession should proceed to deal with these issues.

Will Counselors Take Advantage of Technology to Provide Better Services to Clients?

By their very nature, counselors are people-oriented as opposed to machine- or data-oriented. As a result, many find microprocessors and other technological advances uninviting. However, many of the services offered by counselors can be greatly enhanced by the judicious use of computers. And, perhaps most importantly, the time that counselors have available to spend with clients can be greatly increased if technology is employed properly. As Sampson (1983) put it,

> While aspects of the helping process involving human relationship skills and judgment make good use of human capabilities, other aspects involving data collection, storage and retrieval, statistical computations, actuarial predictions, repetitive instruction, and clerical tasks do not make efficient use of human capabilities and can be better performed by computers. (p. 65).

So the position taken here, and previously by others (Harris-Bowlsby, 1983; Katz & Shatkin, 1983; Sampson, 1983), is that technology has two major functions: enhancing direct service and making counseling services more efficient so that more direct service can be provided.

As was pointed out in Chapter 3, computers are being widely employed to assist with the provision of educational and occupational information and with career decision-making. In Chapter 6, the application of technology in the administration, scoring, and interpretation of tests was noted. These are but three of the ways computers are enhancing counselors' direct service efforts. Sampson (1983) believes that computers can also be utilized to collect routine data from clients in intake situations, to identify appropriate referral sources, to provide computer-assisted instruction to clients with information deficits such as child-rearing techniques, to provide such intervention as systematic desensitization for phobic clients, and to provide biofeedback to aid with problems such as stress control. Sampson also suggests that it may not be outside the realm of possibility of computer programs to provide psychotherapy and that research needs to be conducted on this front as well as on the others already mentioned.

Computers can be readily adapted to perform a wide variety of tasks that now require large amounts of counselors' time in some settings. For example, the scheduling activities performed by many high school and community college counselors can be greatly facilitated by the use of a computer. After a master schedule is developed, students may, with the assistance of an advisor or counselor, construct a schedule and receive a copy of it in minutes. At the same time, the computer keeps track of the availability of spots in each class so that overscheduling will not occur.

Grade point averages can be computed, class ranks determined, transcripts printed and prepared for mailing, personalized letters developed for college admissions offices, and certain tests and inventories administered and scored on the spot. Record keeping of all types can be greatly facilitated with computerized systems. All these activities take extraordinary amounts of time when performed manually.

But the question remains: "Will these resources be embraced by counselors?" At one time, cost was a major barrier to the adoption of technological advances, but inexpensive microprocessors with capacities rivaling very large systems have for the most part removed economic barriers. Certainly the aversion of some counselors to machines has also played a part, as has the concern by some that computers will abridge the human rights of client groups by allowing access to personal data (Ibrahim, 1985) or that they will go awry in performing a routine function such as test administration or test scoring and, thus, damage the people involved (Ibrahim, 1985; Sampson & Loesch, 1985). However, one suspects that it is the issue raised by Sampson and Loesch (1985) that provides the greatest barrier to the full utilization of computers and other technological advances: training.

Sampson and Loesch (1985) note that current training standards for counselors have no stipulations regarding preparation to work with computers. They propose that the Council for Accreditation of Counseling and Related Education Program Standards (CACREP) be altered to include the following standards:

1. The development of an understanding of the relationship between computers and the services provided by counselors.
2. Supervised experiences that involve students with various types of computer-based activities.

While the above purposes are laudable and would, if adopted, prepare counselors trained in CACREP accredited programs to use computers in their work, the fact remains that many counselors are trained in nonaccredited programs, and most counselors who are currently working in the field have inadequate preparation in this area. In-service training programs are being conducted to remedy the deficiencies of the latter group, but the numbers being reached and the impact of these programs is less than optimal.

Recommendations

Given the current situation, it seems that training programs, professional organizations, and agencies that offer counseling services should embark upon a massive effort to develop computer skills in counselors. The result can only be a more effective counseling profession.

Will a Legal Basis for Counseling Be Developed?

At the outset, it should be noted that "legal basis" in the current context refers to a set of laws, policies, and regulations that recognize and support the counseling profession. The licensure and registry laws discussed in Chapter 11 are examples of one form of legal basis for a counselor, but there are many others.

In Chapter 12, counselors in educational settings were discussed and mention was made of cutbacks in counseling programs in some states. These cutbacks occurred partially because statutes were not in place that recognized the importance of school counseling and authorized funds for school counseling services. Some states have statutes that not only recognize but require school counseling services, often in the form of authorization statutes that provide monies to local school districts that underwrite counselors' salaries. In these situations, local school boards are less likely to cut back counseling programs because of pressure from local taxpayers.

State statutes are not the only area of concern. Human Resource Departments often develop personnel classification systems that include social workers and psychologists, but preclude counselors. Insurance companies often have policies that exclude counselors in private practice from receiving payments for the services they render. Accrediting agencies for community colleges may have relatively low standards for the counseling programs, and those that accredit elementary schools may have no standards at all. State boards of education may require that minimal counseling services be offered to high school students before local school districts can receive state support. Federal agencies such as the Veteran's Administration may not recognize counselors as legitimate service providers and do, in fact, preclude from their internship programs students from programs not accredited by the American Psychological Association. Other federal agencies can, and do, discriminate against counselors in a similar way.

Recommendation

The foregoing paragraph has provided some clues regarding what must be accomplished before we can state that a legal basis for the counseling profession has been established. However, what follows is an outline of the needs in this area.

I.   Statutory bases
  A. State
     1. All states must pass licensing laws for counselors.
     2. State statutes authorizing monies for schools must include funds for counselors in sufficient amounts to allow schools to develop effective counseling programs.
     3. Third-party payment at the state level must include counselors as mental health services providers.
  B. Federal
     1. Federal legislation regarding the provision of mental health services must include counselors as providers.
     2. Federal legislation pertaining to counselors (e.g., rehabilitation legislation) should recognize credentialed counselors such as certified rehabilitation counselors.
     3. Federal legislation in the future, such as National Health Insurance statutes, must recognize counselors as mental health services providers.
II. Quasi-legal policies and regulations
  A. School counseling
     1. State boards of education must mandate counseling services for students of sufficient quantity and quality to meet students' needs.
     2. Accrediting agencies must require effective counseling programs before accreditation is accorded.
     3. Local school boards must adopt policies that will require that effective counseling programs be offered.
  B. Mental health settings
     1. Federal agencies such as the Veteran's Administration must recognize counselors as legitimate mental health services providers.
     2. State personnel classifications systems must include categories for counselors.
     3. Insurance companies must recognize counselors as legitimate mental health services providers.

The cost, both in terms of money and volunteer time, is staggering. One lobbyist estimated that it would take $10,000 to make an assault on the third-party legislation in one state, even if volunteers did most of the work. In spite of the costs, there is increasing evidence that state and local professional organizations are preparing themselves to deal with developing the legal basis for the counseling profession.

Will There Be an Empirical Basis for the Practices of Counselors?

In Chapters 8, 15, and elsewhere throughout the book, the matter of the empirical support for counselors' practices has been raised. Remer (1981) indicates that counselors have an ethical, and probably a legal, responsibility to determine the effectiveness of their practices. Lewis and Hutson (1983) characterize the gap between research data and the effectiveness of counseling as a special concern for counselors. Even more recently, Comas (1986) has indicated that research is becoming increasingly important for school counseling programs and outlines a program embarked upon by the American School Counselor Association to strengthen the research basis for school counseling. What is obvious is that after a long period of debate about the importance of research to counselors (see Chapter 15), there is a growing consensus that empirical data are needed to support the counseling practice.

One of the very positive aspects of this issue is that many of the practices used by counselors are also used by psychologists, and they, as a group, tend to produce extensive research to support their activities. Counselors can, therefore, draw upon an increasingly rich body of literature regarding counseling, consultation, testing, computerized information systems, and so forth. It can also be expected that with the increasing emphasis on the importance of research findings, more research will be produced by counselors themselves.

Even with some very positive trends in the area of research, there are some problems, however. One of these is that many counselors are poorly equipped to read research unless it is extremely rudimentary in nature. Counselors accredited by CACREP must acquire some preparation in the areas of statistics and research design. Other training programs are under no similar compunction, and many require little or no research preparation.

Research training would be helpful in preparing counselors to generate research and to apply the results of research generated by others. However, strictly speaking, it is not necessary to do or read research to adopt and apply empirically based approaches if the leaders in the field who write books and articles and conduct workshops draw upon empirical data for their writings and recommendations.

The problem, as a philosopher might note, is an epistemological one. Epistemology is that branch of philsophy that deals with knowing or, more specifically, what one accepts as knowledge. For some, knowledge must be objectively derived, while for others, subjective data, including their own experiences, are sufficient grounds for knowing that something exists *or* that something works. Many counselors apparently fit into this latter category.

We may be on solid philosophical ground when we argue that our experience is as valid a source of knowledge as is empiricism, but the public of the counseling profession is not likely to accept our experiences as a valid source of data since there is usually a suspicion that the data derived from our experiences about our effectiveness tend to be self-serving.

Even if we could overcome a history of debating the worth of research, the philosophical bias against research data by some, and the deficits in the area of conducting and understanding research that some counselors have, it would still be difficult to develop an empirical basis for the practices of counselors. Group counseling, consultation, classroom guidance, parent education, and individual counseling are all complex activities and, as such, are extremely difficult to research. In most instances, designs must be very complex to accommodate the variables that may influence research outcomes, and, in all instances, numerous replications and extensions of an original research design are required to verify that a technique or approach works. The settings in which counseling activities occur makes it quite difficult to implement complex designs and to go through the extensive replications that will be necessary.

As was pointed out in Chapter 15, there are viable options to traditional research designs, such as those in which single subjects are studied. In the short run, and perhaps in the long run as well, individual counselors may have to validate their own practices using these alternatives because the likelihood of developing an empirically based set of practices seems slight, at least in the near future.

Recommendation

The beginning point for establishing an empirical basis for counseling practice is the development of an awareness of research findings of the counselor's practice. We know that there is widespread empirical support for the treatment of phobias and the development of certain social skills such as assertiveness (Rimm & Cunningham, 1985). There is also limited empirical support for most approaches to counseling. Counselors must be made aware of this support in training programs and through the publication of research review articles in professional journals.

Counselor education programs also need to develop basic research skills in counselor trainees. This is a recommendation not for extensive research and statistic training but for the development of fundamental statistical knowledge and a rudimentary understanding of research design, particularly intensive designs that can easily be taught to and applied by practicing counselors.

The current trend among journal editorial boards to require authors to discuss the practical implications of their findings should be continued and strengthened.

Will Counselors Move from a Focus on Career Planning and Counseling to One on Life Career Planning and Counseling?

In Chapter 2, an overview of some of the major theories of life development were presented. In Chapter 3, mention was made of theories of career development that exist as a subset of theories that focus on the career choice and adjustment process. Also introduced in Chapter 3 were the concepts of life career planning and counseling in which the individual is viewed holistically and all life roles are considered potentially important sources of life satisfaction. There is considerable evidence that this holistic approach is gaining acceptance, but whether it can overcome a history of counselors' focusing primarily on the career as a source of life satisfaction remains to be seen.

As noted above, one of the major barriers to adopting a stance favoring a holistic consideration of the individual is history. To be sure, some (e.g., Warnath, 1975; Hesketh, 1985) have been critical of career development theories, and some (e.g., Super, 1984, Tiedeman & Miller-Tiedeman, 1984) have advocated a more holistic approach. However, trait and factor thinking still dominates the career counseling field (Srebalus, Marinelli, & Messing, 1982), and it is probably true that an updated version of trait and factor thinking (Holland, 1985) dominates much of the research and thinking in the area of career choice and testing. This theoretical perspective provides little in the way of assistance in conceptualizing life career planning and counseling.

However, there are strong countertrends, such as an increasing emphasis on a systems perspective that views the individual as being, to some degree, interdependent with the people in his or her environment (Okun, 1984), and research that demonstrates that life roles interact to create or attenuate stress (Zunker, 1986).

It is also important to note that career development theorists such as Super (1984) have set the stage for an approach to life career planning by altering theoretical perspectives and by developing some practical tools such as the Life Career Rainbow to help clients conceputalize their various life roles.

A number of tasks will probably have to be completed before counselors will embrace life career counseling over career counseling. Human develoment and career development theories still need integration.

More importantly, counselors need to be provided with tools that will enable them to engage in life career planning and counseling. Currently, there are numerous interest inventories, occupational aptitude tests, computer programs, and so forth that can be used with client groups to facilitate career planning. In addition, the Department of Labor turns out reams of labor force information, ranging from job descriptions to trends in a given occupational field. There are few instruments and very little other information that would support counselors in their life career counseling efforts.

It also seems that a change in perspective among counselors regarding the importance of work will need to occur before life career counseling will become the norm. Thirteen years ago, Warnath (1975) challenged the assumption that work is the central life role, an assumption that permeates many career development theories, especially those career counseling approaches that fail to consider other life roles. However, many counselors still hold this assumption.

Recommendation

The counseling profession should increasingly emphasize life career planning as opposed to planning educational, career, or marital/family roles separately. The major implication of this is that current theories need to be reconsidered and refocused on all life roles and that new tools (e.g., inventories) need to be developed to assist counselors in this endeavor.

Will the Training Requirements of Counselors Continue to Escalate?

Twenty years ago, few programs required more than 30 hours in their counselor preparation programs. As indicated in Chapter 11, the current recommendation is that a program consist of no less than 48 semester hours (CACREP, 1985), and there is increasing pressure to increase this to 60 hours plus internship experiences to make counselor training commensurate with that of master's degree level psychologists and social workers who have completed a master's in social work.

It is also obvious from much of the material that was presented throughout the book that counselors are under great pressure to provide computerized services, to conduct research, and to provide services to a variety of groups including some (e.g., drug abusers) that would require specialized training.

The counterpressure regarding the length of the training program comes from those who contend that there is little support for lengthening training programs beyond the point that would guarantee minimum competencies, that many counselors, particularly those in schools, are not paid well enough to justify a lengthy training program, and that counselors such as those in employment offices perform a relatively limited set of functions that can be learned in a shorter training program.

One underlying issue that pervades the training issue is the fear among some counselor educators that student enrollment will decline if programs are lengthened and their programs will be threatened. It is interesting to note that many programs that have lengthened their training programs have seen demand go up. However, this may not be true in all cases.

Length of training and quality of training, while related, are not necessarily highly correlated. Some argue that before lengthening programs, every effort should be made to increase the quality of offerings. While there is validity to the argument that quality should be stressed, there is also validity to the argument that in programs training individuals to work with diverse populations, a lengthy program is required.

A number of factors will ultimately play a role in determining the length of training programs for counselors. One of those will be that the general public, legislators, insurance companies, and other professional groups seem to have accepted the mentality that longer is better. On the other hand, counselor preparation programs may have difficulty attracting and preparing enough counselors for some settings, particularly school counseling. Informal reports indicate that some training programs have a great deal of difficulty attracting school counseling candidates, and the escalating demand for those professionals in some sections of the country may bring pressure to keep training programs relatively short.

Recommendation

The counseling profession must do what the other helping professions have not done, namely document the relationship between length of the training period and counselor effectiveness, particularly if it intends to resist the trend toward longer training programs. In the pursuit of this documentation, the overall goal must be to develop guidelines for educating counselors who can most effectively serve the public.

What Will Be the Posture of the Counseling Profession with Regard to Its Approach to Mental Health Problems?

The counseling profession has long asserted that its primary perspective toward mental health problems is a developmental, preventive one, that is, a focus on helping normally functioning people develop the skills and attitudes that will protect them from mental health problems. This perspective is exemplified in the ASCA role statement discussed in Chapter 12, which places a great deal of emphasis on noncounseling roles for school counselors.

What was pointed out in Chapter 12, and what was probably obvious in Chapters 13 and 14 as well, is that counselors are increasingly oriented toward secondary mental health prevention approaches, that is, working with clients who already have mental health problems to prevent these problems from becoming more serious (e.g., problem drinker versus alcoholic). It also should be noted that there is little current pressure for counselors to move into tertiary mental health prevention efforts, that is to work with severely emotionally disabled clients to keep their problems from becoming life threatening.

It has been the history of mental health movements in this country, and perhaps rightly so, that the more severely disturbed individuals receive greatest priority. Because there appear to be more people needing mental health services at this time (one in five is the current estimate), and since more of these people are in client groups served by counselors, the pressure is on to serve these people first. The analogy of the squeaking wheel getting greased comes to mind here.

There may be a bit more status associated with treating individuals with personal problems than there is in organizing a recreational program that will prevent juvenile delinquency. And even if status is not an issue, there is a certain amount of ambiguity associated with preventive efforts since the procedures for conducting these activities are not as well delineated, and the outcomes are more difficult to judge.

It is also probably true that the skill most emphasized in counselor education programs is individual counseling, which by its very nature is usually a secondary prevention activity. A recent survey reveals that group counseling also probably receives considerable attention and that consultation and group educational activities are attended to least among the major intervention strategies (Brown, 1986).

While there is pressure from groups such as the American School Counselor Association to emphasize primary preventive activities, one can only wonder whether a secondary mental health prevention perspective will become the primary orientation of the profession.

Recommendation

In spite of pressure to pursue remedial activities, the counseling profession should continue to emphasize preventive approaches and should redouble its efforts to gain support for these activities.

Will Counselors Be Fully Accepted as Mental Health Practitioners?

As noted in Chapters 1 and 11, counselors have only recently begun to flex their professional muscles and demand legal recognition, third-party payments, equal employment opportunities, and so forth. These moves have not gone unnoticed and, in fact, have resulted in opposition from other mental health professionals. In some instances, the opposition from a single group has led to enhanced relationships among counselors and other groups of mental health workers. For example, social workers and counselors in Texas and Ohio worked together to achieve certain legislative goals.

Drawing upon the somewhat stormy historical relationship of psychology and psychiatry to predict the future, one could readily conclude that relationships among the various mental health groups are likely to be adversarial as counselors make increasing demands. One could also draw upon this same history to predict that if counselors are diligent and persist in their efforts, they will eventually win most of these battles.

There is a more peaceful scenario than the one depicted above. It was mentioned earlier that in some states professional group coalitions have been formed to advance the causes of all the groups concerned. It may well be that increased communication among various professional organizations can reduce tension in some instances and eliminate it in others. At this point, it is unclear whether all groups of mental health professions are willing to engage in these types of discussions, but what is clear is that discussions aimed at finding a common ground have not often been tried.

Recommendation

The counseling profession should take the lead in trying to develop collaborative working relationships with other mental health practitioners such as psychologists and social workers. The focus of these activities should be to find common concerns and to develop joint approaches to solving these problems.

Should collaborative approaches fail, counselors must be prepared to assert themselves in the legislative arena, in the courts, and through direct lobbying with those agencies that regulate mental health services.

Will School Counselors, in the Face of the Back to Basics
Movement in This Country, Be Able to Maintain Their Current
Emphasis on Psychological Development?

Educational achievement has become a dominant social and political issue in this country. The result, in some instances, has been that students have become virtually unavailable to counselors because making them available would reduce the amount of time spent on academic pursuits. In other instances, counselors have been pressured to show the educational relevance of their functioning as it relates to educational achievement. Since the concern regarding educational achievement seems unlikely to abate in the near future, the impact on the functioning of counselors needs careful monitoring.

Recommendation

Counselors in school settings need to demonstrate the link between psychological well-being and academic performance. This can probably be done most effectively through research and evaluation efforts and individual school efforts to monitor the impact of programs designed to foster personal development.

Will Counselors in Educational Settings Be Influenced by the
"Moral Majority" and Their Concerns About Secular Humanism
and the Family's Right to Provide Guidance to Their Youngsters?

In some states laws have been introduced that would preclude counselors from counseling students without parental permission. In some cases counselors have been criticized for engaging in a godless practice because of values clarification exercises that did not result in conclusions consistent with a fundamental interpretation of the Bible. Some materials used by counselors to encourage rational decision-making have also been criticized. The overall impact of these assaults will undoubtedly influence practice in some communities. The long-term impact of right-wing extremism is a continuing matter of concern.

Recommendation

Counselors in educational institutions need to militantly defend their right to offer services to school-age students. However, counselors need to consider carefully the types of services being offered in the light of community norms and expectations in order to ensure that the necessary harmony exists between the school, the family, and the community.

What Is the Future of Counseling Services in Business and Industry?

In Chapter 14, the functioning of counselors in corporate settings was discussed. While it is true, as was suggested in that chapter, that businesses are employing counselors, the future of those services is in doubt for a number of reasons. One of these is that "bottom line" evidence regarding the value of these services has not been produced. The question of whether counseling services produce more effective employees and, thus, more profits need to be addressed.

Another concern that deserves attention is whether services, if they are offered, should be offered internally or contracted for externally? Some corporations have established internal employee assistance programs (EAPs). Others contract with mental health centers or private practitioners to offer these services. Few data are available about the relative value of counseling services, let alone the best way to deliver them.

Recommendations

Counselors need to aggressively pursue major efforts to demonstrate the worth of counseling services in the corporate setting. These efforts should focus on such key variables as employee satisfaction and retention, overall productivity and, of course, profit. Simultaneously, similar efforts need to be mounted to clarify the most efficient and effective ways to deliver services in the corporate setting.

SUMMARY

The counseling profession has made tremendous strides during the last decade, but there is much work to be done. A part of this work involves introspection on the part of the profession. Ultimately, a profession exists for only one purpose, to serve the public. Our introspection should dwell on our ability as a profession to adequately serve.

In addition to self-analysis, the counseling profession must continue to assert itself with other professional groups, with governmental agencies, and with the public at large. Counselors as individuals are often reluctant to advertise their strengths, but as a profession in a competitive environment, we cannot have the same inclination. The continued recognition and advancement of the profession rests on the ability of counselors to continue to make the difficult decisions regarding internal control and also the adeptness with which counselors present themselves to the public.

REVIEW QUESTIONS

1. What theories run through the issues listed in this chapter?
2. What concerns may groups such as psychologists have about increased recognition for counselors? How can these concerns be combatted?
3. Outline the arguments that the "moral majority" might lodge *against* school counselors.
4. Discuss the pros and cons of lengthening the training programs. Speculate about future trends in this area.
5. Corporate and mental health counselors have many similar issues confronting them. Briefly outline these issues and talk about ways of resolving them.
6. Is empirical evidence the only basis for practice? If not, list others and defend them.

REFERENCES

Accreditation of Counseling and Related Educational Programs. (1985). *Accreditation procedures manual and application for counseling and related educational programs.* Alexandria, VA: Author.

American School Counselor Association. (1981). The ASCA role statement: The practice of guidance and counseling by school counselors. *The School Counselor, 29,* 7–12.

Brown, D. (1986). Survey of training practices among master's level counselor educator training programs. Unpublished manuscript. School of Education, University of North Carolina, Chapel Hill, NC.

Comas, R. E. (1986). Research becomes increasingly vital to school counseling programs. *The ASCA Counselor, 24,* 15.

Harris-Bowlsby, J. (1983). The computer and the decider. *The Counseling Psychologist, 11,* 9–15.

Hesketh, B. (1985). In search of a conceptual framework for vocational psychology. *Journal of Counseling and Development, 64,* 26–30.

Holland, J. L. (1985). *Making vocational choices: A theory of careers* (2nd ed.). Englewood Cliffs, NJ: Prentice-Hall.

Ibrahim, F. A. (1985). Human rights and ethical issues in the use of advanced technology. *Journal of Counseling and Development, 64,* 134–135.

Katz, M. R., & Shatkin, L. (1983). Characteristics of computer assisted guidance. *The Counseling Psychologist, 11,* 15–33.

Lewis, W. A., & Hutson, S. P. (1983). The gap between research and practice in the question of counseling effectiveness. *Personnel and Guidance Journal, 61,* 532–535.

Okun, B. F. (1984). *Working with adults: Individual, family, and career development.* Monterey, CA: Brooks/Cole.

Remer, R. (1981). The counselor and research: Introduction. *Personnel and Guidance Journal, 59,* 567–571.

Rimm, D. C., & Cunningham, H. M. (1985). Behavior therapies. In S. J. Lynn & D. Garske (Eds.), *Contemporary psychotherapies: Models and methods* (pp. 220–221). Columbus, OH: Charles E. Merrill.

Sampson, J. P., Jr. (1983). An integrated approach to computer applications in counseling psychology. *The Counseling Psychologist, 11,* 65–74.

Sampson, J. P., Jr., & Loesch, L. C. (1985). Computer preparation standards for counselors and human development specialists. *Journal of Counseling and Development, 64,* 31–34.

Srebalus, D. J., Marinelli, R. P., & Messing, J. L. (1982). *Career development: Concepts and procedures.* Monterey, CA: Brooks/Cole.

Super, D. E. (1984). Career and life development. In D. Brown & L. Brooks (Eds.), *Career choice and development: Applying contemporary theories to practice* (pp. 192–234). San Francisco: Jossey-Bass.

Tiedeman, D. R., & Miller-Tiedeman, A. (1984). Career decision making: An individualistic perspective. In D. Brown & L. Brooks (Eds.), *Career choice and development: Applying contemporary theory to practice* (pp. 235–280). San Francisco: Jossey-Bass.

Warnath, C. F. (1975). Vocational theories: Directions to nowhere. *Personnel and Guidance Journal, 53,* 422–428.

Zunker, V. G. (1986). *Career counseling: Applied concepts of life planning* (2nd ed.). Monterey, CA: Brooks/Cole.

Appendix A

Ethical Standards, American Association for Counseling and Development

(Approved by Executive Committee upon referral of the Board of Directors, January 17, 1981.)

PREAMBLE

The American Personnel and Guidance Association is an educational, scientific, and professional organization whose members are dedicated to the enhancement of the worth, dignity, potential, and uniqueness of each individual and thus to the service of society.

The Association recognizes that the role definitions and work settings of its members include a wide variety of academic disciplines, levels of academic preparation and agency services. This diversity reflects the breadth of the Association's interest and influence. It also poses challenging complexities in efforts to set standards for the performance of members, desired requisite preparation or practice, and supporting social, legal, and ethical controls.

The specification of ethical standards enables the Association to clarify to present and future members and to those served by members, the nature of ethical responsibilities held in common by its members.

Note. From *Ethical Standards—American Association for Counseling and Development* by American Association for Counseling and Development, 1981, Alexandria, VA. Copyright AACD. Reprinted by permission. No further reproduction authorized without further permission of AACD.

The existence of such standards serves to stimulate greater concern by members for their own professional functioning and for the conduct of fellow professionals such as counselors, guidance and student personnel workers, and others in the helping professions. As the ethical code of the Association, this document establishes principles that define the ethical behavior of Association members.

SECTION A: GENERAL

1. The member influences the development of the profession by continuous efforts to improve professional practices, teaching, services, and research. Professional growth is continuous throughout the member's career and is exemplified by the development of a philosophy that explains why and how a member functions in the helping relationship. Members must gather data on their effectiveness and be guided by the findings.

2. The member has a responsibility both to the individual who is served and to the institution within which the service is performed to maintain high standards of professional conduct. The member strives to maintain the highest levels of professional services offered to the individuals to be served. The member also strives to assist the agency, organization, or institution in providing the highest caliber of professional services. The acceptance of employment in an institution implies that the member is in agreement with the general policies and principles of the institution. Therefore the professional activities of the member are also in accord with the objectives of the institution. If, despite concerned efforts, the member cannot reach agreement with the employer as to acceptable standards of conduct that allow for changes in institutional policy conducive to the positive growth and development of clients, then terminating the affiliation should be seriously considered.

3. Ethical behavior among professional associates, both members and nonmembers, must be expected at all times. When information is possessed that raises doubt as to the ethical behavior of professional colleagues, whether Association members or not, the member must take action to attempt to rectify such a condition. Such action shall use the institution's channels first and then use procedures established by the state Branch, Division, or Association.

4. The member neither claims nor implies professional qualifications exceeding those possessed and is responsible for correcting any misrepresentations of these qualifications by others.

5. In establishing fees for professional counseling services, members must consider the financial status of clients and locality. In the event that the established fee structure is inappropriate for a client, assistance must be provided in finding comparable services of acceptable cost.

6. When members provide information to the public or to subordinates, peers or supervisors, they have a responsibility to ensure that the content is general, unidentified client information that is accurate, unbiased, and consists of objective, factual data.

7. With regard to the delivery of professional services, members should accept only those positions for which they are professionally qualified.

8. In the counseling relationship the counselor is aware of the intimacy of the relationship and maintains respect for the client and avoids engaging in activities that seek to meet the counselor's personal needs at the expense of that client. Through awareness of the negative impact of both racial and sexual stereotyping and discrimination, the counselor guards the individual rights and personal dignity of the client in the counseling relationship.

SECTION B: COUNSELING RELATIONSHIP

This section refers to practices and procedures of individual and/or group counseling relationships.

The member must recognize the need for client freedom of choice. Under those circumstances where this is not possible, the member must apprise clients of restrictions that may limit their freedom of choice.

1. The member's *primary* obligation is to respect the integrity and promote the welfare of the client(s), whether the client(s) is (are) assisted individually or in a group relationship. In a group setting, the member is also responsible for taking reasonable precautions to protect individuals from physical and/or psychological trauma resulting from interaction within the group.

2. The counseling relationship and information resulting therefrom [must] be kept confidential, consistent with the obligations of the member as a professional person. In a group counseling setting, the counselor must set a norm of confidentiality regarding all group participants' disclosures.

3. If an individual is already in a counseling relationship with another professional person, the member [must] not enter into a counseling relationship without first contacting and receiving the approval of that other professional. If the member discovers that the client is in another counseling relationship after the counseling relationship begins, the member must gain the consent of the other professional or terminate the relationship, unless the client elects to terminate the other relationship.

4. When the client's condition indicates that there is clear and imminent danger to the client or others, the member must take reasonable per-

sonal action or inform responsible authorities. Consultation with other professionals must be used where possible. The assumption of responsibility for the client's behavior must be taken only after careful deliberation. The client must be involved in the resumption of responsibility as quickly as possible.

5. Records of the counseling relationship, including interview notes, test data, correspondence, tape recordings, and other documents, are to be considered professional information for use in counseling and they should not be considered a part of the records of the institution or agency in which the counselor is employed unless specified by state statute or regulation. Revelation to others of counseling material must occur only upon the expressed consent of the client.

6. Use of data derived from a counseling relationship for purposes of counselor training or research shall be confined to content that can be disguised to ensure full protection of the identity of the subject client.

7. The member must inform the client of the purposes, goals, techniques, rules of procedure and limitations that may affect the relationship at or before the time that the counseling relationship is entered.

8. The member must screen prospective group participants, especially when the emphasis is on self-understanding and growth through self-disclosure. The member must maintain an awareness of the group participants' compatibility throughout the life of the group.

9. The member may choose to consult with any other professionally competent person about a client. In choosing a consultant, the member must avoid placing the consultant in a conflict of interest situation that would preclude the consultant's being a proper party to the member's efforts to help the client.

10. If the member determines an inability to be of professional assistance to the client, the member must either avoid initiating the counseling relationship or immediately terminate that relationship. In either event, the member must suggest appropriate alternatives. (The member must be knowledgeable about referral resources so that a satisfactory referral can be initiated.) In the event the client declines the suggested referral, the member is not obligated to continue the relationship.

11. When the member has other relationships, particularly of an administrative, supervisory and/or evaluative nature with an individual seeking counseling services, the member must not serve as the counselor but should refer the individual to another professional. Only in instances where such an alternative is unavailable and where the individual's situation warrants counseling intervention should the member enter into and/or maintain a counseling relationship. Dual relationships with clients that might impair the member's objectivity and professional judgment (e.g., as with close friends or relatives, sexual intimacies with any

client) must be avoided and/or the counseling relationship terminated through referral to another competent professional.

12. All experimental methods of treatment must be clearly indicated to prospective recipients and safety precautions are to be adhered to by the member.

13. When the member is engaged in short-term group treatment/training programs (e.g., marathons and other encounter-type or growth groups), the member ensures that there is professional assistance available during and following the group experience.

14. Should the member be engaged in a work setting that calls for any variation from the above statements, the member is obligated to consult with other professionals whenever possible to consider justifiable alternatives.

SECTION C: MEASUREMENT AND EVALUATION

The primary purpose of educational and psychological testing is to provide descriptive measures that are objective and interpretable in either comparative or absolute terms. The member must recognize the need to interpret the statements that follow as applying to the whole range of appraisal techniques including test and nontest data. Test results constitute only one of a variety of pertinent sources of information for personnel, guidance, and counseling decisions.

1. The member must provide specific orientation or information to the examinee(s) prior to and following the test administration so that the results of testing may be placed in proper perspective with other relevant factors. In so doing, the member must recognize the effects of socioeconomic, ethnic and cultural factors on test scores. It is the member's professional responsibility to use additional unvalidated information carefully in modifying interpretation of the test results.

2. In selecting tests for use in a given situation or with a particular client, the member must consider carefully the specific validity, reliability, and appropriateness of the test(s). *General* validity, reliability and the like may be questioned legally as well as ethically when tests are used for vocational and educational selection, placement, or counseling.

3. When making any statements to the public about tests and testing, the member must give accurate information and avoid false claims or misconceptions. Special efforts are often required to avoid unwarranted connotations of such terms as *IQ* and *grade equivalent scores*.

4. Different tests demand different levels of competence for administration, scoring, and interpretation. Members must recognize the limits of their

competence and perform only those functions for which they are prepared.

5. Tests must be administered under the same conditions that were established in their standardization. When tests are not administered under standard conditions or when unusual behavior or irregularities occur during the testing session, those conditions must be noted and the results designated as invalid or of questionable validity. Unsupervised or inadequately supervised test-taking, such as the use of tests through the mails, is considered unethical. On the other hand, the use of instruments that are so designed or standardized to be self-administered and self-scored, such as interest inventories, is to be encouraged.

6. The meaningfulness of test results used in personnel, guidance, and counseling functions generally depends on the examinee's unfamiliarity with the specific items on the test. Any prior coaching or dissemination of the test materials can invalidate test results. Therefore, test security is one of the professional obligations of the member. Conditions that produce most favorable test results must be made known to the examinee.

7. The purpose of testing and the explicit use of the results must be made known to the examinee prior to testing. The counselor must ensure that instrument limitations are not exceeded and that periodic review and/or retesting are made to prevent client stereotyping.

8. The examinee's welfare and explicit prior understanding must be the criteria for determining the recipients of the test results. The member must see that specific interpretation accompanies any release of individual or group test data. The interpretation of test data must be related to the examinee's particular concerns.

9. The member must be cautious when interpreting the results of research instruments possessing insufficient technical data. The specific purposes for the use of such instruments must be stated explicitly to examinees.

10. The member must proceed with caution when attempting to evaluate and interpret the performance of minority group members or other persons who are not represented in the norm group on which the instrument was standardized.

11. The member must guard against the appropriation, reproduction, or modifications of published tests or parts thereof without acknowledgment and permission from the previous publisher.

12. Regarding the preparation, publication and distribution of tests, reference should be made to:
    a. *Standards for Educational and Psychological Tests and Manuals*, revised edition, 1974, published by the American Psychological Association on behalf of itself, the American Educational Research Association and the National Council on Measurement in Education.

b. The responsible use of tests: A position paper of AMEG, APGA, and NCME. *Measurement and Evaluation in Guidance*, 1972, 5, 385–388.

c. "Responsibilities of Users of Standardized Tests," APGA, *Guidepost*, October 5, 1978, pp. 5–8.

SECTION D: RESEARCH AND PUBLICATION

1. Guidelines on research with human subjects shall be adhered to, such as:

   a. *Ethical Principles in the Conduct of Research with Human Participants*, Washington, D.C.: American Psychological Association, Inc., 1973.

   b. Code of Federal Regulations, Title 45, Subtitle A, Part 46, as currently issued.

2. In planning any research activity dealing with human subjects, the member must be aware of and responsive to all pertinent ethical principles and ensure that the research problem, design, and execution are in full compliance with them.

3. Responsibility for ethical research practice lies with the principal researcher, while others involved in the research activities share ethical obligation and full responsibility for their own actions.

4. In research with human subjects, researchers are responsible for the subjects' welfare throughout the experiment and they must take all reasonable precautions to avoid causing injurious psychological, physical, or social effects on their subjects.

5. All research subjects must be informed of the purpose of the study except when withholding information or providing misinformation to them is essential to the investigation. In such research the member must be responsible for corrective action as soon as possible following completion of the research.

6. Participation in research must be voluntary. Involuntary participation is appropriate only when it can be demonstrated that participation will have no harmful effects on subjects and is essential to the investigation.

7. When reporting research results, explicit mention must be made of all variables and conditions known to the investigator that might affect the outcome of the investigation or the interpretation of the data.

8. The member must be responsible for conducting and reporting investigations in a manner that minimizes the possibility that results will be misleading.

9. The member has an obligation to make available sufficient original research data to qualified others who may wish to replicate the study.

10. When supplying data, aiding in the research of another person, reporting research results, or in making original data available, due care must

be taken to disguise the identity of the subjects in the absence of specific authorization from such subjects to do otherwise.

11. When conducting and reporting research, the member must be familiar with, and give recognition to, previous work on the topic, as well as . . . observe all copyright laws and follow the principles of giving full credit to all to whom credit is due.

12. The member must give due credit through joint authorship, acknowledgment, footnote statements, or other appropriate means to those who have contributed significantly to the research and/or publication, in accordance with such contributions.

13. The member must communicate to other members the results of any research judged to be of professional or scientific value. Results reflecting unfavorably on institutions, programs, services, or vested interests must not be withheld for such reasons.

14. If members agree to cooperate with another individual in research and/or publication, they incur an obligation to cooperate as promised in terms of punctuality of performance and with full regard to the completeness and accuracy of the information required.

15. Ethical practice requires that authors not submit the same manuscript, or one essentially similar in content, for simultaneous publication consideration by two or more journals. In addition, manuscripts published in whole or in substantial part in another journal or published work should not be submitted for publication without acknowledgment and permission from the previous publication.

SECTION E: CONSULTING

Consultation refers to a voluntary relationship between a professional helper and help-needing individual, group or social unit in which the consultant is providing help to the client(s) in defining and solving a work-related problem or potential problem with a client or client system. (This definition is adapted from Kurpius, DeWayne. Consultation theory and process: An integrated model. *Personnel and Guidance Journal,* 1978, 56.)

1. The member acting as consultant must have a high degree of self-awareness of his/her own values, knowledge, skills, limitations, and needs in entering a helping relationship that involves human and/or organizational change and . . . the focus of the relationship [must] be on the issues to be resolved and not on the person(s) presenting the problem.

2. There must be understanding and agreement between member and client for the problem definition, change goals, and predicted consequences of interventions selected.

3. The member must be reasonably certain that she/he or the organization represented has the necessary competencies and resources for giving the kind of help that is needed now or may develop later and that appropriate referral resources are available to the consultant.

4. The consulting relationship must be one in which client adaptability and growth toward self-direction are encouraged and cultivated. The member must maintain this role consistently and not become a decision maker for the client or create a future dependency on the consultant.

5. When announcing consultant availability for services, the member conscientiously adheres to the Association's *Ethical Standards*.

6. The member must refuse a private fee or other remuneration for consultation with persons who are entitled to these services through the member's employing institution or agency. The policies of a particular agency may make explicit provisions for private practice with agency clients by members of its staff. In such instances, the clients must be apprised of other options open to them should they seek private counseling services.

SECTION F: PRIVATE PRACTICE

1. The member should assist the profession by facilitating the availability of counseling services in private as well as public settings.

2. In advertising services as a private practitioner, the member must advertise the services in such a manner so as to accurately inform the public as to services, expertise, profession, and techniques of counseling in a professional manner. A member who assumes an executive leadership role in the organization shall not permit his/her name to be used in professional notices during periods when not actively engaged in the private practice of counseling.

    The member may list the following: highest relevant degree, type and level of certification or license, type and/or description of services, and other relevant information. Such information must not contain false, inaccurate, misleading, partial, out-of-context, or deceptive material or statements.

3. Members may join in partnership/corporation with other members and/or other professionals provided that each member of the partnership or corporation makes clear the separate specialties by name in compliance with the regulations of the locality.

4. A member has an obligation to withdraw from a counseling relationship if it is believed that employment will result in violation of the *Ethical Standards*. If the mental or physical condition of the member renders it difficult to carry out an effective professional relationship or if the member is discharged by the client because the counseling rela-

tionship is no longer productive for the client, then the member is obligated to terminate the counseling relationship.

5. A member must adhere to the regulations for private practice of the locality where the services are offered.

6. It is unethical to use one's institutional affiliation to recruit clients for one's private practice.

SECTION G: PERSONNEL ADMINISTRATION

It is recognized that most members are employed in public or quasi-public institutions. The functioning of a member within an institution must contribute to the goals of the institution and vice versa if either is to accomplish their respective goals or objectives. It is therefore essential that the member and the institution function in ways to (a) make the institution's goals explicit and public; (b) make the member's contribution to institutional goals specific; and (c) foster mutual accountability for goal achievement.

To accomplish these objectives, it is recognized that the member and the employer must share responsibilities in the formulation and implementation of personnel policies.

1. Members must define and describe the parameters and levels of their professional competency.

2. Members must establish interpersonal relations and working agreements with supervisors and subordinates regarding counseling or clinical relationships, confidentiality, distinction between public and private material, maintenance, and dissemination of recorded information, work load and accountability. Working agreements in each instance must be specified and made known to those concerned.

3. Members must alert their employers to conditions that may be potentially disruptive or damaging.

4. Members must inform employers of conditions that may limit their effectiveness.

5. Members must submit regularly to professional review and evaluation.

6. Members must be responsible for inservice development of self and/or staff.

7. Members must inform their staff of goals and programs.

8. Members must provide personnel practices that guarantee and enhance the rights and welfare of each recipient of their service.

9. Members must select competent persons and assign responsibilities compatible with their skills and experiences.

SECTION H: PREPARATION STANDARDS

Members who are responsible for training others must be guided by the preparation standards of the Association and relevant Division(s). The member who functions in the capacity of trainer assumes unique ethical responsibilities that frequently go beyond that of the member who does not function in a training capacity. These ethical responsibilities are outlined as follows:

1. Members must orient students to program expectations, basic skills development, and employment prospects prior to admission to the program.

2. Members in charge of learning experiences must establish programs that integrate academic study and supervised practice.

3. Members must establish a program directed toward developing students' skills, knowledge, and self-understanding, stated whenever possible in competency or performance terms.

4. Members must identify the levels of competencies of their students in compliance with relevant Division standards. These competencies must accommodate the para-professional as well as the professional.

5. Members, through continual student evaluation and appraisal, must be aware of the personal limitations of the learner that might impede future performance. The instructor must not only assist the learner in securing remedial assistance but also screen from the program those individuals who are unable to provide competent services.

6. Members must provide a program that includes training in research commensurate with levels of role functioning. Para-professional and technician-level personnel must be trained as consumers of research. In addition, these personnel must learn how to evaluate their own and their program's effectiveness. Graduate training, especially at the doctoral level, would include preparation for original research by the member.

7. Members must make students aware of the ethical responsibilities and standards of the profession.

8. Preparatory programs must encourage students to value the ideals of service to individuals and to society. In this regard, direct financial remuneration or lack thereof must not influence the quality of service rendered. Monetary considerations must not be allowed to overshadow professional and humanitarian needs.

9. Members responsible for educational programs must be skilled as teachers and practitioners.

10. Members must present thoroughly varied theoretical positions so that students may make comparisons and have the opportunity to select a position.

11. Members must develop clear policies within their educational institutions regarding field placement and the roles of the student and the instructor in such placements.

12. Members must ensure that forms of learning focusing on self-understanding or growth are voluntary, or if required as part of the education program, are made known to prospective students prior to entering the program. When the education program offers a growth experience with an emphasis on self-disclosure or other relatively intimate or personal involvement, the member must have no administrative, supervisory, or evaluating authority regarding the participant.

13. Members must conduct an educational program in keeping with the current relevant guidelines of the American Personnel and Guidance Association and its Divisions.

Appendix B

Ethical Principles of Psychologists, American Psychological Association

PREAMBLE

Psychologists respect the dignity and worth of the individual and strive for the preservation and protection of fundamental human rights. They are committed to increasing knowledge of human behavior and of people's understanding of themselves and others and to the utilization of such knowledge for the promotion of human welfare. While pursuing these objectives, they make every effort to protect the welfare of those who seek their services and of the research participants that may be the object of study. They use their skills only for purposes consistent with these values and do not knowingly permit their misuse by others. While demanding for themselves freedom of inquiry and communication, psychologists accept the responsibility this freedom requires: competence, objectivity in the application of skills, and concern for the best interests of clients, colleagues, students, research participants, and society. In the pursuit of these ideals, psychologists subscribe to principles in the following areas: 1. Responsibility, 2. Competence, 3. Moral and Legal Standards, 4. Public Statements, 5. Confidentiality, 6. Welfare of the Consumer, 7. Professional Relationships, 8. Assessment Techniques, 9. Research with Human Participants, and 10. Care and Use of Animals.

Note. From *Ethical Principles of Psychologists* by American Psychological Association, 1981, Washington, DC. Copyright 1981 by the American Psychological Association. Reprinted by permission of the publisher.

Acceptance of membership in the American Psychological Association commits the member to adherence to these principles.

Psychologists cooperate with duly constituted committees of the American Psychological Association, in particular, the Committee on Scientific and Professional Ethics and Conduct, by responding to inquiries promptly and completely. Members also respond promptly and completely to inquiries from duly constituted state association ethics committees and professional standards review committees.

PRINCIPLE 1: RESPONSIBILITY

In providing services, psychologists maintain the highest standards of their profession. They accept responsibility for the consequences of their acts and make every effort to ensure that their services are used appropriately.

a. As scientists, psychologists accept responsibility for the selection of their research topics and the methods used in investigation, analysis, and reporting. They plan their research in ways to minimize the possibility that their findings will be misleading. They provide thorough discussion of the limitations of their data, especially where their work touches on social policy or might be construed to the detriment of persons in specific age, sex, ethnic, socioeconomic, or other social groups. In publishing reports of their work, they never suppress disconfirming data, and they acknowledge the existence of alternative hypotheses and explanations of their findings. Psychologists take credit only for work they have actually done.

b. Psychologists clarify in advance with all appropriate persons and agencies the expectations for sharing and utilizing research data. They avoid relationships that may limit their objectivity or create a conflict of interest. Interference with the milieu in which data are collected is kept to a minimum.

c. Psychologists have the responsibility to attempt to prevent distortion, misuse, or suppression of psychological findings by the institution or agency of which they are employees.

d. As members of governmental or other organizational bodies, psychologists remain accountable as individuals to the highest standards of their profession.

e. As teachers, psychologists recognize their primary obligation to help others acquire knowledge and skill. They maintain high standards of scholarship by presenting psychological information objectively, fully, and accurately.

f. As practitioners, psychologists know that they bear a heavy social responsibility because their recommendations and professional actions may alter the lives of others. They are alert to personal, social, organizational, financial, or political situations and pressures that might lead to misuse of their influence.

PRINCIPLE 2: COMPETENCE

The maintenance of high standards of competence is a responsibility shared by all psychologists in the interest of the public and the profession as a whole. Psychologists recognize the boundaries of their competence and the limitations of their techniques. They only provide services and only use techniques for which they are qualifed by training and experience. In those areas in which recognized standards do not yet exist, psychologists take whatever precautions are necessary to protect the welfare of their clients. They maintain knowledge of current scientific and professional information related to the services they render.

a. Psychologists accurately represent their competence, education, training, and experience. They claim as evidence of educational qualifications only those degrees obtained from institutions acceptable under the Bylaws and Rules of the Council of the American Psychological Association.

b. As teachers, psychologists perform their duties on the basis of careful preparation so that their instruction is accurate, current, and scholarly.

c. Psychologists recognize the need for continuing education and are open to new procedures and changes in expectations and values over time.

d. Psychologists recognize differences among people, such as those that may be associated with age, sex, socioeconomic, and ethnic backgrounds. When necessary, they obtain training, experience, or counsel to assure competent service or research relating to such persons.

e. Psychologists responsible for decisions involving individuals or policies based on test results have an understanding of psychological or educational measurement, validation problems, and test research.

f. Psychologists recognize that personal problems and conflicts may interfere with professional effectiveness. Accordingly, they refrain from undertaking any activity in which their personal problems are likely to lead to inadequate performance or harm to a client, colleague, student, or research participant. If engaged in such activity when they become aware of their personal problems, they seek competent professional assistance to determine whether they should suspend, terminate, or limit the scope of their professional and/or scientific activities.

PRINCIPLE 3: MORAL AND LEGAL STANDARDS

Psychologists' moral and ethical standards of behavior are a personal matter to the same degree as they are for any other citizen, except as these may compromise the fulfillment of their professional responsibilities or reduce the public trust in psychology and psychologists. Regarding their own behavior, psychologists are sensitive to prevailing community standards and to the possible impact that conformity to or deviation from these standards may have upon the quality of their performance as psychologists. Psychologists are also aware of the possible impact of their public behavior upon the ability of colleagues to perform their professional duties.

a. As teachers, psychologists are aware of the fact that their personal values may affect the selection and presentation of instructional materials. When dealing with topics that may give offense, they recognize and respect the diverse attitudes that students may have toward such materials.

b. As employees or employers, psychologists do not engage in or condone practices that are inhumane or that result in illegal or unjustifiable actions. Such practices include, but are not limited to, those based on considerations of race, handicap, age, gender, sexual preference, religion, or national origin in hiring, promotion, or training.

c. In their professional roles, psychologists avoid any action that will violate or diminish the legal and civil rights of clients or of others who may be affected by their actions.

d. As practitioners and researchers, psychologists act in accord with Association standards and guidelines related to practice and to the conduct of research with human beings and animals. In the ordinary course of events, psychologists adhere to relevant governmental laws and institutional regulations. When federal, state, provincial, organizational, or institutional laws, regulations, or practices are in conflict with Association standards and guidelines, psychologists make known their commitment to Association standards and guidelines and, wherever possible, work toward a resolution of the conflict. Both practitioners and researchers are concerned with the development of such legal and quasi-legal regulations as best serve the public interest, and they work toward changing existing regulations that are not beneficial to the public interest.

PRINCIPLE 4: PUBLIC STATEMENTS

Public statements, announcements of services, advertising, and promotional activities of psychologists serve the purpose of helping the public make informed judgments and choices. Psychologists represent accurately and objectively their professional qualifications, affiliations, and functions, as well as those of the institutions or organizations with which they or the statements may be associated. In public statements providing psychological information or professional opinions or providing information about the availability of psychological products, publications, and services, psychologists base their statements on scientifically acceptable psychological findings and techniques with full recognition of the limits and uncertainties of such evidence.

a. When announcing or advertising professional services, psychologists may list the following information to describe the provider and services provided: name, highest relevant academic degree earned from a regionally accredited institution, date, type, and level of certification or licensure, diplomate status, APA membership status, address, telephone number, office hours, a brief listing of the type of psychological services offered, an appropriate presentation of fee information, foreign languages spoken, and policy with regard to third-party payments. Additional relevant or important consumer information may be included if not prohibited by other sections of these Ethical Principles.

b. In announcing or advertising the availability of psychological products, publications, or services, psychologists do not present their affiliation with any organization in a manner that falsely implies sponsorship or certification by that organization. In particular and for example, psychologists do not state APA membership or fellow status in a way to suggest that such status implies specialized professional competence or qualifications. Public statements include, but are not limited to, communication by means of periodical, book, list, directory, television, radio, or motion picture. They do not contain (i) a false, fraudulent, misleading, deceptive, or unfair statement; (ii) a misinterpretation of fact or a statement likely to mislead or deceive because in context it makes only a partial disclosure of relevant facts; (iii) a testimonial from a patient regarding the quality of a psychologist's services or products; (iv) a statement intended or likely to create false or unjustified expectations of favorable results; (v) a statement implying unusual, unique, or one-of-a-kind abilities; (vi) a statement intended or likely to appeal to a client's fears, anxieties, or emotions concerning the possible results of failure to obtain the offered services; (vii) a statement concerning the comparative desirability of offered services; (viii) a statement of direct solicitation of individual clients.

c. Psychologists do not compensate or give anything of value to a representative of the press, radio, television, or other communication medium in anticipation of or in return for professional publicity in a news item. A paid advertisement must be identified as such, unless it is apparent from the context that it is a paid advertisement. If communicated to the public by use of radio or television, an advertisement is prerecorded and approved for broadcast by the psychologist, and a recording of the actual transmission is retained by the psychologist.

d. Announcements or advertisements of "personal growth groups," clinics, and agencies give a clear statement of purpose and a clear description of the experiences to be provided. The education, training, and experience of the staff members are appropriately specified.

e. Psychologists associated with the development or promotion of psychological devices, books, or other products offered for commercial sale make reasonable efforts to ensure that announcements and advertisements are presented in a professional, scientifically acceptable, and factually informative manner.

f. Psychologists do not participate for personal gain in commercial announcements or advertisements recommending to the public the purchase or use of proprietary or single-source products or services when that participation is based solely upon their identification as psychologists.

g. Psychologists present the science of psychology and offer their services, products, and publications fairly and accurately, avoiding misrepresentation through sensationalism, exaggeration, or superficiality. Psychologists are guided by the primary obligation to aid the public in developing informed judgments, opinions, and choices.

h. As teachers, psychologists ensure that statements in catalogs and course outlines are accurate and not misleading, particularly in terms of subject matter to be covered, bases for evaluating progress, and the nature of course experiences. Announcements, brochures, or advertisements describing workshops, seminars, or other educational programs accurately describe the audience for which the program is intended as well as eligibility requirements, educational objectives, and nature of the materials to be covered. These announcements also accurately represent the education, training, and experience of the psychologists presenting the programs and any fees involved.

i. Public announcements or advertisements soliciting research participants in which clinical services or other professional services are offered as an inducement make clear the nature of the services as well as the costs and other obligations to be accepted by participants in the research.

j. A psychologist accepts the obligation to correct others who represent the psychologist's professional qualifications, or associations with products or services, in a manner incompatible with these guidelines.

k. Individual diagnostic and therapeutic services are provided only in the context of a professional psychological relationship. When personal advice is given by means of public lectures or demonstrations, newspaper or magazine articles, radio or television programs, mail, or similar media, the psychologists utilizes the most current relevant data and exercises the highest level of professional judgment.

l. Products that are described or presented by means of public lectures or demonstrations, newspaper or magazine articles, radio or television programs, or similar media meet the same recognized standards as exist for products used in the context of a professional relationship.

PRINCIPLE 5: CONFIDENTIALITY

Psychologists have a primary obligation to respect the confidentiality of information obtained from persons in the course of their work as psychologists. They reveal such information to others only with the consent of the person or the person's legal representative, except in those unusual circumstances in which not to do so would result in clear danger to the person or to others. Where appropriate, psychologists inform their clients of the legal limits of confidentiality.

    a. Information obtained in clinical or consulting relationships, or evaluative data concerning children, students, employees, and others, is discussed only for professional purposes and only with persons clearly concerned with the case. Written and oral reports present only data germane to the purposes of the evaluation, and every effort is made to avoid undue invasion of privacy.

    b. Psychologists who present personal information obtained during the course of professional work in writings, lectures, or other public forums either obtain adequate prior consent to do so or adequately disguise all identifying information.

    c. Psychologists make provisions for maintaining confidentiality in the storage and disposal of records.

    d. When working with minors or other persons who are unable to give voluntary, informed consent, psychologists take special care to protect these persons' best interests.

PRINCIPLE 6: WELFARE OF THE CONSUMER

Psychologists respect the integrity and protect the welfare of the people and groups with whom they work. When conflicts of interest arise between clients and psychologists' employing institutions, psychologists clarify the nature and direction of their loyalties and responsibilities and keep all parties informed of their commitments. Psychologists fully inform consumers as to the purpose and nature of an evaluative, treatment, educational, or training procedure, and they freely acknowledge that clients, students, or participants in research have freedom of choice with regard to participation.

    a. Psychologists are continually cognizant of their own needs and of their potentially influential position vis-à-vis persons such as clients, students, and subordinates. They avoid exploiting the trust and dependency of such persons. Psychologists make every effort to avoid dual relationships that could impair their professional judgment or increase the risk of exploitation. Examples of such dual relationships include, but are not limited to, research with and treatment of employees, students, supervisees, close friends, or relatives. Sexual intimacies with clients are unethical.

    b. When a psychologist agrees to provide services to a client at the request of a third party, the psychologist assumes the responsibility of clarifying the nature of the relationships to all parties concerned.

    c. Where the demands of an organization require psychologists to violate these Ethical Principles, psychologists clarify the nature of the conflict between the demands and these principles. They inform all parties of psychologists' ethical responsibilities and take appropriate action.

d. Psychologists make advance financial arrangements that safeguard the best interests of and are clearly understood by their clients. They neither give nor receive any remuneration for referring clients for professional services. They contribute a portion of their services to work for which they receive little or no financial return.

e. Psychologists terminate a clinical or consulting relationship when it is reasonably clear that the consumer is not benefiting from it. They offer to help the consumer locate alternative sources of assistance.

PRINCIPLE 7: PROFESSIONAL RELATIONSHIPS

Psychologists act with due regard for the needs, special competencies, and obligations of their colleagues in psychology and other professions. They respect the prerogatives and obligations of the institutions or organizations with which these other colleagues are associated.

a. Psychologists understand the areas of competence of related professions. They make full use of all the professional, technical, and administrative resources that serve the best interests of consumers. The absence of formal relationships with other professional workers does not relieve psychologists of the responsibility of securing for their clients the best possible professional service, nor does it relieve them of the obligation to exercise foresight, diligence, and tact in obtaining the complementary or alternative assistance needed by clients.

b. Psychologists know and take into account the traditions and practices of other professional groups with whom they work and cooperate fully with such groups. If a person is receiving similar services from another professional, psychologists do not offer their own services directly to such a person. If a psychologist is contacted by a person who is already receiving similar services from another professional, the psychologist carefully considers that professional relationship and proceeds with caution and sensitivity to the therapeutic issues as well as the client's welfare. The psychologist discusses these issues with the client so as to minimize the risk of confusion and conflict.

c. Psychologists who employ or supervise other professionals or professionals in training accept the obligation to facilitate the further professional development of these individuals. They provide appropriate working conditions, timely evaluations, constructive consultation, and experience opportunities.

d. Psychologists do not exploit their professional relationships with clients, supervisees, students, employees, or research participants sexually or otherwise. Psychologists do not condone or engage in sexual harassment. Sexual harassment is defined as deliberate or repeated comments, gestures, or physical contacts of a sexual nature that are unwanted by the recipient.

e. In conducting research in institutions or organizations, psychologists secure appropriate authorization to conduct such research. They are aware of their obligations to future research workers and ensure that host institutions receive adequate information about the research and proper acknowledgment of their contributions.

f. Publication credit is assigned to those who have contributed to a publication in proportion to their professional contributions. Major contributions of a professional character made by several persons to a common project are recognized by joint authorship, with the individual who made the principal contribution listed first. Minor contributions of a professional character and extensive clerical or similar nonprofessional assistance may be acknowledged in footnotes or in an introductory statement. Acknowledgement through specific citations is made for unpublished as well as published material that has directly influenced the research or writing. Psychologists who compile and edit material of others for publication publish the material in the name of the originating group, if appropriate, with their own name appearing as chairperson or editor. All contributors are to be acknowledged and named.

g. When psychologists know of an ethical violation by another psychologist, and it seems appropriate, they informally attempt to resolve the issue by bringing the behavior to the attention of the psychologist. If the misconduct is of a minor nature and/or appears to be due to lack of sensitivity, knowledge, or experience, such an informal solution is usually appropriate. Such informal corrective efforts are made with sensitivity to any rights to confidentiality involved. If the violation does not seem amenable to an informal solution, or is of a more serious nature, psychologists bring it to the attention of the appropriate local, state, and/or national committee on professional ethics and conduct.

PRINCIPLE 8: ASSESSMENT TECHNIQUES

In the development, publication, and utilization of psychological assessment techniques, psychologists make every effort to promote the welfare and best interests of the client. They guard against the misuse of assessment results. They respect the client's right to know the results, the interpretations made, and the bases for their conclusions and recommendations. Psychologists make every effort to maintain the security of tests and other assessment techniques within limits of legal mandates. They strive to ensure the appropriate use of assessment techniques by others.

a. In using assessment techniques, psychologists respect the right of clients to have full explanations of the nature and purpose of the techniques in language the clients can understand, unless an explicit exception to this right has been agreed upon in advance. When the explanations are to be provided by others, psychologists establish procedures for ensuring the adequacy of these explanations.

b. Psychologists responsible for the development and standardization of psychological tests and other assessment techniques utilize established scientific procedures and observe the relevant APA standards.

c. In reporting assessment results, psychologists indicate any reservations that exist regarding validity or reliability because of the circumstances of the assessment or the inappropriateness of the norms for the person tested. Psychologists strive to ensure that the results of assessments and their interpretations are not misused by others.

d. Psychologists recognize that assessment results may become obsolete. They make every effort to avoid and prevent the misuse of obsolete measures.

e. Psychologists offering scoring and interpretation services are able to produce appropriate evidence for the validity of the programs and procedures used in arriving at interpretations. The public offering of an automated interpretation service is considered a professional-to-professional consultation. Psychologists make every effort to avoid misuse of assessment reports.

f. Psychologists do not encourage or promote the use of psychological assessment techniques by inappropriately trained or otherwise unqualified persons through teaching, sponsorship, or supervision.

PRINCIPLE 9: RESEARCH WITH HUMAN PARTICIPANTS

The decision to undertake research rests upon a considered judgment by the individual psychologist about how best to contribute to psychological science and human welfare. Having made the decision to conduct research, the psychologist considers alternative directions in which research energies and resources might be invested. On the basis of this consideration, the psychologist carries out the investigation with respect and concern for the dignity and welfare of the people who participate and with cognizance of federal and state regulations and professional standards governing the conduct of research with human participants.

a. In planning a study, the investigator has the responsibility to make a careful evaluation of its ethical acceptability. To the extent that the weighing of scientific and human values suggests a compromise of any principle, the investigator incurs a correspondingly serious obligation to seek ethical advice and to observe stringent safeguards to protect the rights of human participants.

b. Considering whether a participant in a planned study will be a "subject at risk" or a "subject at minimal risk," according to recognized standards, is of primary ethical concern to the investigator.

c. The investigator always retains the responsibility for ensuring ethical practice in research. The investigator is also responsible for the ethical treatment of research participants by collaborators, assistants, students, and employees, all of whom, however, incur similar obligations.

d. Except in minimal-risk research, the investigator establishes a clear and fair agreement with research participants, prior to their participation, that clarifies the obligations and responsibilities of each. The investigator has the obligation to honor all promises and commitments included in that agreement. The investigator informs the participants of all aspects of the research that might reasonably be expected to influence willingness to participate and explains all other aspects of the research about which the participants inquire. Failure to make full disclosure prior to obtaining informed consent requires additional safeguards to protect the welfare and dignity of the research participants. Research with children or with participants who have impairments that would limit understanding and/or communication requires special safeguarding procedures.

e. Methodological requirements of a study may make the use of concealment or deception necessary. Before conducting such a study, the investigator has a special responsibility to (i) determine whether the use of such techniques is justified by the study's prospective scientific, educational, or applied value; (ii) determine whether alternative procedures are available that do not use concealment or deception; and (iii) ensure that the participants are provided with sufficient explanation as soon as possible.

f. The investigator respects the individual's freedom to decline to participate in or to withdraw from the research at any time. The obligation to protect this freedom requires careful thought and consideration when the investigator is in a position of authority or influence over the participant. Such positions of authority include, but are not limited to, situations in which research participation is required as part of employment or in which the participant is a student, client, or employee of the investigator.

g. The investigator protects the participant from physical and mental discomfort, harm, and danger that may arise from research procedures. If risks of such consequences exist, the investigator informs the participant of that fact. Research procedures likely to cause serious or lasting harm to a participant are not used unless the failure to use these procedures might expose the participant to risk of greater harm, or unless the research has great potential benefit and fully informed and voluntary consent is obtained from each participant. The participant should be informed of procedures for contacting the investigator within a reasonable time period following participation should stress, potential harm, or related questions or concerns arise.

h. After the data are collected, the investigator provides the participant with information about the nature of the study and attempts to remove any misconceptions that may have arisen. Where scientific or humane values justify delaying or withholding this information, the investigator incurs a special responsibility to monitor the research and to ensure that there are no damaging consequences for the participant.

i. Where research procedures result in undesirable consequences for the individual participant, the investigator has the responsibility to detect and remove or correct these consequences, including long-term effects.

j. Information obtained about a research participant during the course of an investigation is confidential unless otherwise agreed upon in advance. When the possibility exists that others may obtain access to such information, this possibility, together with the plans for protecting confidentiality, is explained to the participant as part of the procedure for obtaining informed consent.

PRINCIPLE 10: CARE AND USE OF ANIMALS

An investigator of animal behavior strives to advance understanding of basic behavioral principles and/or to contribute to the improvement of human health and welfare. In seeking these ends, the investigator ensures the welfare of animals and treats them humanely. Laws and regulations notwithstanding, an animal's immediate protection depends upon the scientist's own conscience.

a. The acquisition, care, use, and disposal of all animals are in compliance with current federal, state or provincial, and local laws and regulations.

b. A psychologist trained in research methods and experienced in the care of laboratory animals closely supervises all procedures involving animals and is responsible for ensuring appropriate consideration of their comfort, health, and humane treatment.

c. Psychologists ensure that all individuals using animals under their supervision have received explicit instruction in experimental methods and in the care, maintenance, and handling of the species being used. Responsibilities and activities of individuals participating in a research project are consistent with their respective competencies.

d. Psychologists make every effort to minimize discomfort, illness, and pain of animals. A procedure subjecting animals to pain, strees, or deprivation is used only when an alternative procedure is unavailable and the goal is justified by its prospective scientific, educational, or applied value. Surgical procedures are performed under appropriate anesthesia; techniques to avoid infection and minimize pain are followed during and after surgery.

e. When it is appropriate that the animal's life be terminated, it is done rapidly and painlessly.

Author Index

Subject Index